Engd. by John Sartain. Phil. after Copley

James Habersham

A

HISTORY OF GEORGIA,

FROM ITS

FIRST DISCOVERY BY EUROPEANS

TO THE ADOPTION OF THE

PRESENT CONSTITUTION

IN

MDCCXCVIII.

BY

REV. WILLIAM BACON STEVENS, M.D., D.D.,

FORMERLY PROFESSOR OF BELLES-LETTRES, HISTORY, ETC., IN THE UNIVERSITY OF GEORGIA, ATHENS.

IN TWO VOLUMES.

VOL. II.

PHILADELPHIA:

PUBLISHED BY E. H. BUTLER & CO.

1859.

C. SHERMAN & SON, PRINTERS,
Corner Seventh and Cherry Streets, Philadelphia.

CONTENTS.

BOOK THIRD.

GEORGIA UNDER ROYAL GOVERNMENT.

BOOK FOURTH.

GEORGIA IN THE REVOLUTION.

BOOK FIFTH.

GEORGIA AN INDEPENDENT STATE.

PREFACE.

MORE than eleven years ago the first volume of the History of Georgia was given to the public.

It was then expected that the second and concluding volume would follow within a year or two, and most of the copies of the first volume were kept back from sale, with the hope that the work would be soon completed, and both sent out together.

My removal from Georgia in 1848, at what I deemed the emphatic bidding of God's providence, and the toil and time required in the care of one of the largest city parishes, rendered it almost impossible for me to find sufficient leisure to prosecute those researches which could be conducted only in Georgia; and hence delay succeeded delay until years had passed. While thus almost despairing of bringing the work to a conclusion, the Georgia Historical Society, through a committee, of which Bishop Elliott was chairman, urged me anew, and in the most generous manner, to resume my half-suspended labors, and to permit the work when done to be published at the expense of the Society. Cheered by this confidence, I addressed myself with renewed diligence to the task, and the result is now laid before the public. But for the request of the Georgia Historical Society, made to me through an honorable Committee in 1841, I should never have commenced the work; but for the material of books and manuscripts which their archives and influence opened to my research, I could not have prosecuted my labors; and but for its long-continued confidence and its late resolutions of encouragement and regard, I should not have been able to complete what I began under such auspices.

The delay, however, has not been without its benefits. It has enabled me to bring to my pleasing task greater historic materials, and a more matured judgment; and thus, perhaps, I have written with more soberness, accuracy, and propriety than I should have done had I finished the work ten years earlier.

As the volume has been written mostly from manuscript materials, and as I have but rarely based my statements on the authority of published works, I have deemed it unnecessary to specify every source from which the body of the text is derived, especially as they could not be referred to by the general reader.

In the preparation of this History I have had access to the Manuscripts and printed Journals of the Governors, and Committees of the Council of Safety, the Provincial Congress, the Executive Council, the two Houses of the Assembly, the Conventions of the State, the Meetings of Indian Commissioners, and other public bodies.

I have consulted the private papers and letters of

many who took a prominent part in the affairs of Georgia, together with the manuscript documents obtained by the Legislature from the State Paper Office, the Board of Trade, and the British Museum, in London.

Manuscript notes of former historians, private journals of eminent men, order-books of general officers, and the oral or written reminiscences of old soldiers and settlers, have afforded me much light and aid.

The ground over which I have travelled has, in all instances, been re-examined in the light of original authorities, and thus has been more thoroughly explored than on any previous occasion.

Those who have attempted to write a history from original manuscript material, will fully understand the labor of poring over thousands of pages blurred and faded by age and stains, and the difficulty of adjusting the often discordant materials, and framing out of the mass a true and readable history.

To those who have never attempted such a task, no description will ever convey an adequate idea of the toil and trial.

Having prescribed to myself at the beginning of my work a definite historic period, I stop there, though it leaves the work in the midst of a most interesting state of public affairs. It has been my aim to trace the great current of events from the settlement of Georgia to the adoption of the Constitution of 1798, and in order to keep the volume from swelling beyond its proper dimensions I have been obliged to omit many interesting personal and collateral events, which, however, would have led me aside from the main channel of my History.

To the many friends who have, by the loan of papers, and by kind suggestions and encouraging words, aided me in this work, I tender my special thanks. Especially are such thanks due to I. K. Tefft, Esq., of Savannah, in whose library the idea of writing this History was conceived; in whose rich collection of autographs and manuscripts I obtained the material for many of my most interesting pages; in whose untiring zeal to serve me I have found an invaluable helper; and to whom I here tender the gratitude of a heart which, for more than a quarter of a century, has ever found in him a true and generous friend.

For the excellent Index to this volume, I am indebted to the kindness of my nephew, the Rev. Wm. Stevens Perry, M.A., for which I return my sincere thanks.

Grateful to God, who has enabled me to complete this work, I commit it to the citizens of Georgia, conscious indeed of its imperfections, yet happy in the assurance that it is written with the single desire to display the truth, free from all personal or political bias, and in the hope that it will prove a reliable, and therefore an enduring history of a colony,—the youngest and the weakest of the old thirteen; of a State,—one of the greatest and most influential of the confederated sovereignties which make up the American Union.

PHILADELPHIA, Oct. 1, 1859.

HISTORY OF GEORGIA.

BOOK THIRD.

GEORGIA UNDER ROYAL GOVERNMENT.

CHAPTER IV.

THE NEW GOVERNOR, JAMES WRIGHT.

On the 11th October, 1760, Lieutenant-Governor James Wright arrived in Georgia.

This gentleman, whose subsequent career forms so interesting a portion of our history, was descended from the ancient family of Wright of Kilverstone, whose possessions in the county of Norfolk, England, date from Henry VIII. His grandfather, Sir Robert Wright, Knight, was Chief Justice of the Court of King's Bench, in the time of James II, and presided in that capacity in the celebrated trial of the seven Bishops, in 1688. His grandmother was the daughter of Matthew Wren, Lord Bishop of Ely (nephew of Sir Christopher Wren).

James Wright was born in South Carolina, of which province his father, the Honorable Robert Wright, was Chief Justice. At an early age he was appointed Attorney-General of his native colony, an office which he retained twenty-one years, discharging its duties with ability and diligence.

In many respects he was peculiarly qualified for his new position, as Lieutenant-Governor of Georgia: his American birth, his long residence in Carolina, his familiarity with colonial affairs, his business habits and legal acquirements, pointed him out as one who would secure the confidence of the Georgians, and administer the government with dignity and prudence.

Governor Ellis left Savannah on the 2d November, 1760, and the commission of Mr. Wright was immediately published, with the usual formalities.

The General Assembly met the day following, and in his opening speech he called the attention of both houses to the dangers to which the province was exposed, from the Creek Indians, who were rendered insolent and threatening by the partial successes of the Cherokees in Carolina, and by the intrigues of the French at Mobile and the Alabama Fort. He also spoke of the defenceless state of Savannah, of the necessity of finishing the fortifications already begun, and of erecting such other as the exigencies of the times required.

The entire military strength of the colony, at this time, consisted[1] of two troops of Rangers, three small Regiments of militia, and a detachment of fifty men from South Carolina; the whole number, from the sea-

[1] MS. Documents from Board of Trade, ix, 78.

board to Augusta, and from the Alatamaha to the Savannah, including alarm-men and superannuated citizens, did not exceed eleven hundred men. Of this force only one-half could be considered as effective troops; and those who might be relied upon were so badly provided with arms and ammunition that they could give but slight protection in time of danger.

The removal of the seat of government to Hardwicke, which had received the favorable notice of former Governors, was discouraged by Mr. Wright, who argued, that if the object of a removal was to obtain a more central position, Hardwicke was too near; while, on the other hand, a removal there would be very disadvantageous to the present capital, which was conveniently settled for intercourse with the Indians and for trade with South Carolina. The project was therefore abandoned, and the attention of the Assembly was directed to enlarging and strengthening the city which Oglethorpe had founded.

The death of George II occurred on the 25th October, 1760; the official intelligence of it did not reach Savannah until February, 1761, when, in consequence, the Assembly was dissolved, and the Governor in Council ordered, as was customary on such occasions, writs of election to issue for a new Assembly, to meet on the 24th March following. Funeral honors to the late sovereign were paid on the 9th February, and, on the day following, George III was proclaimed King in the most solemn manner, with the utmost civil and military pomp which the Province could display. It was the only time this ceremony of proclaiming a King was witnessed in Georgia.

The first session of the third General Assembly met

in March, 1761, and the Governor, in his opening speech, congratulated them on the happy accession of the young King to the throne of his grandfather. The speech called forth a loyal echo from both houses, and they proceeded to business, resolving "to make it their study[2] to promote his majesty's service, and pay all due obedience to his loyal commands."

But little business of historical importance was transacted by this Assembly. The principal object of desire was that the King should approve of the act passed on the 1st of May, 1760, for stamping, imprinting, issuing, and making current, the sum of £7410 in paper bills of credit, and for applying and sinking the same. To secure this purpose, both the Council and lower House addressed the Governor, intreating him to use his good offices with the Lords Commissioners for Trade and Plantations, that they would please to intercede with his majesty for his royal approbation and allowance of the same. This act was essentially necessary to the trade and commerce of Savannah, which greatly suffered for lack of more pecuniary facilities than the limited supply of sterling money or colonial currency permitted. Though Governors Reynolds and Ellis had, under legislative sanction, issued paper bills of credit to a small extent, yet Mr. Wright assured the Board of Trade[3] that, at the time this last act was passed, the entire currency for trade, Indian affairs, and other purposes, amounted to only about £5500, which sum was being annually reduced, by calling in and sinking a certain per cent., according to the original intention of the acts. The Governor ac-

[2] MS. Journal of Council in Assembly, 457.

[3] MS. Documents, ix, 97.

cordingly represented to the Board of Trade that, unless the new act and emission were allowed, "they should really be involved in very great difficulties." The King's Solicitor, Sir Matthew Lamb, made no objection to the bill, and the money was put in circulation.

The importance of fortifying the island of Cockspur early forced itself upon the attention of the Governor, "not only as being necessary in time of war, for the protection of trade and of the province, but also useful in time of peace, for enforcing a due obedience to our laws." Accordingly, what Captain De Brahm, the engineer, employed for the purpose, called a "redoubted caponiere," was erected on the south side of the island, while a small battery of three eighteen-pounders only was deemed sufficient to protect the channel on the northern side. About the same time, "to prevent all clandestine trade and his majesty's enemies from being supplied with provisions," the Governor, by the advice and consent of his Council, declared and established Sunbury to be a port of entry, and appointed Thomas Carr collector, John Martin naval officer, and Francis Lee searcher; which officers were approved by the Commissioners of his Majesty's Customs.

On the 20th March, 1761, the King conferred upon Mr. Wright full executive powers, with the title of Captain-General and Governor-in-Chief. This promotion was deserved, for the zeal which he had displayed in advancing every interest connected with Georgia, and for the distinguished ability which marked his intercourse with the Indians, during a period when the slightest imprudence would have involved the people in the horrors of a savage warfare. His commission—such was then the slow transit between the two countries—did not reach Savannah until the 28th January, 1762, when it was published with the usual formalities. The regiment of militia, commanded by Colonel Noble Jones, was drawn up in Johnson Square, and, after the commission was read, fired three volleys, which were answered by the cannon from Fort Halifax, and by all the ships in the river. In the evening, the Governor gave a ball to the ladies, "at which there was the most numerous and brilliant appearance ever known in the town."[4] Nearly every house was illuminated, and the chronicle of the day declares that "there never was an occasion on which the joy and satisfaction of the people were more apparent." But, while the Governor, by his approved abilities and unsullied integrity, was securing the confidence and affections of the people, there were sources of disquietude around him, which demanded wisdom, prudence, and unquailing firmness. The first sore trial to his patience, was the conduct of William Grover, the Chief Justice of Georgia. This person had been appointed to his distinguished station by the Earl of Halifax, during the administration of Governor Ellis; but, failing to agree with the Governor, he absented himself from the Council board, and began that peculiar course of conduct which gave such just offence to the Governor and the whole province. After waiting a sufficient time to ascertain whether he would resume his seat in the Council, the Governor sent to require his attendance. This he refused to do, and shortly resigned his seat; and, declining all intercourse with

[4] South Carolina Gazette, February 20, 1762.

the executive, he directed the whole force of his official and personal character to thwart and derange the course and counsels of the government. The Governor, in a very temperate manner, laid the case before his Council, and, after a full investigation, they unanimously declared,[5] "That Mr. Grover's conduct has been and is dishonorable, partial, arbitrary, illegal, indecent, and not consistent with the character, duty, and dignity of his office," and recommended his suspension until the pleasure of the King was known. He was accordingly suspended, and a memorial was sent to the Board of Trade, setting forth that he had intrigued with the Assembly, and hindered the course of legislation—that he was illegal, arbitrary, and oppressive in his judicial acts;—in short, that his conduct, in every respect, seemed exceptionable—derogatory to his station and prejudicial to the honor and interest of both his majesty and the province in which he was the great law-officer of the crown. These complaints were amply substantiated, and, the Board of Trade concurring in the view of the Governor and Council, the King removed him from office in March, 1763.

The mal-conduct of Mr. Grover produced serious effects on the legal and legislative condition of the province. He was the first Chief Justice of Georgia, and his position as the law adviser of the executive and the supreme legal authority in the province, demanded of him a conduct consonant to the eminence of his rank and the dignity of his profession. In so small a community, the character of a Chief Justice

[5] Documents Board of Trade, x, 8.

must have an important influence in moulding the legal proceedings of the colony, and in shaping, indeed, the moral character of the community. It was truly unfortunate that Georgia's first Governor (Reynolds) and first Chief Justice (Grover) should have been men so unworthy of their station, and so derelict to their high and responsible trusts. Their conduct retarded, to a great extent, the advancement and prosperity of the province.

Another source of anxiety to the Governor, was the fluctuating and uncertain state of the Indian affairs. The French, before the declaration of war, on the 17th May, 1756, and especially since, had spared no effort to instigate the Creeks and Cherokees against the colonists, and thus harass, if not effectually extirpate, the southern plantations. The aim of the French seemed to be to involve all the colonies in a general Indian war. By means of presents of warlike stores and flattering speeches, they at last succeeded in effecting a rupture between the Cherokees and the English, which resulted in a tedious and wasting war, which was only finally quelled by Colonels Montgomery and Grant, at a vast expense of treasure, suffering, and blood. In this war South Carolina, North Carolina, and Virginia were the chief sufferers, as Georgia, through the unwearied assiduity of Governor Ellis, was saved from ruin—for he not only calmed the Creeks and pacified the Cherokees, but dissuaded them from their base designs, and engaged them to a strict neutrality.[6]

Mr. Wright aimed to pursue towards the Indians the same mild and judicious course; and had the wise

[6] Adair's History of American Indians, 256.

counsels of Governor Bull and himself been followed, a rupture might have been avoided.

The emissaries of the French, however, were unremitting in their efforts to detach all the southern Indians from the English interests; and it required all the talent, patience, and boldness of which Wright was master, to counteract their arts and bring them to act in concert as allies of the British crown. The Spaniards pursued a course similar to the French; encouraging the savages in their interest to acts of massacre and deeds of incendiarism worthy of their cruel and relentless nature.

Dangers from both these powers menaced the colony several years; while to counteract them, and secure tranquillity to the weakest and most exposed of the thirteen colonies, Mr. Wright was compelled to rely for defence, not so much on arms and military strength, as upon the prudence of his measures, the wisdom of his counsels, and the firmness of his conduct. These did not fail him in the time of trial, and with them he was enabled to secure peace, and pave the way for those future benefits which resulted from his well-planned administration.

By the Peace of Paris (February 10th, 1763) he was somewhat relieved from these vexing troubles, for though that treaty was stoutly opposed in England, as "premature and inconclusive," yet to the American colonies it proved an invaluable blessing. By the sixth article of this treaty, it was stipulated that the western boundary line between Great Britain and France should be the middle of the Mississippi River, and by the twentieth article his Catholic majesty of Spain ceded to England the Floridas, and all that Spain possessed on the Continent, to the east or southeast of the Mississippi, except the island of New Orleans. This removal of the Spanish rule from St. Augustine and Pensacola, and of the French from the Alabama Fort and Mobile, relieved the colony of some of its most grievous troubles, those which were fomented by the rivalry and jealousy of these national enemies of our religion and government.

Another great advantage to Georgia incidental to this cession of territory was, that Florida was divided into two provinces, and was erected into two separate English governments, with a full colonial establishment in each; thus leaving Georgia no longer the southern and western frontier, but protected on her lower boundaries by the new colonies of East and West Florida. Not only had enemies been dislodged, but friends had been introduced in their place; and it now possessed security from its three potent enemies, the French, the Spanish and the Indians, which it had never obtained before. The effect was most salutary: inhabitants flocked in, lands were taken up and cleared, new settlements projected, trade was enlarged, wealth increased, and a day bright with many promises of future aggrandizement dawned upon the long harassed and afflicted colony. But though the formidable European enemies of the province were removed, the Indians in their interest, who occupied lands ceded to the crown, still remained. For the purpose of apprising them of the change, as well as to secure their amity and confidence, the Earl of Egremont, then principal Secretary of State for the Southern Department, wrote, by command of his majesty, to the Governors of Virginia, North Carolina, South Carolina, and Georgia, directing them, together with Captain Stuart, Superintendent of Indian Affairs, to hold a congress with the Creeks, Cherokees, Catawbas, Chickasaws and Choctaws, at Augusta, or elsewhere, as they should deem expedient.

In opposition to the views of the other Governors, who wished to hold the congress in South Carolina, Governor Wright suggested that it would evince the confiding trust of the English in the tribes, as well as secure a larger attendance of the chiefs and warriors from their various towns, if they met at Augusta, which, after some delay, they agreed to do, as most of the Indians positively refused to go to South Carolina. The necessary arrangements having been made, the session of this novel yet important congress opened at Augusta, on Saturday morning, the 5th November, 1763. There were present on the part of the English government, James Wright, Governor of Georgia; Arthur Dobbs, Governor of North Carolina; Thomas Boone, Governor of South Carolina; Francis Fauquier, Lieutenant-Governor of Virginia, and Captain John Stuart, Superintendent of Indian Affairs for the Southern District. On the part of the Indians, there appeared twenty-seven chiefs of the Upper and Lower Chickasaws, two of the Choctaws, nine of the Upper and Lower Creeks, fifteen of the Cherokees, and one of the Catawbas, accompanied by their squaws and friends, making in all about seven hundred Indians.

After seven persons had been sworn in as interpreters, Governor Wright opened the session, by observing, "that the day was fair, and hoped that the talks would not prove otherwise; that the several Governors had pitched upon Captain Stuart to deliver their sentiments; that they were agreed upon the declarations to be made to the Indians; and desired them to pay attention to what Captain Stuart uttered, as they were the words of all the Governors." Accordingly, Captain Stuart began his talk to them as friends and brothers, assuring them, that "no conference was ever intended to be more general, none more friendly;" for now, "at a time when he has nothing to apprehend from any of his enemies, the King of England opens his arms to receive his red children," doing it "the rather at this juncture, as he knows the insinuations and falsehoods which have been formerly circulated among you by the perfidious and cruel French." He then proceeded to tell them that, having defeated and humbled that nation, as also the Spaniards, "the King had now given peace to both nations; and to prevent the revival of such disturbances, by repetition of such dangerous proceedings, and for this purpose only, he insisted in the treaty of peace that the French and Spanish should be removed beyond the river Mississippi, that the Indians and white people may hereafter live in peace and brotherly friendship. It will be your faults if this does not happen, for we are authorized by the great King to give you the most substantial proofs of our good intention and desire to live like brothers with you." He also assured them that all past offences should be buried in oblivion; that they should be plentifully supplied with goods; that justice should be done them on all occasions, and that the forts ceded to the English by the French and Spanish should be employed for their protection, assistance, and convenience.

To this exposition of English views the Indians replied on the following Monday and Tuesday, and, after mutual explanations and promises, a treaty for the preservation and continuance of a fair and perfect peace and friendship between his most sacred majesty George III and the several kings, head men, and warriors of the Chickasaws, Upper and Lower Creeks, Choctaws, Cherokees, and Catawbas, was concluded on the 10th November, and the congress adjourned, under a salute from the guns of Fort Augusta.[7]

The results of this treaty were beneficial both to the Indians and to the colonists. It insured protection to the former, and tranquillity to the latter; and, by the further acquisition of territory, so enlarged the boundaries of Georgia, as to afford ample tracts of land to the new settlers, who were now daily flocking to the colony.

Among the applicants for lands within the newly acquired territory, were Denys Rolles and the Earl of Eglintoun. The former gentleman was the brother of Lord Rolles, Baron of Stevenstone, one of the most distinguished families in Devonshire, and who sat in Parliament for the county of Devon.

In the beginning of 1764, this gentleman, in company with William Reynolds, an Elder Brother of the Trinity House, Colonel George Buch, Captain John Buch, and Dr. Robert Willan, petitioned the Board of Trade for a tract of land, "from the Georgia line on the north to another line southward, to be drawn parallel to the equator, from two miles below the forks of the Apalachicola River to the Alatamaha, to be bounded

[7] Journal of the Proceedings of the Southern Congress, at Augusta, in 1763. Printed at Charleston, South Carolina, in 1764; only fifty copies printed.

on the west by the first, and on the east by the last of these rivers."[8]

They proposed to build a town on the south side of the Alatamaha, and a larger one, designed for the capital, was to be erected on the Apalachicola. Their objects were to cultivate silk, indigo, and cotton; to collect ship timber, and especially knees of live-oak, and naval stores; to open a more easy communication with the Creeks than by way of Augusta, and a freer access to the Gulf of Mexico than by the dangerous route round the keys of Florida. Mr. Rolles purposed to go over himself to superintend the first embarkation and planting of this new colony, and solicited that a regular government, with proper courts of justice, might be appointed; at first, to be supported by the crown, vesting the proper powers in the petitioners as proprietors, in the same way as was formerly done in Pennsylvania and Maryland.

This plan not meeting the approbation of the Board of Trade, the petitioners made a request to the Earl of Hillsborough, and the other Lords Commissioners for Trade and Plantations, for the grant of Cumberland Island, on the coast of Georgia, "for the purpose of raising cotton, silk, oil and wine, and such other commodities as may be hoped for in a warm climate." This also was denied; and the failure of such plans in their inception prevented the still deeper reverses and miscarriages, that must have attended the putting in operation schemes so ideal in their design, and so expensive in their construction.

Not six months after the application of Mr. Rolles,

[8] Board of Trade, x, 68.

Alexander Montgomerie, the tenth Earl of Eglintoun, with others, presented a petition to the King in council, setting forth,[9] that "your petitioners, Alexander, Earl of Eglintoun, and others, are willing to introduce into these provinces 100,000 settlers, viz.: 10,000 the first five years, and 18,000 every five years after, till the whole is completed, at their own expense, for the property of the soil only, the crown reserving the entire jurisdiction, with power to order and direct the proprietors to give what grants your majesty shall be pleased to signify to them by your Secretary of State or the Lords of Trade and Plantations.

"1st. We most humbly beg that one of the royal family will be graciously pleased to be at the head of this great and expensive undertaking.

"2d. We are willing to oblige ourselves to comply with the terms of your majesty's late proclamation for encouraging the settlement of that country.

"3d. We desire our legal grants of lands already made in these countries may be confirmed, and that the proprietors may be restrained from making grants to any one person exceeding five hundred acres (except to such as have greater allowance by your majesty's proclamation), which grants to contain indispensable terms and conditions of cultivation, and to subject the new settlers to no higher quit-rents than what is at present paid in those provinces.

"4th. We will give full and sufficient security to pay into your majesty's exchequer, free of all charges and deductions, one shilling per annum for every one hundred acres that is already and may be hereafter

[9] Board of Trade, x, 137.

granted away: provided, such quit-rents be not exacted or payable till fifteen years from the date of the respective grants.

"And all these conditions we will be obliged to perform, upon a penalty of the resumption of the grants, and the loss of whatever we may have laid out previous to the forfeiture, together with any other security that may be judged necessary for the performance of this task, particularly against a monopoly of the lands, by being subject to such directions respecting grants as your majesty shall from time to time signify to us by your Secretary of State and Lords of Trade and Plantations, whereby we shall be as much under the control of your majesty's Government as the present Governors and Councils of those provinces, or any other part of the Continent of America, who are now vested with a power of granting lands under your majesty's commissions and instructions; and we are also ready to submit to any other measures for the true and reasonable interest of the colony and mother country, which can be contrived so as to make the one grow and flourish under the protection and superintendency of the other."

This strange petition succeeded no better than those of Mr. Rolles. Had the request been granted, the scheme could never have been carried out, as it embraced conditions which it was next to impossible to fulfil. The tragical death of the Earl shortly after put a sudden termination to a plan as Utopian as it was impracticable.

The extension of boundaries by the recent treaties made it necessary to revoke the former letters patent to Mr. Wright as Captain-General and Governor-in-

Chief of Georgia, and accordingly a new commission to him received the great seal at Westminster, on the 20th January, 1764, extending his authority over the new territory included within the extended limits of the colony.

Relieved now from the maraudings of the French and the Spaniards; in peace and amity with most of the adjacent Indian tribes; its boundaries enlarged on the one side to the Mississippi, and on the other to the St. Mary's, and protected on the south by two new English colonies, Georgia occupied a position which it had never before attained. Its population, though small, was substantial and industrious; its agricultural resources were rapidly increasing; its commerce called into requisition several thousand tons of shipping; its Indian trade was large and productive, and it was presided over by a Governor who knew its best interests and who closely studied to advance its welfare. The province rose in importance day by day, and was fast becoming what its founder intended it should be, noble, vigorous, and flourishing.

But just as Georgia had attained this longed for position, and was beginning to realize the benefits for which its wise Governor had so diligently striven; just as the clouds which had hung round its morning hours broke away, and the sun of peace and prosperity shone out with its gladdening light; another and a darker cloud rose in the opposite horizon, small indeed at the first, as that which the prophet saw from the top of Carmel, but one which was destined to cover the colonial firmament with blackness, and pour forth the storms of revolution and civil war.

Fortunate was it for Georgia that it had thus been

consolidated and strengthened by these flanking colonies, and by this Indian treaty: but for these, it must necessarily have been swept away in the first irruption of the invader; for there was no subsequent period, prior to the Revolution, when the colony could have thus girded up its strength, because dissension in council, opposition in politics, uneasiness among the people, and rebellion to government, soon absorbed the public mind and engaged the energies of the people. It was a fortunate thing, also, for all the colonies, that before they were called upon to enter into contest with the mother country, the other enemies on their frontiers had been silenced and removed; and, furthermore, that in the very treaties which removed them, were contained germs of dissatisfaction with Great Britain, which, when the war of the Revolution did come, caused the Indians to rank themselves as our friends and allies, against the power which had stripped them to such an extent of their American possessions.

CHAPTER V.

THE STAMP ACT IN GEORGIA.

The colony of Georgia presents itself to the historian under two aspects: one, as it respects its own internal affairs, and the other, in its relation to the other colonies and to the parent state. Up to this time, we have considered Georgia as a province by itself, and have confined ourselves to its history alone; we must now look at its other aspect, and examine its historical connections with its sister colonies and the mother country. Hitherto, the only ties which bound it to the provinces which skirted the Atlantic coast were those of continental interest, and the derivation of governmental powers through the same common source, the King and Parliament of Great Britain. But other links were soon forged, which were to bring into yet closer union the leading colonies of North America, and to exhibit these it is necessary to merge, for a time, the narrative of Georgia in the common history of our American confederacy. The liberty which we now enjoy was not the sudden disenthralment of a nation from monarchical rule, effected in the heat of political excitement, by men acting under the impulses of fevered passion. The seeds of that liberty had been brought by the colonists from their fatherland—they had been scattered broadcast from the Kennebec to the Alatamaha—they had taken root and sprung up, and the Revolution was the fruit of their long but effective germination.

It would not come within the province of this history to trace the progress of free principles in America, yet a brief review of their development is necessary to a full understanding of the revolutionary history of Georgia.

It is not saying too much to declare, that the fundamental doctrines of civil and religious freedom were better understood in the American colonies than in any other portion of the globe. Their several charters conferred upon them rights and immunities which they cherished with peculiar tenacity, and which strengthened them in that spirit of liberty which manifested itself so often during their colonial existence. From the time that the Virginians, under the wise administration of Sir George Yeardly, in 1619, gave the New World the first example of representative legislation, onward to the eventful epoch of American independence, the leading principles of political liberty were boldly proclaimed and firmly supported. Of these principles, that which recognized resistance to taxation without representation, was the first developed, and the soonest tested.

When Virginia capitulated to the commonwealth of Cromwell, in 1652, it was expressly stated in the deed of surrender, that no taxes or customs should be levied, except by their own representatives.

When the "West India Company" attempted to tax the inhabitants of New Netherlands (now New York), the province drew up a remonstrance, which declared,

"We, who have transformed the wilderness into fruitful farms, demand that no new laws shall be enacted, but with consent of the people;" and they refused to pay them.

When the tyrannical Lovelace insisted upon taxing the people of New York, even for the ostensive purpose of defence, seven villages entered their protest to an act which took from them the rights and privileges of Englishmen; and, though the votes of these towns against this arbitrary decree of the Governor were, by his order, publicly burned in the streets of New York, yet the spirit which cast them remained unchecked.

The efforts of Sir Edmund Andros, in 1688–9, to levy a tax at the pleasure of himself and council, though seconded by imprisonment and fines, resulted in a revolution which overthrew his government, and reinstated on its ruins their old and equitable charter rights.

Not only did the attempt to tax the colonists without representation provoke resistance, but legislative enactments were passed, declaring, with all the emphasis which charters and laws could give, that taxation without representation was contrary to the rights and privileges of Englishmen, and subversive of the liberties of the people.

The frequent agitation of these measures implanted in the minds of the colonists the clearest ideas of their rights as subjects and as men, and prepared the way for resisting, on a broader arena, the flagitious schemes of Parliament in 1765.

One of the results of the English Revolution of 1688, was the recognition of that principle which Magna Charta, signed at Runnymede nearly five hundred years before, had dimly shadowed forth, that property could not be taxed, but with the consent of its proper representatives; and the royal Assembly of New York, catching the spirit of this fundamental principle, resolved, three years after, that no tax whatever shall be levied on his majesty's subjects in the province, or on their estates, on any pretence whatever, but by the act and consent of the representatives of the people in General Assembly convened. The act, indeed, was rejected by King William, and severe taskmasters were sent over to discipline them into obedience, but the very efforts to eradicate or coerce this spirit, only caused it to take deeper root and acquire greater strength.

In 1696, a pamphlet appeared in England, asserting the power of Parliament to tax the colonies, and recommending the plan; but it was immediately answered from this side of the Atlantic by several replies, which denied the right and reprobated the design. It is indeed remarkable, when the tendency of the Americans to self-government was so early discovered, that a different course was not pursued, rather than those oppressive subjugating measures, which the common experience of humanity should have taught the Cabinet could only result in resistance and alienation.

As far back as 1701, the Lords of Trade publicly declared, that "the independency the colonies thirst after is now notorious;" and in 1705, it was openly published in England, that "the colonists will, in process of time, cast off their allegiance, and set up a government of their own;" and yet that same year a memorial, urging a direct tax on the colonists, was transmitted by a royalist to the Lords of Trade; but both the Board and the Ministry wisely suffered it to pass unnoticed. In 1728, Sir William Keith suggested to the King to extend the duties of stamps upon parchment and paper, already existing in England, to the plantations in America; but the plan of the ex-Governor, as also a similar suggestion made to Walpole in 1739, received no serious consideration from the high officers of state. Mr. Pitt, indeed, meditated a plan for the raising of a revenue from the Americans, and towards the close of 1759 wrote to Governor Fauquier, of Virginia, announcing his design; but, on receiving the reply of the Governor, which represented the disturbance it would occasion, he was induced to relinquish his scheme.

At the ratification of peace, in 1763, the American colonies were all loyal provinces, reposing in peace and prosperity, under the guarantee of chartered rights and the plighted faith of the English government; but their quietude was of short duration.

The late war, which Great Britain had engaged in principally at the solicitation of the colonies, and for their defence, had cost the nation over three hundred millions of dollars; which, added to its already overgrown debt, made the condition of its finances desperate. How to reduce this debt, and at the same time so to reduce it as not by new and large taxation to create alarm among the people, already laden with most onerous imposts, called for all the skill and ingenuity of the fiscal minister. Under the pressure of these circumstances, it was resolved to carry into effect what had so long remained a mere speculative scheme. The way for this had been already prepared, by the resolution of the House of Commons, in March, 1764, by which the members determined, almost unanimously, that they had the *right* to tax America. The declaration of their *right* was soon followed by a vote declaring that it was *expedient*, and the resolve of expediency was in a few days succeeded by an act carrying out the asserted right, commonly known as "The Sugar or Molasses Act."

The spirited remonstrances which this act and declaration drew forth from the colonists did not deter the ministers from enlarging their plans for gathering a revenue from America; and accordingly, on the 22d March, 1765, George Grenville's bill, entitled "An Act for granting and applying stamp duties and other duties in the British Colonies and Plantations of America,." etc., received the assent of the King.

This plan was suggested to Mr. Grenville, it is said, by Mr. Huske, a native of New Hampshire, but who then represented the town of Malden in Essex, in the House of Commons, and who proposed by this means to raise £500,000 per annum from the colonies. This man, a nephew of the distinguished General Huske, is represented as "a flashy, superficial fellow, who, by stock-jobbing and servility to the Townshend family, raised himself from poverty and obscurity to a seat in Parliament;" and the first use which he made of his position was to injure the country which gave him birth. But the idea is not altogether his own; for it has been asserted, by one[1] who possessed great knowledge of state secrets, that Grenville "adopted from Lord Bute a plan of taxation formed by Jenkinson,"

[1] Walpole's George III, ii, 28.

the first Lord Liverpool. The plan, by whomsoever devised, was adopted by the Ministry, and George Grenville's bill, intituled "An Act for granting and applying stamp duties and other duties in the British Colonies and Plantations in America," etc., embracing fifty-five resolutions, received, on the 22d March, 1765, the assent of the King.

The Assembly of Virginia, the only provincial legislature in session when the news of the passage of the act arrived, immediately passed resolves, denying the right of Parliament to tax the colonies. Nearly every province echoed the sentiment of the Old Dominion.

The Assembly of Massachusetts, foreseeing the importance of union among the aggrieved colonies, addressed a circular to each of the Assemblies, soliciting the formation of a general congress, to meet in New York, on the first Tuesday in October, 1765.

As soon as Mr. Wylly, the Speaker of the Commons House of Assembly, received the letter, he dispatched expresses to the members, and sixteen members—nearly two-thirds of the entire number—responded to his call, by convening in Savannah, on the 2d September, 1765. This body replied to the Massachusetts resolutions, by a letter intimating their hearty co-operation in every measure for the support of their common rights; but, through the influence of Governor Wright, they were prevented from sending delegates to the proposed congress. How far he had succeeded in calming the excitement which began to appear concerning the Stamp Act, may be inferred from his assertion to the Earl of Halifax, under date September 20, 1765, "that everything in the province is well and doing well at present."

The Assembly met on the 22d October, and on the 28th, an order was made, requiring their Committee of Correspondence to lay before the house the communications between their agent, William Knox, and themselves; and the result was, that the lower house "resolved to give instruction to their Committee of Correspondence to acquaint William Knox, agent for this province, that the province has no further occasion for his services." Not that they found aught objectionable in his correspondence, but they believed that he could not act independently for them, when he was at the same time Crown Agent for East Florida; and they took especial objection to his pamphlet, entitled "The Claims of the Colonies to an Exemption from Internal Taxes imposed by authority of Parliament examined;" in which he defended the proceedings of Parliament, and supported its most obnoxious measures. Had Mr. Knox considered what was due to the colony he represented, he certainly would not thus have obtruded himself in a controversy, which, on the side he advocated, compromised the very privileges and liberties of Englishmen. But, like others in that day, he wrote for advancement, and his promotion, not long after, as "Under-Secretary of State," was doubtless the reward of his devotion to ministerial designs. John Campbell, Esq., the Crown Agent for Georgia, also published an octavo tract of over a hundred pages, on the "Regulations lately made concerning the Colonies, and the Taxes imposed upon them." From him nothing better was expected; it was quite natural that he should kiss the hand that fed him; but that Mr. Knox, who had resided in Savannah, and held high offices in Georgia, and who was supposed to be devoted to the interests of the colonies, should take the part he did, was not only unlooked for, but was regarded first with amazement, and then with indignation.

As the time drew near when this act was to take effect, the spirit of the people became more excited, and occasions were not long wanting, in which it was fully manifested.

On the 26th of October, the anniversary of his majesty's accession, the Governor ordered a general muster in Savannah, which drew together a large concourse of people, and in the evening there was a great tumult, occasioned by burning the effigies of several obnoxious persons, having first paraded them through the streets with insulting mockery. The Governor, by proclamation, condemned such proceedings; and this, having no effect, was in a few days followed by another, "against riots and tumultuous and unlawful assemblies." This also was unheeded; and the Governor himself declared, that "from that time the spirit of faction and sedition increased."

The act was to take effect from the 1st November, 1765, yet, as neither the papers nor distributing officer had arrived, the Governor, by advice of his Council, on the 31st October, stopped the issue of all warrants and grants for land, and gave "let-passes" to the vessels, certifying the non-arrival of any stamped papers or officer in the province, while at the same time he wrote to the Board of Trade:—

"I am, my lords, under great difficulty with respect to the Stamp Act, not having received the act of Parliament, or one scrape of the pen about it; nor is any stampt paper or officer yet arrived here. I fear, my lords, there has been an omission somewhere, relative to this matter, which embarrasses me greatly. The moment I receive the act, it shall be punctually observed, to the utmost of my power; but am very sorry to acquaint your lordships that too much of the rebellious spirit in the northern colonies has already shown itself here; indeed, for many months past, stimulated by letters, papers, etc., sent them from the northward to follow their example."

On the 5th of December, his majesty's ship Speedwell, Captain Fanshawe, with the stamps, arrived in the river, and the papers were secretly transferred to Fort Halifax, and placed under the care of the commissary; for the "Liberty Boys," as they were then termed, had entered into an association to prevent the distribution of the papers, and to compel the officer to resign as soon as he arrived. To oppose these measures, Governor Wright summoned all his energies, and labored day and night, in public and in private, and, by his commanding influence, ably seconded by his Council, was partially successful. Secret meetings, however, were often held, all business was stopped, and the province remained in a state of anxious agitation. Burdensome as the Stamp Act was felt to be by all the colonies, it was peculiarly oppressive to Georgia. "The annual tax raised here," says the excellent James Habersham (President of his majesty's Council, a true loyalist, but a true patriot), "for the support of our internal policy, is full as much as the inhabitants can bear; and suppose the stamps produce only one-eighth of what they would in South Carolina, it would amount to as much in one year as our tax laws will raise in three; and perhaps we have not five thousand pounds, in gold and silver, come into the province in five years, though the act requires it in one. If this is really the case, as I really believe it is, how must every inhabitant shudder at the thought of the act taking place, which, according to my present apprehension, must inevitably ruin them." It was not possible, therefore, for the Georgians to remain passive under such exactions; for not only was the tax onerous in itself, but the act which levied it involved a question, on the issue of which depended the liberty or the slavery of America. It is a just remark of the profound Locke, "Men can never be secure from tyranny, if there be no means to escape it, till they are perfectly under it; and therefore it is, that they have not only a right to get out of it, but to prevent it;" and to prevent it the colonists were determined, or to perish in the attempt.

On the 2d of January, 1766, about 3 P. M., Captains Milledge and Powell informed the Governor that nearly two hundred "Liberty Boys" had assembled together, threatening to break open the fort and destroy the papers. The Governor immediately ordered the two companies of rangers, numbering fifty-four men, to attend him, and marched to the fort, took out the stamps, placed them in a cart, and, escorted by the military, conveyed them to the guard-house. The people looked on in sullen silence; but it was a silence which gave the Governor so much alarm, that for many days he kept a guard of forty men over his house, and during four nights was in such anxiety and fear, that he did not remove his clothes.

The next day, about ten o'clock, the Governor, by preconcerted signals, was made acquainted with the arrival of Mr. Agnus, the stamp distributer, at Tybee, and, fearing the rage of the citizens, immediately despatched an armed scout-boat, with two or three of his particular friends, who, with much secrecy and a charge to allow him to speak to no one, brought him to the Governor's house, on the 4th, where he took the required oath. But a few days' residence here, even with a guard mounted night and day, convinced Mr. Agnus of his insecurity, and in a fortnight he left the town.

Nor were these feelings confined to Savannah. The whole province was aroused; parties of armed men assembled in various places; society was convulsed, and its tumultuous heavings threatened general ruin and desolation. Then was exhibited in an eminent degree the zeal and energy of the Governor; and such was his resolution and weight of character, that for a time all rebellious proceedings ceased; so much so, that he wrote, on the 15th January, 1766, "Everything, at present, is easy and quiet, and I hope peace and confidence will be restored in general." A few days served to dissipate this hope. About the 20th, menacing letters were sent to Governor Wright. President Habersham was waylaid at night, his new and well-stored house was threatened with destruction, and he was obliged to take refuge in the garrisoned mansion of the Governor. Towards the close of January, a body of six hundred men assembled within a few miles of the town, and intimated to the Governor that, unless the papers were removed, they would march to Savannah, attack his house and fort, and destroy the stamps. Immediately he sent the papers down to Fort George, at Cockspur Island, and placed them in charge of the rangers. But even this was not deemed sufficient security, and on the 3d of February, they were once more removed, and deposited on board the man-of-war Speedwell, which had brought them to the colony.

The next day the town was again alarmed, by the appearance on the common of between two and three hundred men, with arms and colors, clamorous for the redress of their grievances. The company of rangers was ordered up from Cockspur, and all the regulars and volunteers, together with a party of marines and seamen from the Speedwell, were marshalled for the defence of the town. For several hours the state of affairs was critical, and suspense added its harrowing influences to the trepidation of alarm. By evening, however, nearly all the provincials had dispersed, though a few at night burned an effigy of the Governor, holding in his hand the offensive circular of Secretary Conway, of the 24th October, 1765.

The situation of Mr. Wright was one of singular trial and difficulty. The province was on the verge of civil war, and one act of indiscretion would have plunged it into its ensanguined horrors. The whole military force of the colony consisted of two troops of rangers, of sixty men each, and thirty of the Royal American Regiment—in all one hundred and fifty men, officers and privates; who were distributed in five forts widely separated, and totally inadequate to sustain the executive authority. With this handful of soldiers, the Governor had to contend with faction and disloyalty, and so inefficient did he deem them, that he was on the point of writing to General Gage and Lord Colville for support.

On the arrival of the stamps there were between sixty and seventy sail in port waiting for clearance, and the necessities of the case seemed so urgent, that, though the people refused to use stamps for any other purpose, they consented to employ them to clear out their ships, by which means the port was opened, though the courts remained closed, and every species of judicial business was suspended. Such a course gave great umbrage to the other colonies, and particularly to South Carolina. Governor Wright was termed by the Carolinians "a parricide," and Georgia "a pensioned government," which had "sold her birthright for a mess of pottage, and whose inhabitants should be treated as slaves without ceremony." Nor did they stop at invectives; they resolved "that no provision should be shipped to that infamous colony," Georgia; "that every vessel trading there should be burnt;" and that "whosoever should traffic with them should be put to death;" and these were not idle threats; for two vessels, about sailing for Savannah, were captured before they had cleared Charleston bar, were taken back to the city, condemned, and, with their cargoes, destroyed.

But the injustice of these measures towards Georgia will be evident, when it is remembered, that through the irresolution of Governor Bull, the port of Charleston itself was open, under pretence that no stamped papers could be had, when in fact they were lodged, by his authority, in Fort Johnson, whence, overawed by the populace, he dared not remove, nor did he dare to use them. Charleston, also, was a city of many thousand inhabitants, and its Governor hesitating or timorous; while Savannah had hardly as many hundreds, controlled by a chief magistrate whose energy and decision could neither be wearied by, importunity, nor daunted by danger. Georgia, therefore, did not deserve the reproach which Carolina cast upon her; for everything which a province similarly situated could do, was done; and she rested not from her efforts until the repeal of the act, and a change of ministry brought with them temporary quiet and repose.

The course of Governor Wright, during these difficulties, was approved by the King; and though it was reported at one time that his conduct had given offence to his majesty, who had resolved to send over a Lieutenant-Governor to supersede him, yet the Earl of Shelburne assured him that this was untrue, "the King having no thought of recalling or superseding him."

The displacement of the obnoxious ministry in June, 1765; and the repeal of the Stamp Act, February 22d, 1766; removed, for a time, some of the causes of colonial discontent; and order and approval took the place of anarchy and opposition. The official announcement of this repeal was received by the Governor on the 6th of July; and he immediately by proclamation convened the General Assembly, which met in Savannah on the 16th of the same month.

Addressing the Assembly, the Governor said: "I think myself happy that I have it in my power to congratulate you on this province having no injuries or damages, either of a public or private nature, with respect to property to compensate, and that you, Gentlemen of the Assembly, have no votes or resolutions injurious to the honor of His Majesty's Government, or tending to destroy the legal or constitutional dependency of the Colonies on the Imperial Crown and Parliament of Great Britain, to reconsider; I say, Gentlemen, these are points that give me, and I dare say must give you, the greatest satisfaction.

"When you consider the papers I shall now lay before you, I am persuaded your hearts must be filled with the highest veneration and filial gratitude, with a most ardent zeal to declare and express your grateful feelings and acknowledgments, and to make a dutiful and proper return, and show a cheerful obedience to the laws and legislative authority of Great Britain."

To this the Commons' House of Assembly returned the following answer: "We, His Majesty's most dutiful and loyal subjects, beg leave to return your Excellency our sincere thanks for your affectionate speech. Hopeful as we were that no occasion would have offered of calling us together till the usual season of our meeting, yet it is with the highest pleasure and satisfaction, and with hearts overflowing with filial affection and gratitude to our most gracious Sovereign, that we embrace the opportunity now presented to us of expressing our most dutiful acknowledgments to the best of kings for his paternal and princely attention and regard manifested to his faithful subjects in these remote parts of his dominions, in graciously condescending to lend his royal ear to their supplications, and removing from them those evils they lamented. Nor can we sufficiently venerate and admire the magnanimity and justice of the British Parliament in so speedily redressing the grievances by them complained of."

"We cannot, indeed, but felicitate ourselves in that we have no injuries or damages, either of a public or a private nature, nor any votes or resolutions derogatory to the honor of his Majesty's government, or tending to destroy the true constitutional dependency of the Colonies on the Imperial Crown and Parliament of Great Britain to reconsider."

"We will immediately proceed to take into our most serious consideration the papers laid before us by your Excellency, and we shall upon all occasions be ready to testify our loyalty to our king and firm attachment to our mother country."

Both Houses also united in the following loyal address to the king, couched in terms of almost abject servility, yet not exceeding the usual character of such papers at that period:

"To the King's most excellent Majesty, the humble address of both Houses of Assembly of the Province of Georgia.

Most Gracious Sovereign:

"We, your Majesty's loyal subjects, the Council and Commons of your Majesty's Province of Georgia, in General Assembly met, beg leave to approach your royal person with hearts full of the most dutiful affection and gratitude. Influenced by principle and animated by your Majesty's exemplary justice and paternal care in redressing the grievances of your faithful subjects in these remote parts of your wide-extended empire, with the deepest sense of your Majesty's royal clemency and goodness, we humbly offer to your most sacred Majesty our sincere thanks for the repeal of the late Act of the British Parliament, commonly called the American Stamp Act. Nor can we sufficiently admire the magnanimity and justice displayed by the British Parliament on this occasion. Permit us, dread sire, while we endeavor to express our gratitude to the best of kings for affording us so speedy and necessary relief, to assure your Majesty that we shall upon all occasions strive to evince our loyalty and firm attachment to your Majesty's sacred person and Government, being truly sensible of the advantage derived to us from the protection of our mother country; and that it is, and ever will be, our honor, happiness, and true interest to remain connected with and dependent on the Imperial Crown and Parliament of Great Britain upon the solid basis of the British Constitution. That your Majesty's Illustrious House may continue to reign over a free, loyal, and grateful people, to the latest posterity, is, most gracious sovereign, our constant prayer, unfeigned wish, and our most sanguine hope."

Order once more prevailed, and the various avocations and pursuits of industry were resumed with diligence and success, as will fully appear from a comparison, in a few points, with the condition of things some years back.

During the first quarter of a century of the colonial existence of Georgia, there was not even a wharf at Savannah. The few vessels which traded there were landed alongside of the bluff, and their cargoes discharged upon the sandy bank of the river.

The first wharf built in Savannah was constructed in 1759, by Thomas Eaton, under the direction of John G. Wm. De Brahm, Surveyor-General of the Southern Provinces of North America, and an engineer of distinguished attainments. De Brahm says, in his report upon the Province of Georgia, that he advised the builder "to drive two rows of piles as far asunder as he desired his wharf to be wide, and as far toward the river as low-water mark, secure their tops with plates, and to trunnel planks within on the piles. This done, then to brace the insides with dry walls of stones intermixed with willow twigs. In the same manner to shut up the ends of the two rows with a like front along the stream, to build inside what cellars he had occasion for, then to fill up the remainder with the sand nearest at hand, out of the bluff or high shore of the stream under the bay."

"This plan," he says, writing many years later, "has been followed ever since to this day."[1]

The next year, 1760, the number of vessels which entered at the custom house, was forty-one, but in 1766, there were one hundred and seventy-one.

The population in 1760 was 6100 whites and 3600 blacks; but in 1766, notwithstanding the ravages of the small pox, two years before, there were 10,000 whites and 8000 blacks.

There were no manufactures in the colony, for they were rigorously disallowed in all the provinces; but commerce and agriculture were carried on with much zeal, and with the reward usually attendant upon all well-directed industry. Governor Wright, who had travelled extensively through the province, speaks enthusiastically of it, as "the most flourishing colony on the continent;" and in a letter to the Earl of Hillsborough, he assured him, that "it was certain, beyond a doubt, that this province has, must, and will, make a rapid progress, and in a few years will make as considerable a figure as most on the continent." Addressing the Earl of Shelburne, he thus forcibly states the advancing condition of Georgia:

"On Governor Ellis's departure from hence, on the 2d of November, 1760, I took upon me the govern-

[1] De Brahm's Province of Georgia, p. 45, Wormsloe, 1849.

ment of this province; and at that time, my lord, from the returns of the militia officers and the best information I could get, the whole number of white people throughout the province, men, women, and children, amounted only to 6000 (and I had afterwards reason to think there were not so many); of which number there was about sixty men belonging to his majesty's independent companies, and two troops of rangers, consisting of five officers and seventy private men each, and the foot militia amounted to 1025; and now, my lord, by a very careful inquiry from every part of the province, the white people amount to 9900, or say 10,000, of which 1800 are effective militia. We have still the two troops of rangers; but the independents are broke, and we have only thirty Royal Americans.

"When I came, the return made me of negroes in the province amounted to 3578, but which I soon found greatly exceeded the real number then in the province; and now, my lord, we have at least 7800.

"In 1760, they exported, as appears by the custom-house books, only 3400 lbs. of rice, and in 1765, though a short crop, 10,235 lbs. In the year 1761, we loaded only 42 sail of sea-vessels; and the last year we loaded 153, and, on an average, of much greater burden.

"Our crop of rice this year will be short for the quantity planted, owing to the excessive rains and inundations that we had in the spring and fore part of the year.

"The Royal Americans and rangers here, my lord, garrison and do duty at seven different places, viz.: 20 of the Royal Americans at Fort Augusta, about

150 miles by land up this river; also, 30 of the rangers in the town of Augusta. The other 10 Royal Americans are at Frederica, about 80 miles south of the town. 25 rangers at Fort Barrington, on the Altamaha River, about 65 miles from hence; 15 at Fort Argyle, on Ogeechee River, 20 miles from town; 19 at Fort George, near the entrance of this river; and the rest here at Savannah. So that your lordship sees how they are scattered about; but I conceive it to be the most useful manner in which such an handful of men can be employed here.

"We have no manufactures of the least consequence: a trifling quantity of coarse homespun cloth, woollen and cotton mixed; amongst the poorer sort of people, for their own use, a few cotton and yarn stockings; shoes for our negroes; and some occasional blacksmith's work. But all our supplies of silks, linens, woollens, shoes, stockings, nails, locks, hinges, and tools of every sort, etc., etc., etc., are all imported from and through Great Britain. We have no kind of illicit trade carried on here, and our whole strength and attention is employed in planting rice, indigo, corn, and peas, and a small quantity of wheat and rye, and in making pitch, tar, turpentine, shingles, and staves, and sawing lumber and scantling and boards of every kind, and in raising stocks of cattle, mules, horses, and hogs; and next year I hope some essays will be made towards planting and making hemp. And everything here, my lord, is going on extremely well, and the people in general well disposed, except some few republican spirits, who endeavor to inculcate independency and keep up jealousy and ill blood, a small specimen of which your lordship will perceive by the inclosed paper. I think it is my indispensable duty to give your lordship every information that may tend to his majesty's service, or that his ministers ought to know. Your lordship may be assured I shall persevere in my utmost endeavors for his majesty's service, and that I shall, in every respect, discharge my duty as I think a faithful servant and an honest man ought to do.

"The spirit that prevailed here, and our transactions with respect to the Stamp Act, your lordship may see by my letters to Mr. Secretary Conway. Amazing to think, what a propensity to faction, sedition, and almost rebellion, there appeared, even in this infant colony; although I must do them the justice to say, they did not think of it till spirited on by our northern neighbors, who never let them rest or gave them time to cool."

CHAPTER VI.

LEGISLATIVE TROUBLES.

The restoration of order by the repeal of the Stamp Act, was, as Governor Wright well expressed it, "but a temporary calm." On the 6th of January, 1767, Captain Philips, commanding the Royal Americans in South Carolina and Georgia, wrote to the Governor, stating the barrack necessaries he required, and desiring to know where he could procure them. The Governor sent the letter with a message to the Assembly, on the 20th, but the House replied "they humbly conceive their complying with the requisition would be a violation of the trust reposed in them by their constituents, and founding a precedent they by no means think themselves justifiable in introducing," and the Governor finding them inflexible, and that compliance with the terms of the "Mutiny Act" was to be expected, had the mortification to transmit their proceedings to His Majesty's ministers.

This Act of Parliament for quartering troops upon the Americans, and making them answerable for the means of their subsistence and transportation, was but another phase of the plan of taxation, and under whatever form such a principle was avowed, it could never be countenanced or sustained by Americans.

The British Constitution solemnly guaranteed to every man the property which he had honestly acquired; and left the disposal of it to his own choice, with which neither corporations nor government could interfere without his consent, expressed by himself, or his accredited representative. If the Americans could be taxed without their agreement by any laws, of whatever name; or if soldiers could be quartered in their houses without their consent, it was a palpable violation of the indefeasible birthright of a British subject; and justified the language of the Massachusetts Assembly to their agent, that, "if they were taxed without representation, they were slaves." It was in truth making the Americans "tenants at will of liberty," a tenure from which they were liable to be ejected at any moment, and which reduced them from the condition of free subjects to a state of ignominious vassalage.

Nor would the condition of things have been much altered, had the King and Cabinet been of a lenient temper; it was the principle which the colonists contended for; and they justly reasoned, with Cicero, that though the sovereign did not oppress and tyrannize, the condition of his subjects was still miserable; that he had the power if he but exercised his will.

This repudiation of the Mutiny Act was followed by a refusal to comply with a clause appended, at the suggestion of the Governor and Council, to two bills granting ferries, and providing for the free carriage of postmen according to the Statute 9th Ann. ch. 10, sec. 29, because they would not seem to adopt or submit to an Act of Parliament.

When the Assembly displaced Mr. Knox as agent of the colony, the Governor desired the House to appoint Mr. Cumberland; but they refused, and gave the place to Mr. Samuel Grath, agent for the Province of South Carolina; but the Governor and Council declined to recognize him, and used their influence to prevent his being accredited as agent by any of the Boards in London. In this they were right, and the lower House of Assembly wrong; for certainly it was impossible that the same agent for contiguous provinces, between which, causes of altercation sometimes arose (and in the present instance were actually pending), could be impartial to either without meeting opposition from both. But such was the zeal of the Commons for the upholding of their prerogative, that no consideration weighed when a compromise of that was required. Having thus thwarted the Governor, and in a variety of ways evinced their contempt of the authority of Parliament, they presented a petition to the Governor desiring "that he would dissolve them," thereby hoping that by the new election which would ensue, a still larger majority of liberal delegates would be returned, the political strength of the existing House being seven "Royalists" and eighteen "Liberty Boys."

These proceedings were immediately represented to the King; and in reply, the Earl of Shelburne, his majesty's principal Secretary of State for the Southern Colonies, wrote to Governor Wright: "It is scarce possible to conceive to what motives to attribute a conduct so infatuated, in a province lately erected, which has been so singularly favored and protected by the mother country." "And I have it," says the Earl, "in command from his majesty, to inform you that he expects and requires the Commons House of Assembly of

Georgia will render an exact and complete obedience, in all respects whatever, to the terms of the Mutiny Act." To punish the Assembly for their conduct, General Gage withdrew all the troops from the province, thus leaving the fort unmanned, and the settlement without defence.

This was a chastisement, as arbitrary as it was severe; but it was a two-edged sword; for while the people complained of it, as exposing them to the mercy of their slave population, and the attacks of the Indians, whose hostile intentions had already been strongly evinced, the Governor also lamented the measure, as cutting him off from the only means whereby to enforce his majesty's authority; and so the matter, at the next session, was mutually and happily adjusted.

While, however, Georgia, in common with other colonies, suffered under the evil legislation of Parliament, she had grievances peculiar to herself, which greatly increased her opposition to the mother country. To facilitate the operations of trade, provincial paper, to the amount of £7410, had been issued by act of Assembly, in 1761, which bills were current at par, both in Georgia and Florida. The merchants and traders, finding this sum insufficient for mercantile purposes, now petitioned both houses for relief "from the want of a sufficient currency in a province where, by the peculiar situation of its commerce and produce, they are precluded from the advantage of receiving any quantity of bullion, or retaining what little they may receive." It was proposed, therefore, to recall the old emission, and issue new paper to the amount of £20,000. But the Governor, though he thought the present bills of credit too limited, also thought that the sum of £20,000 was too large, believing that £12,000 would meet the emergency; as every hundred pounds more of paper currency than is really necessary for the daily or common occurrences, would prove injurious, by depreciating its value and increasing the rate of exchange, and would prevent the circulation of sterling money, and produce a fictitious wealth, which the intrinsic condition of the colony could not by any means support. His counsel, however, was unheeded; the question was made tributary to the absorbing one of parliamentary wrongs, and both the upper and lower house presented a petition to the King for the relief desired; but his majesty refused their prayer.

On the 25th March, 1765, the Assembly passed an act "for the better ordering and governing of Negroes," etc., and the following year, "An Act for encouraging Settlers to come into the Province." Both these laws were founded on strong necessity—the security of the province greatly depended on the former; and its prosperity and increase on the latter; but, when sent over for royal approval, both were disallowed. The Governor, as well as the Assembly, was astounded at this unlooked for result; and the Governor, who declared, that "without the negro law no man's life or property would be safe a moment," was compelled to disobey his instructions, and frame a new bill with a different title, but with the same provisions.

Operating on minds already excited, these refusals of the King to sanction laws enacted for the extension of trade and commerce; and for the protection, prosperity and increase, of the colony; irritated the people to an intense degree; so much so, that the Governor declared, "that though he had hitherto kept the Assembly within tolerably decent bounds, yet that he had lately discovered more than ever a strong propensity to be as considerable and independent, as they term it, of the British Parliament, or of the sovereignty of Great Britain, as any of the northern colonies."

The necessity of sending every law to England for confirmation, before it could be made operative in the province where it was enacted, was a serious hindrance to legislative action in many of the colonies; and not only in the cases just mentioned, but in many others, was this requirement felt to be a sore grievance, and a cause of great disquietude. When the Assembly enacted a law, it must first receive the approbation of the Governor; if vetoed by him, there it ended; if approved, he sent it to England, to be examined by the King's Attorney, who made his report to the Lords of Trade; if this Board approved it, it was sent for confirmation to the King's Council; if it passed the ordeal of this body, it received the sign manual of the King, and became a law. It was then returned to the Board of Trade, thence sent to the Crown Agent, who despatched it to the Governor; thus causing sometimes a detention of two years, from the passage of an act by the Assembly, before, having gone this tedious circuit, and escaped the chances of five negatives, it returned ratified by the King.

On the 11th of April, 1768, Benjamin Franklin was appointed Agent "to represent, solicit, and transact the affairs of this province in Great Britain;" and a committee of both houses was appointed to correspond with him. This committee consisted, on the part of the Council, of James Habersham, Noble Jones, James Edward Powell, Lewis Johnstone, and Clement Martin; and, on the part of the lower house, of Alexander Wylly, John Mulryne, John Smith, Noble Wimberly Jones, John Milledge, John Simpson, Archibald Bulloch, William Ewen, and Joseph Gibbons.

The fame of Franklin had extended over Europe. His dignified manners, his profound knowledge, his grand discoveries in physical science, and his uncompromising support of colonial rights, conspired to render him the best representative which Georgia could select for that critical period. During five years he represented Georgia at the several offices in England, and was her undaunted champion in every hour of danger and of trial.

The onerous enactments of Parliament, by which duties were laid on paper, glass, painters' colors, and teas imported into the provinces; the establishing of a general civil list throughout North America; the demanding that quarters and other barrack necessaries should be furnished to troops; and the restraining the New York Assembly from passing any act, because it had failed to make this provision for the soldiers stationed there, drew forth from nearly all the colonies petitions, remonstrances, and addresses.

On the 11th of February, 1768, the Massachusetts House of Representatives, through their Speaker, addressed a circular letter to the several provincial Assemblies, stating the condition of American grievances, and soliciting a union of petitions to the two houses of Parliament and to the King, having, as they expressed it in the close of their letter, "firm confidence in the King, our common head and father, that the united and dutiful supplication of his distressed American subjects will meet with his royal and favorable acceptance."

When this circular reached Savannah, the Assembly had adjourned; but Mr. Alexander Wylly, the Speaker, replied to it, "as a private person," and stated that "the Assembly had instructed Dr. Franklin to join with the Agents in soliciting a repeal of those acts, and in remonstrating against any of like nature in the future." The Assembly again met on the 17th November, and chose Noble Wimberly Jones Speaker, the late Speaker not being present. The Governor, in his opening speech, remarked: "I have observed, in your Gazette of the 31st of August, a letter from your late Speaker to the Speaker of the House of Representatives of Massachusetts, acknowledging the reception of a letter, dated 11th February last, assuring him, that when the Assembly meets, he will lay the same before the House. I am to acquaint you that his majesty considers that measure to be of a most dangerous tendency. I have it in charge to endeavor to prevail on you not to give any countenance to that letter; but, if I should find any disposition in you to give any countenance thereto, it will be my duty immediately to put an end to your sitting."

For a time the ordinary business proceeded without interruption, and such laws were passed as the necessities of the colonies required. But on Saturday, the 24th December, 1768, after all the bills of the session were prepared for the Governor's assent, prior to adjournment, Mr. Wylly laid before the House the letter from Massachusetts, and also a letter from Peyton Randolph, Speaker of the Commons House of Assembly, Virginia. Both of these were ordered to be entered on the journals, and they then adopted the following resolutions:

"Resolved, That from the inherent right of the subject to petition the throne for redress of grievances, a right allowed and confirmed by the Act of William and Mary, the said letters[1] do not appear to the House of a dangerous or factious tendency, but on the contrary, in the opinion of this House, only tend to a justifiable union of subjects aggrieved, in lawful and laudable endeavors to obtain redress by an application founded upon and expressive of duty and loyalty to the best of kings, a becoming respect for the Parliament of Great Britain, and an equitable and natural affection for our mother country, and arises from the tender and commendable attention of those colonies to the natural rights and liberties of the British subjects in America, and to which they are undeniably entitled upon the happy principles of our constitution.

"Resolved, That copies of this resolution be, by the Speaker of the House, transmitted to the Speaker of the House of Representatives of the Province of Massachusetts Bay, and to the Speaker of the House of Burgesses in Virginia, and that they be acquainted by him that this House approves of the measures by them pursued to obtain redress of our common grievances, also of the method by them taken of communicating these measures to the other provinces of the continent.

"Ordered, that the several proceedings and resolu-

[1] Letters from the Assemblies of Massachusetts and Virginia.

tions respecting the said letters be published in the Gazette of this province, and that the clerk do furnish the printer with a copy of the same."

Governor Wright had used every means to prevent their countenancing "the Boston letter," expostulating with the leading members, and according to his own idea, had "clearly convinced them of the absurdity of it." He was quite surprised, therefore, when informed that similar resolves had been entered on their journal, for so quietly had it been effected, that the Governor said, "everything was prepared and done before I could prevent it." He immediately repaired to the council chamber, and summoning the Commons House to attend, made them a long and earnest address, in which he uttered the prediction, which time has not verified, "that if America was to become independent, from that day you may date the foundation of your ruin and misery."[2] He then, "by virtue of his Majesty's authority and in his name, dissolved the Assembly."

Anticipating this dissolution, the Commons House had previously drawn up the following address:

To the King's most Excellent Majesty.

The humble address of the Commons House of Assembly of the Province of Georgia, 24th December, 1768.

Most Gracious Sovereign:

Your dutiful and loyal subjects, the Commons House of Assembly of Georgia, with the greatest humility beg leave to represent to your sacred person the grievances this province labors under by the late Acts of the Parliament of Great Britain, for raising a revenue in America.

[2] Board of Trade, xiii, 98.

Equally attached by interest, principle, and affection for our mother country, we readily acknowledge a constitutional subordination to its supreme Legislature, at the same time, with inexpressible concern, we much lament that by their imposition of internal taxes we are deprived of the privilege which with humble deference we apprehend to be our indubitable right, that of granting away our own property, and are thereby prevented from a ready compliance with any requisition your Majesty may please to make, and which to the utmost extent of our small abilities, we have hitherto always most cheerfully obeyed.

From your Majesty's equity, wisdom, and truly paternal regard for the rights and liberties of your subjects, however remote, we flatter ourselves with and firmly rely upon redress in this our unhappy situation, and as we of this province experience your Majesty's particular countenance and protection in our present infant state, for which we are impressed with the deepest sense of gratitude, so we most earnestly hope we shall also experience in general with our sister colonies on this occasion fresh marks of your Majesty's royal justice and attention to the supplications of your distressed subjects.

We beg leave to assure your Majesty that none of your numerous subjects can or do more ardently wish and pray for a continuance of your most auspicious reign, and that your latest posterity may happily rule over a free, grateful, and loyal people, than your faithful Commons of Georgia.

By order of the House.

N. W. Jones,
December 24th, 1768. Speaker.

This address was sent by the Speaker to Benjamin Franklin, who was requested to concur with the other "agents of the American colonies in endeavors to obtain a repeal of those acts of Parliament so grievous to his Majesty's loyal subjects of the Continent, and destructive of that harmony which ought, and they earnestly wish may, subsist between our mother country and its colonies."[3]

This address Franklin presented to the King, through the Earl of Hillsborough;[4] but his majesty objected to the transmission of it, through any other channel than that of his Governor, as irregular and disrespectful, and directed the Earl to signify to Governor Wright that, because "it does, both in the letter and spirit, deny and draw into question the authority of Parliament to enact laws binding upon the colonies, in all cases whatsoever, he disapproved of it, being firmly resolved to support the Constitution as by law established, and not to countenance any claims inconsistent with its true principles."

Governor Wright dissolved the Assembly: but this act being expected and prepared for, produced no excitement. The representatives of the people felt that they had done their part, in placing the letters of the Massachusetts and Virginia Assembly on their journals, and in passing resolves and addresses expressing their sympathy with the former, and their determination to support the true principles of English liberty. The affairs of the colony, thus temporarily disturbed, soon resumed their usual tranquil state, and

[3] MS. copies of Letters of Franklin, furnished by Hon. Jared Sparks.

[4] State Paper Office, iv, 127.

the rapid progress of the province, in every respect, was quite observable.

But the legislation of Parliament was still directed towards sustaining, in their most extravagant extent, the prerogatives of the crown, and pursued, for this end, a course as impolitic for Great Britain as for America: and thus the colonists, finding that their respectful appeals to the throne and to Parliament were unheeded, resolved to redress themselves.

One of the primary measures adopted for this purpose, was a suspension of all commercial dealings with Great Britain, except for such articles as were absolutely and unequivocally necessary. Such non-intercourse could not fail of producing disastrous results in the mother country, the prosperity of which was so intimately connected with the colonial trade. Mr. Grenville, first lord of the Treasury, asserted, that "every inhabitant of the colonies employs four at home." "It was American trade," said the Earl of Chatham to the Peers, "which triumphantly carried you through the last war;" and the eloquent Burke declared in the House of Commons, "that whatever England had been growing to, by a progressive increase of improvements brought in by varieties of people, by succession of civilizing conquests and civilizing settlements in a series of seventeen hundred years, you shall see as much added to her by America in a single life." It was hoped, therefore, that the withdrawal of such important resources, and the misery consequent on such a procedure, might work that change in the Ministry, which all the petitions and remonstrances had failed to effect. This plan was suggested as early as April, 1768, by the Boston merchants; but the Assembly of Virginia, in June, 1769, was the first legislative body which adopted resolves of non-importation, which, ere long, were sanctioned by the other colonies.

On the 16th of September, 1769, a meeting of the merchants and traders of Savannah was held at the house of Mr. Alexander Creighton, at which they resolved, "that any person or persons whatsoever, importing any of the articles subject to parliamentary duties, after having it in their power to prevent it, ought not only to be treated with contempt, but also as enemies of their country." Three days after, a larger meeting was convened, with the Hon. Jonathan Bryan, one of the Governor's Council, in the chair; at which the same subject was renewedly canvassed, and resolves of non-importation, mostly similar to the other colonies, unanimously passed. One of the resolves, based on the sentiments of the Bostonians in 1765, was to abolish mourning at funerals, as the black stuffs used for such purposes were of British manufacture.

For the part which Mr. Bryan took in this meeting, he was, by command of the King, displaced from the Council, and thus became the first object of royal vengeance in Georgia. Carrying out into detail the fundamental principle, that there should be no taxation where there was no representation, the Assembly, in 1769, inserted a clause in the annual tax-bill, exempting the four southern parishes from taxation, because they were allowed no members in the legislature, and this decisive stand produced, in due time, the required writs of election for the vacant parishes. There was a constant struggle between the Governor and the Assembly; the former, asserting that they arrogated to themselves the prerogatives of Parliament—that they exercised indecorous privileges, and usurped authority which the royal instructions never invested in that body; and the latter, claiming to be the sole legislative body, the only exponents of constitutional rights, and the only depository of political power—declared that they would be under no executive dictation, and submit to no infringement of their rights. Twice had the Governor dissolved the Assembly; but the time had now arrived when a new agent of royal power was to be employed in humbling their pretensions to the supreme control of the colony.

At the opening of the Assembly in 1770, Dr. Noble Wimberly Jones, one of the morning stars of liberty in Georgia, was unanimously elected Speaker; but the Governor put a negative on his election, and sent the House back to make a new choice. This proscription, which was designed as a rebuke to Dr. Jones, was more honorable to him than the commission which authorized it; and ranked him at once with Otis, negatived by Sir Francis Bernard; and with Hancock, negatived by Hutchinson. To them, the intended stigma, though for the moment mortifying to personal ambition, was like the honorable wound of the soldier, the proud scar of a contest, which rescued almost a hemisphere from thraldom. The Assembly resented this insult to their elective franchise; and passed a resolution complimenting Dr. Jones, and declaring, "that the sense and approbation this House entertain of his conduct, can never be lessened by any slight cast upon him, in opposition to the unanimous voice of the Commons House of Assembly in particular, and the province in general." And they furthermore resolved:

"that this rejection by the Governor of a Speaker unanimously elected, was a high breach of the privileges of the House, and tended to subvert the most valuable rights and liberties of the people and their representatives." This bold assertion was termed by the Council, a "most indecent and insolent denial of his Majesty's authority;" and the Governor, on the 22d February, 1770, dissolved the Assembly.

At a meeting of the Council, on the 2d July, 1771, Governor Wright laid before the board a letter from the Earl of Hillsborough, stating that the King had disapproved of the conduct of the late legislature, and approved the course of the Governor in dissolving that body. He further informed the Council, that he had his Majesty's permission to visit England; and on the 10th July, he left Savannah, on his voyage thither.

On the 13th July, James Habersham, the President of the Council, took the customary oaths of office, and entered upon the gubernatorial duties which devolved upon him during the absence of Mr. Wright. Mr. Habersham was a man whose thorough knowledge of the colony, whose long experience in public affairs, whose pure and upright character, and whose great firmness eminently fitted him for this responsible station. But the part which he was called to act by the royal mandate was exceedingly repugnant to his generous nature. His orders, however, were imperative, and compliance was unavoidable. In consequence of the resolutions of the last Assembly, which denied the authority of the Governor to negative their choice of a speaker, the king commanded Mr. Habersham to signify his disapprobation of their conduct, and that he should, for the purpose of renewedly testing the question, and to compel them to obedience, negative whoever might be first chosen as their next speaker. The Assembly met on the 21st of April, 1772, and Doctor Jones was elected, who, on being presented to President Habersham, was, by virtue of his instructions, negatived. On a second ballot he was again elected, and again rejected. At the third trial he was still their choice, but declining to serve, Archibald Bullock was chosen, whom the president accepted. But when, on examining the journal of the House the next day, he ascertained the third election of Dr. Jones, of which he was hitherto ignorant, he sent them word to suspend all business until that minute was erased; but as the House resolutely refused to expunge it, he ordered the Assembly to be dissolved. These repeated interruptions in colonial legislation produced serious and alarming consequences. The treasury was overdrawn, and no provision was made to replenish it; statutes of importance had expired, and no new enactments supplied their places; the judiciary was deranged, and no means were adopted to rectify it; and new necessities, civil and legal, had arisen, requiring legislative action, but the meetings of the Assembly had been rudely dissolved, and the political existence of the colony was vitally endangered. These oppressions increased the adherents of the colonial cause. The flattering promises of the ministry to redress their grievances, had not been fulfilled; but new sources of distress had augmented those already existing, and cloud upon cloud, each darker and more foreboding than the former, was casting its gloom over their firmament. The passage of the Boston Port Bill, March 31, 1774, by which Parliament precluded all commerce with that city;

followed by another which deprived Massachusetts of its chartered privileges; together with a law for sending state criminals to England "to be butchered in the King's Bench," hurried on the catastrophe of war.

The zeal of Governor Wright in his Majesty's service, and the wisdom and prudence, as well as capacity, which marked his executive character, procured him on his arrival in England a favorable audience of the King; who, on the 8th December, 1772, created him a Baronet of Great Britain. He sailed on his return to Georgia, from Falmouth, England, towards the close of December, 1772, in his Majesty's Packet-boat Eagle, being accompanied by his two daughters.[5] He reached Charleston on the 4th February, 1773, and Savannah about the middle of that month. As, on his departure nineteen months before, affectionate addresses had been presented to him by the Council, the bench, the merchants, and the public officers, so now, on his return, tokens of respect were freely tendered to him, and he was received by the Georgians with great friendliness and rejoicing. Despite the differences of opinion which existed between Governor Wright and some of the leading minds of the colony in reference to the late measures of Parliament, there was a universal feeling that he had honestly discharged his duty to his king, and had exhibited qualities inspiring respect and commanding esteem.

[5] Anne, subsequently married to Rear-Admiral Sir James Wallace; and Mary, afterwards the wife of General Barron.

BOOK FOURTH.

GEORGIA IN THE REVOLUTION.

CHAPTER I.

DAWNINGS OF LIBERTY—INDIAN TROUBLES, ETC.

THE designs of George the Third were now unmasked; and Lord North boldly declared that he would not listen to the complaints of America until she was at his feet. The words, indeed, were those of the favorite minister, but the sentiment was the King's; for his feelings had been so wrought up by the resistance of his prerogative, not only by the Americans, but also by the opposition which he experienced in Parliament, where "that trumpet of sedition," as he termed Lord Chatham, made the walls of St. Stephen's ring with the defence of oppressed millions, that he said several times "if the people will not stand by me, they shall have another king;" and when Lord North, like a wise Palinurus, foreseeing the danger, desired to retire from the helm of state, it was the constraining importunity of the king which alone kept him at his post. The Machiavelian fiction, which, making the ministers amenable for political failures, assert that "the king can do no wrong," turned, indeed, the nation's wrath from the monarch to his officials, but it is nevertheless true, that the severe measures pursued toward America, oftener originated with the king, than with the premier; and that the very effort to accomplish the absorbing idea of George the Third, "the preservation of the empire," resulted through his obdurate rancour in its irretrievable disunion. Whatever might have been the effect of conciliatory measures prior to the recent Acts of Parliament, it was now too late. The favorable moment had passed, and the thirteen colonies of America were lost to him forever. Remonstrances, petitions, resolutions, had all failed in producing a change of policy, and in common with the other provinces, Georgia, the last settled, and the last to renounce allegiance to the crown, addressed herself to the sacrifice of everything but liberty.

The spirit of indignation which was aroused throughout the land by the closing of the port of Boston, and divesting that town of commercial rights, was participated in by many Georgians, and a notice accordingly appeared in the Georgia Gazette, of the 20th July, 1774, stating that "the critical situation to which the British Provinces in America are likely to be reduced, from the alarming and arbitrary imposition of the late act of the British Parliament, respecting the town of Boston, as well as the acts that at present exist tending to the raising of a perpetual revenue, without the consent of the people or their representatives, is considered as an object extremely important at this critical juncture, and particularly calculated to deprive the

American subjects of their constitutional rights and liberties as parts of the British Empire." It concluded by requesting "that all persons within the limits of this province do attend at the liberty pole at Tondee's Tavern, in Savannah, on Wednesday, the 27th inst., in order that the said matter may be taken under consideration, and such other constitutional measures pursued as may then appear most eligible." This invitation, signed by Noble Wimberly Jones, Archibald Bullock, John Houstoun, and George Walton, was promptly responded to; and a large number convened at the watch-house at the time appointed. But little business was done at this meeting, because it was objected, "that many of the out parishes might not have a sufficient notice of the intended meeting;" and, therefore, after reading letters from the various committees of Charleston, Wilmington, Williamsburg, Annapolis, Philadelphia, and Boston, it was "resolved that all further business be postponed till the 10th of August next, and that in the meantime, notice be given to the inhabitants of the several parishes, in order to afford them an opportunity of sending down deputies to deliver their sense upon this very important occasion." This notice was sent by Mr. John Glen, the chairman of the Savannah Committee, to the different parishes, requesting that they would send a number "to join the committee agreeable to the number of representatives each parish sends to the General Assembly."

Such proceedings could not pass unnoticed. The Governor was now fairly excited at the threatening aspect of affairs, and at the array of respectable names on this Savannah Committee of thirty-one persons.

True to his purpose of treading out the first sparks of rebellion, he issued his proclamation, "notifying that all such summonses and calls by private persons, and all assembling and meetings of the people, which may tend to raise fears and jealousies in the minds of his Majesty's subjects, under the pretence of consulting together for redress of public grievances or imaginary grievances, are unconstitutional, illegal, and punishable by law. And I do hereby require," says the Governor, "all his Majesty's liege subjects within this Province to pay due regard to this my Proclamation, as they will answer the contrary at their peril."

Undaunted by such warnings, the patriots of Georgia met at the appointed place, on the 10th August, and unanimously passed the following resolutions:

"Resolved, *nemine contradicente*, That his Majesty's subjects in America owe the same allegiance, and are entitled to the same rights, privileges, and immunities with their fellow-subjects in Great Britain.

"Resolved, *nemine contradicente*, That, as protection and allegiance are reciprocal, and under the British Constitution correlative terms, his Majesty's liege subjects in America have a clear and indisputable right, as well from the general laws of mankind, as from the ancient and established customs of the land, so often recognized, to petition the throne upon every emergency.

"Resolved, *nemine contradicente*, That an act of Parliament, lately passed, for blockading the port and harbor of Boston, is contrary to our idea of the British Constitution: First, for that it in effect deprives good and lawful men of the use of their property without judgment of their peers; and, secondly, for that it is in nature of an *ex post facto* law, and indiscriminately blends, as objects of punishment, the innocent with the guilty. Neither do we conceive the same justified upon a principle of necessity; for that numerous instances evince that the laws and executive power of Boston have made sufficient provision for the punishment of all offenders against persons and property.

"Resolved, *nemine contradicente;* That the act for abolishing the charter of Massachusetts Bay tends to the subversion of American rights; for, besides those general liberties the original settlers brought over with them as their birthright, particular immunities were granted by such charter, as an inducement and means of settling the province; and we apprehend the said charter cannot be dissolved, but by a voluntary surrender of the people, representatively declared.

"Resolved, *nemine contradicente,* That we apprehend the Parliament of Great Britain hath not, nor ever had, any right to tax his Majesty's American subjects; for it is evident beyond contradiction, the Constitution admits of no taxation without representation; that they are coeval and inseparable; and every demand for the support of Government should be by requisition made to the several Houses of Representatives.

"Resolved, *nemine contradicente,* That it is contrary to natural justice and the established law of the land, to transport any person to Great Britain, or elsewhere, to be tried under indictment for a crime committed in any of the colonies, as the party prosecuted would thereby be deprived of the privilege of trial by his peers from the vicinage; the injured perhaps prevented from legal reparation, and both lose the full benefit of their witnesses.

"Resolved, *nemine contradicente*, That we will concur with our sister colonies in every constitutional measure to obtain redress of American grievances, and will by every lawful means in our power maintain those inestimable blessings for which we are indebted to God and the Constitution of our country—a Constitution founded upon reason and justice, and the indelible rights of mankind.

"Resolved, *nemine contradicente*, That the committee appointed by the meeting of the inhabitants of this province, on Wednesday the 27th of July last, together with the deputies who have appeared here on this day from the different parishes, be a general committee to act; and that any eleven or more of them shall have full power to correspond with the committees of the several provinces upon the Continent; and that copies of these resolutions, as well as all other proceedings, be transmitted without delay to the Committees of Correspondence in the respective provinces.

"A committee was appointed to receive subscriptions for the suffering poor of Boston, consisting of William Ewen, William Young, Joseph Clay, John Houstoun, Noble Wimberly Jones, Edward Telfair, John Smith, Samuel Farley, and Andrew Elton Wells, Esquires."

The question was also discussed, whether six deputies should be sent to join with the deputies of the other colonies at the General Congress; but, after much debate, it was negatived, though it was asserted that this negative was brought about by the suffrages of those who had no right to vote in the matter.

The parish of St. John (now Liberty County) was

unanimous and remarkably spirited in furnishing supplies for the oppressed; and of the 579 barrels of rice contributed by the province for the suffering Bostonians, 200 barrels came from this parish. They were also exceedingly anxious to be united with the others in every constitutional measure for the removal of public grievances, and expressed their willingness, in this noble struggle, "to exert themselves to the utmost, to make every sacrifice that men impressed with the strongest sense of their rights and liberties, and warm with the most benevolent feelings for their oppressed brethren, can make, to stand firmly or fall gloriously in the common cause." Unwilling to abide by this decision of the meeting, not to send delegates to the General Congress, the parish of St. John called a meeting on the 30th August, at which deputies from St. George's and St. David's united with the people of St. John's, who "Resolved, that if the majority of the parishes would join with them, they would send deputies to join the General Congress, and faithfully and religiously abide by and conform to such determination as should be there entered into, and come from thence recommended."

The adherents of Government strove to cast odium on these meetings, by representing them as the mere gatherings of factious demagogues, self-appointed and unauthorized representatives,[1] forcing their measures by the low tricks of cunning, and palming off "as the voice of the province" resolutions, "unfairly and insolently made by a junto of twenty-five or six."

With the assent of the Governor, petitions opposing the positions taken by the liberty party were prepared,

[1] State Paper Office, vi, 130–3.

and freely circulated, by artful and interested men, who were to receive a certain sum for each name signed; consequently, the number of those, who by these petitions protested against the liberty proceedings, exceeded in some instances the number of free white persons in the respective parishes; the names of several in fact were put upon the papers who had been dead several years.[2]

The meetings of the friends of liberty, and the growing discontent of the people, under the harrowing legislation of Parliament, justly alarmed the Governor, and he frankly told the Earl of Dartmouth that "it required the interposition of higher authority than the executive power, for however coercion or lenient measures might for a time smother the flame, it would only break out again at some future day with greater violence."[3] He was anxious that things "should be brought to a point at once;" but the "point" to which he wished to have them brought,—"entire submission and obedience to the sovereignty of Great Britain,"—was the very point at issue, and one to which Americans could never again be brought.

A temporary lull in the political elements around him enabled the Governor to give attention to the precarious and threatening condition of Indian affairs.

To manage the complicated relations of the Indian tribes with the government, with the traders, and with each other; to redress their grievances, and to claim redress when they were the aggressors; to preserve their friendship and secure peace; required great tact, unquailing firmness, indomitable energy, blended with patience and wisdom. Governor Wright understood

[2] State Paper Office, vi, 147-59. [3] State Paper Office, vi, 122.

the Indian character, and dealing wisely with them in all his plans, secured their confidence, and often saved the colony from their savage incursions.

In 1770, the Cherokees proposed to cede to the traders certain portions of land to liquidate the claims upon them, which, in consequence of a scarcity of game they were unable to pay to their creditors. The amount of their indebtedness to the traders was over $200,000, and the matter having been brought before the Governor by a memorial from the traders, he took occasion, while in England, to represent the matter in such a light to the Board of Trade and his Majesty's Council, that they agreed to his proposals, and gave him full powers to carry out his plan.

On his return to Georgia, he united with Captain Stuart, the Superintendent of Indian Affairs, in sending a message to the Creeks and Cherokees to meet him in congress at Augusta.

They convened at the appointed place on the 1st June, 1773, and having in a long preamble stated their inability to pay the debts justly due from them to the traders, and their desire to cancel these claims by grants of territory, they ceded to his Majesty over 2,100,000 acres, comprising most of the land now lying in the counties of Wilkes, Lincoln, Taliaferro, Green, Oglethorpe, and Elbert.

The Governor anticipated the most beneficial results from this concession, and told the ministry[4] that he expected it would add 10,000 families to the present population; give an increase of 15,000 effective men on the militia muster roll; bring over $500,000 worth of produce into the market; add greater security to the

[4] State Paper Office, v, 168.

present settlements; and remove still farther off the Indians; who, with all their promises of peace, were still troublesome and dangerous. A plan for the settlement of this fertile and healthy region was arranged by the Governor, and Messrs. Bartlett, Maddox, Holland, and Young were vested with powers to carry out this scheme. Two hundred acres were granted to every head of a family, and fifty acres to each member, black and white; warrants for the survey being granted when the entrance money, £5 per one hundred acres, was paid into the Land Courts at Augusta, or Fort James (now Petersburg), at the confluence of the Broad and Savannah Rivers.

A portion of these benefits would no doubt have accrued to Georgia, but for an unfortunate rupture between the Creeks and frontier settlers, owing to which seventeen white persons were murdered by them at Sherrill's Fort, in the beginning of the year 1774. The Indians, led on by Big Elk, secretly approached the fort in the morning, and suddenly firing upon the people then at work, killed three persons, among whom was Sherrill, at the first fire. They hoped to complete their work of destruction by setting fire in several places to the building into which the women and children had retreated, but being suddenly attacked by a party of men under Captain Bernard, they quickly retreated, not, however, until they left several of their number dead upon the field. The attack on Sherrill's Fort was followed up by other skirmishes, in which many lives were lost on both sides; though the great body of the Creeks repudiated these maraudings of a portion of their tribe. These events blasted for a time the fair prospect which dawned on the newly ceded lands, as the inhabitants who ventured there and opened plantations were driven off, by the insecurity of their position, so that the settlement of this noble tract was for some time delayed. In consequence of these frequent ruptures, the Governor and Captain Stuart solicited an interview with the Upper and Lower Creeks at Savannah, and accordingly twenty chiefs met them there on the 18th October, 1774, when a new treaty of peace and amity was made and signed, giving the strongest assurances of mutual good will, and of the pacific disposition of the Indians. It is difficult for us, hemmed in by no savage tribes and exposed to no merciless warfare with infuriated Indians, to appreciate the dangers to which Georgia was then so constantly exposed. Their causes of anger were so slight, their irruption into the settlements was so sudden, their revenge so cruel, that the bold pioneer and the hardy settler quailed before the terrors of the wilderness, and few were sufficiently daring to strike out new paths in the forest, and detach themselves from the stronger settlements. The exertions of the Governor now gave to the population a security they had never before enjoyed, and his negotiations with so many and conflicting tribes, reflected the highest praise upon his sagacity and his fair and equitable dealings. Success was not always commensurate with his hopes; but the failure was caused by the disjointed times, rather than by any defect in his well-matured schemes. He merited and received for his zeal and labors in Indian affairs, the thanks of Georgia, the ministry, and the king.

The autumn of 1774 passed without any public demonstrations in favor of liberty. Both parties were now fairly arrayed, and each labored to secure ascendency; and whatever could be effected by the allurements of office, by promises of favor, by the smiles of the Governor, by political favoritism; was done, and that most sedulously, to keep the province loyal to the King, and free from the innovations of continental reform.

During the second week in January, 1775, a district Congress was held by the inhabitants of St. Andrew's Parish (now Darien), at which a series of resolutions were passed, embodying with great force and earnestness the views of the freeholders of that large and flourishing parish. These resolutions, six in number, expressed, first, their approbation of "the unparalleled moderation, the decent, but firm and manly, conduct of the loyal and brave people of Boston and Massachusetts Bay, to preserve their liberty;" their acquiescence "in all the resolutions of the Grand American Congress," and their hearty and "cheerful accession to the association entered into by them, as the wisest and most moderate measure that could be adopted." The second resolution condemned the shutting of the land offices, to the great detriment of colonial growth, and to the injury of the industrious poor, declaring "that all encouragement should be given to the poor of every nation by every generous American." The third, animadverted upon the ministerial mandates which prevented colonial Assemblies from passing such laws as the several exigencies of the provinces required, an especial grievance, as they declared, "in this young colony, where our internal police is not yet well settled." The fourth, reprobated the practice of making colonial officers dependent for salaries on Great

Britain, "thus making them independent of the people, who should support them according to their usefulness and behavior." In the fifth resolution, the parish declare "our disapprobation and abhorrence of the unnatural practice of slavery in America," and their purpose to urge "the manumission of our slaves in this colony, upon the most safe and equitable footing for the masters and themselves." And, lastly, they thereby choose delegates to represent the district in provincial congress, and instruct them to urge the appointment of two delegates from this colony to the Continental Congress, to be held in Philadelphia in May.

Appended to these resolutions were the following articles of agreement or association:

"Being persuaded that the salvation of the rights and liberties of America depend, under God, on the firm union of the inhabitants in its vigorous prosecution of the measures necessary for its safety, and convinced of the necessity of preventing the anarchy and confusion which attend the dissolution of the powers of government, we, the freemen, freeholders, and inhabitants of the province of Georgia, being greatly alarmed at the avowed design of the Ministry to raise a revenue in America, and shocked by the bloody scene now acting in the Massachusetts Bay, do, in the most solemn manner, resolve never to become slaves; and do associate, under all the ties of religion, honor, and love of country, to adopt and endeavor to carry into execution, whatever may be recommended by the Continental Congress, or resolved upon by our Provincial Convention that shall be appointed, for the purpose of preserving our Constitution, and opposing the execution of the several arbitrary and oppressive acts of the British Parliament, until a reconciliation between Great Britain and America, on constitutional principles, which we most ardently desire, can be obtained; and that we will in all things follow the advice of our general committee, to be appointed, respecting the purposes aforesaid, the preservation of peace and good order, and the safety of individuals and private property.

(Signed)

LACHN. McINTOSH,
GEO. THREADCRAFT,
CHARLES McDONALD,
JOHN McINTOSH,
RAYD. DEMERE,
JILES MOORE,
SAMUEL McCLELAND,
PETER SALLENS, JUN.,
JAMES CLARK,
JOHN WITHERSPOON, JUN.,
JOHN WITHERSPOON,
JOHN FULTON,
SAMUEL FULTON,
ISAAC CUTHBERT,
ISAAC HALL,
JONES NEWSOM,
A. DANIEL CUTHBERT,
JOHN HALL,
JNO. McCOLLUGH, SEN.,
JNO. McCOLLUGH, JUN.,
WILLIAM McCOLLUGH,
REU. SHUTTLEWORTH,
JOHN McCLELAND,
RICHARD COOPER,
SETH McCULLUGH,
THOMAS KING,
PAUL JUDTON,
JOHN ROLAND,
PR. SHUTTLEWORTH,
JOSEPH STOBE,
TO. BIERRY.

On the 18th January, six days after the above association was signed, a Provincial Congress met in Savannah, upon invitation of a committee of the citizens of Christ Church Parish, and elected John Glen chairman. The General Assembly of the province met there, also, on the same day, and was opened by an earnest, affectionate, and argumentative speech from Sir James Wright, in which he cautioned them not to be "led away by the voices and opinions of men of overheated ideas; consider coolly and sensibly of the terrible consequences which may attend adopting resolutions and measures expressly contrary to law, and hostile to the mother country;" and he hoped that their "prudence and regard for the welfare and happiness of the province, of themselves, and of their posterity, would deter them from entering into similar resolutions."

The reply of the Council, sitting as an upper house, was loyal, and echoed the sentiments of the Governor; but the address of the Commons' house, though respectful, expressed their sense of the numerous grievances under which they suffered, and their desire of redress; as "it is the enjoyment of constitutional rights and liberty that softens every care of life, and renders existence itself supportable."

The upper house proposed a conference with the lower house upon the subject of American grievances, and, after several days' delay, the two bodies met in the Council chamber; but they could not unite in their views, and the Commons' house declined acceding to the measures proposed by the other branch of the Legislature.

Unintimidated by the Governor and Council, the lower house proceeded to take into consideration the papers and letters received from the other colonies, and they passed a series of resolves, laid before them by the Provincial Congress, then sitting, embracing the substance, and generally the language, of the resolutions adopted on the 14th October, 1774, adding to them three resolutions; one, presenting "their most grateful acknowledgments to those truly noble, honorable, and patriotic advocates of civil and religious liberty, who have so generously and powerfully, though unsuccessfully, espoused and defended the cause of America, both in and out of Parliament. The second, gave thanks "to the members of the late Continental Congress, for their wise and able exertions in the cause of American liberty;" and the last resolved, that certain persons, not named, "be deputies to represent this province in the intended American Continental Congress, proposed to be held at the city of Philadelphia, on the 10th May next."

An early day was appointed to take definite action on this important paper; but before it arrived, the Governor adjourned the Assembly, from the 10th February to the 9th May, the day prior to the appointed time for the Philadelphia Congress to assemble.

In the Provincial Congress, which had convened simultaneously with the Assembly; it was found, that out of twelve parishes invited, only five sent deputies, and some of these had laid their delegates under instruction as to the form of the proposed association. Embarrassed by this inaction of the colony, brought about by the most diligent efforts of the Governor; the friends of liberty adopted the expedient of laying their papers and articles of association before the Commons' house; and it was these resolutions which the Governor suppressed, by adjourning the Assembly. Thwarted in this design, which, it must be confessed, was not a correct mode of procedure, the Provincial Congress, if such it could be called, entered into articles of association, differing, however, in some important respects, from the model proposed by the Continental Congress.

This course, forced upon the congress by prudential reasons, gave umbrage to the deputies from St. John's, which parish had fully acceded to the resolutions and association adopted in Philadelphia. On the first day of the session, the committee from St. John's sent a message to their fellow-deputies, stating what the parish had done, and expressing the hope that they would adopt similar measures. This message remaining unanswered two days, a second one was sent, and a reply at once disrespectful and evasive was returned. The St. John's deputies immediately adopted resolutions declaring "that the committees of the several parishes now sitting are not and cannot be called a Provincial Congress," that they are not and will not be bound by their proceedings, and reaffirming their adherence to the Continental Association.

To these impolitic resolutions, they were impelled by the slow and cautious policy of the Provincial Congress; but surely it was a sad breach of the spirit of unity thus to withdraw from, and stigmatize as unconstitutional, a body which they would have acknowledged as authoritative in every repect, had it but responded favorably to their parochial views. Liberty required union, and the eye of the Governor must have gleamed with pleasure when he saw its few friends disagree, and break asunder, at a time when concord was essential to success.

The Provincial Congress adjourned on the 23d January, having elected Noble Wimberly Jones, Archibald Bullock, and John Houstoun delegates to represent Georgia in the Continental Congress, to assemble in Philadelphia in May following.

As they failed to comply with all the requisitions of the General Association, the Carolinians resolved to hold no intercourse with Georgians, but "to consider them as unworthy of the rights of freemen, and as inimical to the liberties of their country."

The parish of St. John's sought to be exempted from the operation of this harsh sentence; and sent a deputation, consisting of Joseph Wood, Daniel Roberts, and Samuel Stevens, to solicit an alliance with them, on the ground that they were detached from the colony by their resolutions, distinct by local situation, and of sufficient size to merit notice, especially as the Continental Congress had already noticed them by a particular address; but their petition was politely refused, as they constituted a part of the Colony of Georgia, which, as a province, came under the law of the fourteenth resolution of the General Association.

Painful as was this refusal, it did not deter them from further efforts; and on the 21st of March, they elected Lyman Hall to represent that parish in the General Congress, binding themselves faithfully to adhere to and abide by the determination of him and other honorable members of the same.

At this period the parish of St. John's possessed nearly one-third of the entire wealth of the province, and its inhabitants were remarkable for their upright and independent character. Of New England origin, they sympathized more strongly with northern distresses than other parts of Georgia; and being removed from the immediate supervision of the Governor and Council, it pressed on more resolutely in the cause of freedom, than the surrounding parishes. The time for action had arrived, and irresolution and supineness found no place in its decisive councils. With great unanimity the people renounced every fellowship that savored not of freedom; and refused to use any luxury the tax on which contributed to swell the ministerial coffers; and while, as yet, the cause of American freedom was involved in gloom and uncertainty, they boldly cast in their lot with the fortunes of the country, to live with her rights, or die in their defence.

The hesitation on the part of the other parishes to adopt all the measures of Congress, was the theme of violent and unjustifiable denunciation; but a momentary glance at the condition of Georgia will remove these aspersions. According to the returns of the Governor to the Lords of Trade, the population in 1774 was but 17,000 whites and 15,000 blacks; and the militia between the ages of sixteen and sixty, only numbered 2828, scattered from Augusta to St. Mary's. Within its borders, and along its frontiers, were the Creeks with 4000 gun-men; the Chickesas with 450 gun-men; the Cherokees with 3000 gun-men; and the Choctaws with 2500 gun-men; comprising all together over 40,000 Indians, 10,000 of whom were warriors, and all, by means of presents, and the influence of Captain Stuart and Mr. Cameron, were firm in their alliance with the royal party, and could be brought in any numbers against the colony. On the south, lay the garrisoned Province of Florida, with a large military force under Governor Tonyn, and numerous tory bandits, waiting for the signal of the spoiler. On the east was a long line of seaboard, with many fine harbors, sheltered bays, large rivers, and well-stocked islands, inviting naval depredations.

Besides these motives which addressed themselves to the fears of the colonists, there were others of a moral character. Since its settlement, Georgia had received by grant of Parliament nearly a million of dollars in addition to the bounties which had been lavished on the silk culture, indigo, and other agricultural products. This consideration weighed with much force on many minds; and on such, the Governor took every occasion to impress the baseness of ingratitude towards a Sovereign, whose paternal care had been so peculiarly exerted in their behalf. Each of the other colonies, also, had a charter, upon which to base some right or claim to redress; but Georgia had none. When the Trustees' patent expired, in 1752, all its chartered privileges became extinct; and on its erection into a royal province, the commission of the Governor was its only constitution—living upon the will of the monarch, the mere creature of royal volition. At the head of the government was Sir James Wright, Bart., who, during fourteen years, had presided over it with ability and acceptance. When he arrived, in 1760, the colony was languishing under the accumulated mismanagement of the former Trustees, and the more recent Governors; but his zeal and efforts soon changed its aspect to health and vigor. He guided it into the avenues of wealth, sought out the means of its advancement, prudently secured the amity of the Indians, and by his negotiations added millions of acres to its territory. Diligent in his official duties, firm in his resolves, loyal in his opinions, courteous in his manners, and possessed of a vigorous and well-balanced mind, he was respected and loved by his people; and, though he differed from the majority of them as to the cause of their distresses, and the means of their removal; he never allowed himself to be betrayed into one act of violence, or into any course of outrage and revenge. The few years of his administration were the only happy ones Georgia had enjoyed, and to his energy and devotedness may be attributed its civil and commercial prosperity. With these obstacles within and around her, is it a matter of wonder that Georgia hesitated and wavered? that she feared to assume a course of action which threatened inevitable destruction? Her little phalanx of patriots, scarcely outnumbering the band of Leonidas, were men indeed of Spartan hearts; but Spartan hearts, even at Thermopylæ, could not resist the hosts of the despot. And what had they to hope in their feeble state—the parishes divided, the metropolis filled with placemen and officers, the sea-coast guarded by a fleet, and the frontier of two hundred and fifty miles gleaming with the tomahawks of the scalper and the fires of the Indian wigwam? Georgia did falter, but only for a moment; for, soon summoning her energies, she cast aside all fear, and commending her cause to the God of battles, joined in the sacred league which now united thirteen colonies.

When the 9th of May—the day named in the executive proclamation for the convening of the General Assembly—arrived, there were not sufficient members in attendance to form a House. No more came on the 10th; and on the 11th, the House adjourned to the 15th, to afford time for the country members to come in. But the Governor, understanding, or professing to understand, that the Commons did not intend to make a house, or proceed to business, with the unanimous advice of the Executive Council, prorogued the Assembly to the 7th of November, at which time, a quorum not being formed, it was still further prorogued; though, when the time for its meeting arrived, the province was in the hands of the republicans, and royal government, for a time at least, had ceased in Georgia.

The General Congress met in Philadelphia on the 10th May; and on the 13th, Dr. Lyman Hall presented to that body his credentials as deputy from the parish of St. John's, accompanied by an address from his constituents, containing a brief summary of their proceedings. Both were read and approved, and he was permitted to take his seat, "subject to such regulations as the Congress shall determine relative to voting."

The delegates elected to this General Congress by the Provincial Congress in Savannah, did not attend; but sent a letter to the President, dated April 8, 1775, stating at length the reasons which deterred them from uniting with the other colonies. The letter illustrates the spirit which then reigned in Georgia, and is too important to be omitted in a history, which aims to give a faithful delineation of those exciting times. It began by stating, that "The unworthy part which the province of Georgia has acted in the great and general contest leaves room to expect little less than the censure, or even indignation, of every virtuous man in America. Although, on the one hand, we feel the justice of such a consequence, with respect to the province in general, yet, on the other, we claim an exemption from it, in favor of some individuals, who wished a better conduct. Permit us, therefore, in behalf of ourselves, and many others, our fellow-citizens, warmly attached to the cause, to lay before the respectable body over which you preside, a few facts, which, we trust, will not only acquit us of supineness, but also render our conduct to be approved by all candid and dispassionate men." After recapitulating the proceedings already detailed, they ask :—

"What, then, could the Congress do? On the one hand, truth forbid them to call their proceedings the voice of the province, there being but five out of twelve parishes concerned; and, on the other, they wanted strength sufficient to enforce them, on the principle of necessity, to which all ought for a time to submit. They found the inhabitants of Savannah not likely soon to give matters a favorable turn. The importers were mostly against any interruption, and the consumers very much divided. There were some of the latter virtuously for the measures; others strenuously against them; but more who called themselves neutrals than either.

"Thus situated, there appeared nothing before us but the alternative, of either immediately commencing a civil war among ourselves, or else of patiently waiting the measures to be recommended by the General Congress. Among a powerful people, provided with men, money, and conveniences, and by whose conduct others were to be regulated, the former would certainly be the resolution that would suggest itself to every man removed from the condition of a coward; but in a small community like that of Savannah (whose members are mostly in their first advance towards wealth and independence, destitute of even the necessaries of life within themselves, and from whose junction or silence so little would be added or lost to the general cause), the latter presented itself as the most eligible plan, and was adopted by the people. Party disputes and animosities have occasionally prevailed, which show that the spirit of freedom is not extinguished, but only restrained for a time, till an opportunity should offer for calling it forth.

"The Congress convened at Savannah did us the honor of choosing us delegates to meet your respectable body at Philadelphia, on the tenth of next month. We were sensible of the honor and weight of the appointment, and would gladly have rendered our country any services our poor abilities would have admitted of; but, alas! with what face could we have appeared for a province, whose inhabitants had refused to sacrifice the most trifling advantages to the public cause, and in whose behalf we did not think we could safely pledge ourselves for the execution of any one measure whatsoever.

"We do not mean to insinuate that those who appointed us would prove apostates, or desert their opinion; but that the tide of opposition was great—that all the strength and virtue of these our friends might be insufficient for the purpose. We very early saw the difficulties that would occur, and therefore repeatedly and constantly requested the people to proceed to the choice of other delegates in our stead; but this they refused to do. We beg, sir, you will view our reasons for not attending in a liberal point of light. Be pleased to make the most favorable representation of them to the honorable the members of the Congress. We believe we may take upon us to say, notwithstanding all that is past, there are still men in Georgia who, when an occasion shall require, will be ready to evince a steady, religious, and manly attachment to the liberties of America. To the consolation of these, they find themselves in the neighborhood of a province, whose virtue and magnanimity must, and will, do lasting honor to the cause, and in whose fate they seemed disposed freely to involve their own."

In connection with this matter, it should be observed, that the Earl of Dartmouth had particularly enjoined upon Governor Wright to check any provincial associations, and to thwart every measure designed to carry out the views of the Continental Congress. These directions, so consonant to the loyalty of Sir James Wright, were rigidly enforced; and he declared, in his letter to the Earl, that "he had given them every kind of opposition he could," and had, he believed, "succeeded in his endeavors."[5] The civil and judicial power of the colony was combined to put down the rising spirit of liberty, and retain the colony in its allegiance to the crown. The struggle was one between power and office, and the stern principles of human liberty; and it was arduous and severe. But each attempt to crush them gave it new vigor, each new exercise of arbitrary power added to the votaries of freedom, until the shedding of blood announced that a crisis had arrived, and that the hopes of America now rested on an appeal to arms.

[5] State Paper Office, vi, pt. 2, 108.

CHAPTER II.

THE FIRST BATTLE IN GEORGIA.

The news of the battle of Lexington reached Savannah on the night of the 10th of May, 1775, and produced intense excitement among all classes. On the night of the 11th, Noble Wimberly Jones, Joseph Habersham, Edward Telfair, and a few others, impressed with the necessity of securing all military stores, and preserving them for colonial use, took from the King's magazine, in Savannah, about five hundred pounds of powder. On its discovery, the next day, the Council advised his excellency to offer a reward of £150 to any who would give information of the offenders; but, though the gentlemen engaged in this act were well known, none informed, and no proceedings were ever instituted against them. Tradition asserts, that part of this powder was sent to Boston, and used by the militia at the battle of Bunker Hill. This is rendered probable, by the fact that contributions of other articles were forwarded to Massachusetts, among which were sixty-three barrels rice and £122 in specie; "which," says the chairman, in his letter, dated 1st June, notifying the Bostonians of the remittance, "we desire you will please appropriate towards the relief of those who have lately left the town of Boston."

On Monday, the 5th June, the first liberty pole was erected in Georgia; yet, such was still the desire of the people for reconciliation on constitutional principles, that it was set up on his Majesty's birthday, and at the dinner immediately after, the first toast drank was, "The King," the second, "American Liberty." The following week, thirty-four of the principal friends of liberty held a meeting, and passed a number of very decided resolutions, one of which declared, "that this province ought, and it is hoped will, forthwith join the other provinces, in every just and legal measure to secure and restore the liberties of all America, and for healing the unhappy dissensions now subsisting between Great Britain and her colonies." Another meeting, for the purpose of choosing a committee to enforce the Continental Association, was held, on the 22d June, at which time a Council of Safety was also appointed, consisting of William Ewen, President; Seth John Cuthbert, Secretary; Joseph Habersham, Edward Telfair, William Le Conte, Basil Cowper, Joseph Clay, George Walton, John Glen, Samuel Elbert, William Young, Elisha Butler, George Houstoun, John Smith, Francis H. Harris, and John Morel.

The activity of the Liberty party, and its rapid increase, especially since the attempted seizure by General Gage of the military stores at Concord and Lexington, gave Governor Wright just cause for alarm; and he wrote to General Gage, expressing his amazement "that these southern provinces should be left in the situation they are, and the Governors and King's officers, and friends of Government, naked and exposed to the resentment of an enraged people; the Governors had much better be in England than remain in America, and have the mortification to see their powers executed by committees and mobs."

General Gage had indeed directed Sir James, in case of necessity, to call upon Major Furlong, then stationed at St. Augustine, for a company of one hundred men; but both the Governor and Council agreed, that while this force might have sufficed to crush rebellion a few months before, its presence then would only tend to irritate and inflame still more the minds of the people, and therefore he declined making the requisition until the force could be largely increased.[1]

Under the same date of the letter to the Commander-in-chief of all his Majesty's forces in America, the Governor also wrote to Admiral Graves, the naval commander on the North American station, stating that the port was blockaded by four or five boats from South Carolina, and therefore prayed for immediate assistance, assuring the admiral, however, that "nothing less than a sloop-of-war of some force" would answer for the defence of the harbor.[2]

The assistance so earnestly solicited in these letters would have been promptly rendered, but that they never reached their destination. The Committee of Safety at Charleston withdrew them from their envelopes, as they passed through the port, and substituted others, stating that Georgia was quiet, and there existed no need either of troops or vessels. These being transmitted in the original envelopes, completely deceived the several commanders; and it was not until Sir James met General Gage in London, some time

[1] MS. Minutes of Governor's Council.

[2] Drayton's Memoirs of the American Revolution, i, 346.

after, and inquired the cause of his not sending troops to Georgia, that the forgery was discovered.

The statement of Sir James, that the port of Savannah was blockaded by four or five boats from South Carolina, was an exaggeration of the Governor. The real facts of the case were these. The secret Carolina committee, having been notified of the sailing of a ship for Georgia, having on board a large supply of powder, designed by the Governor and Captain John Stuart for the Indians, and the service of the royalists, determined to capture it. Accordingly, Captain John Barnwell and Captain Joyner, of Beaufort, were directed to use all means in their power to seize the military stores on board the expected ship. They therefore embarked forty men, well armed, in two barges, and, proceeding toward the mouth of the Savannah River, encamped on Bloody Point, in full view of the Tybee light-house. The Georgia Provincial Congress offered every kind of assistance to Captains Barnwell and Joyner, and told them, that if they desired it, they would assist them in taking the British armed schooner which was stationed in the river. Arrangements were therefore made for the junction of the Georgia and Carolina forces, and a schooner was commissioned by the Georgia Congress, and placed under the command of Captain Bowen and Joseph Habersham. The British armed schooner put to sea, on the approach of the Georgia schooner, which latter vessel had taken post beyond the bar but a few days, when, on the 10th July, Captain Maitland's ship, with the powder, was descried in the offing. Maitland for a while sailed boldly in, but suspecting the design of the schooner, tacked and stood to sea. Captain Bowen soon overhauled her and brought her to, and, with the assistance of the Carolina party, boarded her and secured their prize. This was the first provincial vessel commissioned for naval warfare in the Revolution; and the first capture made by order of any Congress in America was made by this Georgia schooner, in June, 1775. Of the powder taken in this ship, nine thousand pounds fell to the share of Georgia, and, at the urgent solicitation of the Continental Congress at Philadelphia, five thousand pounds were sent thither; and it was by the arrival there of this powder, that the American arms were enabled to penetrate into Canada, and that Washington drove the British army out of Boston.

On the 4th July, 1775, the Provincial Congress met at Tondees's Long Room, Savannah. Every parish and district was represented. After organizing by the choice of Archibald Bulloch as President, and George Walton as Secretary, they proceeded in a body to the meeting-house of the Rev. Dr. Zubly, one of their associates, and heard from him a sermon on the alarming state of American affairs, based on the words of St. James, ii, 12: "So speak ye, and so do as they that shall be judged by the law of liberty."

The following is a list of the members of this Congress:—

From the Town and District of Savannah: Archibald Bulloch, Noble Wimberly Jones, Joseph Habersham, Jonathan Bryan, Ambrose Wright, William Young, John Glen, Samuel Elbert, John Houstoun, Joseph Reynolds, John Smith, Oliver Bowen, John McClure, Edward Telfair, Thomas Lee, George Houstoun, William Ewen, John Martin, Dr. Zubly, William

Bryan, Philip Box, Philip Allman, William O'Bryen, Joseph Clay, John Cuthbert.

District of Vernonburgh: Joseph Butler, Andrew Elton Wells, Matthew Roach, Jr.

District of Acton: David Zubly, Basil Cowper, William Gibbons.

Sea Island District: Col. Deveaux, Col. Delegall, James Bulloch, John Morel, John Bohun Girardeau, John Barnard, Robert Gibson.

District of Little Ogechee: Francis Henry Harris, Joseph Gibbons, James Robertson.

Parish of St. Matthew: John Stirk, John Adam Treutlen, George Walton, Edward Jones, Jacob Wauldhauer, Philip Howell, Isaac Young, Jenkin Davis, John Morel, John Flert, Charles McKay, Christopher Crumer.

Parish of St. Philip: Col. Butler, William Le Conte, William Maxwell, James Maxwell, Stephen Drayton, Adam Fowler Brisbain, Luke Mann, Hugh Bryan.

Parish of St. George: Henry Jones, John Greene, Thomas Burton, William Lord, David Lewis, Benjamin Lewis, James Pugh, John Fulton.

Parish of St. Andrew: Jonathan Cochran, William Jones, Peter Tarlin, Lachlan McIntosh, Wm. McIntosh, George Theadcraft, John Wesent, Roderick McIntosh, John Witherspoon, George McIntosh, Allen Stuart, John McIntosh, Raymond Demeré.

Parish of St. David: Seth John Cuthbert, William Williams, Sr.

Parish of St. Mary: Daniel Ryan.

Parish of St. Thomas: John Roberts.

Parish of St. Paul: John Walton, Joseph Maddock, Andrew Burns, Robert Rae, Andrew Moon, Andrew Burney, Leonard Marbury.

Parish of St John: James Screven, Nathan Brownson, Daniel Roberts, John Baker, Sr., John Bacon, Sr., James Maxwell, Edward Ball, William Baker, Sr., William Bacon, Jr., John Stevens, John Winn, Sr.

Only Joseph Butler, James Robertson, and Joseph Maddock declined taking their seats.

The first business transacted the next day was the nominating of a committee to wait upon Governor Wright, and request him "to appoint a day of fasting and prayer to be observed throughout this province, that a happy reconciliation may soon take place between America and the parent State." The Governor acceded to the request, and designated the 19th, the day prior to the one set apart by the Continental Congress for the same purpose.

Having first sought Divine aid and enlightenment, Congress proceeded with great promptness and vigor to the work before them, as the following extracts from their proceedings will show:—

"The president being informed by the messenger that John Jamison and John Simpson, Esq'rs, were in waiting, and desired to be admitted, which being agreed to, they were desired to walk in; they then produced and delivered in to the president a paper containing several resolutions entered into by a number of persons inhabitants of the town of Savannah, which was ordered to be read, and is as follows, viz.:—

"At a meeting of several of the inhabitants of the town of Savannah, at Mrs. Cuyler's, on Friday the 13th June, 1775, present John Mullryne, Esq., in the chair, Joseph Clay, James Mossman, Rev. Mr. J. J. Zubly, John Simpson, Noble Wimberly Jones, John Jamison, William Moss, John Glen, Josiah Tatnall, John Grayham, Lewis Johnson, William Yonge, Richard Wylly, Andrew McLean, Basil Cowper, Philip Moore, George Houstoun, Joseph Butler, James Read, Thomas Read, William Paxton, James Edward Powell, William Stuthers, Alexander McGowen, John C. Lucena, Thomas Sherman, J. N. Faming, Levi Sheftall, Charles Hamilton, George Spencer, William Brown, Jr., Francis Courvoizie, James Anderson.

"Whereas public confusion and grievances are much increased by private dissensions and animosities,

"Resolved, therefore, *nem. con.*,

"That we will use our utmost endeavors to preserve the peace and good order of this province, and that no person, behaving himself peaceably and inoffensively, shall be molested in his person or property, or even in his private sentiments, while he expresses them with decency, and without any illiberal reflections upon others.

"Whereas the acts for raising a perpetual revenue in America, and all the measures used to enforce these acts, are not partial, but general grievances, and it is more likely that redress be obtained by the joint endeavors of all who may think these acts unconstitutional or oppressive, than by any measure that might be taken singly by individuals,

"Therefore, Resolved,

"That it is the opinion of this meeting (as a proper measure to be pursued, because the General Assembly is not now sitting, from whom an application to the throne must be very proper, and as no time should be lost), that a humble, dutiful, and decent petition be addressed to his Majesty, expressive of the sense and feelings of all such as may choose to subscribe such petition, which it is hoped will be done by every man in the province; and it is, therefore, the wish of this meeting, that such a measure may be adopted by the Provincial Congress, intended to be held on Tuesday next, the 4th of July.

"Resolved, That the interest of this province is inseparable from the mother country and all the sister colonies, and that to separate themselves from the latter would only be throwing difficulties in the way of its own relief, and that of the other colonies, and justly incurring the resentment of all those to whose distress our disunion might cause an addition.

"Resolved, That this province ought, and it is hoped will forthwith join the other provinces in every just and legal measure, to secure and restore the liberties of all America, and for healing the unhappy divisions now subsisting between Great Britain and her colonies.

"Resolved, That the proceedings of this meeting be laid before the Provincial Congress on Tuesday, the 4th day of July next, and that Mr. Jamison and Mr. Simpson do wait upon them with the same, as recommended to them by this meeting.

"By order of the meeting.

"JOHN MULLRYNE."

"A motion was made and seconded, that the paper above mentioned do lie upon the table for the perusal of the members, which being carried, the same was ordered to lie upon the table accordingly.

"A motion was made and seconded, that this Congress do put this province upon the same footing with our sister colonies; which being put, it was ordered that it be taken into consideration to-morrow morning.

"Thursday, July 6, 1775. The order of the day being read, the same was taken into consideration, and, after some deliberation, it was unanimously

"1st. Resolved, That this province will adopt and carry into execution, all and singular, the measures and recommendations of the late Continental Congress.

"2d. Resolved, in particular, That we, in behalf of ourselves and constituents, do adopt and approve of the American Declaration or Bill of Rights, published by the late Continental Congress, in consequence of several infractions thereof.

"3d. That we will not receive into the province any goods, wares, or merchandise, shipped from Great Britain or Ireland, or from any other place, any such goods, wares, or merchandise, as shall have been exported from Great Britain or Ireland after this day; nor will we import any East India tea from any part of the world; nor any molasses, syrups, paneles, coffee, or pimento; nor wines from Madeira or the Western Islands, nor foreign indigo.

"4th. That we will neither import or purchase any slave imported from Africa, or elsewhere, after this day.

"5th. As a non-consumption agreement, strictly adhered to, will give an effectual security for the observation of non-importation, we, as above, solemnly agree and associate, that from this day we will not purchase or use any tea imported on account of the East India Company, or any on which a duty hath or shall be paid; and we will not purchase or use any East India tea whatever; nor will we, nor shall any person for or under us, purchase any of those goods, wares, or merchandise, we have agreed not to import, which we shall know, or have cause to suspect, were imported after this day.

"6th. The earnest desire we have not to injure our fellow-subjects in Great Britain and Ireland and the West Indies, induces us to suspend non-importation until the 10th day of September, 1775, at which time, if the acts and parts of acts of the British Parliament, hereinafter mentioned, are not repealed, we will not, directly or indirectly, export any merchandise or commodity whatsoever to Great Britain, Ireland, or the West Indies, except rice, to Europe.

"7th. Such as are merchants and use the British and Irish trade, will give orders to their factors, agents, and correspondents, as soon as possible, in Great Britain and Ireland, not to ship any goods to them, on any pretence whatever, as they cannot be received in this province; and if any merchant, residing in Great Britain or Ireland, shall, directly or indirectly, ship any goods, wares, or merchandise, to America, in order to break the said non-importation agreement, or in any manner contravene the same, on such unworthy conduct being well attested, it ought to be made public; and, on the same being done so, we will not, from thenceforth, have any commercial connections with such merchant.

"8th. That such as are owners of vessels will give positive orders to their captains or masters, not to receive on board their vessels any goods prohibited by the said non-importation agreement, on pain of immediate dismission from their service.

"9th. We will use our utmost endeavors to improve

the breed of sheep, and increase their numbers to the greatest extent; and to that end, we will kill them as sparingly as may be, especially those of the most profitable kind; nor will we export any to the West Indies or elsewhere; and those of us who are or may become overstocked with, or can conveniently spare any sheep, will dispose of them to our neighbors, especially to the poorer sort, on moderate terms.

"10th. That we will, in our several stations, encourage frugality, economy, and industry, and promote agriculture, arts, and the manufactures of British America, especially that of wool; and will discountenance and discourage every species of extravagance and dissipation, especially horse-racing, and every kind of gaming, cock-fighting, exhibiting of shows, plays, and other expensive diversions and entertainments; and, on the death of any relation or friend, none of us, or any of our families, will go into any farther mourning dress than a black crape or ribbon on the arm or hat for gentlemen, and a black ribbon and necklace for ladies; and we will discontinue the giving of gloves and scarfs at funerals.

"11th. That such as are venders of goods or merchandise will not take advantage of the scarcity of goods that may be occasioned by this Association, but will sell the same at the rates we have been respectively accustomed to do for twelve months last past; and if any vender of goods or merchandise shall sell any such goods or merchandise on higher terms, or shall in any manner, or by any device whatsoever, violate or depart from this agreement, no person ought, nor will any of us, deal with any such person, or his or her factor or agent, at any time thereafter, for any commodity whatever.

"12th. In case any merchant, trader, or other persons, shall attempt to import any goods or merchandise into this province, after this day, the same shall be forthwith sent back again, without breaking any of the packages thereof.

"13th. That a committee be chosen in every town, district, and parish within this province, by those who pay towards the general tax, whose business it shall be attentively to observe the conduct of all persons touching this Association; and when it shall be made to appear, to the satisfaction of a majority of any such committee, that any person, within the limits of their appointment, has violated this Association, that such majority do forthwith cause the truth of the case to be published in the Gazette, to the end that all such foes to the rights of British America may be publicly known, and universally contemned as the enemies of American liberty; and thenceforth we will break off all connection with him or her.

"14th. That the Committee of Correspondence in this province do frequently inspect the entries of the custom-house, and inform the committees of other colonies which have acceded to the Continental Association, from time to time, of the true state thereof, and of every other material circumstance that may occur relative to this association.

"15th. That all manufactures of this province be sold at reasonable prices, so that no undue advantage be taken of a future scarcity of goods.

"16th. And we do further agree and resolve, that we will have no trade, commerce, dealings, or intercourse whatsoever, with any colony or province in North America, which shall not accede to, or which shall hereafter violate, this Association; but will hold them as unworthy of the rights of freemen, and as inimical to the liberties of their country.

"And we do solemnly bind ourselves and our constituents, under the ties of virtue, honor, and love to our country, to adhere to this Association, until such parts of the several acts of Parliament, passed since the close of the last war, as impose or continue duties upon tea, wines, molasses, syrups, paneles, coffee, sugar, pimento, indigo, foreign paper, glass, and painters' colors, imported into America, and extend the powers of the Admiralty Courts beyond their ancient limits; deprive American subjects of trial by jury; authorize to Judges certificate to indemnify the prosecutor from damages, that he might otherwise be liable to from a trial by his peers; require oppressive security from claimants of ships or goods seized, before he is allowed to defend his property, are repealed; and until that part of the act of the 12th George III, ch. 24, entitled 'An Act for the better securing his Majesty's Dock-yards, Magazines, Ships, Ammunition, and Stores,' by which any person charged with committing any of the offences therein described, in America, may be tried within any shire or county within the realm, is repealed; and until the four acts passed in the last session of Parliament, viz., that for stopping the port and blocking up the harbor of Boston; that for altering the charter and government of the Massachusetts Bay; and that which is entitled, 'An Act for the better Administration,' etc.; and that for extending the limits of Quebec, etc., are repealed;

and until the two acts passed in the present session of Parliament, the one entitled, 'A Bill to restrain the Trade and Commerce of the Colonies of New Jersey, Pennsylvania, Maryland, Virginia, and South Carolina, to Great Britain, Ireland, and the British Islands in the West Indies, under certain Conditions and Limitations;' and the other, an act commonly called the 'Fishery Bill.'"

On Friday, the 7th of July, the Provincial Congress elected John Houstoun, Archibald Bulloch, Rev. Dr. Zubly, Noble Wimberly Jones, and Dr. Lyman Hall delegates to the Continental Congress, then sitting in Philadelphia, and ordered "that any three of them be a quorum."

The Congress also passed the following strong preamble and resolutions:—

"Whereas, by the unrelenting fury of a despotic ministry, and with a view to enforce the most oppressive acts of a venal and corrupted Parliament, an army of mercenaries under an unfeeling commander has actually begun a civil war in America: And whereas, the apparent iniquity and cruelty of these obstructive measures have, however, had this good effect, to unite men of all ranks in the common cause: And whereas, to consult on means of safety, and the method of obtaining redress, the good people of this province of Georgia have thought proper to appoint a Provincial Congress, the delegates met at the said Congress now assembled from every part of the province, besides adopting the resolution of the late Continental Congress, find it prudent to enter into such other resolutions as may best express their own sense and the sense of their constituents on the present unhappy situation of things, and therefore thought fit and necessary to resolve as follows:—

"Resolved, That we are born free, have all the feelings of men, and are entitled to all the natural rights of mankind.

"Resolved, That by birth or incorporation, we are all Britons, and whatever Britons may claim as their birthrights, is also ours.

"Resolved, That in the British Empire, to which we belong, the constitution is superior to every man, or set of men whatever, and that it is a crime of the deepest dye in any instance to impair or take it away, or deprive the meanest subject of its benefits.

"Resolved, That part of the American Continent which we inhabit was originally granted by the Crown, and the charter expressly from Charles the Second, makes its constitutional dependence on the Crown only.

"Resolved, That those who now would subject all America, or this province, to dependency on the Crown and Parliament, are guilty of a very dangerous innovation, which in time will appear as injurious to the Crown as it is inconsistent with the liberty of the American subject.

"Resolved, That, by the law of nature and the British constitution, no man can legally be deprived of his property without his consent, given by himself or his representatives.

"Resolved, That the acts of the British Parliament for raising a perpetual revenue on the Americans, by laying a tax on them without their consent, and contrary to their protestations, are diametrically opposite to every idea of property, to the spirit of the constitution, and at one stroke deprived this vast continent of all liberty and property, and, as such, must be detested by every well-wisher of Great Britain and America.

"Resolved, That the subsequent laws made with a view to enforce these acts, namely, the Boston Port Bill, the alteration of their charter, the act to carry beyond sea for trial, and what refines upon every species of cruelty, the Fishery Bill, are of such a complexion, that we can say nothing about them, for want of words to express our abhorrence and detestation.

"Resolved, That the loyalty, patience, and prudence of the inhabitants of New England, under their unparalleled passions, having been construed into timidity and a dread of regular troops, a civil war, in support of acts extremely oppressive in themselves, hath actually been begun, and that there is too much reason to believe that plans have been in agitation, big with everything horrible to other provinces, plans as rash, barbarous, and destructive, as the cause they were intended to serve.

"Resolved, That in these times of extreme danger, our Assembly not being permitted to sit, we must have either been a people without all thought or counsel, or have assembled, as we now are, in Provincial Congress, to consult upon measures, which, under God, may prove the means of a perpetual union with the mother country, and tend to the honor, freedom, and safety of both.

"Resolved, That this province bears all true allegiance to our own rightful sovereign, King George the Third, and always will, and ought to bear it, agreeable to the constitution of Great Britain, by virtue of which only the king is now our sovereign, and which equally binds majesty and subjects.

"Resolved, That we are truly sensible how much our safety and happiness depend on a constitutional connection with Great Britain, and that nothing but the being deprived of the privileges and natural rights of Britons, would ever make the thought of a separation otherwise than intolerable.

"Resolved, That in case his Majesty, or his successors, shall, at any time hereafter, make any requisition to the good people of this province, by his representatives, it will be just and right that such sums should be granted as the nature of the service may require, and the ability and situation of this province will admit of.

"Resolved, That this province joins with all the provinces in America, now met by delegates in Continental Congress; and that John Houstoun, and Archibald Bulloch, Esq'rs, the Rev. Dr. Zubly, Lyman Hall, and Noble Wimberly Jones, Esq'rs, be the delegates from this province for that purpose.

"Resolved, That a committee be appointed, whose duty it shall be to see to it, that the resolutions of the Continental and Provincial Congress be duly observed; and that every person who shall act in opposition thereto have his name transmitted to the Continental Congress, and his misdeeds published in every American paper.

"Resolved, That with all such persons, except the indispensable duties that we owe all mankind (bad men and enemies not excepted), we will have no dealings nor connection; and we extend this, our resolution, also to all such persons or corporations in Great Britain, who have shown themselves enemies to America.

"Resolved, That we will do what in us lies to preserve and promote the peace and good order of this province; and, should any person become an innocent sufferer on account of these grievances, we will do whatever we justly may for his relief and assistance.

"Resolved, That, in such calamitous times as the present, every possible indulgence ought to be given to honest debtors; that it would be ungenerous (unless there appears intention of fraud) in any gentleman of the law to sue without previous notice, and any person so sued may apply to the Committee, and, should it appear to them that the creditor is in no danger of losing his money, or can be properly secured, they shall interpose their friendly offices to persuade him to drop the prosecution; and every prosecutor that shall appear to take advantage of the confusion of the times, to distress his debtor, ought to be publicly pointed out and held in abhorrence.

"Resolved, That, notwithstanding in a late bill for restraining the trade in the several provinces in America, this province is excepted, we declare that we look upon this exception rather as an insult than a favor, as being meant to break the union of provinces, and as being grounded on the supposition that the inhabitants of such excepted province can be base enough to turn the oppression of America into a mean advantage.

"By order of the Congress.

"A true copy from the minutes.

"George Walton,
"Secretary."

Of the five delegates elected to the Continental

Congress, Messrs. Bulloch, Houstoun, and Zubly attended its sessions at Philadelphia, and took part in its important proceedings.

When, however, the discussions in Congress developed the views of some of the patriots for a republican and independent government, and when these ideas began to take legitimate shape, and call for definite action, Dr. Zubly became alarmed at the aspect of affairs, and opposed the growing desires for independence.

In the beginning of the contest with the Parliament, Dr. Zubly took a bold and prominent part in the proceedings at Savannah. Occupying the position of minister of the Presbyterian congregation, and fitted by his learning and abilities to exercise a large influence on the public mind, his opinions carried with them great weight, and he proved a most able auxiliary to the American cause.

In his sermon before the Provincial Congress at Savannah; in his correspondence with Dr. N. W. Jones; and especially in his letter to the Earl of Dartmouth; he showed a zeal, an industry, and a patriotism that justly won for him the esteem of the friends of liberty, and the honorable place of a Delegate from Georgia, to the Continental Congress.

His letter to the Earl of Dartmouth, dated 3d September, 1775, which was published in the London Magazine, for January, 1775, at the request, as we have reason to believe, of General Oglethorpe, was one of the best state papers of that period, written with clearness, force, calmness, and a full knowledge of the position of American affairs, and a full vindication of American rights. Alluding to the suggestions made in England, to arm the slaves of the southern colonies in order to reduce their masters to British obedience, he says, "Proposals publicly made by ministerial writers relative to American domestics, laid the southern provinces under the necessity of arming themselves. A proposal to put it in the power of domestics to cut the throats of their masters, can only serve to cover the proposers and abettors with everlasting infamy. The Americans have been called 'a rope of sand,' but *blood* and *sand* will make a firm cementation; and enough American blood has been already shed to cement them together into a threefold cord, not easily to be broken." When, however, he found himself pressed with the question of sundering the ties which bound this country to the English crown, and substituting a republican for a monarchical government, Dr. Zubly, like many others, hesitated to embrace what seemed to him a fearful issue; and in a moment of undue zeal for the established order of things, he wrote to Sir James Wright from Philadelphia, giving him an account of the purposes and plans of the Continental Congress, and thus forewarning him of the coming rupture.

His conduct and language having aroused suspicion as to his fidelity to the cause of America, he was closely watched, and his treasonable correspondence discovered. Judge Chase, of Maryland, hinted on the floor of Congress, that his letter had been seized and its contents were known; which so alarmed the Doctor, that the next day he left for home, leaving on his table, in his room, a letter for Messrs. Houstoun and Bulloch, stating, "I am off for Georgia, greatly indisposed."

On his return to Savannah, he openly took sides against the Liberty party, and became of course very obnoxious to the people; so much so, that in 1777, he was banished from Savannah, and half of his estate taken from him. He wrote and published an earnest remonstrance against this summary proceeding, addressing it to the Grand Jury of the County of Chatham, but it did not avail, and he removed to South Carolina. There he remained until the royal government was re-established in Georgia, when he returned to his ministerial charge, and remained there during the subsequent siege of the town.

He died on the 23d July, 1781, at the age of fifty-six, broken in heart, and broken in fortune, yet nobly struggling against misfortune, aiming to be faithful in the discharge of his ministerial duties, and earnestly laboring to enter himself into that rest which remains for the people of God. His political defection, while it did no harm to Georgia or the colonies, brought misery upon himself and family, and tarnished a name which shone among the earlier patriots of Georgia with peculiar brightness. Savannah still bears the record of this learned man in the names of two of its streets, "Joachim" and "Zubly," and one of the hamlets of the city is called St. Gall, in honor of his birthplace in Switzerland.

In addition to directing a petition to the King, and addresses to the Governor and people of Georgia, Congress appointed a Committee of Intelligence, consisting of nine persons, resolved to raise £10,000, conferred upon the Council of Safety "full power upon every emergency during the recess of Congress," and having "strongly recommended to the friends of America in this province, that they use their utmost endeavors to preserve peace and good order, and to cultivate harmony with one another, they adjourned, on the 17th July, to the 19th August.

Thus the whole province of Georgia was fully committed to the measures of the Continental Congress, and embarked her fortunes with those of her sister colonies in the struggle for freedom and independence.

The resolves of non-importation passed by the Provincial Congress on the 6th July, 1775, were to take effect on the 10th of September, and by these all trade with Great Britain, the West Indies, and every colony which had not agreed to the rules of the Continental Association, ceased. By no circumstance was the firmness of Georgia more tested than by supporting this association. Nearly half of its population were slaves, grouped in various numbers on scattered plantations, dependent on their masters, whose supplies were thus cut off, without a possibility of present relief. Vessels, indeed, frequently arrived with the necessaries required; but the Continental articles were rigidly enforced, and they departed without opening their cargo or coming up to town. The self-denial of the Georgians was the more conspicuous, in that they had none of the internal resources possessed by the northern colonies. Their staple products were rice, lumber, indigo, skins, etc., which found their market in the West Indies or Great Britain, and were there exchanged for commodities needed at home; but this traffic was now closed. Of bullion they had been nearly drained by northern traders, who would take only specie in payment, and their paper currency was daily depreciating. They had no manufactures, and the precarious trade upon which they depended for supplies was not at all adequate to their demands;

for, in addition to the usual dangers of the sea, their proximity to the naval rendezvous at Bermuda, the refugee province of Florida, and the fleet-covered Archipelago of the West Indies, enhanced to such a degree the hazards of commercial intercourse, even with ports which were open, that twenty per cent. was often demanded for insuring vessels bound to the southern provinces, and soon no policy, at any premium, could be obtained for a vessel bound to Savannah. The ships, with their cargoes, lay idly in our waters, or, attempting to run out, were seized by the enemy. The whole industrial machinery of the province was suddenly arrested, and distress was everywhere apparent; but patriotism hushed every murmur, and Georgians counted not their own lives dear unto them, if they might but successfully maintain the cause of freedom.

On the 20th July, the Continental Congress received official notice that Georgia had acceded to the general Association and appointed delegates to attend at Philadelphia. Thenceforward she was regarded as one of the United Colonies, and her name was stricken from the resolution of the 17th May, which placed her, with the exception of the parish of St. John, under the ban of colonial intercourse.

On the 8th August, 1775, the Council of Safety addressed a letter to Governor Wright, bearing the signatures of George Walton, William Le Conte, Francis H. Harris, William Yonge, George Houstoun, William Ewen, John Glen, Samuel Elbert, Basil Cowper, and Joseph Clay, urging him to permit the several companies of militia to elect their own officers, as "many of the commissioned officers in the militia are disagreeable to the people over whom they command." This request the Governor regarded "as of a very extraordinary nature, and to have a dangerous tendency, as calculated to wrest the power and command of the militia from the Crown, and out of his hands." He however laid the letter before the Council, at the same time denying its statements, arguing against its principles, and denouncing the men and the Association which produced it. To this letter, the Council replied through the clerk, "that for many very substantial reasons, the Governor could not comply with their request."

That, however, which the Governor and Council denied, the people themselves accomplished.

On the 28th July, the 1st company of the 1st regiment of foot militia was summoned to the parade-ground, by beat of drum, by order of Captain Quintin Pooler. As John Charles Lucena and John B. Randall had not signed the Articles of Association, they were accordingly rejected by the regiment, and William Jones and Peter Lavein were elected officers in their places. On the same day, the 4th company, under Captain Stirk, paraded; and as William Stephens, first lieutenant, and William Johnson, had not subscribed, others were chosen into their several offices. In the 8th company, Dr. David Brydie and Seth John Cuthbert were elected respectively first and second lieutenants, vice James Robertson and James Ross.

These were but instances of that influence which was at work, purging out the loyal element from the commissioned officers of the militia, and preparing the soldiery to act with obedience and valor, under men chosen of their own free-will, and pledged to sustain the liberty of their country.

At the opening of the Continental Congress, on the 13th September, 1775, Zubly, Hall, Bulloch, and Houstoun presented their credentials as delegates from Georgia, and took their seats. Noble Wimberly Jones, also a delegate, and one of the earliest, firmest, and most intelligent supporters of the cause of liberty, did not appear, in deference to the earnest entreaties of his aged father, who had been for many years a crown officer, and one of the councillors under the royal government. This session was one of great importance. Out of the civil disorganization consequent on the overturning of the royal government, Congress was required to frame new and peculiar institutions; to create an army and navy; to gather the various resources demanded by the war, and disburse them so as best to meet the exigencies of the times; to raise immense sums of money; to harmonize discordant interests; to concentrate provincial efforts, and to guide the movements and deliberations of a great people struggling for constitutional liberty.

The power of the royal government in Georgia was now at an end. With no means of enforcing obedience, and with a strong Liberty party working against him, Governor Wright could do nothing but take affidavits of the various transactions as they occurred, and transmit them, with his observations, to the foreign Secretaries. In one of these letters he solicited a recall, "thinking that a King's Governor has little or no business here." In truth, his position was one peculiarly annoying. His conduct had been severely commented on, in a formal address from the Provincial Congress, wherein they had charged him with preventing the meeting of the Legislature, and misrepresenting the condition of things in the province; and being destitute of troops, without a government, with the courts of law closed, his call for an Assembly disregarded, the church even shut up because of the contumacious conduct of its loyal rector, the Rev. Mr. Smith; exposed to daily insults, which he could not resent, and compelled to witness proceedings which he totally condemned; he might well be pardoned for asking to be released from a condition fraught with many trials, and attended with not a single benefit.

Georgia was now in the hands of the Provincial Congress, who vested all executive and legislative power in "The Council of Safety." On the 1st of December, Congress took under its supervision all courts of law, and appointed a committee of fifteen to sit quarterly in Savannah, as a Court of Appeal, "to hear and determine between the parties, and sanction or prohibit processes, according to the circumstances of the case." To counteract, however, the license which many might take, in times of such judicial laxity, Congress required all persons, who designed leaving their parochial districts or the province, to give such notice of their intention as would enable creditors to secure their just demands.

The Council of Safety, consisting of George Walton, William Ewen, Stephen Drayton, Noble Wimberly Jones, Basil Cowper, Edward Telfair, John Bohun Girardeau, John Smith, Jonathan Bryan, William Gibbons, John Martin, Oliver Bowen, Ambrose

Wright, Samuel Elbert, Joseph Habersham, and Francis Henry Harris, was organized on the 11th December, 1775, by the election of George Walton as President, and Edward Langworthy as Secretary. The Council resolved to meet at Tondee's Long Room every Monday at 10 A. M., and at such other times as the emergency of affairs might require. At their first meeting, they commissioned Andrew Maybank, Joseph Woodruffe, Hezekiah Wade, and John Dooly, as captains; James Cochran, John Morrison, Jeremiah Beale, and Thomas Dooly, as first lieutenants; James Galoche, Moses Way, Jacob Blunt, Zephaniah Beale, and William Bugg, second lieutenants; and Thomas Dowly, George Philips, and Joshua Smith, third lieutenants, of the battalion of troops which the Continental Congress, on the 4th November, had ordered to be raised, at the Continental expense, for the protection of Georgia, and towards which they appropriated five thousand dollars.[3] On the 7th January following, this battalion was fully organized, by the appointment of the following field-officers: Lachlan McIntosh, colonel; Samuel Elbert, lieutenant-colonel; and Joseph Habersham, major.

In consequence of the arrival at Tybee, on the 12th January, of two men-of-war and a transport, from Boston, with a detachment of King's troops, under Majors Maitland and Grant, the Council of Safety resolved, on the 18th, "that the persons of his Excellency Sir James Wright, Bart., and of John Mullryne, Josiah Tatnall, and Anthony Stokes, Esqs., be forthwith arrested and secured, and that all non-associates

[3] MS. Journal of the Council of Safety.

be forthwith disarmed, except those who will give their parole, assuring that they will not aid, assist, or comfort any of the persons on board his Majesty's ships-of-war, or take up arms against America in the present unhappy dispute." To secure the person of the Governor was of course the first object, and Major Joseph Habersham undertook to perform the difficult duty. Proceeding that very evening to the house of the Governor, who had assembled the Council to consider what was proper to be done, he passed the sentinel at the door, entered the hall, then marched to the head of the table, and laying his hand upon the shoulder of the Governor, said, "Sir James, you are my prisoner." The party, astonished at his boldness, and supposing, from his firm manner, that a large force was surrounding them, fled in the utmost precipitation, through doors and windows. This was one of the most signal instances of deliberate and successful daring in the history of the war. For a youth of twenty-four, unarmed and unsupported, to enter the mansion of the chief magistrate, and at his own table, amidst a circle of councillors, place him under arrest, is an act of heroism ranking with the most brilliant exploits in American history. The Governor gave his solemn parole not to go out of town, or hold any correspondence with any officers or others on board the ships at Tybee, and was suffered to remain in his house, under guard. But his confinement proving irksome and painful, as well from the insults to which he was subjected, as from the danger to which he was exposed, from bullets wantonly fired into his house by the guard, he contrived, on the night of the 11th February, to escape, went in haste to

Bonaventure, and thence, in an open boat, to his Majesty's ship Scarborough, Captain Barclay, on board of which he was taken at three o'clock in the morning.

In the mean time the Provincial Congress, which had been called to meet on the 20th January, 1776, at Savannah, was opened, on Monday, the 22d, by a sermon from the Rev. Dr. Piercy, and was organized by the choice of Archibald Bulloch as President. The principal business of this Congress, was the election of delegates to attend the Continental Congress; and on the 2d of February, Archibald Bulloch, John Houstoun, Lyman Hall, Button Gwinnett, and George Walton, were duly chosen; to whom, three days later, was given the following letter of instruction, brief, indeed, but pertinent, and exhibiting an enlarged and unsectional spirit:—

"GENTLEMEN—Our remote situation from both the seat of power and arms, keeps us so very ignorant of the counsels and ultimate designs of the Congress, and of the transactions in the field, that we shall decline giving any particular instructions, other than strongly to recommend it to you that you never lose sight of the peculiar situation of the province you are appointed to represent: the Indians, both south and northwestwardly, upon our backs; the fortified town of St. Augustine made a continual rendezvous for soldiers in our very neighborhood; together with our blacks and tories with us; let these weighty truths be the powerful arguments for support. At the same time we also recommend it to you, always to keep in view the general utility, remembering that the great and righteous cause in which we are engaged is not provincial, but continental. We, therefore, gentlemen, shall rely upon your patriotism, abilities, firmness, and integrity, to propose, join, and concur, in all such measures as you shall think calculated for the common good, and to oppose such as shall appear destructive.

"By order of the Congress.

"ARCHIBALD BULLOCH, President.

"SAVANNAH, April 5, 1776."

The organization of the militia was also a subject of earnest deliberation; and the most efficient measures were taken to enrol, officer, arm, and equip the inhabitants, and to put them in readiness for any emergency. Volunteer companies, as riflemen, rangers, and infantry, were also formed in several of the parishes, and reported themselves for service.

The Council of Safety also passed resolutions, releasing all vessels importing gunpowder, saltpetre, sulphur, brass field-pieces, or muskets, within nine months, from the operation of the non-exportation agreement, and appointed Samuel Elbert, Edward Telfair, and Joseph Habersham, a committee to supply the province with arms and ammunition; who were recommended to contract for 400 stand of arms with bayonets; 20,000 pounds of gunpowder; 60,000 pounds of balls, bullets, bar-lead, grape, swan, and goose shot; and, furthermore, the Council ordered the stores at the Fort of Frederica to be immediately secured.

To meet the pecuniary wants of the colony, bills of credit were issued, in the form of certificates, which were to be accepted, "upon the faith of the public of this province," and it was made a penal offence to refuse to receive them in payment, or to depreciate their value.

From his retreat on the Scarborough, Governor Wright, on the 13th February, wrote a letter to the members of his Council, which he desired to be laid before the Provincial Congress, in which he says: "After having examined and duly weighed and considered my several letters from England, and General Howe, at Boston; and after having had a full conversation with his Majesty's officers here, I have the great satisfaction to be able to affirm, from the best authority, that the forces now here will not commit any hostilities against this province, although fully sufficient to reduce and overcome every opposition that could be attempted to be made; and that nothing is meant or wanted, but a friendly intercourse and a supply of fresh provisions. This his Majesty's officers have an undoubted right to effect, and what they insist upon; and this I not only solemnly require, in his Majesty's name, but also as (probably) the best friend the people of Georgia have, advise them, without the least hesitation, to comply with; or it may not be in my power to insure them the continuance of the peace and quietude they now have, if it may be called so."

Having stated that he had the King's leave to return to England, he proceeds: "My regard for the province is such that I cannot avoid, and possibly for the last time, exhorting the people to save themselves and their posterity from that total ruin and destruction which, although they may not, yet I most clearly see at the threshold of their doors; and I cannot leave them without again warning them, in the most earnest and friendly manner, to desist from their present plans and resolutions. It is still in their power; and, if they will enable me to do it, I will, as far as I can, engage to give, and endeavor to obtain, for them full pardon and forgiveness for all past crimes and offences; and this I conjure you to consider well and most seriously of, before it's too late. But let things happen as they may, be it remembered, that I this day, in the King's name, offer the people of Georgia the olive branch; that most desirable object and inestimable blessing, the return of peace and happiness to them and their posterity."

The "olive branch," which Sir James thus earnestly and honestly tendered, was not accepted, as the Georgians preferred war for liberty, to peace with slavery. Mr. Bulloch, as President of Congress, briefly answered this letter, declining a compliance with its propositions, and assenting to the requests made in it, on the part of Captain Barclay, the naval commander at Cockspur, only upon such conditions that he refused to accept them. This letter the Governor said he could not consider as an answer to his, "as they have not taken any notice of the most serious part, with respect to themselves and the province;" but he adds, "if they will not be their own friends, the province will blame them, and not me, who, through friendship, put it in their power to be happy."[4]

The refusal of Congress, and the vigilance of the Council of Safety, having prevented Captain Barclay from supplying the fleet with the necessaries desired, he determined to resort to force, and capture the

[4] Original MS. Journal of the Council of Safety.

eleven rice ships which lay under the bluff, waiting the departure of the men of war to proceed to sea. On the last of February, 1776, the Scarborough, Hinchinbroke, St. John, and two large transports with soldiers, came up the river and anchored at five fathom. In view of this demonstration, the Council of Safety, on the 2d March, passed unanimously a resolution, "that all the shipping in port be dismantled, and that the valuation of the houses of those appertaining to the friends of America be taken, for the purpose of burning the same, rather than suffer the British to possess them." This patriotic measure elicited great applause from the Carolinians, and the same council which a few months before termed Georgia "that infamous colony," and resolved to hold her inhabitants as inimical to the liberties of their country, now declared, in a letter signed by its president, that it was "noble, patriotic, and vigorous," "an instance of heroic principle, not exceeded by any, and equalled by but few, in history." The Carolinians still further evinced their interest, by sending a detachment of militia, under Colonel Bull, to join the troops in Savannah in repelling the attack, which it was anticipated would be made, by the Cherokee and other armed vessels, which had sailed from Charleston for Savannah.

Having previously sounded Back River, two of the vessels, on the 2d March, sailed up that channel: one anchored directly opposite the town; and the other, in attempting to go round Hutchinson's Island, and so come down upon the shipping from above, grounded at the west end of the island, opposite Brampton, the plantation of Jonathan Bryan, Esquire.

During the night, between two and three hundred troops from the first vessel, under the command of Majors Maitland and Grant, were silently marched across Hutchinson's Island, and, by collusion with the captains, were embarked by 4 A. M. in the merchant vessels which lay near the store on that island. When the morning of Sunday the 3d March revealed the proximity of the naval force, the inhabitants were filled with the utmost indignation. The grounded vessel, which proved to be the Hinchinbroke,[5] was immediately attacked by two companies of riflemen, under Major Habersham, who soon drove every man from its deck. It was not, however, until nine o'clock that the people had any knowledge that troops were secreted on board the merchantmen lying at the store on Hutchinson's Island, a fact that became known through two sailors, who, on pretence of going on shore to get their clothes, communicated the intelligence that Captain Rice, to whom was committed the carrying out of the order to dismantle the ships in port, had gone on board one of the vessels in pursuance of his duty, and himself and boat's crew had been forcibly detained by the officers. This news created intense excitement, and three hundred men, under command of Colonel McIntosh, were marched to Yamacraw Bluff, opposite the shipping, and threw up a hasty breastwork, through which they trained three four-pounders to bear upon the vessels. Anxious, however, to avoid bloodshed, Lieutenant Daniel Roberts, of the St. John's Rangers, and Mr. Raymond

[5] The Hinchinbroke was a merchantman, which was sheathed with wood, taken into the naval service, and mounted with twenty-eight guns. Lord Nelson and Lord Collingwood were both made post-captains in this vessel.

Demeré, of St. Andrew's Parish, solicited, and were permitted by the commanding officer, to go on board and demand a surrender of Rice and his people. They were accordingly rowed on board the vessel, in which were Captain Barclay and Major Grant; but, though they were unarmed and on a mission of peace, they were immediately arrested and detained as prisoners. After waiting half an hour, and the deputies not returning, the people on shore hailed the vessel through a speaking-trumpet, and demanded the return of Rice, Roberts, and Demeré; but receiving only insulting replies, two four-pounders were discharged at the vessel; whereupon they replied, that if the people would send on board two men, in whom they most confided, they would treat with them. Accordingly, Captain Screven, of the St. John's Rangers, Captain Baker, of the St. John's Riflemen, and about twelve of the Rangers, rowed immediately under the stern of the vessel, and in peremptory terms demanded the deputies. Captain Baker, doubtless incensed by some insulting language, fired a shot on board, which immediately drew down upon the boat a discharge of swivels and small arms from the vessel, which was kept up as long as the boat was within reach, though only one man was wounded. The firing from the vessel was the signal for the batteries to open, which were as briskly answered for the space of four hours.

At four o'clock, a meeting of the Council of Safety was held, and the resolution adopted to set fire to the vessels; and a party, consisting of Captain Bowen, Lieutenant James Jackson, John Morel, and six others, proceeded to the ship Inverness, which they set on fire, and, cutting her cable, she drifted upon the brig Nelly, which was also soon in flames. The officers and soldiers on board the vessels fled, in the utmost precipitation, across the low marshes and half-drained rice-fields, several being killed by the grape-shot played upon them from the intrenchments, and most of them losing their arms and ammunition.

The scenes of that day and night were solemn and terrific: the sudden marshalling of troops, the alarm of the people, the roll of artillery, the vessels wrapped in flames, every mast a pinnacle of fire, combined to form a scene of awful and soul-stirring excitement.

As Messrs. Roberts, Demeré, and Rice were still kept prisoners by the King's troops, the Council of Safety, on the 6th March, put under arrest all the members of the Royal Council that were then in Savannah, and menaced the officers of the ships at Tybee with still further measures of redress, if the prisoners, so unjustly detained by them, were not liberated. Various negotiations followed, and on the 27th March an exchange was effected; Roberts, Demeré, and others were released, and the crown officers put on the footing of prisoners on parole.

Finding that the houses on Great Tybee Island afforded comfortable shelter for the King's officers and tory refugees, the Council of Safety resolved to send a detachment of troops there, to destroy them and rout the tories. The execution of this order, rendered perilous by the peculiar situation of the place, and the protection afforded by the men-of-war, was committed to Archibald Bulloch, who, with a party of men composed of detachments from the riflemen, light infantry, fusiliers, volunteers, and a few Creek Indians, burnt all the houses, except one, in which was a sick woman and several children, killed two marines and one tory, and took one marine and several tories prisoners. The Cherokee man-of-war and an armed sloop kept up an incessant fire upon the party; but none of them were injured, and they retired from the island in perfect safety. Hitherto the Georgians had only heard of British aggressions; but now their own soil was moistened with the blood of the slain; their quiet homes had been assailed; their property pillaged; and their province threatened with devastation and ruin. The crisis had arrived; they met it like heroes.

CHAPTER III.

SOUTHERN EXPEDITIONS.

LORD NORTH'S "Prohibitory Bill" passed the House of Commons on the 11th December, 1775. By this act all trade and intercourse with the thirteen American colonies was prohibited, "during the continuance of the present rebellion within the said colonies respectively."

This was the first parliamentary act that involved Georgia; and while it was under discussion in the House of Commons, this fact was made the ground of particular objection and remark. On the sixth day of the debate, Edmund Burke moved an humble address to his Majesty, "that he will be graciously pleased to order to be laid before this House such advices as may enable this House to judge of the present state and condition of his Majesty's loyal and dutiful province of Georgia, in North America." His motion, however, met with little favor, and was negatived. On the Monday following, Governor Johnstone moved, "that no evidence has been produced to this House to show that many persons in his Majesty's colony of Georgia have set themselves in open rebellion and defiance to the just and legal authority of the King and Parliament of Great Britain, or have assembled together an armed force, or engaged his Majesty's troops, or attacked his forts, or prohibited all trade and commerce with this kingdom and the other parts of his Majesty's dominion." This motion led to an animated debate between Lord North, Governor Johnstone, and Mr. Burke, relative to the position of Georgia at this period. Governor Johnstone deplored that Georgia should now "be entered in the black catalogue;" that it should be marked out for destruction, as well as Massachusetts; "the latter, for defending their liberties, which were immediately invaded—the former, because they disapproved of the inhuman measure of condemning people unheard and untried." On the side of the Georgians, it was insisted that "it had not even been urged in debate, much less proved, that they had committed a single act, which the most willing, ingenious, most-expecting, or best-paid lawyer in the House could stretch even so far as a misdemeanor;" and the certain consequences of the "Prohibitory Bill" would be, "that a whole province was to be proscribed, its trade ruined, and its inhabitants declared rebels, and compelled to submit to tyranny, or consent to be starved."

Lord North professed that he had no objection to have the loyalty or disloyalty of Georgia the subject of evidence; but declared, that though Georgia was not actually in arms, or in a state of open rebellion, it was well known that they acted in conjunction with the other colonies, and there could not be a more decisive proof of their disposition, and the part they meant to take, than their sending delegates to the Continental Congress.

Mr. Dempster animadverted very severely upon

Lord North's presuming Georgia guilty, and, upon this presumption, including her in his prohibitory bill; declaring it "more horrible in its consequences, and more repugnant to the generally established ideas of justice, than anything yet imputed to that bloody tribunal, the Inquisition; that it was the very language of Charles the First to his Parliament, and of every other tyrant, from William the Conqueror to this day."

The Secretary of the Board of Trade (Mr. Pownall) replied, by detailing the different proofs the Georgians had given of their rebellious disposition. In answer to an expression dropped by this gentleman, that "their own newspapers were filled with accounts of these exploits," Burke said, "this was the first time he had ever heard newspaper information made a foundation for any solemn proceedings in that House;" and he commented with sarcastic raillery upon Mr. Pownall's referring the House to the public gazettes for information which it was his duty officially to announce.

The motion of Governor Johnstone met the fate of Edmund Burke's, and the bill, to use the words of Burke, "so diabolically constructed; for it inflicted punishment for acts thought innocent at the time they were committed, and legalized others, which were acts of atrocious plunder and robbery," was, with a few modifications, carried through the House of Lords, and received the royal assent on the 22d December, 1775.

Thus was Georgia by her own act, by the act of the Continental Congress, and by the act of the British Parliament, bound up with the other American colonies, to enjoy with them the freedom which they sought to gain, or share with them the disgrace and slavery that an ignorant Parliament, a vindictive ministry, a foreign soldiery, and an insane monarch were striving to fasten upon them.

This prohibitory bill reached Georgia only a few days after the attack on Savannah previously narrated. A number of vessels were lying in the river, some ready to sail, and his Majesty's ships Tamar and Cherokee were at Cockspur, to facilitate their departure. Several of these were laden (besides rice, the export of which was allowed by the Continental Congress, until the 1st March, 1776) with indigo, deer-skins, &c., and designed to circumvent the non-exportation resolves, by clearances dated prior to the 10th September.

Owing to the want of a sufficient force to overawe the disaffected, several irregularities had been passed over by the Georgians, which, however, had not escaped the notice and censure of the Carolinians. The Council of Safety in Charleston represented these to the committee in Savannah, and the latter resolved, at all hazards, to comply with the strict letter of the Congressional resolves upon this point, and therefore ordered, "that the rudders be unshipped, and the rigging and sails taken away and secured from the several vessels now riding in the port of Savannah."[1]

The absence of sufficient military power to enforce this order, caused it to be imperfectly obeyed; but the arrival of Colonel Stephen Bull, on the 10th March, with various detachments of Carolina troops, to the number of about 250, gave confidence to the patriots,

[1] Drayton, ii, 130.

who immediately proceeded to carry out the resolve, and dismantle the ships. Colonel Bull, having effected the object of his visit, returned to Charleston, leaving the defence of Savannah to the Georgia Battalion, under Colonel McIntosh, numbering only 236, rank and file, of which number only 100 were on duty, and these, of course, confined to Savannah.

The seaboard and inlets were infested by armed vessels, of light draft, for the purpose of securing provisions and carrying off prisoners, and there was not a vessel in the colony to protect the coast. Along the Florida line, there was stationed a troop of sixty horse, to prevent the driving off of cattle; and on the western frontier, a similar body of cavalry was raised, to guard the settlements from the threatened invasion of the Indians. This was all the military strength of this large, yet weakest and most exposed, of the American colonies. In the midst of these dangers, the patriots showed no alarm, but proceeded steadily to their work of organizing a government suited to the exigencies of the time, and accordingly, on the 15th April, adopted a constitution or form of government, and thus became an independent State.

Thus the prediction of Mr. Adams, that in consequence of this "prohibitory bill," which was looked upon throughout the colonies "as the last stretch of oppression," "governments will be up everywhere before midsummer, and an end to royal style, titles, and authority," came true; and with no less truth than force did he add, "It requires more serenity of temper, a deeper understanding, and more courage than fell to the lot of a Marlborough, to ride out this whirlwind."

Though Governor Wright and most of his Majesty's officers had left Georgia; though the royal authority was entirely overthrown; though a new government had been organized by the will of the majority; yet there were many disaffected persons resident in the province, and many causes of internal and external alarm. These demanded of the new executive a firmness tempered with prudence, and a sagacity blended with wisdom, that could only belong to one who thoroughly understood his position, and who, rising above all personal and party schemes, dared to carry out the requirements of duty, and maintain that supremacy which the tumult of the times demanded. Mr. Bulloch proved himself worthy of his trust; diligent, active, unflinching, he sustained himself in the executive chair with an ability suited to the station, and an energy adequate to the crisis. His modesty and republicanism were very happily displayed at his first assumption of executive power. When Colonel McIntosh, the commander of the Continental battalion in Savannah, tendered President Bulloch the military courtesy which had usually been paid to Governor Wright, and posted a sentinel at his door, he addressed him a note, saying, "I beg you will immediately order the sentinel to be withdrawn from my door; the grenadiers are already removed, in consequence of my orders. I act for a free people, in whom I have an entire confidence and dependence, and would wish upon all occasions to avoid ostentation."[2]

In addition to her other troubles, Georgia, in common with South Carolina, was now menaced with an

[2] Original letter of President Bulloch, in collection of I. K. Tefft, Esq.

Indian war. Through the agency of Captain Stuart, his Majesty's Superintendent of the Southern Indian Department; and Mr. Cameron, his deputy; the Cherokee Indians had been incited to fall upon the frontier settlements and perpetrate the most atrocious massacres. To reduce them to order, the colonies of Georgia, South Carolina, North Carolina, and Virginia, sent detachments of troops, commanded respectively by Colonel Jack, Colonel Williamson, General Rutherford, and Colonel Christy; who penetrated into the northern parts of Georgia and South Carolina, and carried the war with such vigor into the Indian country, that the savage foe, after fighting bravely and losing many men, were completely humbled. Cameron, through whose instrumentality they had taken up arms, was driven from the country; and the following year a treaty of peace, concluded at Dewitt's Corner, between Georgia, South Carolina, and the Cherokees, gave a temporary respite to the long-harassed and stricken frontier.[3]

On the 18th June, 1776, the President laid before the Council of Safety a letter from President Rutledge, informing him that General Lee (who had recently been appointed to command in the Southern Department) desired that they would send two of their body to Charleston, "to confer with him upon the state of Georgia, and the mode of putting it in the best posture of defence against all enemies, external and internal." The Council accordingly deputed Jonathan Bryan, John Houstoun, and Colonel McIntosh, to wait upon the General; which they did,

[3] Moultrie's Memoirs, i, 154.

shortly after the brilliant repulse of the English fleet from Fort Moultrie.

On the 5th July, the delegation handed in a report of their proceedings to the Council, in which they state that, "from the weak and defenceless situation of the colony, surrounded as it is with enemies, it stands in immediate need of assistance from the General Congress; and when they consider, that however small the colony may be of itself, in a comparative point of view, yet that, from the great plenty of provisions, numerous stocks of cattle, excellent inlets, harbors, and rivers, with which the colony abounds, and above all, the firm attachment of its inhabitants to the American cause, they are led to trust that the protection and security of that colony will be held an object of considerable importance. Not one of the thirteen United Colonies is so weak within, or so exposed from without. To the east, the inhabitants suffer the ravages of British cruisers; their negroes are daily inveigled and carried away from their plantations; British fleets may be supplied with beef from several large islands, well stocked with cattle, which line their coasts, and round which large ships may sail. To the south, they have the province of East Florida, the inhabitants and soldiery of which must, of necessity, make inroads upon Georgia for the article of provision with which they have been heretofore chiefly supplied. Georgia here stands as a barrier to South Carolina, and effectually secures that province against the like depredation." "We have certain accounts of there being at this time upwards of one thousand British troops in St. Augustine. To the west, and almost down upon the Georgia line, are the most numerous tribes of Indians now in North America, in the whole, at least 15,000 gunmen. They are so situated as to make it extremely convenient for our enemies to supply them, from East and West Florida, with ammunition and everything that they want. There seems to be the greatest reason to apprehend a rupture with them; in such a case, the fate of Georgia may be easily conceived. Add to these considerations the vast number of negroes we have, perhaps of themselves sufficient to subdue us.

"The conquest of Georgia would be considered as a great acquisition by Great Britain. It is a most excellent provision country; abounds with ship-timber and lumber of all kinds, and is most conveniently situated for a place of rendezvous to their shipping. Under all these circumstances, it must certainly appear indispensably necessary that measures be immediately taken for the defence and security of that province; but the low situation in point of means or ability of its inhabitants, puts it out of their power to do it of themselves, more especially as they have been already put to a very great expense in consequence of the late descent upon them." "The great objects seem to be, then, fortifications, and a good understanding with the Indians."

The deputies conclude their report with the following propositions:—

"1st. That his excellency General Lee be requested to state the peculiar situation of the province of Georgia to the General Congress, and to obtain directions from them to raise, and take into Continental pay, so many men as may be conceived to be sufficient to defend this province. In our opinion, less than six battalions will not answer the purpose; but as we do not conceive that any of these men can be recruited in Georgia, we would apprehend it full as eligible (if that can be done), to order some of the regiments already raised to march thither; and further, that the four troops of horse already raised be augmented to a regiment, and put upon the Continental establishment.

"2d. That the sum of —— sterling be granted by the General Congress, for building fortifications and guard-boats in the province of Georgia. The reason why we conceive this ought to be a general charge, is because it is evident the same will serve against attacks from the south, and for cutting off the communication between East and West Florida and the Indians, upon which the peace of the back inhabitants of Georgia, South Carolina, North Carolina, and Virginia depends.

"3d. It is a fixed principle with the Indians, to be paid for their good offices; and in this controversy, we conceive that they will expect to be well paid, even for neutrality. The articles they prefer will doubtless be ammunition and clothing; but these we have it not in our power to give them. We would then propose cattle, as a substitute, and are inclined to think, that if the communication between them and our enemies were cut off, they would soon be brought to be well satisfied with a present of this kind. It is, therefore, submitted to the General Congress, whether it would not be worth while to give direction that —— head of cattle be purchased, and distributed among the Indians by the Commissioners. We are of opinion this step would answer many valuable purposes, and would have a tendency not only of attaching them to our interest, from gratitude, but would also be a means of civilizing them, and by fixing the idea of property, would keep them honest and peaceable with us, for fear of reprisals."

The representations of this committee had such an effect on General Lee, that the morning after his interview with them, he paraded the North Carolina and Virginia troops, and told them that he had planned a secret expedition, one free from danger, certain of success, and productive of a large booty. His scheme, when unfolded, was embraced by the soldiers, and after some delay, President Rutledge furnished him with 460 men, drawn from the several regiments of infantry, rangers, and artillery, and the necessary ammunition to carry on his design. The second week in August, however, arrived, before he could put even a portion of his troops in motion; and then, in that unhealthy season, they were marched to Georgia, "without even a field-piece or medicine-chest." The remaining portion, with the artillery and baggage, went round by water, and reached Savannah on the 17th of August. Generals Howe and Moultrie accompanied the troops, while General James Moore, of North Carolina, was left in command at Charleston.

On the 19th August, General Lee waited on the President and Council, and proposed these questions for their consideration: "1st. Whether, as the port on St. Mary's is now abandoned, and the whole country between that river and the St. John's broken up, and as there is no probability of transporting cannon, ammunition, provisions, or collecting a sufficient number of men for the siege and reduction of St. Augustine, an irruption into East Florida can be productive of so important advantages to the general cause, or to this State of Georgia in particular, as to compensate for the trouble and expense? and what these advantages are? 2d. What are the means of certainly supplying the troops with grain and meat? How their baggage can be transported? whether safely by water? If not, whether wagons can pass? or, if the road is practicable only to horses, how pack-saddles are to be provided?"

The Council referred the questions to a committee, consisting of Jonathan Bryan and Nathan Brownson, who reported, "that an irruption into the province of East Florida will be attended with the most salutary consequences to this province, and of course render service to the whole continent." This opinion they supported by several reasons, all of which, however, were based rather on their hopes, than on the real facts of the case.

But so earnest were all the members of the Council for this expedition, that the report of the committee was accepted, and a resolution was passed[4] promising "all assistance in their power to forward the said expedition." General Moultrie was placed in command of the enterprise, and, in conjunction with General Lee and the other officers, set about collecting supplies, and organizing and pushing forward his troops. Everything wore a favorable aspect, and the hopes of the Georgians rose high as they beheld such active preparations to annoy, if not to conquer, their troublesome neighbor on the south. But, in September, as General Moultrie, having nearly completed his arrange-

[4] MS. Journal Council of Safety.

ments, was about to take up his march to join the advance guard already posted in Sunbury, an express reached Savannah from Congress, recalling General Lee to the northward; who immediately left Georgia, directing the Virginia and North Carolina troops to follow.

This sudden blow to the enterprise was soon succeeded by the recall of the South Carolina regiment; and the expedition terminated as suddenly as it was suddenly projected. The whole affair reflected very little honor upon the skill and military forethought of General Lee. The season of the year was the worst that could have been chosen; and as a consequence, officers and men suffered severely from sickness, the deaths averaging fourteen a day while the South Carolina battalion and Colonel Muhlenburg's regiment were encamped at Sunbury.

It was resolved upon after only one night's consideration; planned upon imperfect information; commenced with means inadequate to secure the desired end; and the troops began their march, when as yet neither boats, artillery, wagons, pack-horses, ammunition, nor stores of any kind, were provided for them.

Washington, it is true, said of General Lee, "He is the first officer in military knowledge and experience we have in the whole army;" but, judging from this display of his abilities as a general officer, he is not entitled to this encomium of the commander-in-chief. The consequences of the failure of this expedition were seen not only in the disheartening influence it had upon the troops, but it gave strength to the disaffected, and furnished matter of taunting exultation to the loyal Floridians.

While Georgia was thus deeply solicitous for her defence, Congress was not unmindful of her necessities, and, on the 15th June, appointed a committee, consisting of Messrs. Hopkins of Rhode Island, Harrison of Virginia, and Samuel Adams of Massachusetts, to take into consideration the state of Georgia. Their report was made on the 5th July, whereupon it was resolved[5] to raise two additional battalions (one of them to consist of riflemen) to serve in Georgia; that blank commissions be sent to the Convention of Georgia, to be filled up with the names of such persons as the said Convention shall think proper; also that the Legislatures or Assemblies of Virginia, North Carolina, and South Carolina be recommended to allow recruits for these battalions to be enlisted in their several States. It was furthermore ordered to build four galleys for the defence of the sea-coast, and to raise two artillery companies of fifty men each, to garrison two forts which the State was to erect at Savannah and Sunbury.

On the 8th, Congress appropriated $60,000 to pay the battalions thus ordered to be raised.

The Declaration of Independence was not received in Savannah until the 8th of August; when a copy of it, together with a letter from John Hancock, was laid before the Council of Safety, who directed that it should be proclaimed at the Assembly House, Liberty Pole, and Battery with military honors, on Saturday at 11 o'clock. This was accordingly done, and after the Declaration had been publicly read in the square fronting the Government House, a procession, composed of

[5] Journal of Congress, i, 375.

the military and civil officers, soldiers, and citizens, proceeded to the Liberty Pole, where the 1st battalion of the Georgia Continentals saluted them with thirteen volleys; thence the procession marched to the Battery, where another national salute was fired. After a public dinner, the procession was again formed, in reversed order; and with muffled drums and trailed arms, they solemnly buried the Royal Government of Georgia. At night they celebrated their joy by bonfires and a general illumination. Thus were severed the ties which bound Georgia to the mother country; thus was established the liberty and independence of this youngest of the thirteen colonies.

The importance of having a provincial marine early impressed itself on the minds of the Council, and they accordingly accredited Captain Bowen to the Governor of Cape François for the purpose of obtaining armed vessels, arms, and warlike stores; to procure articles for the building and fitting out of vessels, and also an assortment of medicines suitable to the climate. Captain Pray was also directed by the Council of Safety, October 18th, 1776, to proceed to St. Thomas, and to procure as many seamen, arms, ammunition, and swivels as he possibly could, with permission to mount as many carriage-guns as the vessel can bear on his return hither.

At this early period there were no national vessels; and each State was left to defend its own seaboard, and protect its own harbors. Georgia offered such good harbors, so near to the Province of Florida; and was so unprotected, that she was frequently visited by the English cruisers, who committed many depredations on the islands, and largely supplied themselves with cattle and other provisions.

To secure these as much as possible, Colonel McIntosh was ordered to station troops along the points likely to be assailed, and an express was sent to General Howe to send back that portion of the Georgia battalion doing duty in South Carolina, as also the boats and ammunition forwarded from Georgia. The militia of the State were also drafted into three divisions; one of which was required to be in readiness at a moment's warning; for danger menaced the State, not merely from the seaboard, but also from the Indian and Floridian borders.

For a long time, a sort of predatory warfare had been carried on by both parties on the southern boundaries of Georgia; but the incursions on the part of the British now assumed a more formidable shape. A large body of troops, consisting of about five hundred regulars, loyalists, and Indians, with several pieces of artillery, under the command of Colonel Fuser, with whom were associated the noted refugee officers, Colonels Brown, McGirth, and Cunningham, marched from St. Augustine, and invested Fort McIntosh, on the northeast side of the St. Illa River. This was a mere stockade fort, about one hundred feet square, situated on a rising ground near the banks of the river, and was garrisoned by seventy men, under the command of Captain Richard Winn. An attempt to surprise the fort, on the morning of the 17th of February, 1777, having failed, through the vigilance of its young commander, it was regularly invested; and all hopes of a reinforcement being cut off, the provisions being reduced to one day's supply, and the rage of the invading force rising with delay, Captain Winn surrendered himself and party as prisoners of war; after evincing as much skill and firmness in obtaining proper articles of capitulation, as he had done in bravely defending his little fort against such an overwhelming force. The main point of this capitulation required, that the Americans should return to Fort Howe, and not serve until regularly exchanged; two of their officers, Lieutenant Milton, of the Georgia brigade, and Lieutenant Caldwell, of the Carolina regiment, being sent to St. Augustine, as hostages for the fulfilment of these stipulations.

The news of the capture of Fort McIntosh, and of the faithlessness of the British commander to carry out all the terms of surrender, roused the whole province, and, with a unanimity and enthusiasm never before known,[6] the inhabitants prepared to repel the invaders. Notice was immediately sent to General Howe, then at Charleston, acquainting him with the threatened invasion, and he at once set off for Savannah, directing General Moultrie to send on a strong detachment to his assistance. Accordingly, Lieutenant-Colonel Marion, with six hundred men, four field-pieces, and ample ammunition, stores, and provisions, sailed through the inland passages; but did not reach Savannah until the 28th of February, a few days after General McIntosh, with the remains of the first battalion of his brigade, had driven the invaders back from the Alatamaha.

So great was the alarm, and so imminent the danger, that a large part of the militia of the State were or-

[6] MS. letter of Joseph Clay.

dered into service, and a camp was formed at Medway Meeting-house. The rest of the militia were commanded to hold themselves ready to turn out with arms at a moment's warning; while the President, finding it sometimes impossible to collect the Council of Safety, was desired, by a resolution of the Council, passed on the 22d February, 1777, "to take upon himself the whole executive powers of government, calling to his assistance not less than five persons of his own choosing, to consult and advise with on every urgent occasion, when a sufficient number of councillors cannot be convened to make a board."

This was giving to the President extraordinary powers; but the Council knew the prudence and reliability of the man to whom they intrusted them, and hence confided fully in his wisdom and patriotism. Mr. Bulloch did not long hold these dictator-like powers; for, before the close of the month, he died, and Button Gwinnett was elected to succeed him as President of the Council of Safety.

Mr. Bulloch seemed to be just the man for the critical time in which he lived, and for the responsible station which he held. He was one of the foremost to assert and maintain the liberties of his country, even before the rupture with Great Britain, and when the friends of American rights in Georgia were few and fearful. When Bryan had been ejected from the Governor's Council; and Wylly from the clerkship; and Jones from the Speaker's chair; for their freedom of thought and speech; when it was hazardous to come in collision with the royal power, and provoke the wrath of a King's Governor; when it was almost treason to talk the honest sentiments of a freeman,

Archibald Bulloch and three others came out, over their own signatures, with a call for a meeting of those opposed to the unjust acts of England, and anxious for a redress of their grievances.

His death was a heavy loss to Georgia, at a moment when it could hardly be borne;—for all parties of Liberty men were united on him, and on him alone; and when he was called hence, by the fiat of God, divisions and discord rent the ranks of the Americans, and it was not until blood had flowed, and years of animosity passed, that harmony again pervaded our councils. Had not Mr. Bulloch been so deeply engaged in provincial affairs, as to prevent his attendance at Philadelphia in the Congress of 1776, to which he was elected, his name would have gone down to posterity as one of the signers of the Declaration of Independence. If he failed, however, of securing this distinction, he gained the honor of being the first republican Governor of Georgia—the people's first choice to their highest office—one who sacrificed his private views for the public good, and who died in the very harness of executive authority, revered and cherished by his native province.

Scarcely had Button Gwinnett seated himself in the executive chair, before he became anxious of military as well as civil renown; and, desirous of signalizing his administration by some brilliant stroke of arms, he planned an expedition against Florida, in order to return upon St. Augustine the attack lately made upon our southern forts. But it was an expedition ill-judged, ill-planned, ill-executed; resulting in disaster to the troops, evil to the province, and death to its projector.

It was ill-judged, to think of attacking with a few half-disciplined Continentals and militia a stronghold like St. Augustine, which had recently been reinforced by a thousand British troops; while the whole military force in Georgia, numbering some seven or eight hundred men, was not sufficient to man its own forts and frontier posts.

It was ill-planned, as being resolved upon by a civilian, without consulting the commanding officer of the Georgia Brigade, or even asking his assistance, as the President determined to rely solely on the militia and State Continentals.

It was an ill-executed measure, as only one portion of the troops, the militia, under Colonel Baker, reached Saw-pit Bluff, near the mouth of the St. John's, the appointed place of rendezvous, Colonel Sumter, with the Carolina troops by land, and Colonel Elbert, with his Continentals and little armament by water, being unable to join their forces at the appointed time and place.

It was disastrous to the troops, as they suffered much in this fruitless campaign, and acquired for the service an almost unconquerable distaste.

It was disastrous to the province, as it originated crimination and recrimination, splitting up the State into feuds and parties; dividing, and consequently weakening, their power; perilling the great interest of liberty in the bickerings of party strife and personal jealousies; seeking to cover the mortification of defeat and the odium of ill-judged schemes, by criminations as foolish as they were unjust.

It was disastrous to the President, because his highly improper conduct involved him in controversies with General McIntosh, then commanding the Georgia Brigade. A duel resulted from their misunderstanding, in which both were wounded at the first fire; but, while General McIntosh recovered, Gwinnett, after lingering twelve days, expired on the 19th May, 1777.

The death of Gwinnett roused the malevolence of his party: irritated at the loss of their leader, they threw so many obstacles in the way of General McIntosh, and so retarded all his efforts, that, feeling he could do but little good in a State and among a people so unjustly arrayed against him, he applied, through the President of Congress, to be transferred to a northern command. His request was granted; and, taking with him his son, Captain Lachlan McIntosh, and Captain John Berrien, of his staff, he repaired to Pittsburg, to take command of the western army, to which important post he had been appointed by Congress, on the recommendation of Washington. The removal of this excellent officer, who, more than any other, was fitted to command in a State with whose inhabitants, resources, and localities, he was so intimately acquainted, was a very serious loss to the State; not only by taking away from it so valuable a citizen, and a general, but also, as it was the means of having it placed under the command of a weak, unmilitary, and inefficient officer, General Robert Howe.

Painful, however, as was the removal of General McIntosh to his own feelings, and unfortunate as it was for Georgia, no other course was left open to him. The petty persecutions, the contemptible jealousies, the open opposition, and the secret undermining at work in reference to him, were sources of such constant annoyance that his abilities were cramped for want of scope; his power weakened by the usurpation of civil officers; his energy fettered by executive restrictions, and his life was exposed not to the fire of the enemy, but to the jealousy of hating and murderous rivals.

CHAPTER IV.

SOUTHERN INVASIONS—CAPTURE OF SAVANNAH.

In the beginning of 1778, the State was very much disturbed by the irruption into its northern portion of a band of insurgents, who, from being under the command of a fuming and illiterate partisan, Colonel Scophal, were named "Scophalites." This band, numbering five or six hundred men, came from the upper part of Carolina, crossed the Savannah River just below Augusta, and captured a number of well-laden trading-boats as they passed. On their route they were joined by the disaffected of the district through which they passed, and committed great depredations, before they reached Florida, whither they hastened, to swell the garrison of St. Augustine, and aid the British in their projected conquest of Georgia.

The movements of these loyalists, combined with the many rumors concerning the operations of Colonel Prevost, induced a resolution on the part of General Howe to anticipate their meditated attack on Georgia by an invasion of the Floridian capital.

Yet, how little prepared Georgia was to make such an invasion may be known from General Howe's own statement, wherein he declares:[1] "That the country

[1] Moultrie, i, 204.

was assailable on every side, and nowhere prepared for defence; many of the people disaffected to the cause, and those who wish it well not united among themselves, exceedingly weak in numbers as to militia, and these ill armed; and it is a melancholy truth that our regulars do not exceed 550 effectives."

Notwithstanding these adverse circumstances, which should have counselled more prudent measures, General Howe ordered to Savannah 200 men from the brigade of General Moultrie, who detached 150 from Thompson's, and 50 from Sumter's regiment. These were subsequently increased to 600 Continentals, in addition to a force of several hundred militia under Colonel Williamson, who marched down to his assistance from Ninety-six in Carolina. Fort Howe was the place appointed for the rendezvous of the several detachments.

Colonel Elbert, who commanded here, had recently signalized himself by a brilliant exploit, which he thus narrates in a letter to General Howe:—

"FREDERICA, April 19th, 1778.

"DEAR GENERAL:—

"I have the happiness to inform you, that about 10 o'clock this forenoon, the brigantine Hinchinbrooke, the sloop Rebecca, and a prize brig, all struck the British tyrant's colors, and surrendered to the American arms.

"Having received intelligence that the above vessels were at this place, I put about three hundred men by detachment from the troops under my command at Fort Howe, on board the three galleys, the Washington, Captain Hardy; the Lee, Captain Braddock; and the Bulloch, Captain Hutcher; and a detachment of artillery, with two field-pieces, under Captain Young, I put on board a boat. With this little army, we embarked at Darien, and last evening effected a landing at a bluff about a mile below the town; leaving Colonel White on board the Lee, Captain Melvin on board the Washington, and Lieutenant Petty on board the Bulloch, each with a sufficient party of troops. Immediately on landing, I despatched Lieutenant-Colonel Ray and Major Roberts, with about one hundred men; who marched directly up to the town, and made prisoners three marines and two sailors belonging to the Hinchinbrooke.

"It being late, the galleys did not engage until this morning. You must imagine what my feelings were to see our three little men-of-war going on to the attack of these three vessels, who have spread terror on our coast, and who were drawn up in order of battle; but the weight of our metal soon damped the courage of these heroes, who soon took to their boats; and as many as could, abandoned the vessel with everything on board, of which we immediately took possession. What is extraordinary, we have not one man hurt. Captain Ellis, of the Hinchinbrooke, is drowned, and Captain Mowbray, of the Rebecca, made his escape. As soon as I see Colonel White, who has not yet come to us with his prizes, I shall consult with him, the three other officers, and the commanding officers of the galleys, on the expediency of attacking the Galatea, now lying at Jekyl."

The contemplated attack on the Galatea was thwarted by the departure of that vessel, just as Colonel Elbert was completing his preparations for its seizure or destruction. General Howe reached Fort Howe on the 20th May, and on the 25th, he crossed the Alatamaha and encamped at Reid's Bluff. Here he was kept waiting nearly two weeks by the sickness of his troops, the tardiness of the militia, and the non-arrival of those supplies which were to come round by water from South Carolina.

These supplies were greatly needed, as tents were so scarce that ten and twelve were often crowded into one, or else they slept in the heavy dews. One camp kettle sufficed for twelve or fifteen, one small canteen was distributed to six or eight, and though many were sick, they had but few and inferior medicines. It was not until the 7th June, that General Howe was enabled to march off the Georgia brigade from Reid's Bluff, as the van of his little army destined for the conquest of Florida. This brigade, under Colonel Elbert, was advanced to the Satilla River, to collect boats for the passage of the troops; and the main body of the army under Howe, finding no interruption of a serious nature, was enabled to reach the St. Mary's River, where a junction was formed with Commodore Bowen, who had gone round by sea.

Fort Tonyn, which they had expected to have found fully manned, was evacuated and demolished, and the enemy had made a stand at Alligator Creek, fourteen miles to the south. To dislodge them, General Howe ordered three hundred men to reconnoitre their position, and if it seemed practicable, to give them battle.

The camp of the enemy was only surrounded by a ditch, while a number of recently felled trees constituted a simple abatis. Satisfied that a camp thus slightly entrenched could be easily captured, the commanding officer ordered a body of cavalry, under Colonel Elijah Clarke, to attack them on one side, while the main body, seizing the opportunity of the confusion created among the enemy by the onset of Clarke, would rush upon them in front, and gain the day. Clarke, after great difficulty, penetrated the outward barrier of trees and brush; but found, when about to leap the ditch, that it was too wide, and his horses, being made fractious by the fire and huzzas which greeted their arrival at the ditch, he was unable to effect his design, and being wounded in the thigh, ordered a retreat, losing three killed and nine wounded. Owing to this failure, no attack was made in front, and the whole force returned to the main army.

The failure of this plan was the natural result of the peculiar and unmilitary state of affairs in the American forces. Some of these are thus hinted at by General Howe:—

"I have been waiting for the galleys first, and, after their arrival, a tedious time for the militia of this State, and for the long-expected coming of Colonel Williamson and our countrymen with him. In short, if I am ever again to depend upon operations I have no right to guide, and men I have no right to command, I shall deem it then, as I now do, one of the most unfortunate incidents of my life. Had we been able to move at once, and those I expected would have been foremost had only been as ready as we were, a blow might have been given to our enemies which would have put it out of their power to have disturbed us, at least not hastily; and perhaps have been attended with consequences more important than the most sanguine could have expected; but delayed beyond all possible supposition, embarrassed, disappointed, perplexed, and distressed beyond expression, the utmost we could now achieve, will be a poor compensation for the trouble and fatigue we have undergone; excepting we may be allowed to suppose (what I truly think has been effected) that the movements we have made have drove back the enemy, and prevented an impending invasion of the State of Georgia, which would otherwise inevitably have overwhelmed it, and also a dangerous defection of both States. This good, I am persuaded, has resulted from it, and this is our consolation. The enemy were, two or three days since, at Alligator Creek, fourteen miles from this place; their forces, by all accounts, are at least equal to either the Governor's troops or mine, and we are on contrary sides of the river, and not within eight miles of each other. Ask me not how this happened, but rest assured that it has not been my fault. I believe, however, that the Governor will encamp near me to-night, and if the enemy are still where they were, which I hope to know to-night or to-morrow morning, we shall probably beat up their quarters."

Though the 12th of June was the time appointed for the junction of troops at St. Mary's, Governor Houstoun, with the State militia, did not reach there until the 4th July, and Colonel Williamson on the 11th; and when the four portions, severally commanded by General Howe, Commodore Bowen, Governor John Houstoun, and Colonel Williamson, reached their destination, so far from amalgamating into one command, under the general officer; Commodore Bowen insisted on his exclusive right to control the galleys; Governor Houstoun refused to surrender his right as commander-in-chief of the militia; and Colonel Williamson's troops refused to obey any orders but such as emanated from him.

It was an army cursed with four heads, each jealous of the other; and an army without unity, like "a house divided against itself," cannot stand. Sickness also came into camp, and struck down one half of the troops. Their horses were so reduced in number, that they had scarcely enough to drag the artillery, ammunition, and baggage, so that had their retreat been cut off by water, they could scarcely have effected it by land, "and if we do not retreat soon," said a distinguished officer of the expedition, "we shall not be able to retreat at all, and may crown this expedition with another Saratoga affair in reverse."

It now became very evident that the enemy, while they were in large force at St. Augustine, designed waiting for the Americans on the south side of the St. John's, and concentrated there a force of twelve hundred; consisting of regulars, royalists, and Scophalites, besides Indians, to dispute the passage to St. Augustine. The middle of summer had arrived, and two months and a half had been consumed in getting the troops to the St. Mary's, under disadvantages, arising in part from the roads and climate; but mostly, from the tardiness of the militia, the sickness of the soldiers, the want of co-operation among the commanders, and the lack of those military stores, which common prudence and military foresight should have anticipated and provided. In the perplexing emergency in which General Howe was now placed, he called a council of war of the principal officers on the 11th of July. He stated to the board the reasons which induced the undertaking, the results thus far in driving the enemy from Georgia, and obliging them to evacuate Fort Tonyn, and the various impediments in the way of a further advance over roads rendered impassable to the artillery. He added that he had not sufficient horse power to carry the necessary baggage and ammunition; that his force was reduced by sickness, from eleven hundred to three hundred and fifty men fit for duty, and that he could not expect the co-operation of the naval armament. He then proposed to the officers the following questions:—

1st. "As driving the enemy out of Georgia, and demolishing Fort Tonyn, were the objects principally aimed at; have not these purposes been effected?

"Resolved unanimously in the affirmative.

2d. "As it appears from information above recited, that the enemy do not mean to oppose us in force on this side of St. John's River; is there any other object important enough in our present situation to warrant our proceeding?

"Resolved unanimously in the negative.

3d. "Is the army in a situation to cross St. John's River, attack the enemy, and secure a retreat in case of accident, though they should be aided by the militia, now embodied under Governor Houstoun and Colonel Williamson?

"Resolved unanimously in the negative.

4th. "Does not the sickness which so fatally prevails in the army, render a retreat immediately requisite?

"Resolved unanimously in the affirmative.

"The general then proceeded to inform the council that the Governor had denied him the right to command the militia, even if a junction had been formed between them and the Continental troops, notwithstanding the resolution of Congress declaring 'that as to the propriety of undertaking distant expeditions and enterprises, or other military operations, and the mode of conducting them, the general or commanding officer, must finally judge and determine at his peril.'"

The General therefore thought proper to put the following questions :—

1st. "Can he, with propriety, honor, and safety to himself, or consistent with the service, relinquish the command to the Governor?

"Resolved unanimously in the negative.

2d. "Can the army, whilst the command is divided, act with security, vigor, decision, or benefit to the common cause?"

"Resolved unanimously in the negative."

These resolutions were agréed to and signed by all the officers who composed the council of war.

Agreeably to the advice thus given, the army began its retreat by water to Sunbury, and thence in small parties returned to their several posts or homes. This abortive attempt upon St. Augustine resulted in an immense loss to the invaders. More than one-third of the troops were either dead or were disabled, and, although it had the temporary effect of driving the enemy out of Georgia, yet the weakness of the measures pursued, the vacillation of purpose in the commanding officers, and the waste of life and money incurred by the expedition, were such as lost the confidence of the Georgians in their own efforts, and incited to new attacks the loyalists of Florida, who now waited but a proper opportunity to return invasion for invasion, with every prospect of success.

General Howe soon repaired to Charleston, and Georgia was left in her feebleness to bear the innumerable troubles created and fostered by this disastrous expedition. Throughout the summer the southern borders of the Province were constantly assailed by small marauding parties of five or six from Florida, who, attacking single houses, destroyed the people, cattle, and crops, and then, suddenly retiring, eluded pursuit. The Creeks on the north, were restless and turbulent; and many murders were committed by the Indians, though there was no general rising of the tribes, such as demanded military subjugation. In addition to these troubles from without, the patriot Georgians were harassed by the disaffected and the disappointed, and by the partisan broils and jealousies which disgraced the conduct of many of the leading politicians of that day.

Harmony and wisdom seemed to forsake the counsels, as success did the efforts of the Georgians; and though some remained firm and devoted, many wavered, many despaired, and all suffered in the additional distresses which gathered around them. The rumors of an invasion from Florida, which had so long floated through the Province, gathered strength and probability as the autumn advanced; and General Howe returned to Georgia to prepare for any emergency that might occur.

Sir Henry Clinton had failed in many of his schemes at the north, and the Commissioners appointed by his Majesty "to treat, consult, and agree upon the means of quieting the disorders now subsisting in certain of the colonies, plantations, and provinces in North America," having received no overtures, nor seen any prospect of effecting a reconciliation, the British General resolved to secure the southern provinces; and for this purpose, designated Georgia as the first point to be attacked, proposing, if successful, to follow it up with the subjugation of the Carolinas.

In pursuance of this design, Sir Henry Clinton planned two expeditions against the province: one from the north, under Lieutenant-Colonel Archibald Campbell; and one from Florida, under Colonel Augustin Prevost, who commanded in East Florida, and who was directed, on the junction of the two bodies of troops, to take command of the whole. Colonel Prevost received his orders on the 27th November, but previously to this had sent off two parties of troops, one under his brother, Lieutenant-Colonel James Mark Prevost, and the other under Lieutenant-Colonel Fuser, purposing to follow himself in time to effect the desired junction with Colonel Campbell.

The troops under Lieutenant-Colonel Prevost (consisting of about one hundred regulars and three hundred refugees and Indians, under the deserter McGirth, who joined him at Fort Howe) ravaged the country as they advanced, meeting the Americans first at Bull Town Swamp, who, being entrapped in an ambuscade, after a slight skirmish, retreated; the commander of the Americans, Colonel Baker, and two officers, being wounded. A more general engagement took place about a mile and a half south of Medway Meeting-house, when both parties, seeking to ensnare each other in an ambuscade, were brought into direct collision. General Scriven, who commanded the American side, fell early in the fight, of a wound that proved mortal the next day. This misfortune did not altogether damp the ardor of his troops; for they fought so bravely, that at one time the enemy were thrown into confusion, and the shout of victory rose from the lips of Major James Jackson, one of the gallant officers; but the cry was premature: the British, momentarily confused by the unhorsing of Lieutenant-Colonel Prevost, were rallied, when he was remounted, and returned to the struggle with such spirit, that Colonel White, on whom the command now devolved, retreated with order, first to the Meeting-house, and then, pressed by superior numbers, to the Ogeechee, where a slight breastwork had been thrown up by Colonel Elbert. Prevost advanced only about six or seven miles north of the Medway Meeting-house, when, learning that Colonel Fuser had not arrived at Sunbury, nor any transports from New York at Savannah, and that Colonel Elbert was prepared to dispute the passage of the Ogeechee, "he suddenly decamped, and began a retreat,"[2] blackening his march with the ruins of settlements, crops, and families; for his force was but a horde of freebooters, glutting themselves with blood and spoil.

Owing to head winds, Lieutenant-Colonel Fuser did not reach his destination, Sunbury, until after Lieutenant-Colonel Prevost had retreated to Florida. He had with him a large force, and siege-guns, light artillery, and mortars. Encamping before the fort, he summoned it to surrender, in terms of marked ferocity. Lieutenant-Colonel John McIntosh, though he

[2] Steadman's History of the War, 68.

had under him scarcely a hundred men, and was conscious that the place could not hold out against an ordinary assault, sent back the laconic answer, "Come and take it!" This courageous and unexpected reply, combined with the fact that Lieutenant-Colonel Prevost had retreated, and that the American troops were marching from Savannah to oppose him, caused him to raise the siege at once, and return to Florida.

General Howe arrived at Sunbury shortly after the retreat of Fuser. "The town," he said, "is not defensible for half an hour, should it be attacked the least formidably; and its present safety is entirely owing to the spirited conduct of the troops in the fort, and the want of enterprise in the enemy."

The expedition under Lieutenant-Colonel Campbell sailed from New York on the 27th November, 1778. The squadron that was to convoy and assist, consisted of the Phœnix forty-four, the Fowey twenty-four, the Rose twenty-four, the Vigilant twenty-eight, the Keppel, an armed brig; the Greenwich, an armed sloop, and the Comet galley; besides several transport ships, under command of Commodore Hyde Parker, having on board the 71st Regiment of foot; the Wellworth and Wissenbach battalions of Hessians;[3] 1st and 2d battalion of De Lancey's corps, New York volunteers; 4th battalion of Skinner's corps; and a detachment of the Royal Artillery; numbering, in the whole, 3500 men.

Of this designed attack upon Savannah, the Georgians had no notice, until the 6th of December, when a deserter from one of the transports gave the alarm.

[3] Beatson's Naval and Military Memoirs of Great Britain, iv, 371; Steadman's History of the American War, ii, 66.

General Howe was then at Sunbury, where, conjointly with this news, he received an express from the south, notifying him of the northward march of Colonel A. Prevost, with all his available troops. General Howe hurried to Savannah; the Governor called out the militia; Continental troops were ordered from South Carolina; and every effort was made to prepare for the threatened invasion.

Bad weather prevented the arrival of this squadron off Tybee, until the 23d December, though it was not until the 27th, that all the vessels anchored inside the bar. Both the naval and military officers were ignorant of the condition of things in Georgia; and to gain the desired information, Sir James Baird, with a company of light infantry, and Lieutenant Clark, of the Phœnix, were despatched in two flat-boats, on the night of the 25th, to scour Wilmington Island, and secure all persons on it. They found but two men, and such was the information which they gave of the defenceless state of Georgia, that Colonel Campbell resolved to land at once, and attack Savannah, without waiting for the arrival of Colonel Augustine Prevost. Owing to the grounding of several galleys, it was not until daybreak on the 29th, that the troops of the first division, consisting of all the light infantry, the New York volunteers, and the 1st battalion of the 71st, under Lieutenant-Colonel Maitland, were landed on the river, down in front of Gerridoe's plantation, about two miles, in a straight line, from Savannah. From this embankment a narrow causeway, one-third of a mile long, led to a bluff about thirty feet high, called Brewton's Hill, and distant, by road, three or four miles from town. Captain Cameron's company of light infantry—the first that effected a landing—pushed on to this bluff, where they were opposed by Captain John C. Smith, of South Carolina, with about forty men, who opened an effective fire on the assailants, killing Captain Cameron and two Highlanders, and wounding five more; but, overpowered by numbers and the impetuous charge of the British, the hill was soon cleared, as Captain Smith had received orders to retreat, as soon as it was untenable, to the main works.

As the several portions of the army landed, they formed in order of battle on the high ground in front of Mr. Gerridoe's house, and there remained, until Colonel Campbell, by reconnoitring, could ascertain the force and position of the Americans. These, under the command of General Howe, were drawn up about half a mile to the southeast of Savannah, in two brigades, one commanded by Colonel Huger, and the other by Colonel Elbert: the whole did not amount to eight hundred, a portion of whom were militia; the suddenness of the attack not allowing the calling in of the militia in greater numbers, to protect the capital. Expecting the attack on the great road leading to Brewton's Hill, General Howe had burnt down a little bridge that crossed a small rivulet, and about three hundred feet in the rear of this marshy rivulet, a trench was cut, which soon filled with water, so that the trench, the stream, and the marsh through which it flowed, offered serious embarrassment to the advance of the enemy. At this point General Howe had placed two cannon, that flanked the causeway, and three that bore directly on its front. Thus stationed, the Americans awaited the onset.

Colonel Campbell had discovered their position, and having detailed a proper guard to cover the landing, pressed on to the attack. The light infantry, under Sir James Baird, advanced first, supported by the New York volunteers, under De Lancey. These were followed by the first battalion of the 71st, with two six-pounders; the Wellworth battalion of Hessians, with two three-pounders; and part of Wissenbach's battalion of Hessians, which formed the rear. By 3 P. M., they had reached the open country near Tatnall's plantation, and halted awhile, as if preparing for the battle.

Advantageously posted as the Americans were, it would have been quite hazardous to have offered them battle in front, for they were too well protected by the intervening marsh and stream and ditch. The aim of Colonel Campbell, therefore, was to gain, if possible, their rear, or turn their extended flanks. In this desire he was fortunately aided by an old negro, Quash Dolly, who informed him of a private path, leading through the wooded swamp, by which he could gain, unperceived, the rear of the Americans. This path had been pointed out to General Howe, in the morning, by Colonel Walton, as being a place necessary to guard and secure; but it was culpably and, as the event proved, disastrously neglected. Manœuvring in front, as if about to attack the left flank of General Howe, the Americans opened their fire upon the enemy, who, however, received it in silence, not a gun being fired in return. Perceiving the Americans thus deceived by the feint, the British commander lost no time in directing Sir James Baird, with the light infantry and the New York volunteers, to follow the guidance of the negro, and secure the rear of the Americans. They reached their destined point, unperceived by General Howe, and suddenly issuing from the swamp, attacked a body of militia, which had been posted to secure the great road leading to the Ogeechee. As soon as this firing gave notice to the commander that Major Baird had effected his purpose, he gave orders for the whole British column to advance at a rapid pace; while the artillery, which had been previously formed behind a slight rising ground, to conceal it from view, was instantly run forward to the eminence, and began to play upon the Americans. With a destructive fire thus unexpectedly pouring in upon them in front and rear, our troops were thrown into confusion, and thus were compelled to make a hasty retreat. The centre of the American line, with the commanding General, were enabled, by the exertions of Colonel Daniel Roberts, —who had partially secured the road leading to the causeway over Musgrove's Swamp,—to pass in comparative safety; the right flank, under Colonel Huger, attempting to go through the town, rushed between two fires, and many were bayoneted in the streets; the left, under Colonel Elbert, finding it impracticable to pass the causeway, now in possession of the British, cast away their arms and accoutrements, and, throwing themselves into the swamps and rice-fields, sought, by swimming the creek, then in full tide, to reach the Augusta road, though thirty lost their lives in this perilous attempt.

While Colonel Campbell had been thus successful

by land, Sir Hyde Parker had not remitted his vigilance in the fleet. As soon as he discovered that the troops had made an impression on the American line, he moved up the small armed vessels to the town, sending the Comet galley as high up as the ebb-tide would permit, securing the shipping and commanding the town from all approaches on the Carolina side. This movement completely shut in Savannah from succor, and was effected with the loss of only one seaman killed and five wounded; while the squadron captured one hundred and twenty-six prisoners, and seized three ships, three brigs, and eight smaller vessels.

The British entered Savannah without opposition, and, notwithstanding the assurance of Colonel Campbell in his official despatches, "that little or no depredation took place, and that even less than had ever happened to a town under similar circumstances," yet the soldiers and officers did commit atrocities and cruelties upon the inhabitants, of a character more worthy of savages than of men. The houses of the "rebels," as they were called, were given up a prey to the spoiler, and their pilfering hands and brutal outrages carried terror to every heart, and made Savannah a scene of anguish and distress. Nothing could exceed the consternation of the inhabitants, when they saw their defenders flying before the victorious march of the enemy, and that enemy, with rolling drums and flying colors, and a thirst for blood and spoil made keen by victory, enter their streets, with their hands and bayonets dripping with the blood of their husbands, fathers, brothers, and sons; their faces begrimed with sweat, and dust, and powder, and their countenances lowering with rage and the pent-up lusts, that chafed to be let loose upon the vanquished.

In this encounter—for it can hardly be called a battle—the English lost but two captains and five privates killed, and one officer and eight privates wounded; while the American loss was nearly one hundred killed and wounded, besides thirty, who lost their lives in the swamp; and seven officers and four hundred and sixteen non-commissioned officers and privates taken prisoners. With the town, they captured, of course, the fort, having in it forty-five pieces of cannon, nine of which were brass, twenty-three mortars and howitzers, ninety-four barrels of powder, and six hundred and thirty-seven small arms, besides shell and shot.

Thus, the expedition of Colonel Campbell had been entirely successful. An army had been defeated, and mostly captured; the capital of the State was taken; its commerce destroyed; the officers of government dispersed; provincial rule was broken, and the yoke of ministerial tyranny was again fastened on its neck.

The military author of the Memoirs of the War of the Southern Department has well said:[4] "However we must applaud the judgment displayed by the American general in selecting and improving his position; however, we must honor his gallant determination to receive the enemy's attack with an inferior force, yet, as this resolution in prudence must have been formed in the advantages of his ground, we cannot excuse the negligence betrayed by his ignorance of the avenues leading to his camp. How happens it that he who had been in command

[4] Lee's Memoirs, ii, 70.

of that country for many months should not have discovered the by-way, passing to his rear, when Lieutenant-Colonel Campbell contrived to discover it in a few hours? The faithful historian cannot withhold his condemnation of such supineness." His conduct in this matter has been severely animadverted on by military critics, and as severely censured by the people whom he was expected to defend. It became a matter of inquiry, by a committee of the General Assembly of Georgia, who, on the 17th January, 1780, brought in the following report: "The committee appointed to take into consideration the situation of the State since the 29th of December, 1778, report, that the capital and troops in this State were sacrificed on the said 29th of December, which was the first cause of the distresses and consequences which ensued. Your committee are of opinion that the delegates of this State should be directed to promote a trial of Major-General Howe, who commanded on that day. They find that the good people of the State were still further discouraged by the said Major-General Howe crossing Savannah River the next day, with the troops that escaped from Savannah, and ordering those at Sunbury and Augusta to do the same; leaving the State at the mercy of the enemy, without any Continental troops; instead of retreating to the back country, and gathering the inhabitants. The country, thus abandoned, became an easy prey to the British troops, they marching up, and taking post at Augusta, and sending detachments to every part of the State."

General Howe was subsequently brought before a Court of Inquiry, but was acquitted, though he was never after employed in active service. In fact, at the capture of Savannah, he was only holding his command until the arrival of General Benjamin Lincoln, who, on the 26th of September, 1778, was appointed by Congress to the command of the army in the Southern Department of the United States, and whose arrival was looked for by the people of the South with hope and satisfaction.

CHAPTER V.

BATTLES OF KETTLE CREEK AND BRIER CREEK.

As soon as Colonel Campbell had secured Savannah, he placed it under the command of Lieutenant-Colonel Innes, aid-de-camp to Sir Henry Clinton, and pushed forward a portion of his army to Cherokee Hill, which was taken possession of on the 1st January, 1779. The next day he took the town of Ebenezer, after securing all the intermediate posts. On his march, he collected twenty horses for dragoons, and several hundred head of cattle; and the day after the last scattered remains of General Howe's army had crossed over Sister's Ferry into Carolina, he established a post at that ferry. He then proceeded, with his corps of infantry and cavalry to Mount Venture, scouring the country for fifty miles above the town, "without finding," as he says, "a single rebel to oppose him."

On the 4th of January, Colonel Campbell and Commodore Parker jointly issued a proclamation, setting forth, that "a fleet and army were now actually arrived in Georgia, for the protection of the friends of lawful government, and to rescue them from the bloody persecution of their deluded fellow-citizens." It assured all those well-disposed citizens, who reprobated the idea of supporting a French league, and who wished to embrace the happy occasion of cementing a firm union with the parent state, free from the imposition of taxes by the Parliament of Great Britain, and secured in the irrevocable enjoyment of every privilege, consistent with that union of force on which their mutual interests depend, should meet with the most ample protection, on condition "they forthwith returned to the class of peaceful citizens, and acknowledged their just allegiance to the crown." But to those who should attempt to oppose the re-establishment of legal government, the proclamation denounced against them "the utmost rigors of war." This paper, sustained by the presence of so large a force, and the expected arrival of still further reinforcements, induced many to accept its proffered mercy and protection; and they accordingly took an oath, swearing allegiance to the King, and support of his government, renouncing, as "unlawful and iniquitous," the confederacy called the "General Continental Congress;" also, "the claim set up by them to independency, and jurisdiction of any sort, assumed by or under their authority."

It was the boast of the British commander, and one too much verified by the conduct of those who took the offered protection, that "many respectable inhabitants joined the army on this occasion, with their rifles and horses." These were organized into a corps of rifle dragoons, for the purpose of patrolling the country between the advanced posts of the English; and some of the Germans at Ebenezer, also formed themselves into a corps of militia, to act in the same capacity in the vicinity of their settlement.

A second proclamation soon followed, offering "a reward of ten guineas for every Committee or Assembly man taken within the limits of Georgia, and two guineas for every lurking villain"—(for thus courteously did it style the patriots of the Revolution)—"who might be sent from Carolina to molest the inhabitants." This was done, with the ostensible pretext of "establishing public security, and checking every attempt to disturb the peace of individuals."

The prisoners taken in the capture of Savannah, met with severe and cruel usage. A few enlisted in the enemy's ranks; but those who refused, after being alternately threatened and coaxed, were hurried on board ships in the river—crowded together like slaves—tyrannized over by every petty officer—stinted in provisions and every necessary of life, and treated with savage barbarity, so that four or five died every day. Nor was this treatment confined to common soldiers alone: civilians of standing and property were thrown indiscriminately into these prison-ships; and in some instances officers, who had a military right to different treatment, were—as in the case of Mordecai Sheftall, Commissary-General of the Georgia Line, and Sheftall Sheftall, his assistant, and the Rev. Moses Allen, Chaplain—thus immured.

The spirit which then animated the English officers, was often very alien to that high sense of honor and gentlemanly bearing, of which they so loudly boasted; and painfully, at times, did the atrocious spirit of war glut itself, in revenge of a personal and most malignant kind.

Nothing of the American army now remained in Georgia, save the garrison at Sunbury, under the command of Major Lane, which Colonel Campbell "thought too insignificant for early attention;" but which he now purposed to subdue, though, as he was about starting on the expedition, he learned that it had been reduced by Colonel A. Prevost, then on his way to Savannah. As soon as Colonel Prevost heard of the arrival of the troops from the north, he collected all the soldiers who could be spared from St. Augustine, and, agreeably to the instructions of General Sir Henry Clinton, marched to join Lieutenant-Colonel Campbell, and assume the command. Being retarded in his movements by the difficulty of finding conveyance for his artillery and ammunition, he sent on before him his brother, Lieutenant-Colonel James Mark Prevost, who, by a forced march in the night, surrounded the town of Sunbury; and the remainder of the troops soon coming up, they regularly invested the place; and after three days' resistance, during which the besieged had a captain and two men killed, and three wounded, Major Lane surrendered at discretion; while the British had only one private killed, and three wounded. Two hundred and twelve officers[1] and soldiers, two galleys, forty pieces of ordnance of various sizes, and some shot and small arms, were surrendered with the fort to Colonel Prevost, who, changing its name to Fort George, settled in it a garrison, to secure the dependence of that portion of the country.

In defending this post, Major Lane went contrary to the commands of General Howe; for on the day of the capture of Savannah, he despatched Lieutenant Aaron Smith, of the 3d South Carolina Regiment, to Major Lane, ordering him to evacuate his post at Sunbury, retreat across the country, and join him at Sister's

[1] Colonel Prevost's Letter, in Gentleman's Magazine, 1779.

Ferry. His refusal caused the loss of his command and the loss of his commission; for he was tried by a court-martial, and dismissed the army, for disobeying the orders of the commanding general.

On the arrival at Savannah of Colonel Prevost, he took the command of the combined forces from Florida and New York, and on the 24th of February he was gazetted major-general.

The Province of Georgia having been mostly reduced by the King's troops, civil government was re-established, on the 4th March, 1779; and on the 13th of July following, Governor Wright and the other crown officers, who had taken refuge in England, returned to Georgia, and entered anew upon the administration of their several offices.

General Lincoln relieved General Howe in the command of the Southern Department, and reached Purysburg on the 3d January, 1779, five days after the capture of Savannah. The loss of Howe's army was a more severe blow than the loss of the capital; its dispiriting influence on the soldiers themselves, and its disheartening effect upon the State, did much to prostrate its energies, and rob it of the strength and confidence which were necessary for its very existence.

General Lincoln found the army in anything but a gratifying condition. It numbered five hundred Continentals and seven hundred North Carolinians; and so near were they encamped to the enemy's posts, that they could hear their drums beat every morning, and the challenge of the sentinels. In a few days afterwards, this force was doubled; but many of the troops were exceedingly restive, as their time was nearly expired—all the State levies refused to come under Continental regulations—military obedience was reluctantly yielded—discipline was feebly enforced, and "the greatest military crime they could be guilty of, was only punishable by a small pecuniary fine."

The enemy, in the mean time, had stretched their posts along the Savannah; six hundred being stationed at Sister's Ferry, two hundred at Zubly's Ferry, while the main body of the army, under Colonel Campbell, took post at the little village of Abercorn, six miles below the American camp. Notwithstanding so many took protection, or enrolled themselves in the British troops, yet a few resolute spirits, in Burke and Richmond Counties, took the field, and, with a mere handful of Continentals, called in the militia to their aid, and roused the upper district of Georgia in its defence.

A party of royalists, under Colonel Brown, consisting of four hundred mounted men, was ordered to form a junction, at the jail in Burke County, with Colonel Thomas, the commander of the militia of the county, who, with many of his men, had sided with the enemy. Colonels Benjamin and William Few hastily gathered the Americans, and being joined by Colonel Twiggs, numbering in all about two hundred and fifty, fell suddenly upon Brown, after a forced march, and defeated him, with a small loss; but, expecting that the royalists would be reinforced, Colonel Twiggs thought it prudent to retire, and wait another opportunity, when, by another dashing movement, he could secure a more brilliant victory. The opportunity was not long wanting. Major Harry Sharp and two other Tory majors from South Carolina, raised a partisan corps, by which they greatly distressed the inhabitants of Burke County and its vicinity. Having watched them for some time, they were at length observed to encamp in such a position as would allow them to be very advantageously attacked; when Colonel Twiggs and Captain Joshua Inman rushed upon and totally defeated them. This sudden onset cost Captain Inman his life—not, however, until he had killed all three of the British majors with his own hands.[2]

This complete discomfiture of the Tories gave a temporary peace to the long-harassed residents of that vicinity; though it did not arrest the upward march of Colonel Campbell, who reached and took possession of Augusta by the close of January. Stopping but a few days in Augusta, he marched up some thirty or forty miles in the interior; and his presence, together with the fall of Augusta and Savannah, caused many of the inhabitants to take the oath of allegiance and come under the British protection. Those who declined, finding themselves insulted, pilfered, threatened—in terror by day and by night—their effects taken before their eyes—their children slain in their yards—their stock slaughtered or driven off to the English — their crops ruthlessly destroyed — their houses burnt over their heads — gathered what few things they could save from the general ruin, and moved across the river. The few who remained faithful to the American cause, after securing, as they hoped, the safety of their families, reassembled, at the earnest call of Colonel John Dooly, at a point on the Savannah River, five miles above the line of McGirth,

[2] Jackson's MS. Notes on Ramsey.

who, with three hundred loyalists, had encamped at a creek, for the purpose of watching the movements of the Americans and intercepting their passage across the river. By crossing a few miles higher up, Dooly effected a landing in Georgia; but only to retire again, before a detachment under Major Hamilton, who pursued him so closely, that the rear of Dooly's party and the van of Hamilton's were within musket distance when the Americans recrossed the Savannah River. Dooly remained upon the Carolina banks, anxiously watching another opportunity to fall upon his antagonist, and at the same time rousing up the Whigs in the vicinity to join him in expelling the marauders from their once happy homes.

Colonel Pickens, with about two hundred and fifty men of his regiment, promptly responded to the call; and joining Dooly, who, though the senior officer, waived the command in favor of Pickens, the united force marched to the attack of Hamilton, then supposed to be encamped in security about three miles below Cowan's Ferry. Hamilton, however, not anticipating any movement on the part of the Americans, had marched off on a few days' tour, for the purpose of bringing all within his military district under the oath of strict allegiance, and of changing the garrisons in the several small forts scattered through the neighboring country. The two little armies met at Carr's Fort; and a detachment of the Americans, under Captain William Freeman, having, by an act of daring bravery, secured a new log-house, which commanded the spring by which the fort was supplied with water, the British were locked in without food and water. Their horses and baggage were captured, and nothing but the humane desire of Colonel Pickens to save the few women and children in the fort, deterred the assailants from setting fire to the fort and compelling instant submission. But while the Americans waited for a more tardy, yet apparently certain surrender, news was brought to Colonel Pickens of the advance of the notorious royalist Boyd; who, just returned from a conference with Sir Henry Clinton at New York, had, under a commission, organized a partisan corps in the upper district, and was now, with a body of eight hundred loyalists, on his desolating march towards Georgia. This induced an instant abandonment of the fort, though within a few hours it must necessarily have yielded; and raising the siege, the Americans recrossed the Savannah; while Major Hamilton, rejoicing in his unexpected fortune, retreated to Wrightsborough, and thence, in a few days, to Augusta, where he joined Colonel Campbell, losing nine killed and three wounded during the siege.

Boyd, aware of their intention to attack him, and unwilling at this juncture to hazard a battle, changed his route; but Captain Anderson, with about a hundred men, who had been detached to watch his movements, ascertained his point of fording the river, and stationing his few troops in the thick canebrakes, poured a destructive fire upon the main body, as it crossed the river, and continued the havoc until a portion of the enemy, which had crossed a little higher up, came suddenly upon his rear, and compelled a retreat, with the loss of thirty-two killed, wounded, and taken prisoners, while Boyd's loss was three times this number.

The enemy having effected a passage into Georgia,

Pickens and Dooly, now joined by Colonel Clarke, resolved to follow; and they accordingly crossed the Savannah on the 12th February, and the following night encamped within four miles of the enemy. Forming the line of march in the order of battle, the Americans now prepared once more, at a great disadvantage of numbers, to contest with the Tories for the supremacy in Upper Georgia. Much depended on this battle. If Boyd should be successful in driving back the Americans, under such men as Pickens, and Dooly, and Clarke, he might rest assured that no farther molestation, at least for a very long time, would follow, and all would yield to the British power; while, on the other hand, should the Americans be successful, it would not only crush the Tory power, already so galling to the people, but protect them from further insult, and give a stimulus to American courage, which a long series of disasters made especially necessary; it was a moment big with the fate of Upper Georgia.

Boyd, with a carelessness evincing great lack of military skill and prudence, had halted, on the morning of the 14th, at a farm near Kettle Creek, in Wilkes County, having no suspicion of the near approach of the Americans, and his army were dispersed in various directions, killing and gathering stock, cooking, and other operations. Having reconnoitred the enemy's position, the Americans, under Pickens, advanced in three divisions: the right under Colonel Dooly, the left under Clarke, the centre led by the commander himself, with orders not to fire a gun until within at least thirty-five paces.

As the centre, led by Pickens, marched to the attack, Boyd met them, at the head of a select party, his line being protected by a fence filled in with fallen timber, which gave him great advantage over troops displaying in his front. Observing this half-formed abatis, Pickens filed off to a rising ground on his right, and thence gaining the flank of Boyd, rushed upon him with great bravery—the enemy fleeing, when they saw their leader shot down before them. Sustained in this charge by Dooly and Clarke, the enemy, after fighting with great bravery, retired across the creek; but were rallied by Major Spurgen, on a hill beyond, where the battle was again renewed with fierceness; but Colonel Clarke, with about fifty Georgians, having discovered a path leading to a ford, pushed through it, though in doing so he encountered a severe fire, and had his horse shot down under him, and, by a circuitous route, rose upon the hill in the rear of Spurgen, when, opening a deadly fire, the enemy, hemmed in on both sides, fled, and were hotly pursued by the victors, until their conquest was complete. For one hour and a half, under great disadvantage, and against a force almost double, had the Americans maintained the unequal contest, and though once or twice it seemed as if they must give way, especially when the Tories had gained the hill, and were re-formed under Spurgen; yet the masterly stroke of Clarke, with his few brave Georgians, turned the scale, and victory, bloody indeed, but complete, was theirs.

Pickens and Dooly lost thirty-two killed and wounded, while Boyd and seventy of his men were killed, and as many more wounded and taken prisoners. Not two hundred and fifty, however, of his party ever reached Augusta,—the rest fled in every direction;

some cast themselves on the mercy of the Whig government, some were hung as traitors and miscreants, whose barbarities entitled them to the most horrid deaths, and some skulked among the mountain passes of North Carolina. The Tory force was broken, and only in small parties and petty skirmishes, did they again take the field. This victory was one of the most important in Georgia, and secured, for a time, the Whig ascendency in all that section. A few hours' delay in making this attack might have proved fatal to the Americans, as a party of five hundred men, under McGirth, was even then on its march to join Boyd, at Little River; but, the intelligence of his defeat and death, and the confusion it produced among the loyalists, determined him to return at once to Augusta, lest they also should fall before the victorious Americans.

The success of the Americans at Kettle Creek gave new vigor to their cause, and nerved the arms of the officers and soldiers to deeds of daring and bravery. Some feat of arms was almost daily performed, and generally resulted in advantage to the Americans. One of these consisted in the surprise of the British post at Herbert, consisting of seventy regulars, by a party of militia under Colonels Twiggs, McIntosh, and Hammond, killing and taking prisoners the entire corps. Another deed of valor was performed by Captain Cooper and twelve dragoons, who charged upon a reconnoitring party of the British Rangers, twenty in number, commanded by three officers, as they were advancing upon Brownsburg, and took them all prisoners. Instances of individual valor were of daily occurrence. One only need be related here. While the American troops lay near Augusta, General Elbert, anxious to obtain an accurate notion of the force and situation of the British, sent Lieutenant Hawkins to spy out their post. He departed alone; but, as he neared their camp, he was overtaken at the Bear Swamp by three men whom he knew to be noted Tories, and to avoid them was now too late. Resolutely advancing towards them, he demanded who they were, and whither they were going. They answered, to join Colonel Daniel McGirth. Hawkins, who had on an old British uniform, told them that he was McGirth, and did not believe a word that they said, that they were rebels, and he would hand them over to his party that were near. They protested to the contrary; when Hawkins told them that if what they said was true, to ground their rifles and hold up their right hands. As they did this, he advanced with cocked pistols, and, taking up their rifles, ordered them to march, and the first one that turned round he would shoot. Thus preceded, he arrived at the camp, and delivered his three prisoners to the General.

Finding the Tories thus defeated and dispersed, and all his hopes of help from these insurgents disappointed; and being unable, with any degree of safety, to occupy so long a chain of military posts, General Prevost abandoned Augusta, and all his line north of Hudson's Ferry, twenty-four miles above Ebenezer.

On the retreat of Campbell from Augusta (for such his precipitate departure may well be termed), his rear was harassed by parties of Americans, and a more vigorous pursuit was prevented only by his burning or breaking down all the bridges on his route until he got within supporting distance of Colonel J. M. Prevost, who marched up a little distance from Hudson's Ferry, to conduct him within the lines.

The Americans had now a large force along the Savannah River, distributed in several camps. At Augusta there were twelve hundred troops under General Williamson; at Black Swamp, seven hundred under General Rutherford; at Brier Creek, two thousand three hundred under General Ash; and at Purysburg, where General Lincoln had his head-quarters, were between three and four thousand men,—making, in all, a force of between eight and nine thousand. At a consultation, held at General Rutherford's camp, it was resolved by General Lincoln, and the principal officers, to march the army from Purysburg (leaving, however, a strong guard there to watch the enemy) to General Rutherford's, at Black Swamp,—there to cross the river and join General Ash, at Brier Creek. The position occupied by General Ash at the creek, was deemed by him perfectly secure, and he even believed that the enemy, having magnified his numbers, were afraid to cope with the troops under his command. On the other hand, the British commander, anticipating that the troops at Brier Creek might soon be joined by the main army, and feeling the ill effects which their presence had upon his movements, shutting him up so closely within his lines, he deemed it advisable to strike at General Ash before he could be reinforced, and thus prevent the attack which General Lincoln designed to make with his whole force upon the British at Hudson's Ferry and Ebenezer.

The plans of the enemy were secretly, but most effectively laid. To draw off attention from the main attack, which it was designed should be on the American front, Lieutenant-Colonel Prevost, with the 2d battalion, took a circuitous route of fifty miles to cross the creek above them, as if to turn their flank and gain the rear of the Americans; while, to keep General Lincoln in ignorance of their main design, General Prevost made a feint on the river bank, as if he purposed crossing the stream. The attacking columns found some difficulty in getting into their proper position, owing to the swollen current and the absence of bridges which they themselves had previously destroyed; but, on the morning of the 3d they were ready for action. Three grenadier companies of the 60th regiment; one of light infantry, under Sir James Baird; the 2d battalion of the 71st regiment; a troop of light dragoons, a body of provincial rangers, &c., with five pieces of artillery, numbering in all one thousand, moved on to the scene of slaughter.

General Ash was not prepared for such an encounter, encamped as he was in a place totally unfitted for defence. On his right was a deep lake, made by the overflowing of the surrounding streams into the low and matted swamp. On his left was Brier Creek, swollen, rapid, and impassable by recent rain; and his rear was bounded by the Savannah, with not a boat to cross it; while his only means of exit from this trap, into which, with entire lack of military skill, he had led his troops, was by an open field in front, and even this he had failed adequately to secure. Not suspecting his danger, he had sent off two detachments, one under Major Ross, of 300 dragoons, to reconnoitre the enemy at Hudson's Ferry; and the other under Colonel Marbury, to watch the upper pass of Brier Creek. This latter officer discovered the van of Prevost's army, and exchanged a few shots with them at Paris's Mills. He instantly sent an express to inform Ash of the near approach of the enemy, but the rider was captured, and it was only by a vague rumor, transmitted to the General by General Elbert, that he had any idea of their proximity. The enemy had then advanced almost to the picket guard at the bridge, about a mile from the main body, and when the drum sounded to arms, as that body of one hundred fled before the British van, not a soldier or piece of artillery had been served with cartridges, and not a plan of any kind had been formed for action. The confusion of the camp may well be imagined. Ash attempted to rally his troops under three divisions, but, as he confessed, they did not stand fire five minutes, and most of them shamefully fled, the General at full speed leading the way. The only portion of this ill-fated army that did stand their ground was the left division, under Elbert, which fought so gallantly that the English reserve were ordered up to support the line of attack: not until then, when there was no escape, and resistance was hopeless, did Elbert order his men to ground their arms, and surrender themselves prisoners of war.

The surprise and defeat of the Americans were complete. The enemy pursued the routed troops with a vengeance worthy of savages, and the order of Sir James Baird to his light infantry was, that "every one who took a prisoner should lose his ration of rum," and thus many, who on their knees implored mercy, were bayoneted by the brutal soldiery, who would not lose their allowance of grog. The loss of the Americans in battle was about 340, killed, wounded, and prisoners, one-half of whom fell dead on the battlefield, or were drowned in the neighboring waters. They lost also one thousand stand of arms. The British loss was very trifling, being only sixteen killed and wounded. A few of the fugitives, including Generals Ash and Bryant, and Colonel Pickens, reached Matthews's Bluff that evening; and that night, as many as could, crossed over into Carolina.

A court of inquiry sat a week after, at the request of General Ash, to investigate the conduct of this officer at this battle; and while, in its finding, the court acquitted General Ash of any want of personal courage, it declared its opinion that he had not taken all necessary precautions to secure his camp, and obtain timely notice of the movements and approach of the enemy.

But what shall we think of a General who, with an enemy so near at hand, and with two hundred dragoons in camp, should allow himself to be so surprised that not fifteen minutes elapsed from the alarm to the attack? Indeed it is fully evident that General Ash was deficient in almost every requisite of a commanding officer, having neither judgment, skill, foresight, nor self-reliance; and, notwithstanding the judgment of the court, wanting in personal bravery. It was more than suspected by many that he had betrayed his army and his place of encampment. The disposition of his troops and defence, his dilatory movements, and his precipitate flight, certainly gave strength to a report which obtained a very general credence. How unfortunate was it for Georgia that she should have had in her armies as her defenders such men as Howe and Ash, men totally incapacitated for their responsible duties, and whose errors and cowardice brought disgrace and ruin upon the State. Had not the wretched spirit of faction driven McIntosh from our borders, a different story might have been told of the British operations in Georgia.

The defeat of General Ash was very beneficial to the English. It opened to them the upper and back parts of the country and put them in connection with the Indian tribes; and their boast was that fourteen hundred of the inhabitants of these districts had given in their adhesion to the crown, and had organized themselves into twenty companies of militia for the defence of their property against the incursions of the rebels from South Carolina.

To the Americans it was peculiarly disastrous. The well-laid plans of General Lincoln were thwarted, the spirit of the people depressed, and the gathering reinforcements of militia dispersed to their homes, more than ever impressed with the prowess of the British arms, and the hopelessness of the American cause.

The operations during the remainder of the spring and summer were of a very desultory character. A few troops under such gallant leaders as Colonels Twiggs, Dooly, and Clarke, kept the field as skirmishers, moving rapidly here and there, as the exigencies of the times required; now striking down a body of Tories, and now fighting hand to hand with perfidious Indians. The demonstrations which the enemy now made upon Carolina, and especially Charleston, diverted for a time their attention from Georgia, which they regarded as completely in their power. There were not wanting, however, gallant men and gallant deeds to signalize this sad period, when hope of freedom seemed to have fled from Georgia forever. The surprise of a party of officers at Medway, on the 4th of June, by Captain Spencer, and his capture of a British vessel of six guns in Sapello Sound; the total defeat of Captain Muller and his grenadiers, by Twiggs, at Hickory Hill, on the Ogeechee; the rout which this same gallant officer made of the party of McGirth; and the victory which Major Baker gained the same day over a detachment under Captain Goldsmith; diversified the history of the war, and infused for a time new energy into the few and faithful adherents of the cause of freedom.

CHAPTER V.

SIEGE OF SAVANNAH.

THE treaty between France and the United States which engaged France as our revolutionary ally, was signed at Versailles on the 6th of February, 1778, and was hailed by Americans as a happy presage of victory and independence. Agreeably to the provisions of this treaty, the French government sent to America a fleet, which sailed from Toulon on the 12th of April, 1778, composed of twelve ships of the line and four frigates, and placed it under the command of Count d'Estaing. The special object of the fleet was, by a secret and rapid movement, to blockade the mouth of the Delaware, then occupied by the British fleet; and, with Washington's forces on the land, besiege the British troops in Philadelphia, and thus compel Lord Howe to surrender both fleet and army to the allied powers. A passage of nearly three months across the Atlantic threw d'Estaing upon the coast twenty days too late, and the whole design was therefore frustrated. A variety of joint operations were subsequently concerted by the American and French officers, but misfortune seemed to attend all; and, somewhat discouraged, d'Estaing sailed with his ships for the West Indies, and there captured Grenada and St. Vincent. While at the West Indies, he was met by letters from M. Gerard (the French minister who came out in the fleet), General Lincoln, and M. Plombard, the French consul of Charleston, soliciting his co-operation with General Lincoln in the capture of Savannah, which they represented might be carried by a *coup-de-main.*

The Count acceded to the proposal; sailed for America, and arrived off the coast of Georgia on the 3d of September, 1779, with twenty line of battle, two fifty-gun ships, and eleven frigates. So sudden was his appearance off the bar, that he captured part of the fleet of Sir James Wallace (the son-in-law of Sir James Wright,) who was then in command of the Tybee station. The arrangements for the combined operation of the armies had been determined on in Charleston between General Lincoln and the Vicomte de Fontanges, Adjutant-General of d'Estaing's army. Colonel Cambray, Major Thomas Pinckney, and Captain Gadsden were requested by Lincoln to join d'Estaing, who had desired some American officers conversant with the French to assist in the deliberations and interpretation necessary between the two nations. The time fixed upon for the junction of Lincoln and d'Estaing before Savannah, was the 17th September, previous to which the former was engaged in crossing the river with his army, rallying the militia, and calling in recruits; while the latter proceeded with his ships to Tybee,—which post the British immediately evacuated,—and thence to Ossaba, where he was met by Colonel Joseph Habersham, who had been despatched to point out a place of landing, and make every arrangement necessary for the debarkation of the troops. At nightfall, on the 12th September, the soldiers were transferred to the boats of the fleet, and vessels of light draught furnished by Carolina, and proceeded twelve miles up the river to Beaulieu, the old seat of President William Stephens. The 13th, 14th and 15th were consumed in landing the troops and artillery at Beaulieu, and in sending ashore entrenching tools at Thunderbolt. By the evening of the 15th it had all been effected. Count Pulaski, with his cavalry, had joined the French; and, on the morning of the 16th, the French army took up the line of march for Savannah, and encamped at Greenwich, within three miles of the town. The Georgia Continentals, under General Lachlan McIntosh, stationed at Augusta, were ordered down by Lincoln, to secure the British outposts, and open the way to the seaboard, which McIntosh effected, and then fell back to Millen's plantation, a short distance from Savannah, to await the arrival of the troops under Lincoln.

The preparations made by the British commander, for the reception of this combined army, were also prompt and vigorous.

On the 4th September, General Prevost received the first intelligence of the arrival of the French fleet off the bar. He immediately sent orders to all the outposts to hold themselves in readiness to join him, as it was yet uncertain whether the French designed to proceed to Charleston, or land at Savannah. But, on the 7th, when it was ascertained that the fleet was designed for Georgia, expresses were sent to all the outposts, requiring them to join the commanding General at Savannah.

On the 9th, the Fowey and the Rose, of twenty

guns each, and the Keppel and the Germain, armed vessels, retired up the river; the battery on Tybee was destroyed, the guns spiked, and the munitions removed. On the same day the following orders were issued from the head-quarters in Savannah:—

"The Regiment of Wissenbach to take their ground of encampment; likewise the 2d battalion of General Delancey's. In case of an alarm, which will be known by the beating to arms, both at the Barracks and main guard, the troops are to repair to their several posts, without confusion or tumult.

"Captain Stuart, of the British Legion, will take post with his men in the work on the right, near the river.

"The main guard to be relieved by convalescents from the Hessians.

"Major Wright's corps to send their convalescents in the old fort. Twenty-four men in the small redoubt, and seventy men in the left flank redoubt, upon the road to Tatnall's.

"The militia to assemble in rear of the Barracks.

"The Light Infantry, the Dragoons, and Carolina Light Horse, as a reserve, two hundred yards behind the Barracks.

"The King's Rangers, commanded by Lieutenant-Colonel Brown, in the small redoubt on the right, with fifty men, the remainder extending towards the larger redoubt on the right.

"The Carolinians divided equally in the two large redoubts.

"The battalion men of the 60th Regiment in the right redoubt. The Grenadiers on the left, extending along the abatis towards the Barracks; the Hessians on their left, so as to fill up the space to the Barracks.

"On the left of the Barracks, the 3d battalion of Skinner's, General Delancey's, and the New York volunteers; and on their left, the 71st Regiment, lining the abatis to the left flank redoubt, on the road to Tatnall's.

"If all orders are silently and punctually obeyed, the General makes no doubt that, if the enemy should attempt to make an attack, but that they will be repulsed, and the troops maintain their former well-acquired reputation; nor will it be the first time that British and Hessian troops have beat a greater superiority of both French and Americans than it is probable they will have to encounter on this occasion. The General repeats his firm reliance on the spirit and steady coolness of the troops he has the honor to command."[1]

Having confined his views to the sole object of defending the town, General Prevost bent all his energies to make it impregnable. The cannon and ammunition of the ships of war were landed at Savannah; the seamen were appointed to the different batteries, and the marines incorporated with the grenadiers of the 60th Regiment. The troops were employed in making fascines and cutting pickets; while a large body of negroes were at work night and day with the engineer, Major Moncrief, making and strengthening fortifications. Fifteen batteries, thirteen redoubts, communicating, each with each, and protected by an abatis in front, were begun, and when completed manned with seventy-six guns, ranging in calibre from

[1] From the original Order Book of General Prevost, in possession of I. K. Tefft, Esq., of Savannah.

six to eighteen pounds. Even the captains and crews of the merchantmen in the river were assigned to posts of duty; every available resource of men and means being subsidized by General Prevost.

It being apprehended that the French fleet might move up the river, the landmarks which pointed out the ship channel were cut down; the armed vessels, Rose and Savannah, and four transports, were sunk below the town, to stop up the passage; and several small vessels were also sunk above the town, and a boom laid across, to prevent the descent of fire-rafts, or the landing of troops in their rear. Such were the energetic measures taken by the British general to defend his post.

On the arrival of the American troops under General Lincoln at Zubly's Ferry, they met with so many obstacles, that they did not reach Cherokee Hill, on the Louisville road, until the 16th; where they halted, so as to be ready, by an early march on the following morning, to join, as agreed upon, the army of d'Estaing. But d'Estaing had no sooner reached Savannah, on the 16th, than, without waiting for General Lincoln, he demanded of General Prevost a surrender of the city to the arms of the King of France, in the following summons:—

"Count d'Estaing summons his Excellency General Prevost to surrender to the arms of the King of France. He apprises him that he will be personally responsible for all the events and misfortunes that may arise from a defence, which, by the superiority of the force which attacks him, both by sea and land, is rendered manifestly vain and of no effect.

"He gives notice to him, also, that any resolution

he may venture to come to, either before the attack, in the course of it, or at the moment of the assault, of setting fire to the shipping or small craft belonging to the army, or to the merchants, in the river of Savannah, as well as to all the magazines in the town, will be imputable to him only.

"The situation of Hospital Hill, in the Grenadas, the strength of the three intrenchments and stone redoubts, which defended it, and the comparative disposition of the troops before the town of Savannah, with a single detachment which carried the Grenadas by assault, should be a lesson to futurity. Humanity obliges the Count d'Estaing to recall this event to his memory; having so done, he has nothing to reproach himself with.

"Lord Macartney had the good fortune to escape from the first transport of troops who entered a town sword in hand; but, notwithstanding the most valuable effects were deposited in a place supposed by all the officers and engineers to be impregnable, Count d'Estaing could not have the happiness of preventing their being pillaged.

"ESTAING."

"CAMP BEFORE SAVANNAH, the 16th of September, 1779."

The reply of Prevost, to such a grandiloquent summons, was, as might have been expected, calm, but decided.

"CAMP, SAVANNAH, September 16, 1779.

"SIR—I am just now honored with your Excellency's letter of this date, containing a summons for me to surrender this town to the arms of his Majesty the King of France, which I had just delayed to answer, till I had shown it to the King's civil Governor.

"I hope your Excellency will have a better opinion of me, and of British troops, than to think either will surrender on a general summons, without any specific terms.

"If you, sir, have anything to propose that may with honor be accepted of by me, you can mention them, both with regard to civil and military, and I will then give my answer. In the mean time, I will promise, upon my honor, that nothing, with my consent or knowledge, shall be destroyed, in either this town or river."

To this d'Estaing replied:—

"CAMP BEFORE SAVANNAH, Sept. 16, 1779.

"SIR—I have just received your Excellency's answer to the letter I had the honor of writing to you this morning. You are sensible that it is the part of the besieged to propose such terms as they may desire; and you cannot doubt of the satisfaction I shall have in consenting to those which I can accept, consistent with my duty.

"I am informed that you continue intrenching yourself. It is a matter of very little importance to me; however, for form sake, I must desire that you will desist during our conferences together.

"The different columns which I had ordered to stop, will continue their march, but without approaching your post, or reconnoitring your situation.

"P. S. I apprise your Excellency that I have not been able to refuse the army of the United States uniting itself with that of the King.

"The junction will probably be effected this day. If I have not an answer, therefore, immediately, you must confer in future with General Lincoln and me."

As General Prevost was hourly anticipating the arrival of the Honorable Colonel Maitland, with some eight hundred troops, from Beaufort and vicinity, he was anxious to gain time by negotiation, to enable them to reach Savannah before hostilities commenced; and therefore he sent this note to the French commander:—

"September 16th, 1779.

"SIR—I am honored with your Excellency's letter in reply to mine of this day.

"The business we have in hand being of importance, there being various interests to discuss, a just time is absolutely necessary to deliberate. I am, therefore, to propose that a suspension of hostilities shall take place for twenty-four hours from this date; and to request that your Excellency will direct your columns to fall back to a greater distance, and out of sight of our works, or I shall think myself under the necessity to direct their being fired upon. If they did not reconnoitre anything this afternoon, they were sure within the distance.

"A. PREVOST."

D'Estaing suspected, and even intimated his suspicions of the temporizing policy of Prevost, and yet granted the boon, confident of final success over every advantage which this truce could give to the besieged, in the following terms:—

"CAMP BEFORE SAVANNAH, September 16, 1779.

"SIR: I consent to the truce you ask. It shall continue till the signal for retreat to-morrow night, the 17th, which will serve also to announce the recommencement of hostilities. It is unnecessary to observe to your Excellency, that this suspension of arms is entirely in your favor, since I cannot be certain that you will not make use of it to fortify yourself, at the same time that the propositions you shall make may be inadmissible.

"I must observe to you also, how important it is that you should be full aware of your own situation, as well as that of the troops under your command. Be assured that I am thoroughly acquainted with it. Your knowledge of military affairs will not suffer you to be ignorant, that a due examination of that circumstance, always precedes the march of the columns; and that this preliminary is not carried into execution by a mere show of troops.

"I have ordered them to withdraw before night comes on, to prevent any cause of complaint on your part. I understand that my civility in this respect, has been the occasion, that the Chevalier de Chambis, a lieutenant in the navy, has been made a prisoner of war.

"I propose sending out some small advanced posts to-morrow morning. They will place themselves in such a situation, as to have in view the four entrances into the wood, in order to prevent a similar mistake in future. I do not know whether two columns, commanded by the Viscount de Noailles and the Count de Dillon, have shown too much ardor, or whether your cannoniers have not paid a proper respect to the truce subsisting between us; but this I know, that what has happened this night, is a fresh proof that matters will soon come to a decision between us one way or another.

"I have the honor to be, with respect, &c.,

"ESTAING."

The next day General Lincoln joined the French army, and, as mildly as possible, remonstrated against the precipitancy of the Count's movements in demanding a surrender prior to the stipulated junction. By the noon of the 17th, Lieutenant-Colonel Maitland, with eight hundred men from Beaufort, reached Savannah, favored by a thick fog, unperceived by the French; and his presence so stimulated the besieged that, at a consultation of the higher officers of the navy and army, with the Governor and Lieutenant Governor, —it was unanimously determined to defend the place to the last extremity; and the resolution was communicated to Count d'Estaing, with the statement that the evening gun fired an hour before sunset, would be the signal for recommencing hostilities.

Before the arrival of Colonel Maitland, with a force nearly equal to the Continentals and militia of the Americans, serious thoughts, and even incipient measures had been taken for a capitulation; but the accession of so much strength turned the wavering decision to firm resolve and determined resistance.

The feeling of the English, at this succor, may be inferred from the orders of the day for the 17th September, when hostilities were to commence:—

"GENERAL ORDERS.

"CAMP BEFORE SAVANNAH, 17th September, 1779.

"Parole, *Maitland*. Countersign, *St. George*.

"Field officers for to-morrow, Lieutenant-Colonel Cruger and Major Graham.

"The troops to be under arms this afternoon at four o'clock; as the enemy is now very near, an attack may be hourly expected; the General, therefore, desires that the whole may be in instant readiness. By the known steadiness and spirit of the troops, he has the most unlimited dependence, doubting nothing of a glorious victory, should the enemy try their strength. What is it that may not, by the blessing of God, be expected from the united efforts of British sailors and soldiers, and valiant Hessians, against an enemy that they have often beat before? In case of a night attack, the General earnestly requests the utmost silence to be observed, and attention to the officers, who will be careful that the men do not throw away their fire at random, and warn them earnestly not to fire until ordered."[1]

This unexpected decision changed the whole face of affairs, giving disappointment to the combined army, and exultation to the British. A siege was determined on, but as yet neither French nor Americans had the cannon or mortars necessary to conduct it, and time was again lost in bringing them from the fleet. On the 23d September, the armies of Lincoln and d'Estaing broke ground together, about a mile from the enemy's works—the French on the right.

"It appeared now," says an eye-witness,—Major Thomas Pinckney, "to be the determination of the General to endeavor to carry the post by regular approaches: for the enemy's lines of defence, which were scarcely begun when d'Estaing's summons was

[1] Original Order-Book of General Prevost.

given, had in that interval of ten days become formidable; it extended along the sandy ridge or bluff from the swamp, below the ground now occupied by the eastern wharves, to Yamacraw, or Musgrove Creek on the west. It consisted of a chain of redoubts with batteries, the whole covered in front by a strong abatis. The principal battery appeared to be in the centre of the line, where stood, when we first approached it, a large public building of brick, but which disappeared in one night, and in a day or two a formidable battery was opened upon us from its site. The next work in importance was the Spring Hill redoubt, which commanded Yamacraw Creek, at the mouth of which was stationed a British galley. This line was admirably adapted to the enemy's force; if it had been a closed line, their two thousand five hundred troops could not have manned the whole, especially as they were obliged to have some slight works on each flank, and to pay some attention to their front on the river, as the French had sent some vessels of war with a bomb-ketch into Back River."

The besiegers were no less active. Day after day they drew nearer and nearer—mounted more and more cannon; and, from their land and river mortars and cannon, kept up a constant fire upon the town. For two weeks this cannonading and bombarding was continued, relieved only now and then by the sharp discharge of musketry, as parties of skirmishers met, fought, and retired. Sorties were occasionally made by the besieged, and bold attacks planned by the besiegers. Personal prowess was often called into requisition, and daring bravery was often manifested as in an arena before the contending armies. One of these dashing movements was made on the 24th September by three companies of light infantry, under Major Graham, of the 16th. At 9 o'clock he dashed out with his party, and momentarily had possession of the nearest breastwork of the Americans, but he was soon forced to retire. In the haste of pursuit, two columns of French troops pressed so far that they came within range of the guns from the redoubts, and many were slain. The loss in this sortie being, on the part of the British, twenty-one killed and wounded; while the French had over fifty. On the night of the 27th September, a party from a British picket, under Major McArthur, and the chief engineer, advanced towards the Americans in such a manner as to draw out portions of both Americans and French, and then, retiring unperceived, in consequence of the darkness, the Americans and French, each supposing the other the enemy, began a brisk fire upon each other. Several were killed before the mistake was discovered.

On the 4th of October, the batteries of the besieged opened on the land side with nine mortars and thirty-seven cannon, and from the broadside of the frigate La Trinité, of sixteen guns, on the river. The cannonading was now severe; and aware of the dreadful situation of the inhabitants, Prevost beat a parley on the morning of the 6th October, and, sending in a letter to Lincoln and d'Estaing, requested permission to send the women and children down the river, and place them under protection of one of the French men-of-war; but this request the allied Generals refused, for reasons of the most urgent and politic nature, comporting with both the courtesy and discipline of the soldier. Much blame has been cast upon them, both by English and American historians, for this refusal; but not one of them seemed to be aware that General Prevost had actually refused a similar application made by General McIntosh in behalf of his wife and family, and such other females as might choose to avail themselves of his courtesy. Had Prevost granted the request of McIntosh, on the 29th September, the allied Generals would not have refused the petition of Prevost on the 6th October. The fault then lies with the English General, and d'Estaing and Lincoln spoke truly when they wrote, "It is with regret we yield to the austerity of our functions, and we deplore the fate of those persons who will be the victims of your conduct, and the delusion which appears in your mind." Already had d'Estaing remained on shore longer than he had intended; he had landed but for a few days—a month had nearly passed, and he was not as near success as when he first paraded his troops on the bluff of Beaulieu. The tempestuous season for this coast was at hand, and his naval officers, among whom was the celebrated La Perouse, remonstrated with him for keeping the ships so long upon a coast so exposed, without a single harbor in which they could be sheltered; and represented the risk he was running, not only of being wrecked by the hurricane, but of capture, during the absence of so large a part of his force by superior fleets. To continue the siege by the usual advances would therefore be impossible, as, according to the opinion of the engineers, it would take ten days to reach the British lines; and, after much deliberation, it was determined to carry the town by assault, and thus, if possible, gain by a stroke what otherwise would require the operation of days. Such was the determination of the assailants. What was the preparation of the British to receive them?

At the first approach of d'Estaing there were but ten cannon mounted upon the works; now, through the almost incredible exertions of Major Moncrief, the number exceeded one hundred and eighteen. The defences in every respect were ample and effective; every pass and avenue to the city was vigilantly guarded and covered. The Germain, the only ship that had not been dismantled, was carried above the town, and commanded every approach through the low grounds bordering on Musgrove Creek. The troops were well trained, disciplined, and faithful; the guns were well served and judiciously planted, and whatever military science or experience could do in its defence was done by the zealous and able officers in command.

But there was one advantage which served them above all this. As soon as the plan of attack had been agreed upon by the American and French commanders, James Curry, a clerk of Charlestown, but who had been made Sergeant-Major of the volunteer company of grenadiers from that city, deserted to the enemy, with the entire programme of operations; by which the British were apprised of the intended feint, the real attack, and the disposition, strength, and nature of the army, as had been agreed upon by the allied Generals. Of this desertion the French and Americans knew nothing until after the attack.

At 2 o'clock, on the morning of the 9th October, the troops were paraded under arms; and, soon after, the whole force of nearly three thousand French and Americans, in one solid column, marched up to the front of the wood, when, wheeling into their appointed places, they proceeded to their several duties. Unavoidable hindrances had prevènted their appearing before the enemy until it was clear daylight, whereas, they had designed to have attacked before the break of day. Now they were easily seen, as they deployed into several columns, and the enemy, knowing from Sergeant Curry, that the attack of Colonel Huger on the left was a mere feint, concentrated all their strength upon the Spring Hill redoubt, on the right of their lines, on the road leading to Ebenezer, where the French commander, d'Estaing, sword in hand, was gallantly leading up his troops.

Count Dillon, who had orders to lead his column under cover of the night round the swamp and gain the rear of the Ebenezer Road redoubt, mistook his way through the darkness, and did not reach his position till day discovered him to the besieged, who drove him back with a galling fire. The near approach of d'Estaing also drew upon his troops a most destructive cannonade—the guns loaded with grape, chain, and cannister shot; and the muskets of the Hessians, Grenadiers, and Loyalists, made awful havoc amidst those well-drilled troops. They fell like grass before the mower. But animated by their officers, they still rallied to the front, pressed onward to the attack, and still hoped for a victory. Amidst all this slaughter they gained the abatis, while the other columns of French troops having mostly lost their way by the darkness of the night, were crowded together in a morass to the west of the city, and exposed to the deliberate and galling fire of the redoubt and a cross fire from the Germain and its associate gallies.

Colonel Laurens at the head of the Light Infantry, the Second South Carolina Regiment, and the First Battalion of Charleston Militia, also attacked the redoubt, and the colors of the Second South Carolina Regiment, which had been presented to it by Mrs. Elliott, of Charleston, were for a moment planted on the berm by Lieutenants Hume and Bush, who being killed, Lieutenant Grey advanced to their support, but he being wounded, Serjeant Jasper rushed forward, and though mortally wounded, brought off his colors at the expense of his life. Count Pulaski, with his cavalry, followed the attacking columns with the view of charging in the rear of the redoubts at the first vulnerable point; but, finding the front of d'Estaing's troops thrown into confusion by the deadly fire of the British, he left his command to the care of Colonel Horry, and with Captain Bentalou hastened on his black charger to animate by his presence the wavering spirits of the soldiers, and carry out the plans of d'Estaing now twice wounded, and borne from the field. He dashed on, heedless of danger, and anxious only to retrieve the discomfiture into which the head columns had been thrown; he penetrated to the Spring Hill redoubt, the scene of the greatest carnage, and, endeavoring to rally the disordered troops, was struck by a grape-shot from the last gun of the bastion; he reeled upon his horse, which, unguided, plunged madly forward, until his noble rider fell into the arms of his comrades, and was by them borne back from the murderous conflict.

But nothing human could stand before the terrible cannonade from the enemy's lines. Troops the bravest, soldiers the most disciplined, hearts the stoutest, quailed before the Angel of Death, as he seemed to spread out his wings upon that blood-covered plain. When the second American column under McIntosh reached the Spring Hill redoubt, the scene of confusion was dreadful. They marched up over ground strewn with the dead and the dying, and seldom has the sun of a warm October morning looked down upon a scene so mournful and appalling. The smoke of the muskets and cannon hung broodingly over the place, gathering denseness and darkness from every discharge; and the roar of artillery, the rattling of small arms, the calling bugle, the sounded retreat, the stirring drum, and the cries of the wounded blended startlingly together.

Colonel Huger marching through the low rice grounds on the east, reached his appointed post, and was received with music, and a brisk discharge, which killed twenty-eight of his men, and compelled him to retreat. Only the column of General McIntosh was now fresh and ready for action. But the fate of the day was decided; the French and Americans had been slain and wounded by hundreds, and their bodies lined the redoubts and ditches. They had left their camp in anticipation of decisive victory, blood-bought and toil-earned, indeed, but yet victory, and expected to plant the standards of the army over the prostrate ensigns of England; but the betrayal of their plan of attack, and the losing of their way, with the consequent detention till daylight, revealed their position to the enemy, changed the fortunes of the day, and, though bold, valiant, and persevering, they were repulsed and slaughtered. For one hour they had stood gallant and undaunted before the murderous connonade, which struck down rank after rank, and sent dismay by its sweeping fury, into every column; until, finding further attempt but a useless sacrifice of life, a retreat was ordered, and the remains of that gallant army were drawn off the field.

With the exception of Bunker Hill, no battle of the Revolution was more sanguinary or destructive. The British marched into the engagement at Bunker Hill with about 3500 men, and their killed and wounded amounted to 1054. Even at the battle of Minden, one of the bloodiest ever fought in Europe, where the English sustained for a long time the whole force of the French army, the killed and wounded were but 1328; but at this assault of Savannah, there were brought into action not quite 4000 men; and yet the killed and wounded were 1100, or nearly one-third of the army. Of these, 640 were French, and 469 Americans. The loss of the British was about 100.

General Lincoln, with the reserve, covered the retreat; and, notwithstanding the terrible volleys of grape and ball shot, and a sortie in their rear, they were brought off with but little loss. Count d'Estaing was twice wounded,—in the arm and thigh; Vicomte de Fontanges, Vicomte de Bethizy, Baron de Steding, Count Pulaski, and the Chevalier d'Eronville, were also wounded; four majors, two captains, four lieutenants, and several other subalterns, were killed; one major, nine captains, and eleven lieutenants, were among the wounded. About ten o'clock, the allies requested a truce to bury their dead and remove the wounded. It was granted for four hours, and within certain distances; and this most melancholy duty was performed by the comrades of the fallen, with the silence befitting the mournful task.

All hopes of taking Savannah were now extinguished. In a few days, d'Estaing re-embarked his troops, artillery, &c.; but they had hardly got on board, and received the order of d'Estaing, for seven ships of the line to repair to the mouth of the Chesapeake, before the long-dreaded hurricane rose upon them, scattered their ships, and but one vessel, commanded by the Marquis de Vaudreuil, reached its destination.

General Lincoln, immediately after the battle, retreated to Ebenezer Heights, and, on the 19th October, crossed over into Carolina, and repaired to Charleston, from which place he addressed the following letter to Congress:

"CHARLESTON, October 22, 1779.

SIR—In my last, of the 5th ult., I had the honor of informing Congress that Count d'Estaing was arrived off Savannah.

"Orders were immediately given for assembling the troops. They reached Zubly's Ferry and its vicinity on the 11th, and some were thrown over. The 12th and 13th were spent in crossing the troops and baggage, which was effected, though not without great fatigue, from the want of boats, and badness of the roads, through a deep swamp of near three miles, in which are many large creeks. The bridges over them the enemy had broken down. We encamped upon the heights of Ebenezer, twenty-three miles from Savannah, and were there joined by troops from Augusta, under General McIntosh. The 14th, not being able to ascertain whether the Count had yet landed his troops, though several expresses had been sent for that purpose, we remain encamped. On the 15th, being advised that the Count had embarked part of his troops, that he would that night take post nine miles from Savannah, we moved, and encamped at Cherokee Hill, nine miles from the town. The 16th, we formed a junction before Savannah. After reconnoitering the enemy's works, and finding the town well covered, and knowing their determination to defend it, it was deemed necessary to make some approaches, and try the effects of artillery. From the 18th to the 23d, we were employed in landing and getting up the ordinance and stores; a work of difficulty, from the want of proper wheels to transport them, the cannon being on ship-carriages. On the evening of the 23d, ground was broken; and on the 5th instant, the batteries of thirty-three pieces of cannon and nine mortars were opened on the enemy, and continued, with intervals, until the 8th, without the wished-for effect. The period having long since elapsed, which the Count had assigned for this expedition, and the engineers informing him that much more time must be spent, if he expected to reduce the garrison by regular approaches, and his longer stay being impossible, matters were reduced to the alternative of raising the siege immediately, and giving up all thoughts of conquest, or attempting the garrison by assault: the latter was agreed on; and on the morning of the 9th, the attack was made; and it proved unsuccessful, and we were repulsed, with some loss.

"When the Count first arrived, he informed us that he would remain on shore eight days only. He had spent four times that number; his departure, therefore, became indispensable; and to re-embark his ordnance and stores claimed his next attention. This was completed on the 10th. The same evening, having previously sent off our sick, wounded, and heavy baggage, the American troops left the ground, reached Zubly's Ferry the next morning, recrossed, and encamped that night in Carolina.

"The French troops encamped, on the night of the 10th, about two miles from Savannah. They were, after twenty-four hours, re-embarked at Kincaid's Landing.

"Our disappointment is great, and what adds much to our sense of it, is the loss of a number of brave officers and men, among them the late intrepid Count Pulaski.

"Count d'Estaing has undoubtedly the interest of America much at heart. This he has evinced by coming to our assistance, by his constant attention during the siege, his undertaking to reduce the enemy by assault, when he despaired of effecting it otherwise, and by bravely putting himself at the head of his troops, and leading them to the attack. In our service he has freely bled. I feel much for him; for while he is suffering the distress of painful wounds, he has to combat chagrin. I hope he will be consoled by an assurance that, although he has not succeeded according to his wishes and those of America, we regard with high approbation his intentions to serve us, and that his want of success will not lessen our ideas of his merit." * * * * * * *

The lower part of Georgia was now in the possession of the British, rejoicing in their signal deliverance from a superior force, and by almost a miraculous succor. The Governor's council at the suggestion of Sir James Wright, appointed Friday, 29th October, as a day of public and general thanksgiving—the Governor observing to the Board, that "he considered the late deliverance and preservation of the town, garrison, and inhabitants, from the formidable combined force of French and rebel enemies who came against it, as an act of Divine Providence," and therefore worthy of public acknowledgment.

Looking back upon the siege of Savannah, and taking in all its operations at one survey, we are astonished at the number of errors which seemed to mark the contest. The first great error was in the French fleet passing by Beaufort, without capturing Colonel Maitland and his eight hundred men. The overwhelming force of the French could easily have effected this, but the Charleston pilots refused to take the ships over Port Royal bar. Had this regiment been captured, the fate of the city would have been reversed. The second error was in the hasty summons of the city to surrender to the arms of the King of France before d'Estaing had been joined by Lincoln. The joint summons of these generals, backed by the presence of their joint armies, would have produced a different answer from the English commander. The third great error—the fatal error—was in the French General granting a truce for twenty-four hours. That truce saved the city. It was highly impolitic when a sudden impression was desired; it was almost culpable, when the American General was not present, but was hourly expected, to concede such a privilege without his approval. D'Estaing was too much flushed with his late victories at Grenada and St. Vincents to be cautious. Lincoln had been too long schooled in disasters not to be wary and vigilant.

The English officers themselves acknowledged that had the combined armies marched to Savannah at their first junction, they could easily have taken it, so poorly defensible was it at the beginning of the siege. The ignorance of their guides, and the betrayal of their plan of attack, completed the series of misfortunes which resulted in their overthrow.

The season of the year both for land and sea operations was the most improper which could have been chosen. Who that is at all acquainted with our coast does not know its peculiar exposures to the equinoxial gales of September? and who that knows our climate, is not aware of the almost certain sickness which during our fall months attacks the stranger, particularly at that period, when camping near swamps and ditches? The consequence was, that the French officers and troops, both at sea and on land, were continually anxious, restive, longing to depart, fearing the miasma on shore and the hurricane on the ocean. Both came to them too soon, but the destruction of neither, equalled the carnage of the battle. There was a vauntingness at times in the language of d'Estaing, which rendered it too haughty to be brave. His words at his summons;—"I have not been able to refuse the army of the United States uniting itself with the king" is a strange piece of diplomacy, for it implies that he had endeavored to prevent it, when his very purpose in coming to Georgia was to effect it. The conduct of the French troops during the siege was exemplary and praiseworthy. A generous emulation, and nothing more, pervaded both armies; and the bravery of the allies needs no greater comment than the number of dead and wounded they left upon the field of battle. Washington, writing to General Lincoln two months after this attack, concerning its failure, thus alludes to the army: "While I regret the misfortune, I feel a very sensible pleasure in contemplating the gallant behavior of the officers and men of the French and American army; and it adds not a little to my consolation to learn that instead of the mutual reproaches which too often follow the failure of enterprises depending upon the co-operation of troops of different nations, their confidence in and esteem for each other are increased."

Among the English and French officers at the siege of Savannah, were several of historical or family eminence, who deserve more than a passing notice.

Major-General Augustine Prevost, who commanded the British troops, was a native of Geneva, Switzerland, who had settled in England; and entering the army, rose gradually to his high position. His wife was the daughter of the Chevalier George Grand, of Amsterdam. General Prevost died in 1786, leaving four children; the eldest, George, was created a baronet in 1805, was colonel of the 16th regiment, and Governor-General and Commander-in-chief of North America. The second son, James, became a captain in the royal navy. The third son, William Augustus, rose to the rank of a major-general in the English service, and commander of the Bath.

The Commander of the Perseus, at Savannah, in 1779, was George Keith Elphinstone, the son of Charles, the tenth Baron Elphinstone in the Peerage of Scotland. He attained the rank of Post-Captain, in 1775; Rear-Admiral, 1794; and the next year, as Vice-Admiral, conducted the naval part of the successful expedition against the Cape of Good Hope. For his services, on this occasion, he was created, in 1797, Baron Keith of Stonehaven, Ireland. In 1801, he became Admiral of the Blue; obtained, in 1803, the Barony of Keith, in Dumbarton, Scotland; and, in 1814, was created Viscount Keith. His Lordship died in 1823.

Count Arthur Dillon was the son of Henry, the eleventh Viscount Dillon, in the Peerage of Ireland. His father was a Colonel in the French service. His grandfather, Arthur, went into the army of France, and commanded an Irish regiment after his father. Theobold, the seventh Viscount, was outlawed, in 1690, by reason of his attachment to the falling fortunes of James II. The grandfather of Count Dillon was, in 1705, made Marshal of the Camp, and Governor of Toulon; and, subsequently, a Lieutenant-General of France. Dillon's regiment was commanded, after the death of Marshal Dillon, by his son James, a Knight of Malta; and when he fell at the head of this regiment, at Fontenoy, his brother Edward succeeded to his command; and it was this regiment which the young Count Arthur led into action at the siege of Savannah. He was involved in the troubles of the French Revolution, and suffered under the guillotine, in 1794. His daughter, Fanny, was married to Count Bertrand, who adhered so closely to the fortunes of the Emperor Napoleon; and Lady Bertrand was distinguished by her fidelity to the Emperor, during his long imprisonment at St. Helena.

Charles Hector Compte d'Estaing was born in Auvergne, in 1729. He was of an old and distinguished family: being early advanced, he commenced his military career as a Colonel of Infantry; and soon, becoming a Brigadier-General, he was sent under Count de Lally to serve in the East Indies.

Being taken a prisoner at the siege of Madras, in 1759, he was set at liberty by the English on his parole. This parole he violated; was unskilful enough to be again taken; and, was, according to the laws of war, in imminent danger of his life. After a painful confinement, however, in the hulks at Portsmouth, England, he was released; and then took an oath of eternal hatred to the English, which he rigidly kept.

After the peace of 1763, he was made Lieutenant-General of the naval forces. But this appointment gave great dissatisfaction to the navy, and he never obtained even a partial popularity in that service.

In 1778 he was sent, as Vice-Admiral, with twelve ships to aid in establishing American independence; but misfortune mostly attended his movements. Contrary winds kept him back until Lord Howe, with a much smaller squadron in the Delaware, had re-embarked his troops and landed them in New York. Before Rhode Island, he was about to attack Howe, now reinforced by some vessels from Lord Byron's squadron, when a fearful storm separated the hostile fleets, dismasting d'Estaing's ship, and putting both fleets, for the time, *hors du combat.*

Later, however, pursuing the enemy to the West Indies, he attacked and beat Admiral Byron; and, was only deterred from pursuing his victory by the prevalence of contrary winds. After his fruitless expedition to Georgia, he returned, in 1780, to France.

In 1783 he was intrusted with the command of the combined fleets of France and Spain, assembled at Cadiz, and was ready to set sail when the treaty of peace put an end to the expedition.

He threw himself with zeal into the movements

which led to the French Revolution; and, in 1789, was made commandant of the National Guards at Versailles. His revolutionary course, however, is not without some grievous stains; and, in April, 1794, he expiated, under the guillotine, the crime of being a counter-revolutionist.

In the fleet of Count d'Estaing, was La Perouse, the famous navigator. Entering the French navy at the age of fifteen, he served with distinction in several parts of the world, and particularly in the East Indies. After the peace of 1783, he was appointed to command a scientific expedition to the Pacific and Chinese seas. With superior ships and a better corps of scientific men, he followed the track of Captain Cook, and made many valuable discoveries and observations. From the 7th February, 1788, the date of his last communication from Botany Bay, to 1827, a mystery hung over the fate of this distinguished navigator. It was unexpectedly cleared up by the accidental discovery that, both his ships, the Boussole and the Astrolabe, were lost on one of the islands of the New Hebrides group.

The death of Count Pulaski threw a deep gloom over the ill-fated siege of Savannah. Descended from a noble house in Poland; educated under the eye of a father who was one of the ablest jurists in the kingdom; associating with the noble and influential; he early showed his hatred of Russian intrigue, and his opposition to the efforts to place upon the throne of Poland the celebrated Poniatowski, as Stanislaus Augustus, whom he regarded "as a Russian viceroy, rather than as the chief of an independent nation."

Engaging with ardor in the plans devised by his father, for freeing Poland from the chains of its northern oppressor; Casimir Pulaski soon became the most famous chief in his native country for his military successes, his bold daring, and his intense ardor in the cause of freedom. The record of his battles and his struggles evinces courage, skill, and energy worthy of the sacred cause to which his father, his brothers, and himself, had pledged their lives and fortunes. "In those confederacies which were soon formed in various parts of the country, to defend and vindicate its insulted sovereignty, the ardent patriotism of the Count, his implacable hatred of foreign usurpation, his indefatigable zeal, his unshaken constancy, his heroic intrepidity—in short, his towering genius and his stoical and truly republican virtues, rendered him the scourge and terror of the Russians." "During eight succeeding years of a bloody war," says a writer who has eloquently described the situation of Poland in those calamitous times,[1] "the operations of Pulaski were such as almost to challenge belief. Sometimes vanquished, much oftener victorious—equally great in the midst of a defeat, as formidable after victory, and always superior to events, Pulaski attracted and fixed the attention of all Europe, and astonished her by his long and vigorous resistance. Obliged to abandon one province, he made incursions into another, and there performed new prodigies of valor. It was thus that, marching successively throughout all the palitinates, he signalized in each of them that eternal hatred which he had sworn against the enemies of Poland. It was Pulaski who, in 1771, conceived and organized the bold design of forcibly carrying off Stanislaus from Warsaw, and bringing him to his camp; not indeed to assassinate

[1] "Pulaski Vindicated," &c. Baltimore, 1824.

him, as has been basely and falsely asserted by partisans of Russia, but with the view to make him a rallying point for the nobles, and all the patriots of Poland; and, by means of this union of the monarch with the nation, to crush, or, at least, to drive away from the territory of the republic, the satellites of that unprincipled and perfidious power, by whose haughty mandates it had too long been governed. The enterprise, confided to forty brave patriots, succeeded only so far as to seize on the monarch in the very bosom of his capital, and to carry him away some distance from it, in spite of every obstacle and danger. The darkness of the night, and other unforeseen casualties, prevented the final execution of a plan, which might eventually have saved Poland from that political annihilation which has since become her lot.

"When, from nearly the same motives as induce robbers to disguise or suspend, for a time, their jealousies and animosities, and to unite their efforts and their strength, the more easily to secure a common prey, Russia, Prussia, and Austria jointly invaded Poland, in 1772, and at a 'fell swoop' seized upon the fairest portion of her territory, which they divided among themselves, by that right which only kings and freebooters dare to claim, the right of superior physical force, the Polish confederates were compelled either to acquiesce in the degradation of their enslaved, plundered, partitioned country, or to flee from the beloved and hallowed land which had given them birth—from the land which they had disputed, inch by inch, with the lawless potentates who have since entirely erased it from the map of independent nations. Very few submitted; many fell into the hands of the Russians or their adherents, and died martyrs to that noble cause which they had so strenuously supported; others escaped to foreign climes. Pulaski was the last to retire from the noble contest. In a desperate and bloody engagement with the Russians, his army, vastly inferior in numbers, was routed, annihilated; but his courage still remained. To rush furiously on to death would have been useless to his country; he chose to live, in the hope of again serving it, should Heaven and time favor his wishes.

"Through countless fatigues, difficulties, and perils, and after a variety of singular disguises, wonderful adventures, and hairbreadth escapes, he reached Turkey, whose hostilities against Russia accorded with his hatred of that power, and at the same time flattered the patriotic schemes which his ardent spirit had not ceased to cherish. On that side, however, his hopes were frustrated by the peace concluded between Russia and the Porte, 1774.

"In the meantime the situation of Poland had become more deplorable than ever; her king, her senate, her people, yielding to foreign oppression, had sunk into the torpor and apathy of the most abject servitude. Envoys, from the Courts of St. Petersburg, Vienna, and Berlin, swayed her destinies; and, far from assuming a brighter aspect, her horizon daily portended more violent and more tremendous tempests. By the Russian faction, Pulaski had long since been deprived of his estates, degraded from his rank, condemned to lose his head—in short, outlawed. Unable to rouse Turkey to any measure auspicious to his country, he passed into France about the time when the declaration of American independence kindled in every generous breast a holy enthusiasm. The native land of Pulaski had lost her liberties; he resolved to fight for the liberties of America. With him to resolve and to execute were almost simultaneous. In 1777, Philadelphia beheld him tendering his services to the American Congress. The inherent ardor of his warlike spirit, his habits of activity, and the desire of efficiently serving the cause which he had so warmly embraced, did not permit him to wait for the decision of that body on his application, but he immediately joined the army. He was at Brandywine on the day of the battle with the Marquis De La Fayette, and other distinguished foreign officers in the suite of General Washington. At the time when our right wing was turned by the victorious enemy pressing upon us, and the rapid retreat of the right and centre of our army became the natural consequence, Count Pulaski proposed to General Washington to give him command of his body-guard, consisting of about thirty horsemen. This was readily granted, and Pulaski, with his usual intrepidity and judgment, led them to the charge, and succeeded in retarding the advance of the enemy—a delay which was of the highest importance to our retreating army. Moreover, the penetrating military *coup d'œil* of Pulaski soon perceived that the enemy were manœuvreing to take possession of the road leading to Chester, with a view of cutting off our retreat, or, at least, the column of our baggage. He hastened to General Washington to communicate the information, and was immediately authorized by the Commander-in-chief to collect as many of the scattered troops as he could find at hand and make the best of them. This was most fortunately executed by Pulaski, who, by an oblique advance upon the enemy's front and right flank, defeated their object, and effectually protected our baggage, and the retreat of the army. This important service was justly appreciated by General Washington, who did not fail to recommend Pulaski to Congress, and that body passed the following resolution on the 15th of September, 1777:—

"'Resolved, That a commander of the horse be appointed, with the rank of a Brigadier.'

"The ballots being taken, Count Pulaski was elected."

In 1778, Pulaski was authorized by Congress to raise an independent corps, to consist of three companies of cavalry, armed with lances, and three of foot, equipped as light infantry. This corps was called "Pulaski's Legion;" and, such was his known bravery and popularity, that he soon reported his legion as full and ready for service. While engaged on this recruiting duty he was stationed for a time at Bethlehem, Pennsylvania, and some of the choir houses of the Moravians were converted into barracks, hospitals, &c. To protect the single sisters of this religious community from rapine and violence, a guard was posted by Pulaski around their house, and himself in person often shared the duties of the sentinel.

Grateful for this protection from a rough and uncouth soldiery, Susan Von Gersdorf, the spiritual superintendent of the establishment, suggested[1] that the sisters should present Pulaski with a banner for his new legion, as a tribute of respect for his guardianship of their persons, and of sympathy with the cause in which he was engaged.

[1] Bethlehem Seminary Souvenir, 1858, by Wm. C. Reichel, pp. 38–9.

Her suggestion was approved and adopted. The design of the work was intrusted to the sisters Becky Langly and Julia Bader, who planned a banner of double crimson silk, twenty inches square, on one side of which was embroidered, in yellow silk, shaded with green, the All-seeing Eye, inclosed in a triangle, surrounded by thirteen stars, as if God had said to the United States, in the words of the Psalmist, "I will guide thee with Mine eye;" and, above it, the legend, "*Non alius regit.*" No other reigns. On the other side were the initial letters U. S. and the surrounding motto, "*Unitas virtus potior.*" United valor stronger. The silk was heavily fringed with bullion and tassels, and affixed to a handsome lance.

The embroidery was executed with taste and elegance by Anna Bean, Anna Hussy, and Erdmuth Langly, with other associates. The banner was received by Pulaski with expressions of grateful acknowledgment, and it became thenceforth the ensign of the legion.

It was the consecration of this banner which gave occasion for one of those earlier poems of Longfellow, in which, with somewhat indeed of poetic license, he portrayed the scene, and sung the "Hymn of the Moravian Nuns" as they took from the altar

> "The blood-red banner that with prayer
> Had been consecrated there;"

and, presenting it to the gallant Pole, exclaimed—

> "Take thy banner! May it wave
> Proudly o'er the good and brave.
> *   *   *   *   *

Guard it! till our homes are free,
Guard it! God will prosper thee.
Take thy banner! and if e'er
Thou shouldst press the soldier's bier,
And the muffled drum should beat
To the tread of mournful feet,
Then this crimson flag shall be
Martial cloak and shroud for thee."

In February, 1779, Pulaski, with his legion, was ordered to the South, to form part of the Southern army under General Lincoln in South Carolina. Here he did good service, until he was removed to Georgia, to operate with the combined army in the attempt to retake Savannah. How he behaved at this memorable siege has been told. Cool, resolute, daring, vigilant; he entered upon the contest with all the ardor of military fervor, panting to distinguish himself on a field where three nations would witness his bravery, and acknowledge his heroism. When he fell before the lines of Savannah, he was carried back a little distance; and there, on the field, Dr. James Lynah, of Charleston, extracted the ball, an iron grape-shot (now in the possession of the Lynah family), from his groin; an operation which, though exceedingly painful, was borne by Pulaski "with inconceivable fortitude." He was then with Captain Bentalou (who was also wounded) taken on board the U. S. brig "Wasp," where he had the best surgical attendance; but gangrene soon made its appearance, and death speedily followed. "Just as the Wasp got out of the river, Pulaski breathed his last; and the corpse immediately became so offensive, that this officer was compelled, though reluctantly, to consign to a watery grave all that was now left on earth of his beloved and honored commander. The Wasp entered the harbor of Charleston with her flag half hoisted. The mournful signal was repeated by all the shipping in the port; and all the forts and batteries responded to it in the manner usual on such occasions of deep and universal sorrow. The Governor and Council of South Carolina, and the municipal authorities of Charleston, jointly adopted resolutions to pay to the memory of General Pulaski the most respectful and the most splendid funeral honors. A day was set apart for the obsequies, and the Quarter-Master-General of the United States at Charleston, directed to make and to defray all the preparations for the melancholy solemnity. The procession was grand, and suited to the occasion. The pall was carried by three American, and three French officers of the highest rank, followed by the beautiful horse which Pulaski rode when he received his death-wound, with all the armor, accoutrements, and dress, which he then wore. So very large was the mournful procession, that it was found necessary to make a circuit of the whole city to the church, where an eloquent and impressive discourse was delivered by the chaplain of the army."[1]

The banner wrought by the Moravian nuns was saved at the battle of Savannah by one of Pulaski's lieutenants; and delivered by him to Captain Bentalou, who, on retiring from the army, took it with him to Baltimore, his place of residence. In 1824, however, it was used by the young ladies of Philadelphia, on the occasion of welcoming La Fayette to the city; and then deposited in Peale's Museum, where it remained until

[1] "Pulaski Vindicated," &c.

1844, when it was given to the Maryland Historical Society; and now adorns, not with its beauty, for it is faded and tattered, but with its glory, the hall of that institution.

It is a strange, yet remarkable fact, that much controversy has been occasioned concerning the place where Pulaski was buried. The narrative of Captain Bentalou, quoted above, states that he was buried at sea, and others declare that he was buried on land. When the City of Savannah carried into execution a resolution, which, for nearly seventy-five years had been a dead letter on the books of Congress, and erected Launitz's noble monument to Pulaski in Monterey Square; there was placed within the plinth, alongside of the corner-stone, a metallic case, hermetically sealed, containing "what were supposed to be the remains of Pulaski, exhumed on the —— of December, 1853, at Greenwich, on Augustine Creek, distant from the City of Savannah five miles."

As, however, all contemporary evidence, so far as it goes, corroborates the statement of Pulaski's friend and fellow-officer, that he died on board the Wasp, and was buried under the water,—as no contemporary record mentions his death or burial at Greenwich; and as all the evidence offered to support the latter theory is parole, circumstantial, and conjectural, so must we still believe the reports of the time, and say, with a probability amounting almost to certainty, that this brave soldier lies under the tide-waters of the Atlantic, and not beneath the majestic column which bears his name, and is consecrated to his memory, in the City of Savannah.

During the siege of Savannah, occurred one of those

strategic episodes which vary the usual bloodiness of war. So soon as General Prevost heard of the arrival of the French fleet, he ordered in all the outposts; and a portion of Colonel Cruger's command, stationed at Sunbury, under Captain French, attempted to obey the order by passing in vessels through the inland channels. Intercepted in their course up the Ogeechee, they were compelled to land, and entrench themselves for safety; and there they remained in their fortified camp, about twenty-five miles south of Savannah, until the night of the 1st October; when Colonel John White, of the Georgia line, with Captains Melvin and Elholm (an officer of Pulaski's legion), a sergeant, and three privates, having reconnoitered his position, withdrew a little distance, kindled many fires to represent a large encampment, gave loud commands as if guiding the marching of troops, and so simulated by their movements the hurry and bustle of staff-officers, that Captain French, on being boldly summoned by Colonel White to surrender, was convinced that a large force was close beside him. While parleying with Colonel White, Captain Elholm hastily rode up, and abruptly asked of Colonel White where he should place the artillery. Captain French having expressed his wonder that he saw no troops, was told that they were purposely kept back, because they were quite exasperated at an outrage on some prisoners, said to have been committed in Savannah, which they were determined to revenge at the first opportunity.

Captain French being convinced, from what he saw and heard, that it was only by an immediate surrender that he could preserve the lives of his men, capitulated, and one hundred and eleven troops, and five vessels,—some of which were armed,—with their crews and munitions, were delivered up to Colonel White. "The deception," says Ramsey, "was carried on with so much address, that the whole of the prisoners were safely conducted, by three of the captors, for twenty-five miles through the country to the American post at Sunbury."

Rejoining the army before Savannah, Colonel White was severely wounded, eight days after, in the assault on the Spring Hill redoubt, and was taken prisoner by the British. He succeeded, however, in escaping from the enemy, and made his way to Virginia; where, it is said, he shortly after died, from a pulmonary attack produced by fatigue and exposure.

CHAPTER VII.

SIEGE OF AUGUSTA.

The departure of the French fleet, and the repulse of the combined army by the English, opened the way for Sir Henry Clinton, to make further and more important movements.

Leaving the garrison of New York under the command of Lieutenant-General Knyphausen, Sir Henry Clinton, on the 26th of December, 1779, sailed for the South, with an army of three thousand British, Hessian, and loyalist troops, escorted by Admiral Arbuthnot, with an adequate naval force.

The severity of the weather was such, that it was not until the end of January, that the fleet reached Tybee, the place of rendezvous. Here they waited a short time to refit the damaged vessels, and then proceeded to North Edisto Sound, in South Carolina, to carry out the plan of Sir Henry Clinton of besieging Charleston.

Into this city General Lincoln had drawn most of the troops at his disposal, and thus Georgia was left in a most unprotected condition.

Against this step, the Executive Council of Georgia strongly protested, by a series of resolutions, passed on the 3d of February, 1780. The disastrous result of the siege of Charleston, confirmed the judgment of the Council: Augusta, the seat of the republican government, was abandoned, and Heard's Fort (now Washington), in Wilkes County, was the last stronghold of liberty in Georgia. Here the Executive Council sat, and, during the darkest period in Georgia's history, governed the almost deserted State. At this time, there were two distinct governments within the boundaries of Georgia: the lower part of the State, from Hudson's Ferry, just below Brier Creek, to the seaboard, being under the civil government of Sir James Wright; while the upper part of the State, from the same ferry to the mountains, was nominally in the hands of the Republicans.

On the withdrawal of the troops by General Lincoln, many had abandoned their homes, anticipating the re-extension of royal authority over the whole State, and fearing the vengeance of the British regulars, and the more dreaded royalists. The distresses of the inhabitants of what may be termed republican Georgia, were greatly heightened by the plundering parties of Tories, which infested and wasted the farms and dwellings of the citizens. The General Assembly ordered the Governor to take proper measures to prevent, as much as possible, this practice, and annexed a clause to the act, declaring it felony for any person or persons, under any pretence whatever, to plunder or take away from any of the inhabitants of this State, within a line from "Hudson's Ferry to the Ogeechee, any property;" and also ordered "all such as were not well affected to the confederate alliance to remain without the same."

On the 3d March, 1780, Richard Howley, the Governor, issued a proclamation, reciting the above act, and "forbidding all and every person from such illegal and shameful practices, which reflect a disgrace on the sacred cause of America, and assimilate it to the iniquity of that of our enemies;" and he further ordered and required, "that every person well affected to the cause of the United States, should repair, without loss of time, to proper places, within a line from Hudson's Ferry to the Ogeechee, and there remain quiet, demeaning themselves as good citizens of the State."

Many of the best republicans of Georgia had, however, much property in the low country, the removal of which was important, as a means of their future subsistence, as well as to prevent its falling into the hands of the British, and thus adding to the supplies of the enemy. In order to collect these various stores, and to facilitate their removal to the north of the designated line, Colonel Pickens, with a part of his South Carolina regiment, formed a junction, on the 20th March, with a few militia under Colonel Twiggs, and a troop of horse commanded by Captain Inman, the whole force amounting to about three hundred men. Their first aim was to surprise McGirth, who had been laying waste the southeastern part of the State; but in this they failed, owing to the flight of the marauders, when they heard that the Americans were on their track; though several of McGirth's party were killed and taken prisoners. Colonels Pickens and Twiggs formed a post on the Ogeechee, which constituted a rallying point for the Americans; and a point from which incursions could be made into lower Georgia, to the great annoyance of the Governor and the loyalists, who had gathered near the seaboard.

To disperse this body, the British general ordered out a portion of Delancy's corps, under Captain Conklin, which, leaving Savannah before daylight on the 4th April, reached the Ogeechee River by ten o'clock. They were soon engaged in battle with the troops under Pickens and Twiggs, and were completely routed. Captain Conklin died of his wounds the next day, and the discomfited party returned in confusion to the garrison in Savannah.

The fall of Charleston, in May, 1780, was a disastrous event for Georgia. As soon as it was communicated to Governor Howley, he resolved to comply with the resolutions of the General Assembly and the Executive Council, by leaving the State and proceeding to Philadelphia, to take his seat there as a member of Congress, to which he had been previously elected ; and it is recorded, as an evidence of the depreciation of the paper currency, that it cost the State nearly half a million of dollars Continental currency, to pay the expenses of the Governor in Congress. Most of the civil and military officers of the republican party accompanied the Governor as far as North Carolina; and Georgia was left with only the name of a government, and with scarcely a regiment of soldiers to defend its territory.

As soon as Augusta was deserted by the Americans, it was taken possession of by Colonels Brown and Grierson, two notorious partisan officers in the English service. Thomas Brown had been a resident of Augusta, before the breaking out of the war, and had so offended the friends of liberty in that town, by his censures and ridicule, that he was at last taken by the Parish Committee, tried, and sentenced to be tarred and feathered, and to be publicly exposed in a cart drawn by three mules. After this ignominious punishment, he escaped to the British, distinguished himself by his bitterness and hatred towards the Liberty men; and, by his address and daring, was soon entrusted with the command of the town in which he had endured such gross indignities.

He was now in a position to gratify his revenge, and pay back upon the inhabitants of Augusta the ill usage which he had received at their hands, and he did it with no stinted measure. The first plan adopted by him in conjunction with Colonel Grierson, was to sequestrate the property of the whigs, that they might thus possess themselves of all that they owned. The next step was to order all their families beyond the State, under pretence that they held correspondence with the refugees. These wretched families, stripped of nearly all they had, were driven from their homes and their fields, and with a few scanty personal effects, were obliged to travel, under great privations, exposed to gross insults, nearly two hundred miles to the borders of North Carolina, whither they arrived "nearly famished from the want of food, and worn down with the fatigue of so long a way; and the health of many was so much shattered that they could never recover from the effect of such privation."[1]

Induced by the promises of succor held out by General Andrew Williamson,—that southern Arnold,—the patriots of Georgia had somewhat rallied in Wilkes County, in the hope of keeping possession of the upper part of the State; but when his defection was known, Colonel

[1] Jackson's MS. notes on Ramsay.

Elijah Clarke, with about one hundred and fifty men, gathered at Freeman's Fort, in Elbert County, with the view of opposing the British forces in front, on the South Carolina side of the river. This place was called Freeman's Fort from two brothers, Colonel Holman Freeman and John Freeman, who had made a settlement near the place where Lord George Gordon had previously planted a colony of Scotch people, brought over from Scotland under indentures to serve his Lordship for five years, in consideration of his advancing their passage-money and support. At the beginning of the colonial disputes, Lord George returned to England, and his colony was broken up.

The attempt, however, of Colonel Clarke to make anything like a determined stand, at Freeman's Fort, was unsuccessful; and most of his men, being discouraged, were dispersed to their homes, to await a more favorable time. A party of thirty-five, however, under Colonel John Jones, of Burke County, and Stephen Heard, President of the Executive Council, determined to brave every difficulty and make their way to the army in South Carolina.

On their march through the loyalist regions, they represented themselves as loyalists, and under this guise, by boldness and stratagem, captured a party of thirty tories, whom they disarmed, and put upon their parole of honor not to serve again against the Americans. After various other adventures, they reached the Pacolette River; and, on the 16th July, effected a junction with Colonel McDowell and a body of three hundred North Carolina militia.

Colonel Clarke, though disappointed in making his desired stand at Freeman's Fort, and though compelled almost to disband his troops, could not long remain idle, or give up the contest. By great efforts, he succeeded in reassembling most of his regiment; and, striking upwards into the mountainous regions, he joined Colonel Jones at a point where Georgia and the Carolinas intersect each other. They were shortly reinforced by a body of mountaineers from the neighborhood of Holstein River, under Colonel Shelby; and now, feeling themselves sufficiently strong for action, they entered South Carolina, penetrated through Williamson's settlement, fighting their way at almost every step, until, being joined by some Carolina whigs, under Colonel Williams, they resolved to attack a party of the enemy posted at Musgrave's Mills, on the Ennoree River.

Colonel Clarke, as commander of the whole, made a most judicious selection of his ground, and formed his troops with great advantage. The British, under Colonel Jones, advanced to the attack with much courage; but, after sustaining for a few moments a very galling fire, and seven out of the nine officers being either killed or wounded, a retreat was ordered, and the enemy were pursued until they reached Musgave's Mill, being severely annoyed by the fire in flank and rear from the pursuing Americans. In this action Colonel Jones was wounded, sixty-three were killed, and one hundred and sixty were wounded and taken prisoners; while the party under Clarke had but four men killed (among them Captain Inman), and nine wounded, among whom were Colonel Clarke,—who received two sabre cuts on his head and neck,—and Captain John Clark.

This action was so decisive, and its influence upon

the spirits and hopes of the friends of liberty was so elevating, that Colonel Clarke now turned his attention towards the recovery of Augusta from the hands of the loyalists. The present feeble state of the garrison, which had been weakened by the withdrawal of several detachments of troops to join the Earl Cornwallis, near Camden, seemed to hold out some promise of success; and, therefore, in conjunction with Colonel McCall, he resolved to raise soldiers for the enterprise, believing that between them they could muster at least a thousand troops. But when they met at the appointed rendezvous on Soap Creek, in Lincoln County, instead of a thousand men, they had not one-half that number; yet, unwilling to defer longer so important an attempt, Colonel Clarke resolved to march to Augusta; and on the 14th September, 1780, the little army reached the scene of action. The troops were formed into three divisions, and they advanced severally along the middle, lower, and upper roads, and were not discovered by Colonel Brown, until the left division, under Major Samuel Taylor, attacked the Indian camp near Hawk's Creek, when the Indians after a short resistance gave way, and fell back towards the town.

The firing at the Indian Camp induced Colonel Brown to order Grierson to support Captain Johnston, who, with a company of King's Rangers and Indians, had taken post at Seymour's white house, which stood over a mile distant from the town. Brown, himself, followed Grierson with the main body of his troops; and, while they were thus engaged with the division of Taylor, the centre and right divisions, commanded by Colonels Clarke and McCall, entered the town by the other road, and surprising the drained garrison, took possession of Augusta. Hastily placing his prisoners and booty,—consisting of all the Indian presents about to be distributed by the English government to their dark-skinned allies,—under a proper guard, Clarke marched to the aid of Major Taylor, now endeavoring to capture Colonel Brown, who, with Grierson and Johnston, had thrown themselves into Seymour's white house.

The firing was kept up with more or less spirit during the day, but without dislodging the occupants. The Indians, unable to crowd into the house with the Rangers, fought outside, according to their irregular mode of warfare, crouching under the edge of the river's bank, concealing themselves in the shrubbery, and hiding behind trees and fences, and from these places, secure themselves, they delivered their effective discharges against the Americans.

During the night, Brown sought to retreat, but the strong guard posted around the house prevented him, and his only hope was so to secure himself, as to hold out until he could receive the relief which, at the first alarm, he had sent for from Lieutenant-Colonel Cruger, then at Ninety-Six.

Accordingly, himself and Rangers labored with all diligence to make the white house gun-proof, by filling up the spaces between the logs, and barricading the windows with boards ripped up from the floor; and, as the house was loop-holed for muskets, the assailants dared not approach, for the Rangers could take deliberate aim, while, at the same time, they were themselves comparatively secure.

On the morning of the 15th September, two pieces of cannon were drawn up from Fort Grierson; but they were only mounted on trucks, and were so badly served, owing to the want of artillerists, that they proved of little service, and that little was soon lost by the killing of Captain Martin, the only artillerist in Clarke's army. Had these been field, instead of fort pieces, and been well manned, they would soon have compelled Brown to surrender, or battered down the house over his head; as it was, another day was spent in fruitless efforts to dislodge the enemy. Brown was shot through both thighs, the wounded were suffering for want of medical attention, and their distresses were increased on the 16th, by the Americans charging upon the Indian allies, who, the night before, had been reinforced by fifty Cherokee warriors, and completely driving them from the river, thus cutting off all supply of water to the besieged.

Notwithstanding their distressed condition, the many wounded in the house, and the suffering of the Rangers for lack both of food and water, Brown still refused to surrender, though twice summoned by Clarke to do so; haughtily rejecting the summons, with the warning to Clarke, that he would retaliate the calamities of this siege upon the inhabitants of western Georgia, and declaring his intention to defend himself to the last extremity.

Four days of confinement, privation, and suffering, reduced Brown and his party to the very verge of abandoning his defence, and surrendering to the Americans. Still, however, he deferred this humiliating act, in the hope, faint indeed, but yet tenaciously clung to, of relief. Each hour he waited with extreme impatience the appearance of Colonel Cruger; and, as they slowly passed without his coming, he was on the point of sending out a white flag, to settle the terms of capitulation, when the head of the column of British troops was seen emerging from the woods on the other side of the Savannah River, and their appearance was hailed by the despairing Rangers with wild expressions of joy. Had Colonel Clarke a properly organized or well-disciplined force, he could have easily prevented Cruger from crossing the river; but such was the weakness of the Americans, occasioned by the loss of men in the action, and the desertion of others who had joined the army for plunder, rather than patriotism; and such his want of confidence in the men who served under him, that, by ten o'clock, two hours after the appearance of the English troops on the opposite bank of the river, Clarke raised the siege, and, knowing his inability to meet so large a force of regulars, hastily retired, leaving nearly thirty of his wounded men in the town to the mercy of the British commander. How well that mercy was exercised, may be learned from the treatment which these men received, for Brown caused Captain Ashby and twelve of the wounded, to be hung on the stair-case of the white house, so that he could see them swing off as he lay in his sick bed. The other prisoners and wounded men were delivered up to the Indians, who practised on them the refinements of savage cruelty, satiating their revenge by ingenious expedients to prolong the misery of their hapless victims,—seeking, by the horror of their death agonies, to make propitiation to the manes of the seventy warriors who had fallen by the American arms.

Colonel Cruger crossed the river, and entered Augusta without opposition, and the English flag again waved from the fort.

Brown, smarting in body and mind, under painful wounds and remembered indignities, and true to a nature which gloated in revenge, immediately spread around Augusta detachments of troops and Indians, to pick up stragglers from the American army; to surprise such small parties as might still hover near; to seek out every friend of liberty, and ascertain who had relatives among the rebel troops; and these, whether aged men or helpless women, quiet citizens or defenceless children, were visited with cruel treatment; their houses were burned, their plantations laid waste; the men driven off to filthy prisons, under a driver's lash, or at the point of the bayonet; the women abused, dishonored, and, with the children, left to be the sport of the ferocious royalists, whose tender mercies were cruel. No wars exhibit such horrors as those which enlist friends and neighbors in opposing interests and arms. The sudden displacing of kind feelings by political enmity; the hardening influence of such a transition; the private piques and feuds which are engendered; the personal acrimony which embitters the contest; the covetous desires fostered by the easy confiscation of estates; the little value placed upon human life; the intense selfishness which is cherished; these, added to the hardening influences of camp life, and the license accorded to the victor, conspired to make the partizan warfare in Georgia one of the darkest spots in the history of the American Revolution. The minute record of these cruelties is too heart-sickening to be transcribed. War with a foreign power, in well-pitched battles, with disciplined troops, to decide great principles or to enforce great rights, may have in it something noble and stirring, to relieve the dark features of the bloody field, the sacked town, the wasted life; but the social feuds of civil war—the hand-to-hand contests of neighbors—the mutual jealousy of adjoining hamlets—the embittered strife of once bosom friends; and the murders, assassinations, ravishments, burnings, thefts, and barbarities of the most revolting kind, which daily result from such partizan warfare, can be painted by no pencil, written by no pen, told by no tongue; for each case of outrage would, if properly portrayed, fill a large canvas with its sickening details: yet, until each case can be considered in all its bearings, and all these cases, with their various ramifications, be fully spread upon the historic page, we cannot form a true picture of the horrors, or obtain a true idea of the distress, which filled Georgia with blood, and ashes, and tears, during the years of its revolutionary history.

To attempt any further defence of Georgia, was now considered useless; and Colonel Clarke, after collecting such men and families as were unwilling to remain, led them over the Alleghanies, on the northern edge of Georgia, to the borders of Tennessee and Kentucky, where they were welcomed by the hospitable but hardy inhabitants, and where, for a brief season, they rested from their toils; though it was a repose purchased by the sacrifice of all their property, and by enduring sufferings which baffle the most graphic pencil.

From this time until the opening of the next year, the Georgians who kept the field were found doing good service in the adjoining States; and at Blackstock's, and King's Mountain, and Fish-dam Ford, and Long-Cane, the soldiers of our State fought with zeal, and gained unfading honor. In this last battle, Colonel

Clarke was borne from the field severely wounded, and was not able to return to his command for several months. Without a leader, under whom all could rally, the refugee Georgians were broken up into small parties, and acted without concert, as circumstances suggested, keeping up a sort of guerilla warfare against the British. To remedy this defect, by which so much strength and efficiency was wasted, for want of co-operation, General Morgan, from his camp on the Pacolette River, addressed to them, on the 4th January, 1781, the following letter:—

"TO THE REFUGEES OF GEORGIA.

"GENTLEMEN—Having heard of your sufferings, your attachment to the cause of freedom, and your gallantry and address in action, I had formed to myself the pleasing idea of receiving in you a great and valuable acquisition to my force. Judge, then, of my disappointment, when I find you scattered about in parties, subjected to no orders, nor joining in any general plan to promote the public service. The recollections of your past achievements, and the prospects of future laurels, should prevent your acting in such a manner for a moment. You have gained a character; and why should you risk the loss of it for the most trifling gratifications. You must know that, in your present situation, you can neither provide for your safety, nor assist me in annoying the enemy. Let me then entreat you, by the regard you have for your fame, and by your love to your country, to repair to my camp, and subject yourselves to order and discipline. I will ask you to encounter no dangers or difficulties, but what I shall participate in. Should it be thought advisable to form detachments, you may rely on being employed on that business, if it is more agreeable to your wishes; but it is absolutely necessary that your situation and movements should be known to me, so that I may be enabled to direct them in such a manner that they may tend to the advantage of the whole.

"I am, gentlemen, with every sentiment of regard,

"Your obedient servant,

"DANIEL MORGAN."

In consequence of this appeal, many of them rallied around his standard, and were present at the battle of Cowpens, on the 17th January, 1781. On this memorable day, the Georgians were under the immediate command of Major Cunningham, of Clarke's regiment, and were incorporated into the brigade of General Pickens,—James Jackson being Brigade Major.

Major Jackson greatly distinguished himself on this occasion by capturing the colors of the 71st Regiment, and by taking prisoner Major McArthur, the commander of the infantry of Tarlton's Legion; and he received the thanks of General Morgan on the field for his gallant conduct.

The overthrow of Fergusson at King's Mountains, the defeat of Tarlton at the Cowpens, and the march southward of General Green, who had superseded Gates in the command of the Southern Department, revived the flagging spirit of the Americans; and, under the impulse of that rekindled energy, it was determined to make another effort to wrest Augusta, the key of the whole up-country of Georgia, from the hands of the Tories.

Lord Rawdon had not only been held in check, but

had been turned back towards the seaboard by General Green. The outposts of Forts Watson, Motte, Granby, and Orangeburg, had successively yielded to the American arms; and the troops therein had either been taken prisoners, or were withdrawn; and, when the American army reached the Congaree River, its General viewed, with great satisfaction, the successive fall of the advanced British posts, and the rising patriotism of the people, and resolved to press his march with such vigor as to compel the enemy to surrender or retire from the whole interior of Carolina and Georgia, and confine themselves to the seaports of Charleston and Savannah.

On the 16th of May, Lieutenant-Colonel Lee, of the legion, received orders to advance upon Augusta; and, fearing that, in the general abandonment of interior posts, Colonel Cruger would evacuate Ninety-Six, and join Colonel Brown at Augusta, he pushed on with great celerity, relieving the tired infantry by making them occasionally exchange with the dragoons, or mount behind them, and reached Augusta on the 19th.

While Lee was thus pressing on, as the van of General Green's army, on the one side, Colonel Clarke, having again rallied a band of faithful Georgians around him, was prepared to join the expected forces of Pickens and Lee in the reduction of Augusta. As Clarke approached this place on the South, he learned that the boats, laden with the annual presents for the Indian tribes, and with supplies for the garrison, were then ascending the river; and, posting his men among the thick trees which skirted its banks, he so commanded the passage that the boats, unable to ascend without being captured, took shelter at Fort Galphin, or Dreadnought, at Silver Bluff, twelve miles below Augusta, on the north side of the river. While thus engaged in watching these boats, Lee was requested by General Pickens to reduce this post, which was a stockade fort, manned with two companies of infantry. It being important to make the attack at once, as it was evident that neither of the commanding officers at Augusta and Fort Galphin knew of the arrival of Pickens or Lee, Lee, to whom the affair was intrusted, detached a company of infantry and a troop of horse, under command of Major Rudolph, who, by a forced march, reached the pine barrens, in the vicinity of the fort, on the morning of Monday, the 20th of May. Being strengthened here by a strong detachment of Georgia and Carolina militia, under Colonel Clarke, Lee attacked the Fort; and continued the attack with such spirit during the day, that, evening drawing on, and it being impossible to hold out much longer, Captain Roath surrendered the fort by capitulation; and thus, without losing a man, and having only eight or ten wounded, the Americans made one hundred and twenty-six prisoners; and gained a large amount of powder, balls, small arms, blankets, salt, and other articles greatly needed by the army, and of many of which they had been completely destitute.

On Wednesday, the 23d of May, Colonel Clarke formed a junction with Pickens and Lee, near Augusta, and prepared to invest the town. Augusta was then defended by the Forts Grierson and Cornwallis. The former, commanded by the Colonel whose name it bore, was situated near the site of the new market, and was defended by two pieces of artillery and eighty men; and the latter was located half a mile to the east and south, on the spot now occupied by St. Paul's Church. In Fort Cornwallis there were several pieces of cannon, and it was garrisoned by four hundred men, in addition to two hundred negroes, who did duty in the fort. Both forts, as indeed the whole British force in Upper Georgia, were commanded by Colonel Thomas Brown, who had so bravely resisted the former siege under Colonel Clarke.

The first object of the combined forces was to cut off communication between the forts. Pickens, therefore, to whom the honor of conducting these movements was confided, erected field-works on the plain, which equally commanded both forts. This battery opened its fire of artillery on the morning of the 24th, and it was determined, under cover of this fire, to fall upon and destroy Fort Grierson; and then, if possible, take Fort Cornwallis. The troops, destined for the attack on Fort Grierson, were divided into two portions; one, under Pickens and Clarke, being ordered to attack the fort on the north and west; the other, under Majors Eaton and Jackson, was to approach it simultaneously on the south. To prevent any succor being sent to Grierson by Brown, Lieutenant-Colonel Lee, with the infantry and artillery, menaced Fort Cornwallis; while the dragoons, under Eggleston, were so placed, under cover of a neighboring wood, that they could, at a moment's signal, fall upon the rear of Brown, should he attempt a sortie for the rescue of Fort Grierson.

Colonel Grierson finding himself galled by the fire of the American field-works, and fearing that he would be entirely cut off, resolved to abandon the fort, and retreat, under shelter of the river bank, to Fort Cornwallis. As soon as this movement was perceived, he was intercepted, and attacked with such vigor, that he lost his second in command, two field-pieces, thirty men killed, and forty-five wounded or taken prisoners. Grierson and a few others only, escaped to Fort Cornwallis.

In a moment of desperation, at the anticipated capture of Fort Grierson, Brown sallied forth with a body of troops to the aid of his brother commander; but he was promptly met and repulsed by Lee, who drove him back to his fort.

Fort Grierson having fallen into the hands of the assailants, their combined force was now directed upon Fort Cornwallis. Brown, unwilling to surrender, though summoned to do so, exerted himself to the utmost to place the fort in a defensible state by strengthening every assailable part, and resolving to hold out to the last extremity. The peculiar nature of the ground not permitting an assault, it was resolved to invest it by regular approaches, and at these the troops labored with commendable diligence, occasionally interrupted by sallies from the fort, which all resulted in loss to the British. The level plain afforded no eminence from which the besiegers could command the fort by their artillery, and in this emergency, Colonel Lee proposed the plan,—adopted, with so much success, by Lieutenant Mayham, at Fort Watson,—of erecting a square tower of rough logs, about thirty feet high, filled in with fascines, earth, stone, brick, &c., to give it solidity, sufficiently platformed to sustain a six-pounder, and so loopholed as to make it effective, both as an artillery and rifle battery. It was begun on the evening of the 30th of May, under cover of a frame house, which concealed the laborers from the view of the fort, and, by the 1st of June, was raised to a level with the enemy's works.

Brown's attention was now directed to counteracting this novel mode of warfare, and he accordingly erected a platform in the angle of his fort, opposite the Mayham tower, upon which he mounted two of his heaviest pieces, and opened their fire at once upon the besiegers. Not trusting to this alone, and feeling, in the desperate condition of affairs, that he must make a bold and sudden strike, if he would either dislodge or intimidate his foes, Brown resolved to make a general sortie; and, for this purpose, divided his band into two parts, one of which was to attack the American works on the river quarter, as a feint; while the other party, led by Brown himself, was to fall directly upon the troops in front, and gain, if possible, possession of the tower, with a view to burn it down. Shortly after midnight, on the 1st June, the sortie was made; but the British found the Americans prepared to receive them, and they were repulsed, in both attacks, after a long, close, and very bloody conflict, with a steadiness and gallantry worthy of all praise. From this time Brown gave up all such attempts, and sought to do by stratagem what he had failed to do by force.

The Mayham tower being completed, and a six-pounder mounted on its platform, it was pointed and fired with such effect, that before mid-day the two pieces in the angle of Fort Cornwallis, nearest the tower, were dismounted, and the inside of the fort was raked by its balls.

"It was now," says Colonel Lee, who relates the

circumstance,[2] "that Lieutenant-Colonel Brown determined to put in execution his concealed stratagem. In the course of the night a deserter from the fort was sent to Lieutenant-Colonel Lee. He was a Scot, with all the wily sagacity of his country, and a sergeant of the artillery. Upon being questioned upon the effect of our cannonade, and the situation of the enemy, he answered, that the strange log-house, lately erected, gave an advantage which, duly improved, could not fail to force surrender; but, that the garrison had not suffered so much as might be presumed; that it was amply supplied with provisions, and was in high spirits.

"In the course of the conversation which followed, Lee inquired, in what way could the effect of the cannonade be increased? Very readily, replied the crafty sergeant; that knowing the spot where all the powder in the fort was deposited, with red hot balls from the six pounder, directed properly, the magazine might be blown up. This intelligence was received with delight, and the suggestion of the sergeant seized with avidity, although it would be very difficult to prepare our ball, as we were unprovided with a furnace. It was proposed to the sergeant, that he should be sent to the officer commanding our battery, and give his aid to the execution of his suggestion, with assurances of liberal reward in case of success. This proposition was heard with much apparent reluctance, although every disposition to bring the garrison to submission was exhibited by the sergeant, who pretended that Brown had done him many personal injuries in the course of service. But he added, it was impossible for him to put himself

[2] Lee's Memoirs, ii, 105.

in danger of capture, as he well knew he should be executed on a gibbet, if taken. A good supper was now presented to him, with his grog; which, being finished, and being convinced by the arguments of Lee, that his personal safety could not be endangered, as it was not desired or meant that he should take any part in the siege, but merely to attend at the tower to direct the pointing of the piece, he assented; declaring that he entered upon his task with dire apprehensions, and reminding the lieutenant-colonel of his promised reward. Lee instantly put him in care of his adjutant, to be delivered to Captain Finley, with the information communicated, for the purpose of blowing up the enemy's magazine. It was midnight; and Lieutenant-Colonel Lee, expecting on the next day to be much engaged, our preparations being nearly completed, retired to rest. Reflecting upon what had passed, and recurring to the character of his adversary, he became much disquieted by the step he had taken, and soon concluded to withdraw the sergeant from the tower. He had not been many minutes with Captain Finley, before an order remanding him was delivered, committing him to the quarter guard. In the morning we were saluted with a new exhibition, unexpected, though not injurious. Between the quarters of Lee and the fort stood four or five deserted houses; some of them near enough to the fort to be used with effect by riflemen from their upper stories. They had often engaged the attention of Pickens and Lee, with a view of applying them, whenever the enemy should be assaulted, to aid in covering their attack. Brown, sallying out before break of day, set fire to all but two of the houses. No attempt was made to disturb the operation, or to extinguish the flames, after the enemy had returned; it being deemed improper to hazard our troops in effecting any object not material in its consequence. Of the two left, one was most commodious for the purpose originally contemplated by Pickens and Lee in the hour of assault.

"The besiegers being incapable of discovering any reason for the omission to burn the two houses, and especially one nearest the fort, various were their conjectures as to the cause of sparing them; some leading to the conclusion that they were left purposely, and consequently with the view of injuring the assailant. The fire from the tower continued, and being chiefly directed against the parapet fronting the river, in which quarter the proposed attack would be directed, demonstrated satisfactorily that the hour had arrived to make the decisive appeal. Orders were accordingly issued to prepare for the assault, to take place on the next day, at the hour of nine in the forenoon. In the course of the night, a party of the best marksmen were selected from Pickens' militia, and sent to one of the houses nearest to the fort.

"The officer commanding this detachment was ordered to arrange his men in the upper story, for the purpose of ascertaining the number which could with ease use their rifles out of the windows, or any other convenient aperture; then to withdraw, and report to the brigadier. It was intended, before daylight, to have directed the occupation of the house by the same officer, with such a force of riflemen as he should report to be sufficient. Handy was ordered to return to the river quarter at the dawn of day, as to his detachment and the legion infantry the main assault would be committed. These, with all the other preparations being made, the troops continued in their usual stations, pleased that the time was near which would close with success their severe toils.

"About three in the morning of the 4th of June, we were aroused by a violent explosion, which was soon discovered to have shattered the very house intended to be occupied by the rifle party before daybreak. It was severed, and thrown into the air thirty or forty feet high, its fragments falling all over the field. This explained, at once, not only the cause of Brown's omitting its destruction, but also communicated the object of the constant digging which had until lately employed the besieged.

"Brown pushed a sap to this house, which he presumed would be certainly possessed by the besieger, when ready to strike his last blow; and he concluded, from the evident maturity of our works, and from the noise made by the militia, when sent to the house in the first part of the night, for the purpose of ascertaining the number competent to its capacity, that the approaching morning was fixed for the general assault. Not doubting but the house was occupied with the body destined to hold it, he determined to deprive his adversary of every aid from this quarter; hoping, too, by the consternation which the manner of destruction could not fail to excite, to damp the ardor of the troops charged with storming.

"Happily he executed his plan too early for its success, or our gallant band would certainly have shared the fate of the house. This fortunate escape excited grateful sensations in the breasts of the two commandants, for the gracious interposition of Providence; and added another testimonial to the many already received, of the penetration and decision which marked the character of their opponent."

On the 3d June, Pickens and Lee a second time summoned Brown to surrender, who replied, as he had done on the 31st of May, "As it is my duty, it is likewise my inclination, to defend the post to the last extremity." The next day, learning that some of the prisoners in Brown's possession were purposely placed in the most exposed position of the fort, so that the Americans, if they fired, would be likely to kill their own friends, the commanding officers proposed to Brown to send them out of the fort during the contest, to "be considered yours or ours, as the siege may terminate." To this humane proposal Brown refused to accede, and the American commanders determined to carry the fort by a general assault; but its execution was stayed, to receive a flag from Brown, offering to surrender on specified terms; but they were such as could not be granted, though terms were transmitted in reply, which, with some slight modifications, were accepted. On the 5th June, the following articles of capitulation were signed by both parties, and at 12 M. Fort Cornwallis was delivered up to Major Rudolph, the British troops marching out and laying down their arms:—

"ARTICLES OF CAPITULATION

PROPOSED BY LIEUTENANT-COLONEL BROWN, AND ANSWERED BY GENERAL PICKENS AND LIEUTENANT-COLONEL LEE.

"ARTICLE I. That all acts of hostilities and works shall cease between the besiegers and besieged, until the articles of capitulation shall be agreed on, signed, and executed, or collectively rejected.

"*Answer*. Hostilities shall cease for one hour; other operations to continue.

"ARTICLE II. That the fort shall be surrendered to the commanding officer of the American troops, such as it now stands. That the King's troops, three days after signing the articles of capitulation, shall be conducted to Savannah, with their baggage, where they will remain prisoners of war until they are exchanged; that proper conveyances shall be provided by the commanding officer of the American troops for that purpose, together with a sufficient quantity of good and wholesome provisions, till their arrival at Savannah.

"*Answer*. Inadmissible. The prisoners to surrender field-prisoners of war. The officers to be indulged with their paroles; the soldiers to be conducted to such place as the commander-in-chief shall direct.

"ARTICLE III. The militia now in garrison shall be permitted to return to their respective homes, and be secured in their persons and properties.

"*Answer*. Answered by the second article, the militia making part of the garrison.

"ARTICLE IV. The sick and wounded shall be under the care of their own surgeons, and be supplied with such medicines and necessaries as are allowed to the British hospitals.—Agreed.

"ARTICLE V. The officers of the garrison, and citizens who have borne arms during the siege, shall keep their side-arms, pistols, and baggage, which shall not be searched, and retain their servants.

"*Answer*. The officers and citizens who have borne arms during the siege, shall be permitted their side-arms, private baggage, and servants; their side-arms not to be worn; and the baggage to be searched by a person appointed for that purpose.

"ARTICLE VI. The garrison, at an hour appointed, shall march out with shouldered arms and drums beating, to a place agreed on, where they will pile their arms.

"*Answer*. Agreed. The judicious and gallant defence made by the garrison, entitles them to every mark of military respect. The fort to be delivered up to Captain Rudolph at twelve o'clock, who will take possession with a detachment of the legion infantry.

"ARTICLE VII. That the citizens shall be protected in their persons and property.

"*Answer*. Inadmissible.

"ARTICLE VIII. That twelve months shall be allowed to all such as do not choose to reside in this country, to dispose of their effects, real and personal, in this province, without any molestation whatever, or to remove to any part thereof, as they may choose, as well themselves as families.

"*Answer*. Inadmissible.

"ARTICLE IX. That the Indian families now in garrison shall accompany the King's troops to Savannah, where they will remain prisoners of war, until exchanged for an equal number of prisoners in the Creek or Cherokee nations.

"*Answer*. Answered in the second article.

"ARTICLE X. That an express be permitted to go to Savannah, with the commanding officer's despatches, which are not to be opened.

"*Answer*. Agreed.

"ARTICLE XI. Additional. The particular attention

of Colonel Brown is expected towards the just delivery of all public stores, moneys, &c., and that no loans be permitted to defeat the spirit of this article.

"Signed at headquarters, Augusta, June 5, 1781, by

"ANDREW PICKENS, B. G. Mil.
"HENRY LEE, JR., Lieut.-Col. Com.
"THOMAS BROWN, Lieut.-Col.,
commanding King's troops at Augusta."

So exasperated were the Georgians at the wanton cruelties committed by Brown and Grierson, that they were both placed under a strong guard, to secure them from the determined assaults of those whose fathers, brothers, and sons had been massacred by them. Brown, under the care of Captain Armstrong, was, with difficulty, saved from assassination; but Grierson was shot down the day after the capitulation, by a man on horseback, who, riding up to the room where he was confined, and, without dismounting, shot him so that he expired soon after. The American officers exerted themselves to the utmost to check these murderous feelings; but the long course of atrocities perpetrated by these men; the many personal insults, which, in the excited minds of the individuals, demanded personal revenge; and the generally exasperated state of the militia, made it extremely difficult to secure to them the protection which was guaranteed by the articles of capitulation.

Immediately after the surrender of Augusta, the commanding officers, Pickens and Lee, marched their troops to Ninety-Six, and joined the main army under General Greene, leaving Major James Jackson in command at Augusta.

CHAPTER VIII.

EVACUATION OF SAVANNAH.

THE excitement kindled in Georgia by the success of this siege was so great, and the danger to which, in the view of the British, the Province was exposed, was so imminent, that Lord Rawdon felt compelled, even in his own weakness, to send the king's American regiment, in a small craft, and without convoy, from Charleston, in order to reinforce Lieutenant-Colonel James Wright, at Savannah.[1]

Augusta had been a stronghold of the English, by means of which they held in check the whole up-country of Georgia, and preserved an open communication with the tories of Carolina; but, being now driven from this, the British found themselves reduced to narrow limits. With the exception of Savannah, they had but two garrisoned outposts,—at Ebenezer, twenty-five miles northwest, and at Ogeechee, about the same distance southwest of Savannah. Communication was still preserved with Florida, by the seaboard, and through this route the tories and Indians made frequent and harassing incursions; for such was still the influence of the British over the Indians, by means of presents and resident agents, that parties of them

[1] Tarlton's Campaigns, 486.

were ever on the alert, to cut off stragglers from the American forts, and massacre such as were in the American interests.

As the British lines contracted, the spirit of the Georgians expanded; the dawning hope that they might yet drive out the foe, roused many who had heretofore desponded of liberty; while others, who had been kept passive by the overawing force of regulars, tories, and Indians, now joined the American camp, and seemed anxious to atone for long inactivity, by the most energetic efforts. General Greene, also, deeming it a favorable moment, had promised General Twiggs that, so soon as St. Clair, then on his march from the North, should form his camp, he would send Wayne, then lying at Purysburg, with a large detachment, to his help in Georgia. Under these circumstances, Twiggs began a movement southward, cautiously feeling his way, and securing every foot of ground over which his troops passed, until he reached Burke County; when, hearing that a band of loyalists and Indians were collecting on the western frontier of Georgia and Carolina, he retraced his way to Augusta, where the legislature was then sitting, to devise measures to disperse the enemy.

In the meantime Colonel Jackson, to whom Congress had committed the raising and command of a Georgia legion, with a small advance corps, had attempted, on the 2d November, 1781, to surprise the British post at the Ogeechee, commanded by Captain Johnson; but, failing in this plan, through the impetuous conduct of one of his officers, at the very moment that victory seemed certain, he retired towards Ebenezer, having lost sixteen of his command in killed, wounded, and prisoners, while he had inflicted upon the enemy a loss of three officers and nine privates killed, and wounded, and taken prisoners. On the return of General Twiggs to Augusta, after dispersing the Indian and tory bands at the Big Shoals, on the Oconee, which, for a few months, gave peace to that harassed district, he ordered Colonel Jackson to retreat to Burke County, for the purpose of recruiting his force, and then to proceed against Ebenezer. As soon as his corps numbered one hundred and fifty, he completely shut up the garrison at Ebenezer,—cutting off their foraging parties, and so harassing them, that the post was soon broken up by the retreat of the British to Savannah.

On the 4th January, 1782, General St. Clair effected a junction with General Greene, in South Carolina. Upon this accession, the mind of the southern commander turned at once to Georgia, and, agreeably to his promise, he detached General Wayne, on the 10th January, with the 3d regiment of dragoons, under Colonel White, and a party of artillery, to proceed thither, and assume the command of all the American forces there. Colonel Hampton's cavalry had previously been detached from General Sumpter's brigade, in order to report himself for service under Wayne in Georgia.

The distressed situation of Georgia took a deep hold upon the mind of General Greene. The savages had laid waste nearly all the frontier settlements, and often penetrated into the older districts with the torch and scalping-knife. The tories, lost to all feelings of humanity, wreaked their fiery and bloody vengeance upon the plantations and persons of all interested in the American cause. The British soldiers, most of whom were imported loyalists from the north, or German hirelings, ravaged the country with merciless vigor. The continual alarms prevented planting or reaping. The absence of so many males, embodied in the various partisan corps, drew largely on the resources of the country. The havoc and destruction of the whigs upon the tories, and the tories upon the whigs, and the general insecurity of life, and labor, and property, reduced the State to a most pitiable condition. It is not too much to say, that no State suffered more, internally, than Georgia. The legion of Jackson, popular as it was, was subsisted with difficulty; their rations were mostly boiled rice, in small quantities, and even then uncertain. The most common articles of provision were exorbitantly high. Salt often commanded two dollars (specie) a quart. Rice, to keep the people of the upper districts from famishing, was obtained with difficulty from the State of South Carolina. The frontier settlers were grouped chiefly in log forts, and planted and tended their corn by companies. While some guarded the forts with the women and children, the others worked and guarded each other by turns. The utmost distress prevailed. They planted, but knew not that they should reap. They built rude cabins, but knew not how long it would be before they were burnt over their heads. They went out to labor in the morning, not knowing that they should ever return to their little fortress; and each night was a night of horrors and alarm. That General Greene knew much of this distress, is evident from his instructions to General Wayne, in which he says, "The peculiar situation of Georgia, and the great sufferings of the good people of that State, and their uncommon exertions to recover their liberties, induce me to embrace the earliest opportunities to give them more effectual support than has been hitherto in my power." He was particularly enjoined to "invite all the people to join him when he should get into the low country, and to give protection and security to all such as should engage in service under his command." In General Greene's letter to Governor Martin, January 9th, 1782, he gives expression to the following sentiment: "I cannot help recommending to your Excellency to open a door for the disaffected of your State to come in with particular exceptions. It is better to save than destroy, especially when we are obliged to expose good men to destroy bad. It is always dangerous to push people to a state of desperation, and the satisfaction of revenge has but a momentary existence, and is commonly succeeded by pity and remorse. The practice of plundering, which, I am told, has been too much indulged with you, is very destructive to the morals and manners of the people. Habits and dispositions, founded on this practice, soon grow obstinate, and are difficult to restrain; indeed, it is the most direct way of undermining all government, and never fails to bring the laws into contempt, for people will not stop at the barriers which were first intended to bound them, after having tasted the sweets of possessing property by the easy mode of plunder. The preservation of morals, and an encouragement to honest industry, should be the first objects of government,—plundering is the destruction of both. I wish the cause of liberty may never be tarnished with inhumanity, nor the morals of people bartered in exchange for wealth."

Wayne, with his command, reached Sister's Ferry, on

the Savannah, on the 12th, and crossed the river in small canoes, swimming his horses by their side. The artillery, which formed part of his detachment, he was compelled to leave in Carolina, as he had no means of transporting it across the river. The Legislature was at this time in session in Augusta; and immediately, on receiving intelligence from General Wayne of his being in Georgia, accompanied with a suggestion akin to that of General Green, "recommending proclamations to be issued for opening a door for the absent citizens of this State, and to encourage desertion from the enemy," appointed a committee of the Executive Council to wait on General Wayne to devise measures to carry out these views. The result of this conference was, that two proclamations were made, viz., one for opening a door for the reception of citizens; and another to encourage desertion from the enemy, particularly among the Hessian troops, who, from their nearness to the Germans of Ebenezer, were strongly attracted thither. The appearance of General Wayne, and the vigilance and activity of his dragoons, and of the legion of Jackson, drove the enemy within their lines, after they had destroyed all the provisions in the vicinity of Savannah which they could not carry thither.

The proclamations also had a very good effect, especially as they were aided by a general dissatisfaction among the troops in Savannah. Many of the former citizens who had been compelled, from various causes, to take protection under the British Government, and who had even joined the armies of the enemy, availed themselves of the door opened by the proclamation, which had special reference to them, returned to their State allegiance, and joined the camp of General

Wayne, proving their sincerity by the most zealous efforts to merit the pardon and protection extended to them by the Executive. A vindictive and revengeful feeling, however, existed against many of these men, and it required the strong arm of civil and military power to hold in check the ebullitions of feeling which frequently betrayed themselves in a desire to injure and even to murder these reclaimed citizens. Spurred on by passions, which the camp tended to excite, rather than subdue; roused by prejudices, the offspring rather of ignorance than of justice, the militia and other citizens were led to the commission of acts of atrocity for which there can be no extenuation, save in the unbridled spirit which war ever begets, and the jealousy of sharing blood-bought rights with those who had, for a time at least, turned traitors to their country.

The condition of the enemy in Savannah was greatly straitened; and though reinforced by Lord Rawdon with one hundred and fifty men of the 7th regiment, there were, including these, the militia and a corps of one hundred and fifty negroes, armed and equipped as infantry, under the command of the notorious Brown, only about one thousand men. The town, indeed, was well fortified and protected by ordnance, and guarded on the river side by row-gallies and brigs; but so completely had the Americans compressed their operations, that Jackson, with his legion, often pursued the enemy within sight of Savannah, and, in several instances, picked off men and horses even from the town commons. The British spared no pains to form and keep up alliances with the Cherokees, Creeks, and Chickasaws, and aimed to ingratiate themselves into their favor by rivalling them in deeds of cruelty and blood. These savages were induced to visit Savannah under the idea of receiving presents, and were mostly brought round from the Alatamaha by boats, through the inland passage. The peculiar ferocity of the enemy, at this time, is indicated in the following extract of a letter from General Wayne, dated Headquarters, Ebenezer, 26th March, 1782:—

"On receiving intelligence that the enemy were on the point of moving out in force, I determined to more than meet them, and to avail myself of circumstances and position; from a conviction that, although our numbers were not so great as I could wish, yet we were not to be disgraced, and that if we could possibly produce disorder in their ranks, the enemy would have no reason to triumph from the encounter. Our advance guard fell in with a party of their dragoons three miles from Savannah, whom they immediately charged and drove into the lines, and then sounded a charge within the influence of their batteries. This temerity in the officer, drew the enemy out in force, and, in falling back before them, one of his dragoons was killed. However, as soon as they discovered that the advance were supported, they retired into their works, bearing off the scalp of the dragoon, with which they paraded the streets of Savannah, headed by the Lieutenant-Governor and other British officers, who gave an entertainment to the Indians, and had a dance on the occasion. Nor did their barbarity rest here: they mangled and disfigured the dead body in a manner that none but wretches inured in acts of cruelty would possibly be capable of, and ordered it to remain unburied; but the Ethiopians, more humanized, stole it away, and deposited it in the ground, for the commission of which crime, a reward of five guineas is offered for the discovery of any person or persons concerned in that act of humanity."

General Wayne desired to get as many of these Indians as he could into his power, for the purpose of bringing them over to the American side, or at least of making them neutral in the strife. Knowing, therefore, that many of them, unsuspecting the presence of American troops near Savannah, would attempt to get into the town on the land side, he despatched Major John Habersham, with a body of South Carolina cavalry, under Major Francis Moore, and some mounted militia, under Captain Patrick Carr, to collect the various parties known to be on their way to Savannah. The efforts of Habersham were at first quite successful, as he represented himself as Colonel Brown, with whose name they were quite familiar, and his orders, therefore, were promptly obeyed. But the whole plan was foiled by the knavery of a part of his mounted militia, who, with a lieutenant, under pretence that the bad roads would injure their horses, abandoned him in their thirst for blood,—slew several of the Indians, and then threw themselves precipitately into the neighborhood of Sunbury, where they killed eleven loyalists. This transaction opened the eyes of the Indians, and, notwithstanding all the vigilance which Habersham observed, the savages fled by night, carrying tales of outrage and blood into the surrounding tribes. Major Moore was shortly after killed, in a skirmish with some Indians and Tories, at Reed's Bluff, on the Alatamaha, while on his return to headquarters; and Captain Lyons, of that corps, and Captain Carr, were so incensed at his fall, that they, with their several commands, breaking away from the orders of Habersham, determined to repass the Alatamaha, and avenge the death of their gallant comrade. But his death was avenged more speedily and by other hands, as appears from the following extract from the Order-book of General Wayne :—

"HEADQUARTERS, EBENEZER, April 16th, 1782.

"Five of Colonel Jackson's dragoons and young Snyder were surrounded and fired upon a little before daylight on Sunday morning by a party of the enemy, thirty in number, under the command of Major Dill, but without effect. The fire was returned by Snyder with so good a direction, as to leave the Major dead on the spot. A pistol fired by one of the dragoons wounded two men of the party, which was all the arms made use of by our people on this occasion,—the enemy flying with such precipitation to their boats, as to escape the keen cutting swords of their brave pursuers.

"General Wayne requests Mr. Snyder, and those five brave dragoons, to accept his best thanks for their fortitude and gallant conduct in defeating five times their number, although attacked by surprise."

The return home of the Carolina cavalry, and the discharge of the State militia, whose term of service had expired, who, however, in the language of the General, "required some respite from duty and fatigue, which they have gone through with cheerfulness and fortitude becoming the virtuous citizens of America," was in some measure made up by the arrival of one hundred and fifty Virginia troops under Lieutenant-Colonel

Posey. Still the number in his camp was fluctuating, and he was embarrassed greatly by the lack of clothing and subsistence. "We are in great distress for want of shoes, shirts, and overalls; the Virginians have marched upwards of three hundred miles barefoot, in which situation they still continue. I send you," he continues, writing to Colonel Jackson (24th April, 1782), "a gill of spirits for each man with you, and a little for your own use, as we have not a sufficiency to divide among the officers in general. I have directed a distribution between Colonels White, Posey, and yourself, by which means your officers will participate in rotation at your tables."

In the general distress which then prevailed, the civil functionaries suffered equally with the military. A few days after the above letter was written, Governor Martin made a communication to the State Legislature, in which he says: "I am sorry to inform you that my family is frequently destitute of provisions, and that I have no mode of supplying them but through the Commissary, who has it not in his power to prevent it, or is very neglectful; and that, in a fit of illness, from which I have not yet recovered, I was obliged to send to my neighbors for every article but sugar and coffee fit for a sick or weak person to eat. I have not had, since my commencement in office, as much money as would purchase the most trifling necessaries myself or family stands in need of from time to time. My family, such of the members of your body who stay with me (for want of public houses), and the guard, have been for some time, and are now, supported by grain procured on my private credit."

This letter drew a resolve from that body, on the 4th

of May, empowering the Governor to take ten negroes belonging to any person or persons who have forfeited the same, for the purpose of supporting himself and family while in the exercise of government. The aspect of the times will perhaps be still better understood by inserting a report ordered by the House of Assembly, upon certain articles forwarded to Governor Martin from Captain Ignatius Few, a certain portion of which were set aside for the Governor and Council; "the same being inspected by a committee, report, that there is seventy-five pounds sugar, nine bushels salt, and twenty-three gallons rum. To the President two gallons rum, to each member one gallon, the remainder for the Governor, to be disposed of as he may think proper. To the President ten pounds sugar, to each member five pounds, the remainder to be disposed of as the Governor may think proper. The salt to the President two quarts, to each member one, the remainder to be disposed of as the Governor may think proper. To the Messenger of this Board five pounds sugar, one quart of salt, half gallon rum."

At this juncture the State of South Carolina voted the Georgians some rice; but so difficult was its transportation, that one-third of it was "allowed to any person or persons that will bring the said rice from Pocotaligo to Ebenezer." Strange as it may seem, at this time, the very legislature which granted ten negroes to Colonel Martin to support him as Governor, voted five thousand guineas, to be vested in three commissioners, to purchase an estate for General Green; and four thousand guineas to be likewise vested in an estate for General Wayne; so highly did the Georgians estimate the services of these distinguished men, and so liberally did they reward them.[1] But they were not estimated beyond their value, nor rewarded beyond their merit. The grants were the more generous, from the deep poverty of the grantors; for when, a few months before, the Continental Financier had called upon the Executive for the quota of this State, amounting to $25,000, Wereat wrote, 12th March, 1782, there is not "a quarter part of the money in the State without the enemy's lines, neither is there produce to raise it from, or a sufficient provision to last the people until harvest, besides a general want of every necessary."

General Wayne found much difficulty in filling up his regiments, and keeping up a proper force to sustain himself so near the enemy's lines. Yet, under difficulties of the most disheartening character, and in command of a post that demanded anxious vigilance, Wayne not only kept up good appearances toward the enemy, but so disposed his troops, and adjusted his plans, as to keep them in continual fear; hovering around the city, attacking their foraging parties, cutting off their supplies by capture or conflagration, even under cover of the guns of their redoubts. The energy and prowess of Wayne and his soldiers were soon, however, put to a severer test. With the view of escorting into camp a body of Creek Indians, under the command of Guristersigo, who were to rendezvous at Harris's Bridge, on the Ogeechee, seven miles from Savannah, Lieutenant-Colonel Brown, with all the troops that could be spared from Savannah, marched out to conduct their allies into town. As soon as

[1] Johnson's Life of Green, ii, 401, 419.

Wayne heard of this at Ebenezer, on the 21st May, he immediately put White's dragoons and Posey's infantry in motion, who reached Mrs. Gibbons's, within six miles of Savannah, at 5 P.M. An hour after, he received an express from Lieutenant-Colonel Jackson, stating that the enemy were in full force at Harris's Bridge, on the great Ogeechee road, and that a smaller party were at Ogeechee Ferry, which he designed to attack with his corps. Upon inquiry, Wayne found that the only route to the enemy's position was through a tangled swamp of nearly four miles in extent, with many deep and dangerous morasses to pass, and then to intersect the Ogeechee road at an intermediate distance between Savannah and the bridge. He was properly impressed with the difficulty attending a night-march over such ground, as well as the delicacy of a manœuvre that placed him in contact with the whole of the enemy's force in Georgia; but trusting to the experience and gallantry of the officers, and the steady bravery of the troops, he ordered an advance, assured "that the success of a nocturnal attack depended more upon prowess than numbers." The vanguard, under Colonel White, reached the Ogeechee road at a point four miles southwest of Savannah at twelve at night, and there found the enemy advancing, and in good order. Without waiting for the rest of the troops to come up, Wayne ordered the vanguard to charge; which they did with such vivacity as to cause the precipitate flight of Brown and his large force, "without the use of powder." The almost impenetrable woods, deep swamps, and morasses into which they plunged, under cover of night, secured them from total ruin; they lost, however, many of their horses and arms in their hurried efforts to obtain personal safety. This sudden route of a force five times their superior, was effected by a company of light infantry under Captain Parker, and a few dragoons under Captain Hughes and Lieutenant Bowen, led on by Colonel White, under General Wayne; and the only weapons used were the sword and the bayonet. The remainder of Posey's detachment, and of White's dragoons, under Captain Gunn, did not reach the road until after the enemy had broken and fled. The flight was complete. Many were killed and wounded; among whom was Lieutenant-Colonel Douglass. Many prisoners were made, and between twenty and thirty of their best dragoon horses were taken. The discomfited troops reached Savannah by twos and threes; and Colonels Brown and Ingham did not get to town until the next night, when they entered unattended.

This whole affair was as brilliantly achieved as it was daringly conceived, and reflected great honor on Wayne and his enthusiastic troops. After refreshing his men at Mrs. Gibbons's, General Wayne marched within view of Savannah, in the hope of drawing out General Alured Clark and the troops under his command; but that cautious officer declined the virtual challenge, and Wayne therefore returned to Ebenezer, on the morning of the 24th, with the loss of only five privates killed and two wounded.

While these events were transpiring in the lower part of Georgia, active operations were being prosecuted in the upper districts for the suppression of disturbances created by the tories and Indians. In the beginning of the year, General Pickens wrote urgent letters to General Rutherford, Colonels Clarke, Sevier, Shelby, and others, to join him in an expedition against the Cherokees, appointing an early day in February for their setting out, and the middle settlements as a place of junction; stating that he had ordered his own brigade "to be in readiness by that time, with thirty-five days' provision, and pack-horses to carry it;" urging this measure "as a means of saving this country from total ruin, and enabling them to act with their whole force against the enemy below." Owing to the impossibility of mustering men from such remote districts at a given time, the expedition was delayed more than a month; and even then undertaken not as originally designed, as the Tennesseeans and North Carolinians did not reach the ground; for when Pickens reached Choti, where he purposed to rendezvous, he had but two hundred and seventy-five men, "including officers, pack-horse men, and servants." Out of this number, two hundred only had guns, and about fifty swords. Undeterred by this small force, scarcely a fourth of what he anticipated, he determined to march on, until obliged by necessity to turn back. His progress is thus described by himself, in a letter to Colonel Clarke, dated Long Cane, South Carolina, 3d April, 1782:—

"Still in hopes to reach the middle ground and meet the over-mountain men, we crossed the mountains to Catoogojoy, and from there to Quanese and Cheweg, but the Indians had removed from their towns with their provisions. From there we took the road to the middle grounds, and reached the Coosa town, where we were in hopes to get some corn, but did not get an ear in the town. As the snow was excessive, and no cane or corn for our horses, many of them dropped dead on the road that day's march. In the town we met Crittenden and Jack Doharty, with two other young fellows, who were sent from the middle grounds the day before, to spy and watch our motions. Crittenden and one Indian was killed; Doharty and the other was taken, who told us that the Indians had removed with their provisions into the mountains as soon as they heard the Indians with the flag was killed, which appeared to be the case. I told him we had come a great ways to meet their warriors; that I had heard that they wanted much to meet us in that country. He said they were collecting their men to fight us, and that he expected them there that night, but, as the day had been very bad, perhaps they would not come till next day. The next morning I sent out parties with the prisoners to search for corn, and in the whole day found but about thirty bushels. The excessive snows and rains occasioned the loss of the most of our little provisions we had with us. The greatest part of the men were then entirely out. I called a council of the officers; who were unanimous of opinion that it was not possible to proceed any further, as there was no prospect of getting any corn in the Indian towns, and could get no intelligence from the over-mountain men. We staid there two days in that neighborhood, but could not find more than forty bushels of corn and four small beeves, and through absolute necessity we were obliged to return. The officers and men that were out underwent the hardships and fatigues, and done their duty with more cheerfulness and less complaint or murmuring, than I ever saw amongst militia. Though I fear that this important expedition for our frontiers has not been as successful as I could have wished, through the inattention, neglect, or, I fear, the lukewarmness of some of the field officers of the different regiments in this State."

Major John Cunningham, who commanded the Georgians in this expedition, speaks of it "as the most fatiguing expedition I ever had. The weather was so desperate that we were all nigh perishing:" he attributes its failure to the "North Carolina men not meeting agreeably to their repeated promises, and the badness of the weather."

The failure of this well-laid plan reacted with disastrous effect on the people of Wilkes County. They were left in a perishing condition. Over half of them had not a grain of corn, and not the least hope of a supply, and were obliged to live on roots and such fruits as the woods afforded. In addition to this, they were threatened by the Indians and Tories with a retaliating visit, with scarcely a hope of sustaining a contest against such fearful odds.

A week after the defeat of Brown, on the Ogeechee road, Sir James Wright received letters from his Majesty's Secretary of State, inclosing copies of the proceedings of Parliament on the 27th February, 1782, and also his Majesty's answer to this address of the Commons. These Sir James inclosed the next day to General Wayne, expressing his determination to "observe such conduct in *every respect* as may best promote a speedy and happy reconciliation and peace between Great Britain and America;" and he proposed, "as the most effectual means for bringing about that desirable object," "a cessation of arms and hostilities for such time as shall be agreed upon."

This proposition Wayne referred to his commander, General Green, who, of course, referred it to Congress. It was well for Wayne that he did not enter into the proposed terms, for a body of three hundred Indians, under Guristersigo, was at that very time on its march to join General Alured Clark at Savannah, and would augment his force to a dangerous extent. The Indians, which had hitherto been captured by General Wayne, had been returned to their tribes with Mr. Cornell, the interpreter, with friendly talks and kind treatment. This, to a great extent, influenced the mass of the Indians towards pacific measures; but this band, under Guristersigo, having long before determined on aiding the British, now proceeded to carry their resolve into execution. Wayne also, so soon as he heard of their movements, took every precaution to avoid surprise in his camp at Mrs. Gibbons, on the Ogeechee road. But on the night of the 24th they succeeded, by the most stealthy manœuvres and cautious approaches, in gaining undiscovered the rear of Wayne's encampment, and their startling war-whoop was the first notice the army had of their approach. The rear guard, finding the enemy in their midst, retreated, and formed under cover of some of the plantation houses. While the Indians took possession of his field pieces, and, in their futile attempt to turn these upon the Americans, they lost so much time that it gave opportunity for Wayne to rally and form his men and issue his orders, which he did with a promptness and decision that at once banished fear and inspired courage. As Wayne led on his men his horse was shot under him, but, putting himself at the head of Captain Parker's infantry, he ordered his troops to advance with charged bayonets; and his orders were so well executed that the artillery was soon recovered and the enemy fled, leaving their chief, his white guides, and seventeen of their warriors dead on the field. One hundred and seventeen pack-horses, loaded with peltry, were also left on the ground. The pursuit was not long kept up. About thirty Indians were ascertained to have been killed, though many wounded were probably borne off by their friends. No prisoners were taken, for such was the indignation of the soldiers, at the merciless scalping of some of their wounded comrades, that no quarter was given; and twelve, who were captured in the woods, were shot as examples by General Wayne. The American loss was small, four killed and twelve wounded. Wayne received much praise for his coolness and firmness on this trying occasion; and, indeed, but for this promptitude and self-possession, the massacre of Paoli, in 1777, would have been re-enacted, to his own infamy and destruction.

Preparations were now made for bringing the war to a close; and negotiations were going on from the 5th of June, between Sir James Wright and Governor Martin on the one hand, and the British merchants and General Wayne, through Major Hale, on the other, with respect to the property, protection, &c., of the residents in Savannah. These terminating in a manner more satisfactory to the British than they dared to hope, a day was appointed for the formal delivery of the town into the hands of the Americans. That day was the 11th of July, 1782, and by 2 o'clock in the afternoon the last of the English troops had embarked on board the ships in the river, and at 4 P.M. General Wayne issued the following order:—

"HEADQUARTERS, SAVANNAH, 11th July, 1782.

"The light infantry company under Captain Parker to take post in the centre work in front of the town, placing sentries at the respective gateways and sally-ports, to prevent any person or persons going or entering the lines without written permits, until further orders.

"No insults or depredations to be committed upon the persons or property of the inhabitants on any pretext whatever; the civil authority only will take cognizance of the criminals or defaulters belonging to the State, if any there be. The merchants and traders are immediately to make out an exact and true invoice of all goods, wares, or merchandise of every species, dry, wet, or hard, respectively belonging to them, or in their possession, with the original invoices, to the Commissary, who will select such articles as may be necessary for the army and for the public uses of the State, for which a reasonable profit will be allowed; no goods or merchandise of any kind whatever to be removed, secreted, sold, or disposed of, until the public and army are first served, which will be as soon as possible after the receipt of the invoices, &c.

"N. B. Orders will be left with Captain Parker for the immediate admission of the Honorable Executive Council and the Honorable members of the Legislature, with their officers and attendants."

That evening the troops paraded before the lines of Savannah; and Colonel James Jackson, who, "in consideration of his severe and fatiguing service in the advance," had been selected by General Wayne to receive the formal surrender of the town, advanced to the principal gate, where a committee of British officers stood in waiting, and received at their hands the keys of the metropolis of Georgia. The troops then marched into the town, which for three years and a-half had been in the possession of the enemy, and Georgia was once more free and independent.

Wayne received orders to leave Lieutenant-Colonel Jackson's corps and Major Habersham's new recruits in charge of Savannah, and then, with the rest of his troops, to join General Green, encamped on Ashly River in South Carolina. While the evacuation of Savannah, as the first formal and voluntary cession of British to American power, was hailed with joy as an earnest of the disposition of the ministry to comply with the prevailing desire for peace, though no articles or treaty had been signed; yet the manner in which the evacuation was conducted, reflected disgrace on the authorities who permitted such gross disorders. Many of the most notorious Loyalists in the State, whose hands and hearts had been stained with fraternal blood, who had instigated and witnessed the cruelties of their savage allies, were gathered there, and in their anxiety to secure themselves, they laid hands on everything that they could possibly command. All movable property that could be secured was taken away; and five thousand negroes, from three-fourths to seven-eighths of all in Georgia, and many of them plundered from their republican owners, were carried off in the general embarkation. The State was drained of everything that the enemy could avail themselves of, and was left in a crippled and dismantled condition.

BOOK FIFTH.

GEORGIA AN INDEPENDENT STATE.

CHAPTER I.

ESTABLISHMENT OF STATE GOVERNMENT.

HITHERTO we have been chiefly occupied by narrating the military transactions in Georgia, and have alluded to civil affairs mostly to illustrate the condition of things under which the events recorded occurred.

In order to obtain a somewhat connected view of the civil condition of Georgia during this period, when two independent governments, one royal and the other republican, at times exercised jurisdiction in the same province, it will be necessary, in some instances, to state anew facts which have been already related, to avoid the necessity of continually referring the reader to former Chapters, or of making unpleasant breaks in the history.

The first effective organization of the friends of liberty in the province, took place among the deputies from several parishes, who met in Savannah, on the

18th January, 1775, and formed what has been called "A Provincial Congress."

Guided by the action of the other colonies, a "Council of Safety" was created, on the 22d June, 1775, to whom was confided the general direction of the measures proper to be pursued in carrying out resistance to the tyrannical designs of the King and Parliament. William Ewen was the first President of this Council of Safety, and Seth John Cuthbert was the Secretary.

On the 4th July, the Provincial Congress (now properly called such, as every parish and district was represented) met in Savannah, and elected as its presiding officer, Archibald Bulloch. This Congress conferred upon the "Council of Safety," "full power upon every emergency during the recess of Congress." This latter body, which was fully organized on the 11th December, when George Walton was elected its President, and Edward Langworthy its Secretary, assumed now the functions of government—levied troops, commissioned officers, bought supplies, and did whatever else was needed in the peculiar circumstances of the times.

These movements, however, were confessedly imperfect; yet were patiently endured, with their many evils, until a better machinery of government could be constructed, and set in motion. Yet the patriots were not prepared to establish a new and permanent constitution, because it was yet undecided what measures would be ultimately pursued by the Continental Congress. Feeling, however, the need of some broader basis of action, the Provincial Congress, on the 15th April, 1776, adopted the following preamble and resolution, as the groundwork of a more stable and formal government:—

"Whereas, the unwise and iniquitous system of administration obstinately persisted in by the British Parliament and Ministry against the good people of America, hath at length driven the latter to take up arms, as their last resource, for the preservation of their rights and liberties, which God and the Constitution gave them:

"And whereas an armed force, with hostile intentions against the people of this province, having lately arrived at Cockspur, his Excellency Sir James Wright, Baronet, the King's Governor of Georgia, in aid of the views of administration, and with a design to add to those inconveniences which necessarily flow from a state of confusion, suddenly and unexpectedly withdrew himself from his government, carrying off the great seal of the province with him:

"And whereas, in consequence of this and other events, doubts have arisen with the several magistrates how far they are authorized to act under their former appointments, and the greatest part of them have absolutely refused to do so, whereby all judicial powers are become totally suspended, to the great danger of persons and property:

"And whereas, before any general system or form of government can be concluded upon, it is necessary that application be made to the Continental Congress for their advice and directions upon the same; but, nevertheless, in the present state of things, it is indispensably requisite that some temporary expedient be fallen upon to curb the lawless and protect the peaceable:

"This Congress, therefore, as the representatives of the people, with whom all power originates, and for whose benefit all government is intended, deeply impressed with a sense of duty to their constituents, of love to their country, and inviolable attachment to the liberties of America, and seeing how much it will tend to the advantage of each to preserve rules, justice, and order—do take upon them, for the present, and until the further order of the Continental Congress, or of this or any future Provincial Congress, to declare, and they accordingly do declare, order, and direct, that the following Rules and Regulations be adopted in this province—that is to say :—

"1st. That there shall be a President and Commander-in-chief appointed by ballot, in this Congress, for six months, or during the time above specified.

"2d. That there shall, in like manner and for the like time, be also a Council of Safety, consisting of thirteen persons (besides the five delegates to the General Congress), appointed to act in the nature of a Privy Council to the said President or Commander-in-chief.

"3d. That the President shall be invested with all the executive powers of government, not inconsistent with what is hereafter mentioned; but shall be bound to consult and follow the advice of the said Council, in all cases whatsoever; and any seven of the said Council shall be a quorum for the purpose of advising.

"4th. That all the laws, whether common or statute, and the Acts of Assembly which have formerly been acknowledged to be of force in this province, and which do not interfere with the proceedings of the Continental or our Provincial Congresses, and also all and singular the resolves and recommendations of the said Continental and Provincial Congresses, shall be of full force, validity, and effect, until otherwise ordered.

"5th. That there shall be a Chief Justice and two Assistant Judges, an Attorney-General, a Provost-Marshal, and Clerk of the Court of Sessions, appointed by ballot, to serve during the pleasure of the Congress. The Court of Sessions, or Oyer and Terminer, shall be opened and held on the second Tuesday in June and December, and the former rules and method of proceeding, as nearly as may be, shall be observed in regard to summoning of juries, and all other cases whatsoever.

"6th. That the President or Commander-in-chief, with the advice of the Council as before mentioned, shall appoint magistrates to act, during pleasure, in the several parishes throughout this province; and such magistrates shall conform themselves as nearly as may be to the old establishment, form, and methods of proceeding.

"7th. That all legislative powers shall be reserved to the Congress; and no person who holds any place of profit, civil or military, shall be eligible as a member either of the Congress or Council of Safety.

"8th. That the following sums shall be allowed as salaries to the respective officers, for and during the time they shall serve, over and besides all such perquisites and fees as have been formerly annexed to the said officers respectively."

Pursuant to the provisions of this scheme, Archibald Bulloch was elected President and Commander-in-chief of Georgia; John Glen, Chief Justice; William Stephens, Attorney-General; and James Jackson, Clerk of Court.

The "Council of Safety," on the 1st of May, presented to the new President the following address:—

"*To His Excellency Archibald Bulloch, Esquire, President and Commander-in-chief of the Province of Georgia: The Address of the Council of Safety for the said Province.*

"May it please your Excellency:

"The long session of the late Congress, together with the season of the year, called particularly for a speedy recess; and the House having adjourned while you were out of town, it becomes more particularly necessary for us to address your Excellency. All, therefore, with unfeigned confidence and regard, beg leave to congratulate, not only your Excellency on your appointment to, but your country on your acceptance of, the supreme command in this province.

"It would be needless and tedious to recount the various and yet multiplying oppressions which have driven the people of this province to erect that government which they have called upon you to see executed; suffice it, then, to declare, that it was only an alternative of anarchy and misery, and, by consequence, the effect of dire necessity. Your Excellency will know that it was the endeavor of the Congress to stop every avenue of vice and oppression, lest the infant virtue of a still more infant province might in time rankle into corruption; and, we doubt not that, by your Excellency's exertions, all the resolutions made or adopted by Congress will be enforced with firmness, without any regard to any individual, or any set of men; for no government can be said to be established while any part of the community refuses submission to its authority. In the discharge of this arduous and important task, your Excellency may rely on our constant and best endeavors to assist and support you."

To this earnest and confiding address President Bulloch returned the following reply :—

"*To the Honorable the Members of the Council of Safety of the Province of Georgia:*

"Honorable Gentlemen: I am much obliged to you for your kind expressions of congratulation of my appointment to the supreme command of this colony. When I reflect from whence the appointment is derived—that of the free and uncorrupt suffrages of my fellow-citizens, it cannot fail to stimulate me to the most vigorous exertions in the discharge of the important duties to which I am called by our Provincial Congress. While I have the advice and assistance of gentlemen of known integrity and abilities, I doubt not but I shall be enabled to enforce and carry into execution every resolve and law of Congress. And, as far as lies with me, my country may depend I will, with a becoming firmness, and the greatest impartiality, always endeavor to cause justice in mercy to be executed.

"ARCHIBALD BULLOCH."

The Council of Safety still continued to exercise its several functions, his Excellency being the President of the body.

The Declaration of Independence, which had been published in Savannah with impressive ceremonies, put a new aspect on political affairs. It was now no longer a contest of colonies acknowledging fealty to the English Crown, seeking redress of grievances from an obstinate King and a servile Parliament; but a struggle of States for independence. Allegiance to Britain was cast off; the governments which had so long been established in the thirteen colonies were overturned; and, with them, went down the courts of law, and all the instrumentalities by and through which government had been administered. The old civil and political superstructures were taken down, and new establishments were to be reared in their places. To meet the exigency arising from this new attitude of the Continental Congress, in declaring the American Colonies free and independent, President Bulloch issued a proclamation, based on a recommendation of the General Congress, ordering "the several parishes and districts within this State to proceed to the election of delegates between the 1st and 10th days of September next, to form and sit in convention; and the delegates so elected are directed to convene at Savannah on the first Tuesday in October following, when business of the highest consequence to the government and welfare of the State will be opened for their consideration." In a circular letter addressed to the several parishes, he enjoined upon the people "the necessity of making choice of upright and good men to represent them in the ensuing convention — men whose actions had proved their friendship to the cause of freedom, and whose depth of political judgment qualified them to frame a constitution for the future government of the country."

The Deputies met in convention at the time appointed, and took up the important subject before them. Much other business, however, pressed upon them, consequent on putting the State in a proper posture of defence; but after one or two adjournments they accomplished their work, and on the 5th of February, 1777, ratified in convention the first Constitution of the State of Georgia.

This instrument, after reciting in its preamble the causes which led to its origin, was divided into sixty-three articles, covering the whole ground of government in its legislative, executive, and judiciary departments. The second article declared what should be the composition of the Legislature, to wit: a House of Assembly and an Executive Council; and also directed how the Governor and this Executive Council should be elected. The fifth article apportioned the representatives to the several counties. The sixth stated their qualifications. The seventh, the power of the Assembly. The ninth, tenth, eleventh, twelfth, thirteenth, fourteenth, the qualifications and duties of electors. The fifteenth contained the representative's oath. The sixteenth and seventeenth declared who should and who should not, have seats in the Legislature. The articles from the nineteenth to the twenty-fourth, inclusive, set forth the duties of the Governor. Those from the twenty-fifth to the thirtieth, inclusive, stated what were the duties of the Executive Council. The articles from the thirty-sixth to the forty-eighth, were taken up in defining the powers of the Judiciary. The fifty-fourth required the erection of a school, at the public expense, in each county. The fifty-sixth established religious toleration. The sixtieth, the fundamental principle of the habeas corpus. The sixty-first, the inviolate freedom of the press and trial by jury. The sixty-second, the ineligibility of clergymen to seats in the Legislature; and the sixty-third provided, with great caution, for any needed revision of the Constitution. It was a striking indication of the grateful feeling of Georgians for those who had so warmly defended the cause of America in the British Parliament, that the fourth article of this Constitution changed the designation of the old parishes by striking out their former names and substituting therefor, with one exception, the names of the English apologists for America. Thus the old parish of Christ Church, in which was Savannah and a part of the parish of St. Philip, were set off as a new county and called CHATHAM, in honor of the elder Pitt, the venerable Earl of Chatham. The parishes of St. David and St. Patrick, were erected into one county and called GLYNN, after the eminent counsellor of that name. The parishes of St. Matthew and the upper part of St. Philip, were to be known by the name of EFFINGHAM, after Lord Effingham, who had refused to employ his sword against the Americans, and resigned the Colonelcy of the 22d Regiment rather than serve with it in the war of the Revolution. To the parish of St. Paul, in which Augusta was situated, was given the name of RICHMOND, in honor of the Duke of Richmond, who had boldly advocated the cause of America in the House of Lords. The parish of St. George was named BURKE, after that great commoner and wise statesman. The parishes of St. John, St. Andrew, and St. James, were to form one county under the name LIBERTY: a distinction awarded to the parish of St. John for its early and steady devotion to the cause of freedom. The parishes of St. Thomas and St. Mary, were to constitute another county by the name of CAMDEN, after the distinguished Lord Chancellor of England, and firm friend of America. The ceded lands north of the Ogeechee was constituted a county, taking the name of WILKS, the name of that political demagogue who payed his court to liberty only that he might gain notoriety and wealth.

The great seal of the State, adopted by this Convention, had on one side a scroll, whereon was engraved, "The Constitution of the State of Georgia," and the motto, "*Pro bono publico;*" on the other side, an elegant house, and other buildings; fields of corn, and meadows covered with sheep and cattle; a river running through the same, with a ship under full sail; and the motto, "*Deus nobis hæc otia fecit.*"

To carry this Constitution into effect, was now an important object with the President and Council of Safety. But it had scarcely been signed, before Archibald Bulloch died; and on the 4th March, 1777, the Council of Safety elected Button Gwinnett President and Commander-in-chief, until such time as, by the Constitution, a Governor shall be appointed. In the exercise of his gubernatorial powers, he issued a proclamation requiring the parishes to elect delegates to a Legislature, to convene in Savannah on the first Tuesday in May.

The Legislature met at the time and place designated; and at once, after the formalities of opening, proceeded to elect a Governor and Executive Council: when John Adam Treutlen was chosen Governor; and John Houstoun, Thomas Chisholm, William Holzindorf, William Few, John Coleman, William Peacock, John Walton, Arthur Fort, John Fulton, John Jones, and Benjamin Andrews, were chosen as the first Executive Council. Of this body, Benjamin Andrews was elected President, and Samuel Stirk, Clerk. The books and papers of the late Council of Safety were, by a resolution of the Assembly, confided to them, and thenceforth the Council of Safety ceased to exist.

In the latter part of 1776, a resolution was introduced into the General Assembly of South Carolina, and unanimously passed, "that a union between the two States of South Carolina and Georgia would tend effectually to promote their strength, wealth, and dignity, and to secure their liberty, independence, and safety." It was also resolved to send Commissioners to Georgia, to treat with the Legislature upon this matter; and, among others, William Henry Drayton was appointed.

Mr. Drayton reached Savannah in the beginning of January, 1777; but soon found that "every gentleman in public office, with whom he conversed, was strongly against a union." A few others, however, approved the measure. Being honored with an invitation to appear before the Convention, then in session, he stated to that body, in an address of an hour's length, the various reasons which should lead them to seek a union with South Carolina, and the many benefits which would accrue to Georgia thereby. The state of affairs in Georgia, as he painted them, was certainly very highly colored; and some of his prognostications read quite strangely alongside the facts of actual history. Among other things, he declared, "in a state of separation, in all probability, Savannah will be ruined, because it will be our interest to preserve our trade to our own people. A town will rise on the

Carolina side of the Savannah River, which will be sure to preserve our half of the trade of that river, and, by being wisely supported, may draw to it the other half, also."

His arguments failed to produce the desired response; the overtures were rejected, as the Convention, that same afternoon, delivered to Mr. Drayton their answer, declining the proposition.

Button Gwinnett was particularly opposed to this measure, and labored assiduously to check it. After his death, a new plan of action was adopted by the people of South Carolina, who circulated petitions tending to cast odium on the Executive of Georgia; magnifying the grievances, and exciting distrust in the people; and urged them to take some action towards a union of the two most southern States, as the best means of defence and safety. Finding these papers freely circulated, and calculated to be detrimental to the welfare of the State, the Executive Council, on the 14th July, requested Governor Treutlen "to issue a proclamation, offering a reward of one hundred pounds to any person or persons who will apprehend William Henry Drayton and sundry persons," engaged in this project. The next day, therefore, the Governor issued his proclamation to that effect; and it was freely distributed, to counteract the pernicious effect of the Carolina papers.

To this proclamation Mr. Drayton returned a most discourteous and defiant reply. His aim seemed to be to cast ridicule on the Governor and his advisers, of whom he says: "I am inclined to think you are concealed Tories, or their tools, who have clambered up, or have been put into office, in order to *burlesque* government (and I never saw a more extravagant burlesque than you exhibit), that the people might be sick of an American administration, and strive to return under the British dominion, merely for the sake of endeavoring to procure something like law and order. I respect the people of Georgia; but, most *wise* rulers, kissing your hands, I cannot but laugh at some folks. Can you guess who they are?"

Such an insolent communication evinced the *animus* of the men who moved in this matter, and excited general disgust.

These prompt measures of Governor Treutlen put a stop to the efforts of those who sought to reduce Georgia to a state of vassalage to South Carolina; and thenceforward, under difficulties indeed of the most trying kind, her people were permitted to carry on the government of their own affairs, and to place themselves, as an independent State, on the floor of the Continental Congress, on a level with the other colonies.

When the Assembly met in Savannah, 17th January, 1778, John Houstoun, son of Sir Patrick Houstoun, and one of the foremost and most earnest friends of liberty, was, on the 10th instant, elected Governor; John Glen, Chief Justice; William Stephens, Attorney-General; William O'Brien and Nehemiah Wade, Joint Treasurers; James Maxwell, Secretary; and Thomas Chisholm, Surveyor-General. James Jones was elected Collector for the port of Savannah; David Rees, Collector for the port of Sunbury; and Ambrose Wright, Commissary-General of the State, and Superintendent of Public Buildings in the County of Chatham. Registers of Probate for each of the counties, and other minor officers, were also elected.

Thus, gradually, did the State seem to be consolidating itself into a compact government, under judicious leaders, when the threatening aspect of affairs caused the Executive Council to take a step, which showed at once the greatness of the emergency, and the confidence which was reposed in the Chief Magistrate of the State.

At a meeting of the Executive Council, April 16, 1778, to consider and act upon the condition of things, both military and civil, that body adopted the bold and, in most instances, dangerous policy, of investing one man with almost dictatorial powers. In a series of preambles and resolutions spread upon their minutes, they declare, that "the situation of this State is truly alarming, and, without the most spirited and vigorous exertions, the machinations of our enemies threaten to succeed;" that "in such times of danger, it may happen that everything may depend upon instantaneous measures being embraced, which cannot be done should the Governor wait for calling a Council;" and then, having expressed their opinion as to the constitutionality of the proposed measure, they proceed: "The Council, therefore, impressed with a sense of the calamitous situation of this State, and apprehending it as an unavoidable expedient, do request that his honor, the Governor, will be pleased to take upon himself to act in such manner as to him shall seem most eligible; and to exercise all the executive powers of government appertaining to the militia, or the defence of the State, against the present danger which threatens it, or in annoyance of the enemy, independent of the Executive Council, and without calling, consulting, or advising with them, unless when and where he shall find it convenient, and shall choose to do so. And they pledge themselves to support and uphold him in so doing, and to adopt as their own the measures which he shall embrace; and that this shall continue during the present emergency, or until the honorable House of Assembly shall make an order or give their opinion to the contrary."

The Governor, having considered this requisition, answered, that "he was exceedingly unwilling to do any act without the approbation of the Council; but that, as he found by experience during the present alarm, the impossibility of at all times getting them together when too much, perhaps, depended upon a minute; and further, that as the Council had given it as their opinion that the proceeding was justifiable under the Constitution, and as the meeting of the Assembly was so near at hand, and alarms and dangers seemed to thicken on all sides, he agreed to act in the manner the Council requested, during the present emergency, or until the honorable House of Assembly shall make an order, or give their opinion to the contrary."

The practical working of this grant of power to the Executive, was productive of evil, causing disputes with Continental officers as to military rank; and was one of the causes which led to a failure of the expedition on the southern seaboard, to check the Indians and Tories of Florida in their marauding incursions into Georgia.

When the town of Savannah was captured, in December, 1778, the Executive Council removed the seat of government to Augusta. At this place, the members of the Council met at the house of Matthew

Hobson, to choose a President. As, however, no Governor had been elected by the Assembly, "the Convention of the representatives of the State of Georgia, in Assembly met," by a resolution, passed on the 9th, empowered "the members chosen for a Council, or the majority thereof," "to act as a committee to recommend everything they may think expedient, in the place of a Council for this State, until the Convention meet again, to clothe them with power to act as an Executive Council."

Under these instructions, this committee acted until the time came for the next meeting of the Assembly in Augusta. At the designated period, however, a quorum of members did not convene, owing to the disturbed state of the province, and the occupancy of the lower counties by the British troops and government.

The twenty-five members who did meet at this time, though not able to organize the House, and carry on in full the operations of government, felt most deeply the need of certainty and stability, as it respects authority and law; and the great evils which resulted from the absence of an executive head and legislative direction. Impressed with these sentiments, they drew up and subscribed the following remarkable paper:—

"State of Georgia, Richmond County.

"Whereas, from the invasion of the British forces in this State, great evils have arisen, and still exist, to disturb the civil government of the said State, and which, in a great measure, have prevented the Constitution of the land from being carried into such full effect as to answer the purposes of government therein pointed out. And whereas, it becomes incumbent and indispensably necessary at this juncture to adopt such temporary mode as may be most conducive to the welfare, happiness, and security of the rights and privileges of the good people of the said State, and the maintainance and existence of legal and effective authority in the same, as far as the exigence of affairs requires, until a time of less disquiet shall happen, and the Constitution take its regular course; to the end, therefore, that government may prevail, and be acknowledged to prevent, as far as may be, anarchy and confusion from continuing among us, and fully to support the laws of the land derived under the Constitution thereof,

"We, therefore, the representatives of the people of the counties of Wilkes, Richmond, Burke, Effingham, Chatham, Liberty, Glynn, Camden, and other freemen of the State, having convened and met in the county of Richmond, in the State aforesaid, for the purposes of considering the present disturbed situation of the State, and for applying, as far as in our power, some remedy thereto, and having maturely and seriously considered the same, do recommend that the following persons be appointed by the good people of this State to exercise the supreme authority thereof; who shall, before they enter on the execution of their office, take the following oath, viz., I, A. B., elected one of the Supreme Executive Council of the State of Georgia, do solemnly swear that I will, during the term of my appointment, to the best of my skill and judgment, execute the said office faithfully and conscientiously without favor, affection, or partiality; that I will, to the utmost of my power, support, maintain, and defend the State of Georgia, and use my utmost endeavors to support the people thereof in the secure enjoyment of their just rights and privileges; and that I will, to the best of my judgment, execute justice and mercy in all judgments: so help me God.

"And we, and each of us, on our parts, as free citizens of the State of Georgia aforesaid, do for ourselves nominate, authorize, empower, and require you, John Wereat, Joseph Clay, Joseph Habersham, Humphrey Wells, William Few, John Dooley, Seth John Cuthbert, William Gibbons, Sen., and Myrick Davies, Esqr's, or a majority of you, to act as the Executive or Supreme Council of this State; and to execute, from Tuesday, the twenty-seventh instant, to the first Tuesday in January next, unless sooner revoked by a majority of the freemen of this State, every such power as you, the said John Wereat, Joseph Clay, Joseph Habersham, Humphrey Wells, William Few, John Dooley, Seth John Cuthbert, William Gibbons, Sen., and Myrick Davies, Esqr's, or a majority of you, shall deem necessary for the safety and defence of the State and the good citizens thereof: taking care in all your proceedings to keep as near the spirit and meaning of the Constitution of the said State as may be. And you, the said John Wereat, Joseph Clay, Joseph Habersham, Humphrey Wells, William Few, John Dooley, Seth John Cuthbert, William Gibbons, Sen., and Myrick Davies, Esqr's, or a majority of you, hereby have full power and authority, and are authorized, empowered, and required, to elect fit and discrete persons to represent this State in Congress, and to instruct the delegates so chosen in which matters and things as will tend to the interest of this State in particular, and the United States of America in general.

"The said delegates taking care from time to time to transmit to you, the said Council, or other authority of the State for the time being, an account of their proceedings in Congress aforesaid; to regulate the public treasury of the said State, to borrow or otherwise negotiate loans for the public safety; to regulate the militia, and appoint an officer if necessary to command; to appoint, suspend, and discharge all civil officers, if it shall be found expedient; to demand an account of all expenditures of public money, and to regulate the same, and, where necessary, order payments of money; to adopt some mode respecting the current money of this State, and for sinking the same; to direct and commissionate the Chief Justice of the State, or assistant justices, or other justices of the peace, and other officers of each county, to convene courts for the trial of offences cognizable by the laws of the land, in such place or places as you shall think fit: always taking care that trial by jury be preserved inviolate, and that the proceedings had before such courts be in a summary way, so that offenders be brought to a speedy trial, and justice be amply done, as well to the State as to the individuals. You, or a majority of you, the said Council, have full power, and hereby are requested on conviction of offenders, to order punishment to be inflicted, extending to death. And when objects deserving mercy shall be made known to you, to extend that mercy and pardon the offence, remit all fines, mitigate corporal punishments, as the case may be, and as to you or a majority of you shall seem fit and necessary. And you the said Council, or a majority of you, at all times and places, when and where you shall think fit, have hereby full power and competent authority to meet, appoint your own President; settle your own rules; sit, consult, deliberate, advise, direct, and carry in execution, all and every act, special and general, hereby delegated to you, and all and every such other acts, measures, and things, as you, or a majority of you, shall find expedient and necessary for the welfare, safety, and happiness of the freemen of this State.

"And in case any of the persons, herein appointed to exercise the supreme authority as aforesaid, shall refuse to act, die, or depart this State, or shall by any other means be prevented from exercising the same, then, and in such case, you the said Council hereby chosen, or a majority of you, shall, and you are hereby authorized, empowered, and required to fill up such vacancies by choosing fit and discrete persons, or persons to act in his or their room and stead, which person or persons so chosen, is or are hereby invested with every power and authority, in as full and ample a manner, as if they had been appointed by this present instrument of writing.

"And we do hereby declare all officers, civil and military, and all persons, inhabitants of this State, subject to and amenable to your authority, and will ratify and confirm whatever you may do for or concerning the public weal, according to the best of your judgment, knowledge, and ability; and further we do hereby promise you our support, protection, and countenance.

"In witness whereof, we have hereunto set our hands, this twenty-fourth day of July, in the year of our Lord 1779."

The Supreme Executive Council, thus clothed with plenary powers, temporarily organized on Saturday, the 24th July, 1779, by the choice of Seth John Cuthbert, as President *pro tempore;* and fully organized on the 6th August, by electing unanimously, John Wereat, President, who then, together with the other members of the Council, took the oath prescribed by the instrument, which created them the supreme power in Georgia.

It is evident that this whole transaction was illegal and unconstitutional. The appointing body, and the body appointed to office, both felt it to be so; and the Council, in a letter to General Lincoln, say, in reference to the delegates appointing nine members as the Council, "this we assure you they did, but conceive they had sufficient power to establish; but recommended it to the inhabitants of the State, and it has been adopted by a very large majority of them."

Such was the condition of the country at that time, that it was impossible to act under the provisions of the Constitution. A regularly formed government could not then be constructed, and the question was reduced to the dilemma, of having no form of government at all; or, acting as nearly as possible to the letter of the Constitution, and always in its spirit, to set up, by the popular voice, a provisional government, during such period as the Constitution was necessarily inoperative, by reason of the distress and bloodshed and war which filled the land.

How trying to the hearts of the people this period was, and how dark the future appeared, may be learned from a letter written by this Council, under date of August 18th, 1779, to General Lincoln.

Having stated in the beginning, the circumstances which created them the Supreme Executive Council, they remark with an earnestness and a far-sightedness truly commendable :

" A considerable part of the State having been in the immediate possession of the enemy ever since its invasion by them, those counties which have held out against them, have been constantly subject to their incursions and depredations, and, of course, the few militia thereof, much harassed with duty; but their spirits have been kept up with the idea of support from the continent and our sister State, otherwise, we apprehend, a total evacuation would long since have taken place by those who have firmness enough to sacrifice everything to the cause of America, whilst the wavering would have joined the enemy, and assisted them in their operations against Carolina.

" The arrival of the advance of General Scott's army, under Colonel Parker and Major Jamison, at a very critical juncture, has had the most salutary effect that could be expected, for it has infused new spirits into the militia, who are now all cheerfully under arms, to oppose the concerted invasions of the enemy's irregulars and Indians, who are at this time making different inroads upon us. General McIntosh has sent out a part of the Continental troops to support our militia, and we hope that for the present we shall be able to repel the enemy, and to keep them from reaping any considerable advantages from the attempts of small parties. But we presume, sir, that we need not endeavor to impress your mind with an idea of the feeble resistance we should be able to make to any serious attempt of the enemy to sujugate the upper parts of the State, even with the assistance that General McIntosh can at this time afford us. We believe that it is generally allowed, that, unless the enemy are considerably reinforced, they will not make another attempt upon Charleston; and, from a variety of circumstances, we are led to hope that they will not receive such reinforcement. Should this be the case, there can scarce remain a doubt but that they will aim at a total subjugation of Georgia this fall; for we cannot in reason suppose that they will keep a considerable body of troops immured in Savannah whilst the back country, so necessary to their quiet subsistence, as well as their future designs, remains unconquered. The large quantities of grain made in the vicinity of this place, and the numerous herds of cattle through all the upper parts of the country, must be very considerable objects with them, particularly as we know that they cannot even now get sufficient supplies of cattle without coming upwards, and then fighting for them. The frequent skirmishes of our militia with their irregulars, who are employed as drovers, evinces the truth of this observation; and should they gain the upper parts of this State, we are bold to assert that Carolina would be in a very dangerous situation. The great defection of the upper parts of that country is well known; a circumstance on which the enemy found the most sanguine hopes, and we have every reason to believe that they continually receive encouragement from these people to invade the back country. Nor could the enemy wish for a more favorable situation to be joined by them, than that by Augusta, or anywhere above it, where the river is shallow and the swamps all passable.

"Add to the circumstances already mentioned, which might induce the enemy to progress upwards in force, that of having no obstruction to their intercourse with the Indians, is a very capital one, and which will immediately be the case should they effect an entire conquest of this country; and unless they should do this, their intercourse will be very precarious and uncertain, and we shall always have it in our power to give the most considerable interruption to it. We think this point worth paying the most particular attention to, as we are informed that Indian goods are now imported at Savannah, and that the Creek Indians have had no late supply from the Floridas. Should the trade from this country with the Indians be once open and uninterrupted, the enemy will find not the least difficulty, whenever they have a mind, in bringing the savages upon the frontiers of Carolina.

"Besides our apprehensions on the above heads, we are fearful that in case the British troops should move up this way, the greatest part of the inhabitants, worn out with fruitless opposition, and actuated by the fear of losing their all, would make terms for themselves; and as the human mind is too apt to be led by a natural gradation from one step of infamy to another, we have not the least doubt of their joining the enemy against their countrymen in any other State. But even should the British commander not bend his force this way, a great many families, harassed and unsupported, would remove far northwardly (for which they are already thinking of preparing), and this dangerous migration nothing but the appearance of support can prevent.

"With minds forcibly impressed by the operation of

such powerful reasons, we beg leave, sir, to solicit you, in the most serious manner, to order General Scott, who, we understand, is on his march southwardly with the rest of his troops, immediately to this place. We cannot think that the lower parts of Carolina will be endangered by such an order; for we may reasonably presume that the enemy will never penetrate far into that part of the country while a respectable force remains in their rear, which would be the case if General Scott and his troops were in Georgia."

At the same time, the Council addressed a communication to the Governor of South Carolina, briefly reciting their grievances and distress; without representatives in Congress, without a Legislature, without money to pay the services of its soldiery, surrounded by enemies, and expecting still further subjugation; and then they ask assistance, both pecuniary and military, to enable them to maintain their stand, and not abandon Georgia entirely to the British.

Their appeals were not unheeded; and a few weeks saw the combined army of the French and Americans, under Count d'Estaing and General Lincoln, lay siege to Savannah.

The failure of the allied arms to capture this town, and the virtual defeat and withdrawal of the French and American troops, left Georgia in a worse condition than ever; and it seemed almost as if her political existence was at an end. The royal government was re-established, and Sir James Wright issued his proclamation, dated Savannah, the 26th October, 1779, appointing Friday, the 29th, as a day of public thanksgiving to Almighty God, for "His divine interposition" and "signal protection," whose superintending providence, says the Governor, "has at no period been more fully displayed, than in the late deliverance we have experienced from the united efforts of rebellion and our natural enemies." Proclamations were now issued, also, by Governor Wright and by the military commanders, offering protection to such as would lay down their arms, and live at peace under British rule. Many availed themselves of these beguiling offers, and, feeling that all was lost in Georgia, sought to make peace with the enemy, and secure life, even at the expense of liberty.

So soon as Savannah was relieved from the presence of the allied army, Sir James Wright exerted himself to re-establish the royal government, and to bring back the whole province to its former fealty to the crown. His first care was to put Savannah into a proper condition; for it had been so shattered by the destructive fire of the French and Americans, and by the wanton use of the troops within, as well as by the necessary demands of the siege, that it was in a deplorable state. The churches and public buildings had been used for depots, and hospitals, and barracks; private dwellings had been converted into mess-halls and officers' quarters; fire had laid waste some squares of buildings; others had been pulled down, to use the material in the different parts of the fortifications; others had been rendered tenantless by the battering balls; and there was scarcely a house in town which had not been made to suffer, outside or in, in consequence of crowding together so many of the inhabitants, with soldiers, seamen, and negroes, within the narrow limits of the intrenchments.

Scarcely had the town put on the aspect of order and cleanliness, before the small-pox broke out, and produced great consternation among the inhabitants and soldiers. Inoculation was at that time but little practised; and only then, after an order obtained for that purpose from the Governor's Council, who generally refused to grant the order, except the disease had already broken out in the household desiring this preventive operation.

Another serious difficulty, which the Governor had to meet with prompt and decided measures, was the number of armed negroes found in and around the town. These persons had been used as laborers in the works planned and executed by the engineer officers; and, in many cases, it was found necessary to arm them, as they worked at the entrenchments. Knowing to some extent the value of their services, they grew bold and presumptuous; and it was found no easy matter to check their insolence, and reduce them to their proper obedience and position. The petitions which were sent in to the Governor from the inhabitants of Savannah, show how great was the danger, and how unbearable the insolence of these negroes, for several months after the siege was over.

Soon after the allied army had left Georgia, the Governor desired to call a legislative Assembly; and, to this end, put several queries to his Council, on the 30th October, 1779, whether an Assembly could be called without issuing writs of election for all the parishes? how the provost-marshal should do, where the inhabitants would not meet and elect? whether an Assembly, consisting of members from parts of the parishes or districts only, will be a lawful Assembly or representation of the whole province? and whether such a partial Assembly or representation may legally proceed to the business of legislation?

The Chief Justice (Anthony Stokes) and the Attorney-General (James Robertson), to whom these queries were referred, reported to Council, on the 15th November, and decided that "writs of election ought to be issued, in the usual form, for all the parishes and districts that sent members to the last Assembly;" "and if there should be any parish or district without freeholders qualified to elect, or if through the invasion or vicinity of the rebels, the provost-marshal cannot venture to proceed to an election, then he must return such special matter along with the writs of election, and verify it by affidavits. Such a Commons' House of Assembly, convened with the precautions above mentioned, we conceive would be a lawful representation of the whole province."

While this report was approved by the Governor and Council; Sir James and the Council also thought it best to postpone calling an Assembly, and it was not until the following March (1780), that writs were issued for the election of members, returnable on the 5th May.

The following persons were returned to the Council as members of the Commons' House of Assembly.

For the town and district of Savannah: Samuel Farley, James Mossman, John Simpson, and James Robertson.

Little Ogeechee in Christ Church Parish: William Jones.

Great Ogeechee and St. Philip's Parish: James Butler, Thomas Goldsmith, and Simon Monro.

Midway and St. John's: John Irvine, Joseph Fox.

Goshorn and Abercorn in St. Matthew's: Samuel Douglass.

Ebenezer and St. Matthew's: Alexander Wright, Basil Cowper, Nathaniel Hall.

Acton, Christ Church Parish: David Zubly.

Vernonburg, Christ Church Parish: Basil Cowper.

Wilmington, Tybee, &c.: Philip Yonge.

St. Andrew's: Robert Baillie and James Spalding.

Frederica and St. James: William Panton.

St. David's: Samuel Douglass.

St. Patrick's: Robert Porteous.

St. Thomas: Simon Paterson.

St. Mary's: William Ross.

Halifax and St. George's: Alexander Wylly and John Henderson.

On the 9th of May, only fifteen members had qualified, and as the constitutional quorum had been fixed by previous Assemblies at eighteen members, with the Speaker, the Governor was at some loss what to do; but, with the Council, finally decided, "that from the necessity of the thing, they should be taken as a House and proceed to business." Accordingly, the members present organized themselves into a Commons' House of Assembly; elected their Speaker; presented him to the Governor, who approved their choice; and then received from the Governor his speech, and returned the usual replies.

The two principal bills passed by this Royal Assembly, were "An act to attaint of high treason the several persons hereinafter named, who are either absent from this province, or in that part of it which is still in rebellion against his Majesty, and to vest their real and personal estate in his Majesty, &c.;" and a bill entitled, "An Act to disqualify and render incapable the several persons hereinafter named, of holding, or exercising, any office of trust, honor, or profit, in the province of Georgia."

The Governor, with the usual formalities, prorogued the Assembly on the 10th of July, to the 1st November following.

When Augusta was besieged by the Americans, and Colonel Brown and his troops reduced to great extremities, Sir James, by advice of his Council, issued a proclamation on the 21st September, calling a meeting of the Assembly for Monday, the 25th of the same month. In his address to the members on the morning of Wednesday, the 27th, he expressed his regret at being obliged to call them together so soon, "but the exigency of the times requires it."

After stating some of the circumstances "of the late attack on the English troops by a number of rebels from South Carolina, joined by others in the ceded lands," thus showing "clearly, that the spirit and flame of rebellion is not over, and that rigorous measures are still necessary to crush the rebellion in the back part of this province," he urges upon the Assembly: 1. The passage of an act "to compel all persons within such a distance from this town and Augusta as you may judge convenient, forthwith to give in an account of all their male slaves from sixteen years of age to sixty; and that they shall be obliged, when called upon, to send immediately such a proportion of negroes as may be deemed necessary, with proper tools, and for such time as the said works may be found to require their labor."

2. To inquire "whether all the inhabitants in the town should not be obliged to give in an account of, and to send such male slaves as they have in town within the ages as aforesaid, or pay for the same; and whether such male inhabitants in the town who have no hands liable to work, should not be compelled to work themselves or serve as overseer."

3. To rest authority "somewhere" to impress horses, carts, or teams for the public works.

4. To revise the militia laws, so as to make them more stringent in their provisions, and more certain in their operation; and to inquire whether it may be proper at the present time to embody and organize a negro corps as part of the militia of the province?

But little was done by this Assembly; harmony did not prevail in its deliberations; differences continually rose between the upper and lower houses; members absented themselves and were fined, placed under arrest, and reprimanded by the Speaker at the bar of the House; several adjournments over long intervals took place; and the Governor at last, on the 15th November, 1780, adjourned the Commons' House of Assembly to the 17th of January, 1781. Before that day came, at the urgent request of some of the members of the House, and the merchants and traders, Sir James called the Assembly together again on the 11th December, 1780, to "recommend to their serious consideration the present defenceless state of the province, particularly the inlets and sea islands." To remedy this, it was proposed to build a galley from seventy to eighty feet keel, with from fifteen to twenty oars on a side; to carry a six-pounder in the bow, and four two-pounders, twelve swivels and twenty muskets, and fifty whites and ten refugee negroes. But it was found that the cost of such a galley, its equipment, and support, would be beyond the means at command, and the Assembly adjourned, without any definite action in the matter.

All subsequent attempts at royal legislation in Georgia were to little purpose. The British found themselves gradually driven into a smaller compass, as the lines of the so-called "rebels" were pushed on towards Savannah. The headquarters of the American army were shortly after established at Ebenezer, and scarcely anything was left to the Governor but the town of Savannah, which then contained 240 houses and 750 white inhabitants, exclusive of officers and soldiers under General Alured Clarke; and this town, says one of the British officers, "was so closely blockaded by the rebel army, that it was dangerous to go without our lines." This state of things continued until the 14th June, 1782, when orders were received at Savannah, by Sir James Wright, for the evacuation of the province, and measures were accordingly taken to comply with the requisition.

It was during the period when British rule was temporarily re-established and the hopes of the patriots were well-nigh extinct, that the smothered disaffection which had been at first excited in two or three minds, in reference to the manner in which the Executive Council had been constituted, and to the extraordinary powers which had been conferred upon it by an irresponsible meeting of citizens, gathered force, and burst out in a movement which threatened for a time to rend asunder the little liberty that was yet left in Georgia.

George Walton, who had been taken prisoner when

Savannah was captured, in 1778, and had been exchanged after the siege, in 1779; in conjunction with Richard Howley, George Wells, and a few others, spared no pains to spread discontent towards the existing government; they represented some of the members of the Council as favorable to the Tories, and unqualifiedly condemned the whole body "and all their proceedings as illegal, unconstitutional, and dangerous to the liberties of the State." Accordingly, these men called upon the people to choose delegates to an Assembly, to be convened in Augusta, in November, 1779; notwithstanding the Executive Council had issued their writs of election for deputies to the Assembly, as provided for by the Constitution of 1777. The friends of Walton met in Augusta; and, on the 4th November, chose him Governor, for the short remainder of the year; and also a delegate to Congress. The so-called Assembly also appointed a body of councillors, so that there were two Executive Councils exercising authority at the same time, yet neither of them was constitutional, and no act of either was strictly legal. The consequence was, that this aspect of affairs "occasioned the most violent parties and convulsions," and introduced a confusion in civil affairs which the historian, with his present imperfect materials, cannot fully unravel.

While this disaffection was being engendered by the enemies of the first Executive Council; that body, forseeing some of the evils, endeavored to ward them off by publishing a declaration of their powers in these words:—

"Whereas, some jealousies, natural to a people tenacious of their liberties, have arisen among some of the citizens of this State, respecting the power of this

Board; and whereas it behooves the rulers of a free country, at all times, to take every step in their power to give all reasonable satisfaction to the inhabitants thereof, and to put a stop to such jealousies and complaints as may take place; and whereas the citizens of this State above-mentioned conceive, by virtue of the delegation which authorizes this Board to proceed on the executive department of government, they have power to act in the judicial and legislative departments; we do hereby declare and make known to all whom it may concern, that we are not invested with any such judicial or legislative powers, and that it never was nor ever will be our intention to assume to ourselves any such powers by virtue of the above-mentioned delegation, and that we neither mean to contravene or destroy the Constitution of the State, which we think must have due operation, whenever a time of less disquiet will admit of its being adequate to the exigency of Government."

The proceedings of this second self-constituted Assembly and Council, were principally marked by their attempts to traduce the character of General McIntosh; attempts which had begun during the administration of Governor Treutlen, when the General, as a Continental officer, refused to obey the orders of the Executive; and which had been fostered by his enemies with a steadiness and earnestness worthy of a better cause.

The Council of Walton had caused a letter to be prepared and sent to the President of the Continental Congress, expressing the dissatisfaction of the people of Georgia at the appointment of General McIntosh to command in the State; and declaring, that "it is highly necessary that Congress should, whilst that officer is in the service of the United States, direct some distant field for the exercise of his abilities." This letter purported to be from William Glascock, Speaker of the House of Assembly, acting for and in behalf of that body; and was officially transmitted, with other public papers, by George Walton, then the Governor of the State, to the President of Congress. The effect of this was, that Congress, on the 15th February, 1780, voted to "dispense with the services of Brigadier-General McIntosh, until the further order of Congress." It was subsequently proved, however, that Glascock never wrote or saw the letter to which his name was appended; that it did not emanate from the Assembly, nor did it receive its sanction; but that it was the product of Walton, and a few of his ill-judging friends and advisers, for the purpose of blackening the character of McIntosh, and removing him from any command in the State.

Three years later, when the painful subject was again before the public, the whole correspondence and doings of Governor Walton and his Assembly were carefully reviewed by the Legislature, which, upon a report of a committee of the Assembly, voted "that the resolves of Council, dated Augusta, 12th December, 1779, and the letter from the Governor (Walton) to the President of Congress, dated 15th December, 1779, respecting the General, were unjust, illiberal, and a misrepresentation of facts;" that the so-called Glascock letter was "a forgery, in violation of law and truth, and highly injurious to the interests of the State, and dangerous to the rights of its citizens."

The Assembly also expressed their sense of the virtues and merits of General McIntosh, and ordered the Attorney-General "to make the necessary inquiries, and enter such prosecution as may be consistent with his office and duty."

Thus was General McIntosh cleared of the malignant charges of his enemies, and his character publicly indorsed by the Legislature of his State. Yet, strange to say, the very Legislature which passed the resolution condemning the course of Walton, and directing the Attorney-General to enter prosecution, had only the day before elected Walton as Chief Justice of Georgia, and placed him over the very tribunal before which he should have been brought and tried for his "unjust and illiberal" conduct. Of course, the prosecution was never attempted.

The reins of government, which had been usurped by Walton and the Assembly which sat for four or five weeks in the close of 1779, were resumed by an Assembly, called agreeably to the provisions of the Constitution, which met at Augusta, in January, 1780; when Richard Howley was chosen Governor, and William Glascock, Speaker of the House. George Wells, Stephen Heard, John Lindsay, and Humphrey Wells, were appointed members of the Executive Council; George Wells being elected President of that body.

As might have been expected from the constitution of this Assembly, made up mostly of the friends of Walton and Howley, early steps were taken to cast odium upon the Council of State chosen in July, 1779; and on the 15th January, 1780, the Assembly, having recited in a preamble some of the evils which resulted from the action of that Council, such as "exercising powers and authorities unknown to, and subversive of, the Constitution and laws of the State;" "creating different political opinions, and thereby weakening the authority of legal government," and giving the enemy a means whereby they could foment dissensions, where unity was needed; "resolved and declared, and it is hereby resolved and declared, that the said Council, and the powers they exercised, were illegal and unconstitutional."

The condition of the State at this time was truly alarming. Many of its best and most reliable citizens had been driven away, and were in exile in other States; the paper currency had so depreciated, that it was scarcely possible to pay the expenses of government; political power was mostly in the hands of "a triumvirate;" the aspect of affairs was "hastening from bad to worse with great rapidity;" justice had, in some glaring instances, given place to tyranny; boisterous demagoguism, and fealty to the dominant party, passed for patriotism; and many good men who had previously, and who subsequently, occupied high positions in the State, mourned the fearful evils, which they saw so clearly displayed, but which they could not then mitigate or remove.

On the 1st February, 1780, the Assembly, anticipating "from the events of war, it may so happen that the ministers of government of this State might not be able to do or transact the business of the State within the limits of the same," unanimously resolved, "that his honor the Governor, or, in his absence, the President and Executive Council, may do and transact all and every business of government, in as full, ample, and authoritative manner, in any other State within the confederation, touching and respecting of this

State, as though it had been done and transacted within the limits of the State."

The next day, in consequence of hearing "that the British troops in Savannah have received a reinforcement from New York," the Governor issued a proclamation, "to the end that the good people of this State may have notice of the same, and that proper exertions may be made for repelling the common enemy," "commanding and requiring the people to stand firm to their duty, and exert themselves in support and defence of the great and glorious independency of the United States; and also to remember, with gratitude to Heaven, that the Almighty Ruler of human affairs hath been pleased to raise up the spirit and might of the two greatest powers in the world (France and Spain), to join with them, and oppose and destroy the persecutor of their liberties and immunities."

On the 3d February, the Governor was "requested to issue orders for embodying one-half of the militia of this State immediately," to rendezvous at Augusta. Colonel Twiggs was also desired to collect his men, and as many volunteers as possible, and take post at the same place. The Assembly censured General Lincoln for removing the Continental troops, and declared, that he stood "answerable for all the consequences which may follow that unadvised measure."

Aware of the almost defenceless state of Augusta, the seat of government, which, it was stated, "might be surprised by twenty men," and feeling that it was "unsafe and impolitic for the Governor and Council to remain thus exposed," the Assembly designated Heard's Fort, in Wilkes County, as "the place of meeting for transacting the business of the government of this State, as soon after leaving Augusta as may be."

Acting upon this recommendation, the Executive Council, on the 5th February, adjourned to meet at Heard's Fort. Governor Howley was requested to take his seat in the Continental Congress, to which he had been elected by the Assembly; and "the Hon. George Wells, Esq., the President, with three members of this Board," were declared to be "fully competent to the transaction of all public business, as effectually as though the Governor was in the State."

Death shortly removed President Wells from his seat in the Council, and, on the 18th February, Stephen Heard, of Wilkes County, "was appointed to fill that station for the remainder of the year."

At this time, republican Georgia consisted of only two counties, Richmond and Wilkes; as all south of a line drawn from Hudson's Ferry, on the Savannah, to the Ogeechee, was in possession of the British; and this small portion was now menaced with danger from British troops and Indian foes, and reduced to alarming distress; a distress greatly augmented by internal dissensions. While the Assembly was voting the proceedings of the nine members of the body, called "The Supreme Executive Council," illegal, unconstitutional, and dangerous to the liberties of the State; the Grand Jury of Richmond County, the foreman of which was John Wereat, the President of that Council, made a presentment to the General Court, in March, 1780, before the Hon. William Stephens, Chief Justice, and his Associate Justices; in which paper, among other things, they declare on oath, and present as a grievance, "as a manifest breach of the Constitution, a meeting, composed of about the number of twenty, in the month of November last, who called themselves 'The House of Assembly,' and actually assumed and exercised the legislative and executive powers of government, contrary to the express letter and spirit of the Constitution, which we conceive to be a precedent dangerous to the rights and liberties of the good people of this State. 'Tis much to be apprehended, and is the fixed opinion of many of the citizens of this State, that this mutilated Assembly, at the eve of a general election, was rather contrived to answer the private purpose of some artful and designing individuals, than for the real interest and benefit of the State."

Thus discordant were the counsels of the leading men of the times; and the strength of the republican party was wasted by the political animosities of those who should have moved in fraternal union towards the attainment of their great object,—the rescuing the State from the hands of the enemy, and the upholding of its declared independence.

The capture of Charleston not only deprived the South of its army, but enabled Lord Cornwallis to spread his posts in the back country of Carolina and Georgia, and hold both States under his military power. No sooner had the sad news of the capitulation of General Lincoln, in May, 1780, reached Augusta, than the Republican government retreated to Heard's Fort, the place designated by the Assembly. Governor Howley was requested, by a vote of the Executive Council, on the 23d May, "to retire to some place of safety, either South or North Carolina; as, from longer delay, his situation might endanger the liberty of his person;" and the public moneys were directed to "be placed in the hands of the President, and to be paid off as the occasions of public service may require, under his direction and that of the Executive Council in the absence of the Governor."

Thus was Georgia reduced to the verge of political death. The government, such as it was, was administered by President Heard and a few members of the Council in Wilkes County; and when Mr. Heard retreated to North Carolina, Myrick Davies was chosen President in his place. The condition of the republicans in Georgia was indeed deplorable. Driven from Savannah and the seaboard; compelled to evacuate Augusta; hemmed in by hostile Indians on the frontier; and confined mostly to a few settlements in and around Wilkes County, they lived in daily peril; had almost daily skirmishes with regulars, tories, or Indians; were harassed with alarms, were surprised by ambuscades, were pinched with want, and had one long bitter struggle for simple existence, with scarcely a ray of hope to light up the future.

The principal cities of Georgia and South Carolina being now in the hands of the British, and the royal government having been re-established in the Province of Georgia; rumors were heard in various quarters[1] that it was the design of the ministry in England to make new overtures of peace to the Americans, but to leave out of consideration the claims of Georgia and perhaps of South Carolina, regarding Georgia, at least, as now completely restored to the British rule and throne. These accounts reached the ears of the delegates in Congress from Georgia; and with a promptness worthy

[1] Curwan's Journal and Letters, p. 328, speaks of them. Madison Papers, i, 65–71.

of all praise, they immediately issued a small pamphlet entitled "Observations upon the effects of certain late Political Suggestions," by the delegates from Georgia.

These "observations" were written and published in Philadelphia, in January, 1781, and signed by George Walton, W. Few, and R. Howley. To them they appended a valuable table, showing the progressive commerce of Savannah, from 1755 to 1772, compiled by William Brown, Comptroller and Searcher of his Majesty's Customs in Savannah, the truth of which was sworn to before Anthony Stokes, the Chief Justice of the Province.

In the opening paragraph of this tract, they remark: "From the most recent accounts that have been received from Europe, there is the greatest reason to expect, that a new commission will issue from the Court of London for the purpose of again sounding the temper of America upon the subject of pacification; in which the State of Georgia, and perhaps that of South Carolina, will not be regarded as part of the American Union, but excluded as having been again colonized to England by new conquest."

"The *uti possidetis* also has been much talked of in Europe as a probable basis for the peace; and this report, although rejected with marks of abhorrence by all descriptions of men in America, circulates with terror, as it is pretended to be drawn from the armed neutrality."

The delegates then forcibly remark, in reference to Georgia, which would be particularly affected by the operation of such principles: "They united in the one cause, and have sacrificed their blood and fortunes in its support; and, therefore, it would be unjust and inhuman for the other parts of the Union separately to embrace the result of the common efforts, and leave them under the yoke of a bankrupt and enraged tyrant. To preserve the States entire is the object of the alliance with France, and it cannot be the interest of the other great branch of the family compact, that we should again make a part of the British Empire."

Entering at once upon the subject of the importance of Georgia to the Union, they show, that in its commerce and agricultural productions; in its sea-coast and harbors; in its ship-timber and pine forests; in its position as a check to the encroaching power of Spain and England; "Georgia is a material part of the Union, and cannot be given up without affecting its essential interest, if not endangering its existence." With great justice and political sagacity do the delegates declare: "As to America, no part of it could expect to be free long, while England retains both ends of the Continent."

How far this publication prevented the consummation of the rumored *uti possidetis*, is not known. Certain it is, that such a plan as settling a peace to the exclusion of Georgia, was never formally proposed; yet the report of such a movement must have been undoubted, or such a labored defence of the rights and importance of Georgia would not have been published.

The possibility that the *uti possidetis* might be enforced as a basis of treaty by the armed neutrality of Europe, produced alarm in the minds of many. To conciliate Spain, for the double purpose of obtaining from her pecuniary aid and of keeping her from yielding to the British emissaries, who were now at work at Madrid, seeking to detach his Catholic Majesty from the war, the delegates from South Carolina and Georgia, then under military occupancy by the British, were willing to give up the claimed right of navigating the Mississippi, rather than, by insisting upon it, to defeat a peace on a full Continental basis. Mr. Jay had been instructed to insist upon the right of "the free navigation of the river Mississippi, into and from the sea,"[1] as the ultimatum of peace; but the majority of the members of Congress, moved by the impending danger, coincided with the delegates, and the instructions of Mr. Jay were altered, permitting him, if required to do so, to recede from his demand for the free navigation of the Mississippi, below the thirty-first degree of north latitude; provided, above that latitude, the Americans could have equal rights of navigation with the subjects of Spain. As soon, however, as the menacing crisis was over, Congress revoked these instructions, and insisted upon and secured its first demands.

The whole transaction forms an interesting and instructive page in our history; especially when viewed as to what might have been the result, had the concessions authorized by these fears been made by Mr. Jay; and had the outlet of the Mississippi been closed to the commercial enterprise of a people destined soon to find, in the valley of that great river, the heart and centre of the Union.

The policy of the British conqueror of Carolina, in compelling men to take arms against their country, and visiting with almost unparalleled barbarity of punishment the helpless victims which war threw

[1] Vide letter of Madison, in Madison Papers, vol. i, Appen. iv.

into the hands of the enemy; stirred up the masses of the people, and caused them to rally once more under their leaders, for the purpose of recovering their State and their liberties. Under the animation of feeling inspired by these movements, a better state of things dawned upon Georgia, in the year 1781. Augusta had been recovered from the enemy, and an Assembly had convened there, when, on the 16th August, Dr. Nathan Brownson was elected Governor; and Edward Telfair, Colonel William Few, Dr. Noble Wimberley Jones, and Samuel Stirk, were appointed delegates to Congress.

At the next meeting of the Assembly, in January, 1782, held also at Augusta, John Martin was elected Governor; and such was the brighter condition of affairs, that in his inaugural address to the House, he was enabled to say: "I am extremely happy in finding the virtuous struggles made by the good citizens of this State, against our cruel and unnatural enemies, have at length nearly secured to us those blessings for which we have so long contended; and doubt not but, by a continuance of those exertions, and the support we have every reason to expect, we shall, in a short time, reap the happy fruit of our labors." But little business was transacted by this Assembly, and they adjourned to July; but the exigencies of public business, and the necessitous condition of the State, made it necessary for Governor Martin to recall them by proclamation, to meet at Augusta on the third Tuesday in April, 1782.

In his address to the Assembly, Governor Martin stated, that he had called them together for the purpose of requesting them by legislative action, to remove some of the distresses to which they were subjected by "the wanton waste of grain heretofore expended," in consequence of which the people, "for want of common sustenance, are now reduced to a perishing condition;" to devise means for raising the continental quota of troops; and to revise the militia law, "whereby the services may be equally borne."

He also recommended "the establishment of a Court of Claims, to determine the right of contested property;" and further desired them to pass an act defining the boundaries of the State, which might prove the basis of State and Continental negotiation.

For the first time, since the Declaration of Independence, could the Governor say that "the legislative, executive, and judicial powers, now enjoy the free exercise of their respective authorities," the enemy being shut up within the lines of Savannah, whilst the Americans had "full and absolute possession of every other part of the State."

This Assembly, however, did not sit long; having adjourned the first week in May to the 1st of July. This they did, as the Governor said, "for want of provisions." They left undone the most pressing business that was brought before them, and only legislated upon some inconsiderable matters. The Assembly met on the 1st July at Ebenezer, in Effingham County, then the military headquarters of the State, but it soon removed to Savannah, which was evacuated on the 11th July, and became once more the seat of government.

Freed from the presence of the enemy on the seaboard, there yet remained many evils to be redressed, and much confusion and misrule to be reduced to order. One of the earliest efforts of Governor Martin was, by written conference with Patrick Tonyn, Governor of Florida; and through William McIntosh, Samuel Stirk, and John Wereat, who were appointed by the Governor and Council of Georgia Commissioners for that purpose; to check the almost daily massacres and robberies which occurred along and in the vicinity of St. Mary's River. The border war, waged not for glory and liberty, but plunder and lust, which was kept up by alternate parties of Tories and Americans along the boundary lines of Georgia and Florida, was disgraceful to both governments, and productive of benefit to neither; while its atrocities and its bloodshed reduced the contest to nothing less than a strife of savages. Governor Tonyn responded to these efforts of Governor Martin, and thus checked in some measure these predatory incursions, though it was a long time before there was peace in those borders.

The upper part of the State was also sadly harassed by Indian hostilities, incited and directed by those miserable wretches, the frontier Tories and the half-breeds, the vultures and jackals who snuff the carrion breath of war from afar, and who fatten on the carcases of the battle-field. Multitudes of these men, organized into various bands, and incorporated into or acting with different tribes of Indians, saw all their hopes of gain depart, and their trade in blood gone, if war should cease. Hence they still stirred up the spirit of the Indians, urged them by misrepresentations to keep the field, directed their movements for surprise and ambush; that they might continue their marauding life; using the Indians as the instruments of their cruelty, to give greater terror to their movements, and enhance their gains.

CHAPTER II.

EXECUTIVE TROUBLES AND LEGISLATIVE MOVEMENTS.

On the 9th January, 1783, Lyman Hall was elected Governor of Georgia. In notifying him of his election, the Speaker of the House alluded to the "decided part which he had taken in the cause of America; and exertions in the course of the arduous and important struggle which preceded the auspicious dawn of independence;" and stated, that these efforts "confirmed the House in the fullest assurance that, under his administration; a continued practice of Whig principle will prevail, and a strict execution of those wise and salutary laws which have been passed in former Assemblies, for completing the safety and welfare of the State." The Governor replied: "The early and decided part which I took in the cause of America, originated from a full conviction of the justice and rectitude of the cause we engaged in, has uniformly continued as the principles of my heart, and, I trust, will to the last moments of my life."

After making provision for the appointment of a Board of Commissioners to treat with the Creek and Cherokee nations, the Legislature, on the 13th January, voted a congratulatory address to General Greene, then in Savannah, in which they say—

"The Legislature of the State of Georgia wish to assure you of the real happiness your presence in their capital has given them: human language is too mean to convey their true sentiments of your distinguished virtue.

"Your views of ease to the citizens, in drawing your resources through a scattered country; the many difficulties you surmounted during your command in the Southern Department; your well-directed exertions; and the virtuous struggle of your victorious army, will be gratefully remembered by a State, which has felt so particularly the happy consequences.

"They congratulate you, sir, on the signal success wherewith the arms of the United States, under your command, with the blessing of Divine Providence, have been crowned by the total expulsion of the enemy from the Southern States—an annal in the history of our country, which must endear the name of Greene as long as the remembrance of British tyranny is hateful.

"They beg you to accept their unfeigned thanks for your decided and intrepid conduct, and to believe they ardently desire, that your future days may be passed in that ease and tranquillity, to which a glorious and serviceable life, through this grand Revolution, most deservedly entitles you."

To this address General Greene replied in the following letter, which was ordered to be inserted in the minutes:—

"SIR—Your polite and obliging address, to welcome

me to the State, affords me the most singular satisfaction; nor are your liberal acknowledgments for my small services, and generous wishes for my future ease, less pleasing.

"It affords me the most agreeable sensations to contemplate the happy change in the affairs of this country; and it is among the first of my wishes, that you may long, long enjoy the blessings of freedom and independence, free from further alarms; but should it be your misfortune to have the flame of war rekindled in this quarter, my early endeavor shall not be wanting to check its progress; and I cannot but hope, by the smiles of Providence, the virtue and spirit of the army, joined by the genius of the country, we shall triumph over our enemies.

"I beg the Legislature to believe that I am highly sensible of the honor they have done me, and I take the liberty to assure you of my disposition to serve them."

On the 31st January, the House, by ballot, elected as civil officers of the State for the year 1783, George Walton, Chief Justice; Samuel Stirk, Attorney-General; John Martin, Treasurer; John Milton, Secretary; Richard Call, Surveyor-General; Joseph Woodruff, Collector for the town and port of Savannah; John Lawson, Jr., Collector for the town and port of Sunbury; and several gentlemen as Registers of Probate for the several counties.

General McIntosh, John Houstoun, and Edward Telfair, were also, on the 15th February, appointed agents "to settle and adjust the northern boundaries of this State," and to treat with such Commissioners as might be appointed by the State of South Carolina for that purpose.

While matters of such moment to the civil interests of the State were thus engaging the attention of the Legislature, it is gratifying to know that the higher interests of religion and morality were not overlooked. The Revolution found Georgia with only a few settled clergymen. Several of these, being ministers of the Church of England, and, deriving their support, in part at least, from the venerable Society for Propagating the Gospel in Foreign Parts, sided with the mother country, and left the province. Their places were not speedily supplied. The ministers of the other churches were few, widely scattered, and their voices were almost drowned in the turmoil which ruled in a State harassed by war, invaded by Indians, and exposed to all the calamities of a frontier settlement. Religion languished, and morality declined, with the relaxing of civil order, and the absence of the preaching of the holy Gospel. Nor was this a condition of things likely to remedy itself; it required the strong arm of law to arrest the licentiousness which was so widely prevalent; and the loud tone of legislative authority, to speak out its decided approval of the power of true religion to remove crime, promote peace, and exalt a nation to a true and enduring glory.

Such was the feeling entertained by Governor Hall and the leading men of the Legislature, who, with great clearness and force, stated their views on this subject, and bodied forth their desired action thereon, in the following preamble and resolutions, passed on the 26th of February, 1783:—

"Whereas, nothing can have a greater tendency to promote the honor of God, the propagation of the Christian religion, and the spiritual welfare of the citizens residing in this State, than the regular performance of divine service; and whereas, the several churches throughout the county of Chatham, and other counties in this State, are much out of repair, owing to the great neglect of them for many years past—

"Resolved, That it be recommended to the inhabitants of the said county of Chatham, to meet at the different churches therein, on the second Saturday of March next; and the inhabitants of other counties, as soon as may be after the publication thereof; to elect and choose fit and discreet persons for vestrymen and church-wardens, and other officers, for their respective churches, for one year next ensuing."

It was proper and expedient for the State thus to express its opinion through its House of Representatives; but it required something more than legislation to rebuild churches, re-settle pastors, and bring back to our almost deserted State, the blessed influences which accompany the full exhibition of the ordinances of grace.

Great complaint having been made at the distance of the seat of government from the settlers of the back country, and the ceded lands; by which long, expensive, and dangerous journeys were required, in order to transact public business with the several departments of government at Savannah, the Council resolved, in May, 1783, "to afford such relief as is consistent with their duty, and the powers given them by the Constitution; and therefore unanimously adjourned, on Tuesday, the 14th of June, "to meet in the town of Augusta, on the 28th of the same month; and that from and after the said 28th June next, the executive powers of government will be exercised in the aforesaid town of Augusta, for the term of three months."

On the 8th July, the Legislature convened at Augusta; and Governor Hall addressed to that body a message, marked by fervent patriotism, high religious views, sound suggestions of State policy, and earnest appeals to the wisdom and integrity of the House. After an appropriate opening sentence, the Governor said:—

"So great an event as that of a general peace having actually taken place between the belligerent powers, claims your first attention. An event ordered by the decree of Heaven, and brought about by means which, through the various stages of a tedious and distressing war, were evidently marked with a concurrent display of Almighty power, graciously presiding over us and working wonders in our favor;—an event which proclaims the United States *free, and sovereign, and independent,* and surrounded with the blessings of an advantageous and honorable peace, will, when ratified, give us rank and dignity in the grand arrangement of sovereign states and empires.

"The advantages of peace are so numerous and so important that, whilst they demand from us the most devout and fervent expressions of gratitude to the Supreme Ruler of the universe, at the same time cannot fail to inspire sentiments of sincerest joy at the opening of a scene so delightful in prospect, and so diffusive in its blessings; and on this occasion I beg leave to offer you my hearty congratulations.

"From a view of the profligate and wicked lives of many in the community, it appears that some laws to restrain vice and encourage virtue are of the highest importance to the welfare of the State; it being certain that almost all the evils of government originate from men of corrupt principles and abandoned manners. In addition, therefore, to wholesome laws restraining vice, every encouragement ought to be given to introduce religion, and learned clergy to perform divine worship in honor to God, and to cultivate principles of religion and virtue among our citizens. For this purpose, it will be your wisdom to lay an early foundation for endowing seminaries of learning; nor can you, I conceive, lay in a better, than by a grant of a sufficient tract of land, that may, as in other governments, hereafter, by lease or otherwise, raise a revenue sufficient to support such valuable institutions."

The backwardness of the House of Assembly, in taxing their constituents and themselves, gave the Governor and his Council sincere concern; so much so, that the Council, on the 25th July, 1783, sent an address to the lower House, remonstrating against the smallness of the sum proposed in the tax-bill, "as inadequate to the great and pressing exigencies of this State," and suggesting "the absolute necessity of a *sufficient*, as well as *speedy* tax being laid upon the inhabitants of this State; or the government thereof must inevitably fall into extreme distress and confusion." The Council urged the House "to lay a tax of at least one-half a dollar on every negro, mulatto, or other slave; and one-half dollar on every town-lot, in lieu of the quarter of a dollar mentioned in and by said bill." The House, however, did not agree with the Council; and, on the 31st July, passed a bill, imposing a tax "on every one hundred acres of land, one quarter of a dollar; on every negro, mulatto, or slave, one quarter of a dollar; on every town-lot, the same; on every free negro, mulatto, or mestizo, one dollar; and on every male inhabitant, of the age of twenty-one, who does not follow some lawful profession or mechanical trade, or who does not cultivate, or cause to be cultivated, five acres of land, two dollars."

The subject of confiscation and amercement, also occupied the attention of the Legislature, and its deliberations were embodied in an ample and final law, passed on the 29th July.

The first act "for attainting the enemies of American liberty with high treason, and for confiscating their estates, both real and personal, to the use of the State of Georgia," was enacted on the 1st March, 1778. By this bill, all persons residing in this State since the 19th April, 1775, "who have refused their allegiance to the governing powers of the same," were attainted and adjudged guilty of high treason against this State, and their estates, both real and personal, were declared forfeited and confiscated. The first section of this act recited one hundred and seventeen names, beginning with Sir James Wright. By the second section, any of the said persons returning to the State, or being taken in arms, shall be imprisoned and tried for high treason, and suffer death upon conviction. By the third section, the property of these persons was "to be discovered, and applied to the use of the good people of this State." The fifth section created

"Boards of Commissioners in each county, to carry out the provisions of the third section." The remaining portions of this long act were taken up with the necessary details for carrying it into execution. In October of the same year, the Legislature repealed the terms of sale in this act, and made them more stringent. The same Legislature also passed "An Act to compel Non-Residents to return within a certain time, or, in default thereof, that their estates be confiscated." In 1782, certain persons, who, in the language of the preamble, had "withdrawn themselves from the defence of this State," "accepted protection from the enemy," "and, forgetting all the social ties of kindred and humanity, did assist in endeavoring to enforce the laws of British government, and overturn that mild and equitable system of government which they had assisted to raise, and which it was their duty to support," were amerced; some twelve per cent., some eight per cent., "on the true and equitable value of all estates, both real and personal." A deduction from this percentage was to be made, in case any one of the amerced persons enlisted "any able-bodied soldier for the Continental battalion;" though all the persons named in the act were disqualified from exercising any political rights for two years.

The act of confiscation was also made to apply to "all and every person and persons who shall now be, or may have been, within the British lines as British subjects." In May following, this act was enlarged, so as to embrace two hundred and eighty persons, all of whom were banished from the State within sixty days; or, if they remained, they were to be arrested and imprisoned, as guilty of felony; and, on conviction, "suffer death, without benefit of clergy." "A reasonable and temporary maintenance to the families of these persons" was, however, required of the Commissioners appointed to carry out this act, "until the Legislature shall hereafter direct or order a fixed support for the said families."

The Legislature of 1783 revised, and made more perfect in their details, these laws, settled the terms of sale and payment, provided for the expenditure of moneys so received, created a sinking fund to liquidate the State debt, adjusted the jurisdiction of the courts in reference to the sales, and appointed new Commissioners, viz., Charles Odingsells, Hugh Lawson, and Abram Ravolt.

By these acts, a large amount of property, both real and personal, was vested in the government of Georgia; and though, by subsequent repealing clauses, the names of many were taken from the laws confiscating or amercing their estates; yet still negroes, plantations, horses, stock of various kinds, and to a large amount, fell into the hands of the Commissioners, and were sold for the benefit of the State. The confiscated property belonging to Sir James Wright alone was reported, by the Board of Agents of the American Loyalists,[1] to have been worth nearly £34,000, or about $160,000; while many others, whose names appear on the attainting and confiscating list, were gentlemen possessed of large estates, real and personal.

These laws of Georgia were enacted at the suggestion of the Continental Congress, and in accordance

[1] Wilmot's Claims of American Loyalists. London, 1815; p. 47.

with the action of the other colonial Legislatures. By the laws of Massachusetts, as found in two bills, three hundred and thirty-seven persons were banished, and the estates of certain "notorious conspirators" confiscated. New Hampshire banished seventy-six of her inhabitants, and confiscated the estates of twenty-eight. In Rhode Island several acts were passed, sequestering and confiscating the property of the royalists. Connecticut also punished absentees and seekers after royal protection, by laws of varying dates and provisions. New York not only confiscated the estates of those friendly to the King, but laid a tax of nine pence per pound sterling on the estate of every parent whose son was an adherent of the enemy. New Jersey passed four laws in reference to the persons and property of traitors, fugitives, disaffected persons, and political offenders. In Pennsylvania, acts of attainder and confiscation were passed against ninety-eight persons, designated by name. Delaware ordered the property of forty-six adherents to the royal cause to be forfeited to the State. Maryland, by three statutes, confiscated all property belonging to persons holding allegiance to the crown. Virginia made laws upon this subject, but less stringent than in some other colonies; declaring, however, that certain persons should be treated as aliens, and their property be sold. The North Carolina confiscation act named over seventy persons; and South Carolina, dividing, at various stages of the war, the loyalists into four classes: *Addressers* (or those two hundred and ten who "addressed" Sir Henry Clinton, after the fall of Charleston, asking to be readmitted as British subjects), *Petitioners* (or those sixty-three who signed a petition to Sir Henry to be enrolled and armed on the royal side), *Congratulators* (or those thirteen who congratulated Lord Cornwallis on the success of the British arms at Camden), and the *Obnoxious* (or fourteen others, banished "as obnoxious to the American cause"), passed stringent laws against each, stripping many of all their property, and attainting them with high treason against the State.

Georgia, therefore, harsh as her measures seemed, but acted in accordance with the suggestions of Congress, and the views of her sister colonies, in enacting her laws against the obnoxious loyalists.

So long as wars exist, and especially so long as such civil wars shall rage in a nation, causing the ploughshare of party to cut its dividing furrows between those of the same household of political faith, and brethren of the same domestic hearthstone; so long will necessity, and the rules of war, plead for the justice of such confiscations, attainders, and amercements. That many were unjustly condemned; that many were condemned without the privilege of a hearing; that many were enrolled among the attainted because they resided within certain limits, has been made evident to all. Nearly fifty names were, by various rescinding acts of the several Legislatures of Georgia, between the years 1783 and 1800, withdrawn from the acts of confiscation and amercement; and several of these became ornaments to the bar and the senate of the State, which once proscribed them as traitors. Had Great Britain succeeded in the war, she would not only not have allowed any claim for rebel losses, but would have even confiscated all rebel estates, as the property of traitors to the crown.

The English Government, as in duty bound, having by its acts of tyranny caused the war, and having, by its aggressions, made necessary, as a measure of self-defence, these banishments of persons and confiscations of estates, did something towards alleviating the sufferings of the thousands of loyalists who were thrown out of affluence and self-supporting occupations into idleness and want. Parliament appointed its committees of inquiry on the claims of these loyalists, and its Commissioners to adjudge their losses; and the loyalists themselves organized a Board of Agents, of which Sir James Wright was made President, "both from his situation, age, activity, and zeal, as well as abilities and large property;" whose business it was to press these claims to payment, and secure just indemnification for their several losses. Up to 1790, over four thousand claims had been made upon these Parliamentary Commissioners, asking for nearly $40,000,000. The amount allowed, however, was only about $15,-000,000. "After a long examination of his case, the committee reported Sir James Wright, Bart., to have rendered eminent services to Great Britain, to have lost real and personal property to the value of £33,702, and his office of Governor, value £1000 per annum." Sir James did not long survive his political misfortunes, as he died in England in 1786, and was succeeded in his baronetcy by his eldest son, James, who bore till his death, in 1816, his father's title.

John Houstoun was elected Governor by the House of Assembly, on the 9th January, 1783. This gentleman was the son of Sir Patrick Houstoun; had been educated as a lawyer, and early took sides with the Liberty Party against the Royal Government. He had proved himself worthy of the several offices and trusts, hitherto confided to him in the service of the State, at home, and in Congress; and was now, a second time, elevated to the Executive chair.

On the 1st of March, the Governor had the pleasure of laying before the Executive Council, "despatches from Congress, covering a proclamation or ratification of the definitive treaty of peace." The Council, partaking of the happiness felt by the Governor on this joyful occasion, took immediate order to give proper publicity to this state paper, and directed "that it be read and published by the Sheriff through the streets of Savannah, on Wednesday next; that the militia of the town and the vicinity thereof, be paraded and mustered on the occasion, and that the Governor accordingly issue orders for the purpose; and further, that his Honor the Chief Justice be furnished with a certified copy of the said proclamation for his Government, and that he be requested to cause the same to be published and proclaimed in the different counties of this State, at his ensuing circuit."

It must have given peculiar satisfaction to Governor Houstoun, to be occupying the gubernatorial chair at such a period of his country's history. His name was one of the four which were signed to the first call for a meeting of the friends of liberty within the province. He was one of the three persons first selected by the Provincial Congress, in January, 1775, to represent Georgia in the Continental Congress; and for his faithful and unfaltering devotion to the cause of American freedom, his name was placed first on the list appended to the disqualifying act, passed by the Royal Assembly, in Savannah, 1780, and is there styled "Rebel

Governor." He now, not as a "Rebel" Governor, but as a recognized Chief Magistrate of an independent State, had the gratification of publishing the treaty, by which Great Britain made peace with the revolted colonies; and in accordance with which his long-oppressed country took its place as one of the nations of the earth.

In the Assembly which was now convened, there were "very violent struggles," owing to the fact that several persons had been returned as members of the House, who had formerly taken protection under the British Governor. Their right to sit was strenuously contested, and four or five were declared ineligible, "from their not having been long enough under American Government to make them eligible to so important a trust."

In the midst, however, of the troubles incident to the unsettled state of a frontier province, in that transition period, when military law had ceased, and civil law was but imperfectly established; the Legislature, with a forecast which reflects the highest credit upon their wisdom, took measures for the establishment of a State institution of learning. On the 25th February, 1784, a committee of the Legislature was sent to the Executive Council, bearing a resolution, requesting his Honor, the Governor, "to grant eight land warrants for five thousand acres each, in the name of John Houstoun, James Habersham, William Few, Joseph Clay, Abram Baldwin, William Houstoun, and Nathan Brownson, Esqrs., or their successors in office, in trust for the College that is to be established in this State; that one or more of the said Trustees be requested to proceed immediately, with a surveyor or surveyors, and superintend the surveying of the said land in each county, agreeable to the act for that purpose made. That His Honor, the Governor, be requested to draw an order on the Treasurer, in favor of the said Trustees, for the sum of twenty pounds, for the purpose of paying chain-bearers, and defraying the necessary expenses of surveying."

The act to which reference is here made, is "An act for laying out two more counties to the westward," &c., the 11th section of which reads thus: "And whereas, the encouragement of religion and learning is an object of great importance to any community, and must tend to the prosperity, happiness, and advantage of the same. Be it, therefore, enacted by the authority aforesaid, that the county surveyors, immediately after passing of this act, shall proceed to lay out in each county, twenty thousand acres of land of the first quality, in separate tracts of five thousand acres each, for the endowment of a college or seminary of learning, and which said lands shall be vested in and granted to his honor the Governor for the time being. And John Houstoun, James Habersham, William Few, Joseph Clay, Abram Baldwin, William Houstoun, and Nathan Brownson, Esqrs., and their successors in office, are hereby nominated and appointed trustees for the said college or seminary of learning, and empowered to do all such things as to them shall appear requisite and necessary, to forward the establishment and progress of the same: and all vacancies shall be filled up by the said trustees. And the said county surveyors shall, in six months after passing of this act, make return to the trustees hereinbefore mentioned, of all regular plats of all such tracts as he shall have laid out and surveyed by virtue of this act."

To carry out the provisions of this section of the act, the Council, on the 11th March, "ordered that the Secretary of the State do immediately make out eight warrants for the same; that is to say, four for five thousand acres each in Franklin County, and four for five thousand each in Washington County." This most judicious plan was productive of great and beneficial results, and prepared the way for that more definite action which, as we shall see, took place the ensuing year.

The land act—of which the setting apart of these large tracts of country for the endowment of a college constituted one section—was one of the most important results of this Legislature. It brought under survey the large cession of territory made by the Indians, to the north and west of Wilkes; laid out and organized two new counties, and established a Land Court at Augusta, to "be opened on the first Tuesday in April next (1784), by his Honor the Governor, or the Honorable the President, with any three or more of the Executive Council, for the purpose of granting out lands, under and by virtue of this act." This court was to sit for three months, on each Monday, Tuesday, and Wednesday, to grant land and sign warrants; and, each Thursday and Friday, for the purpose of hearing caveats.

It is significant of the unsettled state of the country, that it was deemed necessary, in consequence of "the roads being, at present, infested with robbers," to order, on the 23d March, 1784, "that a guard, consisting of an officer and from six to twelve horsemen, be furnished by the commanding officer of each county, that is to say, the guard of Chatham County to escort the President and members of Council to the lower line of Effingham County; that the guard of Effingham County be ready there, and escort them to the lower line of Burke County; that the guard of Burke County be ready there, and escort them to the lower line of Richmond County; and, that the guard of Richmond be ready there, and escort them to Augusta. That a copy of the foregoing be sent to the respective commanding officers, and that they be informed, at the same time, that the President and members of Council will set out from Savannah on Tuesday, the 30th day of this instant, March. And, that it is required that the several guards do so order themselves as to be in readiness at the several and respective places, before pointed out for them, at the proper times when they may expect the President and members of Council to be along, or one day sooner."

The Land Court was opened at Augusta, at the time designated, by the Hon. John Habersham, President of the Executive Council, and a great number of applicants for warrants appeared. At first, some little order was observed; but, the 17th of May, 1784, being the day appointed for the delivery of the warrants, and the warrants not being fully prepared, the populace became exceedingly impatient, and were with difficulty restrained from acts of violence; but, "on Thursday," says the clerk of the Land Court, writing a graphic description of the scene to the Governor, "a few evil-disposed persons hinted to the people at large, whose minds, by the juice of the cane, were already inflamed, that there was a more concise way of obtaining their warrants; they immediately herded, and, I must confess, looked formidable. Fancy to yourself, my dear sir, the Honorable the President and members of Council, four or five in number, convened on the business of their countrymen, their secretary or clerk, with his assistants, in an adjoining apartment, ready to faint with excessive heat and fatigue, not suffered to open the door or window, whereby a little fresh air might be admitted, and 1500 or, perhaps, 2000 men, set on by designing villains, approaching the doors with threats and menaces, crying out aloud, that their warrants they would have at any rate.

"I once more ventured my humble opinion to the President that it was absolutely necessary, and without hesitation to inform them, that the issuing of the warrants was unavoidably postponed until Monday following, the 24th inst.; at the same time declaring, that at the hour of ten, on the morning of the said day, and not sooner, the warrants would begin to be issued; also that any of the parties concerned might obtain them by appointing a person to receive them on their behalf; this, with Colonel Clarke's remonstrance, seemed to appease them, and many went home thereon. The Fat King, so called in derision, being somewhat intoxicated himself and making others so by lavish treats, not pleased with the said postponement, kicked up another dust, pulled down the notification last mentioned, and insisted that the warrants should be given out the next day. They were now noisy as ever, and ready for any mischief; the house was to stand but two hours at farthest. On this the President engaged that no exertion should be wanting to grant them on the Saturday then next to follow. This emollient produced, like Dr. Franklin's oil on the turbulent Thames, a second calm to appearance; but I degrade the most unruly tempest by a comparison with the savage disposition and brutal temper of lawless and ungovernable men, subject to no control, strangers to order and regularity, and averse to everything that opposes their will. Saturday being come (though I cannot say that those gentlemen who went to their homes on the notice that none should issue before or until Monday morning, had an equal chance), and lists being handed in, by requisition of the several claims for warrants by each individual, and the putting them up accordingly in bundles to be handed out, was going on rapidly: a proposition was made by the most generous and most disinterested of men, the overflowing of a compassionate heart, though fatally unlucky in the consequence, that several individuals, who waited but for their *own* warrants, and when obtained would retire and give room for those who wanted *many*, might have them. I dreaded the confusion that ensued thereon, nor did I omit mentioning it; this having taken place, the general vociferation was, 'Why can't I get my warrant as well as another? Such a one has got his, and I'll have mine.' My office was no longer at my command; the breach being made, the torrent soon widened it, and he thought himself the happiest person that could *grab* the greatest number of them. The alphabetical order that I had observed was soon obliterated, and no trace of regularity or decorum left.

"They soon had the warrants from my table on the floor, at the door, and on the highway. About four or five hundred were soon missing by this outrage; true, great numbers have since been returned under the pretence of being taken away by mistake, &c. &c. The court have endeavored to remedy this evil also, on petitions and testimony that they were so taken away or mislaid. Duplicates have been made out to them and transmitted to the two County Surveyors, with positive orders not to survey on a warrant that a duplicate was issued for.

"I have been ever since busy on this work, hard as the first, and it has been almost too hard for me. I have been very unwell, and still continue so."

There were no less than five different classes of warrants to be prepared, issued and registered by this court. The first, called "Citizens' Rights," were based on the resolution of the Legislature, passed the 20th August, 1781, which declared, that "as many persons were daily absenting themselves from the State, and leaving their fellow-citizens to encounter the difficulties of the war with Great Britain, all who remained and did their duty faithfully, should be entitled to two hundred and fifty acres of good land, which were to be exempt from taxes for ten years." Two thousand nine hundred and twenty-three persons availed themselves of the provisions of this act to obtain certificates which entitled them to "Citizens' Rights" warrants.

On the 12th January, 1782, the Assembly ordered "that the Governor issue certificates to persons who, during their refugeeship, had served their country as good soldiers, for two hundred and fifty acres of land," the officers to receive more, in proportion to rank. Six hundred and ninety-four claimed under this act, by what were called "Refugee Certificates," the designated warrants. Another class of claimants were those who had served the State under the old Congress in the Continental establishment, and nearly two hundred persons received these "Continental Certificates," which entitled them to warrants for land.

A still larger class of applicants presented what were termed "Minute Men Certificates," *i. e.*, such men as were enrolled for service, and liable to be called out at a minute's notice, but who did not do continuous service in the field; and five hundred and fifty-five received land warrants under this provision of the law. There were also issued land warrants to nine persons, under the claim of "Marine Certificates," who had done duty as part of the small naval force in the galleys of the State. Thus rapidly was the territory acquired by treaty absorbed by the people of the State. Persons outside the State also sought to settle here, and General Matthews and some other gentlemen from Virginia, asked that a tract of 200,000 acres be laid off and reserved for them and others, agreeable as they conceived to a clause in the Land Act. As these last petitioners did not comply with the provisions of this act, they did not obtain the grant as desired "in one body of land," though many individuals of that Virginia Company, the most prominent of whom was General Matthews himself, took up lands in Georgia and became residents of the State.

General Samuel Elbert succeeded John Houstoun as Governor, in July, 1785, the Legislature showing its appreciation of him, in placing him, by nearly a unanimous vote, in the Executive chair.

One of his earliest acts was to direct Colonel John Baker, of Liberty County, "to take the most effectual means, to secure the villains who are at this time assembled between the St. Illa and St. Mary's Rivers; with a number of negroes, horses, and other property, supposed to have been stolen from the citizens of this State." As the Governor of Florida was making severe examples of such as fell into their hands, Governor Elbert felt it important to strike terror into this banditti, on this side the St. Mary's also, and thus put a stop to such border pillage and bloodshed.

It was not upon the southern boundary alone, however, that these troubles were felt. Disaffected and mercenary persons were found to be at work among the Indian tribes, committing outrages of the grossest kind, and then attributing them to the Georgians; stimulating the savages to revenge, and driving them on to deeds of cruelty and warfare, which it required the strong arm of military power to put down. But the Governor sent pacific "talks" to the Indians, and urged the most stringent measures of justice to be pursued towards all molesting the Indians, or trespassing upon their lands.

The Assembly, by an act passed on the 27th January, 1785, developed almost into maturity the germ of a university, found in their legislation the previous year. The bill now passed was entitled "An Act for the more full and complete establishment of a public seat of learning in this State," and opens with a preamble, which for its sound principles, and as an expression of the views of the political fathers of those days, well deserves a record here.

"As it is the distinguishing happiness of free governments that civil order should be the result of choice, and not necessity, and the common wishes of the people become the laws of the land, their public prosperity and even existence very much depends upon suitably forming the minds and morals of their citizens. When the minds of the people in general are viciously disposed and unprincipled, and their conduct disorderly, a free government will be attended with greater confusions and evils more horrid than the wild uncultivated state of nature. It can only be happy where the public principles and opinions are properly directed, and their manners regulated. This is an influence beyond the reach of laws and punishments, and can be claimed only by religion and education. It should, therefore, be among the first objects of those who wish well to the national prosperity, to encourage and support the principles of religion and morality, and early to place the youth under the forming hand of society, that by instruction, they may be moulded to the love of virtue and good order. Sending them abroad to other countries for their education, will not answer these purposes; it is too humiliating an acknowledgment of the ignorance or inferiority of our own, and will always be the cause of so great foreign attachments, that upon principles of policy it is inadmissible.

"This country, in the times of our common danger and distress, found security in the principle and abilities which wise regulations had before established in the minds of our countrymen, that our present happiness, joined to the pleasing prospects, should conspire to make us feel ourselves under the strongest obligations to form the youth, the rising hope of our land, to render the like glorious and essential services to our country."

The act provided that the general superintendence

and regulation of the literature of this State should be confided to two bodies, one consisting of the Governor and Council, the Speaker of the House of Assembly, and the Chief Justice, termed a "Board of Visitors;" and the other, consisting of John Houstoun, James Habersham, William Few, Joseph Clay, Abram Baldwin, William Houstoun, Nathan Brownson, John Habersham, Abiel Holmes, Larkin Davis, Hugh Lawson, William Glascock, and Benjamin Talliaferro, to be called the "Board of Trustees." These two bodies, united, were to constitute "The Senatus Academicus of the University of Georgia." This "Senatus Academicus" was to "consult and advise, not only upon the affairs of the University, but also to remedy the defects and advance the interests of literature through the State in general."

The fourteenth section of this bill also declared that "all public schools instituted, or to be supported by funds or public moneys in this State, shall be considered as parts or members of the University, and shall be under the foregoing directions and regulations."

At a meeting of the Trustees, in Augusta, in February, 1786, the Board took steps towards laying out a town in Greene County, directing that eight lots be reserved for a church, academy, court-house, and jails; and that certain others be sold upon specified conditions. This was the beginning of the town of Greensboro, then the contemplated seat of the University.

The first meeting of the "Senatus Academicus" of the State, of which any record remains, was held at Louisville, in November, 1799. The first Professor, Josiah Meigs, was elected by the "Senatus Academicus," the next year, at a salary of $1500.

By an act of the Legislature, in 1800, the General Assembly ordered that the permanent seat of the University should be in the county of Jackson, Franklin, Hancock, Greene, Oglethorpe, Wilkes, or Warren. A new set of trustees was nominated, and a new board, entitled a "Board of Visitors," was appointed, to consist of the Governor, the Judges of the Superior Courts, the President of the Senate, the Speaker of the House, and Senators from certain designated counties.

At the meeting of the Board of Visitors, in June, 1801, the Hon. Abram Baldwin, the President of the Board, stated that the funds of the University admitted the paying of a person as President, whose duty it should be more particularly to superintend the literature of the State; he therefore resigned his position, and Professor Meigs was unanimously elected, took the oath of office, and "entered at once upon the duties of President, by taking his seat as President of the Board of Trustees."[2]

Though the site of the University seemed fixed at Greensboro, yet, as much dissatisfaction appeared, the subject was reconsidered, and the Board therefore appointed Abram Baldwin, John Milledge, John Twiggs, Hugh Lawson, and George Walton, to select a site in Jackson County (then including Clark and Jackson), and to contract for the erection of college buildings to accommodate one hundred students.

In November, 1801, they reported their selection of the present site, and also laid before the Board a conveyance from Mr. Milledge, of nearly seven hundred

[2] Minute Book of "Senatus Academicus."

acres of land (that on which Athens now principally stands), for the benefit of the University.

The location which at that time seemed so adverse to the demands of the population, as it placed the college on the very borders of civilization on its western frontier, now proves to be a most admirable selection. The first commencement was held in May, 1804, and the exercises of that day were held under an arbor formed of branches of trees, upon the Campus. Here, in this rustic chapel, surrounded by the primeval forest, and amidst a gathering of a few friends of the institution, and a still larger number of persons gathered to witness the novel scene; Colonel Gibson Clark, the Honorable Augustine T. Clayton, General Jeptha V. Harris, Colonel William H. Jackson, Professor James Jackson, Thomas Irwin, Jared Irwin, Robert Rutherford, and William Williamson graduated with the honors of the institution.

Considering the age of the colony, the last settled of the original thirteen; the position of the State, a frontier province exposed to incursions from Indians, French, and Spaniards: the feebleness of the State, just recovering from the effects of war, and still suffering from Indian hostilities; the unsettled condition of government, when clashing interests and rival claims were jostling each other in high places, to the prejudice of peace and order: considering these things, and then looking at the broad scope on which the University was planned; the sound principles on which it was based; the zealous efforts of its founders to make it stable and efficient; we must say that Georgia merits peculiar honor in being among the first of the States to make provision for a State University, and in passing most wholesome laws for securing to her sons the blessings of a liberal education on her own soil.

Much of the thought and care of Governor Elbert was taken up with the settlement of Indian difficulties; especially in connection with the proceedings of the Commissioners appointed by Congress to treat with the Cherokees, and the Indians to the south of them; proceedings in which Georgia, indeed, took a part through State Commissioners, but which were, nevertheless, regarded by the Executive with some degree of uneasiness, as if fearful that the rights of Georgia might be trespassed upon, or its true claims overlooked; the lesser power and authority of the State being made to succumb to the overshadowing influence of the General Government. Accordingly, the Executive Council appointed Edward Telfair, William Few, and James Jackson, to attend at Galphinton, in Jefferson County, where the convention was to be held; "and there take cognizance of any matter respecting the same, and to aid and assist them, the said Commissioners of the United States, in forwarding their business as far as they, by the Articles of Confederation and Perpetual Union, are authorized to go; and they are strictly charged to protest against any measures that may appear to them to exceed the powers given by the Confederation aforesaid, and which may be contrary to the Constitution and laws of the State, and to make report thereof to this Board."

This was the first step taken by the General Government, which brought it into seeming conflict with the State Government; and was the beginning of a series of difficulties respecting the jurisdiction of the United States within the limits of the State, which, as they advanced, assumed, at times, even threatening aspects; and which were only really quieted when the Indians were, within a few years back, removed altogether from the Commonwealth of Georgia.

Among the pleasing duties which pertained to General Elbert, at a time when the occupancy of the gubernatorial chair was attended with self-denial and harassing cares, was the notifying the Count d'Estaing of the action of the Legislature, in granting him twenty thousand acres of land, "in testimony of their respect for his meritorious services;" and their further action, in empowering him to receive and hold the grants of land, and in admitting him "to all the privileges, liberties, and immunities of a free citizen of this State."

The letter of the Governor, as well as the official papers concerning the grant, were sent to the Vice-Admiral by the hands of a special agent, John McQueen, Esq., who was directed to deliver them to him in person. The Count received the intelligence with emotions of gratitude. "The mark of its satisfaction," he writes, "which the State of Georgia was pleased to give me, after I had been wounded, was the most healing balm that could have been applied to my pains whenever they were the most acute." "Nothing," he adds, "could be more flattering than to be admitted as a proprietor in a State that has so much distinguished itself in supporting the common cause." And he authorized the Chevalier De La Luzerne to take charge of the property in his name.

From a letter to the Chevalier, by Count d'Estaing, he intimates, as a purpose to which he intended to devote a part of the proceeds of this estate, "to erect to the States, at the entrance of Paris, a monument to the glory of the King, and those patriots who have most contributed to the epoch of liberty."

What the specific design of the Count was we know not. The rising troubles in France, and his own duties, as a Vice-Admiral of the navy, so absorbed his time, that but little was left in which to think upon his American estate. And when, at length, the French Revolution began its reign of terror, d'Estaing was one of the victims of republican proscription, and perished under the guillotine.

On the 9th of January, 1786, Edward Telfair was elected Governor of Georgia. Mr. Telfair, though a native of Scotland, had resided in America nearly thirty years; twenty of which he had passed in Savannah. Engaged there in mercantile business, he gained, by his high and honorable course, wealth and influence; he early took a decided course upon the great questions which agitated America, and openly ranked himself among the friends of liberty. From the time that he attended the first meeting of the "Liberty Boys," he had been uniform, consistent, and earnest in his efforts to protect, make free, and elevate the State of his adoption. As a member of the Council of Safety, as one of the delegates in Congress, and as a commissioner to treat with the Indians, he had proved the integrity of his character, and his great capacity for business; and, having been found faithful in these, he was, by the Legislature, raised to the highest office in the State.

It was a time which required sagacity, promptness, and firmness; and he was enabled to bring to his executive duties not only these qualities, but a ripe and large public experience, so that he was enabled to preside over the State with wisdom and dignity.

Much of the time of Governor Telfair was taken up in preparing for, and warding off, by his prompt and vigorous measures, a threatened war with the Creek Indians. A timid, or a wavering course, at this time, would have proved disastrous to the frontier settlements, and greatly retarded the growth of Georgia. The proceedings of the Council, and commissioners, and military, in reference to these threatened difficulties, will be found briefly stated in the chapter on Indian affairs.

About the middle of 1786, Governor Telfair received notice, from the Secretary of State, that certain books of record, belonging, as was alleged, to the office of the Secretary of State, were detained in Savannah, contrary to an order of the Executive Board, who had directed their removal to the seat of government, at Augusta. To this, it was replied, that the fiftieth Article of the Constitution made each county the custodian of its own records; that the papers, which the assistant of the Secretary had orders to remove, were the records of Chatham County, from the very first settling of the State; that the removal of them would give "great distress" to the inhabitants of that county, as nine-tenths of the records related to the property of the lower counties only; and that a careful inventory had been made of them, and that they were deposited in the office of the Clerk of the County. This letter, to the Governor and Council, was signed by Joseph Clay, William O'Brien, William Gibbons, William Stephens, Richard Wylly, Samuel Stirk, James Jackson, and George Walton,—names of the greatest influence and respectability. "We hope," say these gentlemen, "this measure will meet with your Honor's, and the Honorable Council's approbation, being entirely consistent with justice, public convenience, and the spirit of the Constitution."

The Council, however, thought otherwise. This event, in their eyes, assumed peculiar magnitude, from the character of the actors, and the official position which many of them held; and therefore, on the 17th of March, after a preamble, setting forth that "affairs seemed tending to anarchy, and an infringement of the leading principles of the Constitution, the Board, from the urgent necessity occasioned by such unwarrantable proceedings, and in order, therefore, that the fountain of justice may run pure, and the laws and ordinances may be fully executed in the county of Chatham, have, and do solemnly and unanimously resolve thereupon, as follows:—

"That John Houstoun, Esq., appointed to the office of Chief Justice, be and he is hereby suspended from exercising the duties of the aforesaid office; that Joseph Clay, William O'Brien, and William Gibbons, Esqrs., be and each of them are hereby suspended from the office of Assistant Justice or Justices for the county of Chatham; that William Stephens, Richard Wylly, Peter Deveaux, Samuel Stirk, and James Jackson, Esqrs., be and each of them are hereby suspended from the office of a Justice or Justices of the Peace for the county of Chatham."

This summary proceeding was followed by equally vigorous measures. Eminent counsel were retained by the State, in aid of the Attorney-General; who, without delay, was "required to notify the Chief Justice and Assistant Justices in the county of Chatham, his having in charge, for their deliberation, matters of

State importance; and, upon a court being constituted, that, among other matters and things, he make and demand, in the name of the State, and by the express command of the Executive authority thereof, the immediate surrender of certain State records, now said to be in the hands of James Bulloch, Clerk of the aforesaid Court; and that their honors be informed, that the dignity, interest, and peace of the State, require immediate order to be taken that the aforesaid records be delivered to the State Secretary."

These proceedings, however, did not produce the desired effect; for the several Assistant Justices resigned their commissions; and among these was General Nathaniel Greene, who, having become a citizen of Georgia, was, on the day after the issuing of the order for the suspension of the Chief Justice and Assistant Justices, appointed an Assistant Justice in the new Court. So soon, however, as he learned the true state of things, he refused to serve, and on the 16th April, together with Joseph Habersham, resigned the commissions which had been sent them by the Governor.

The affair caused no little popular commotion; and the real merits of the case were very much distorted, in the personal bickerings and party animosities which it fomented. The Governor laid the matter before the Assembly in July; though it was not until the 20th of November that the Secretary, having informed the Governor that he had received the books, the Council, on the same day, "removed every order and process directed in consequence thereof," and the affair was amicably settled. The gentlemen of Savannah were evidently in the wrong; for, by their own showing, the documents which they retained, were not merely those pertaining to Chatham County; but papers of the Trustees and President and Assistants of the Colony, acting for the whole territory embraced in the chartered limits of Georgia, and also records relating to property in other southern counties. Their action was indeed "disorganizing in its tendency;" and it showed the promptness and vigor of Governor Telfair's administration, that he took such effective measures to sustain the dignity of the Government and the majesty of law. The circumstance is an instructive one, as it shows how a small question, of local interest, can act as the sharp edge of a wedge, which, if driven home with force, may cleave asunder whole communities.

In the midst of these transactions, an event occurred which caused mourning, not in Georgia only, but throughout the land.

At the close of the war, General Nathaniel Greene came to Georgia, to reside, bringing his family with him. They took up their residence, in October, 1785, at the plantation called "Mulberry Grove," fourteen miles above the city, which had been presented to the General, by the Legislature, as a tribute of respect for his merits and services.

In this beautiful place, once the residence of the royal Lieutenant-Governor of Georgia, John Graham, General Greene looked for peace, usefulness, and honor. At the age of forty-three he had achieved a national reputation, and had received almost a nation's ovation, as he journeyed northward the previous year to his native State of Rhode Island. With a mind, so masculine in its power, that he was fitted to command on the broadest scale of military power, he yet possessed sensibilities, which war had not deadened, and which long absence from his loved ones had not crushed; but which, so soon as he had sheltered his family under the rooftree of their new Georgia home, manifested themselves in the sweetness of domestic bliss, and the longing after those social pleasures, which peace now permitted him to enjoy.

Soon after his arrival at "Mulberry Grove," he writes: "We found the house, situation, and out-buildings more convenient and pleasing than we expected. The prospect is delightful, and the house magnificent. The garden is in ruins, but there are still a great variety of shrubs and flowers in it."[3]

"This," says his grandson,[4] "was the happiest period of his life, the months of purest enjoyment that he ever passed: they were destined to be the last."

In consequence of undue exposure to the sun, at the plantation of Mr. William Gibbons, on Tuesday, the 13th of June, 1786, he became quite sick; and though he reached "Mulberry Grove" that evening, and was immediately attended by skilful physicians, yet the disease proved incurable; and, on Monday following, he died. General Wayne and Major Pendleton, a former aid, were with him in his last moment; and the former, in a letter characteristic of his ardent nature, and indicative of his deep affection, thus announced to Colonel James Jackson, the melancholy event:—

"MY DEAR SIR: I have often wrote you, but never on so distressing an occasion. My dear friend General Greene is no more. He departed this morning, six

[3] Johnson's Life of Greene, ii, 418.

[4] Life of Greene, in Sparks's American Biography, new series, 392.

o'clock A. M. He was great as a soldier,—greater as a citizen,—immaculate as a friend. His corpse will be at Major Pendleton's this night; the funeral from thence in the evening. The honors—the greatest honors of war are due his remains. You, as a soldier, will take the proper order on this melancholy affair. Pardon this scrawl, my feelings are but too much affected, because I have seen a great and good man die."

It may well be supposed what sadness and regret would be felt in Savannah, at so sudden and unexpected an event. One emotion of sorrow seemed to pervade all hearts. The town, almost instinctively, put on the habiliments of mourning, and prepared itself to receive his precious remains. His body was brought down the river in a barge, and was met at the town landing by the military, by the civil and judicial officers then in the place, and by the whole populace, which had resorted to the riverside to gaze upon the coffin which contained the remains of him, whom but one week previously, they had seen walking their streets, in the full vigor of healthful and honorable manhood. The funeral procession, long and sad, marched with muffled drums to the graveyard; where, in the absence of a clergyman, the funeral service of the Church of England was read by the Honorable William Stephens, and the remains deposited in the vault prepared for their reception.

This is not the place to enlarge upon the military character of General Greene. His fame was purely military; but, in that, he stood next to Washington. This fame he secured, not by victories, brilliant and important, but by a series of services, skilful manœuvres, and prudent, yet vigorous, generalship, which enabled him to secure, at length, advantages, greater perhaps than would have resulted from a few brilliant conquests. Had he lived, he would doubtless have been called to the councils of the nation; and, though he had already refused to be a member of the Cabinet, yet his countrymen would have demanded, in the Senate, the wisdom and the zeal which were so conspicuous on the field.

At the meeting of the Legislature, in July, 1786, Governor Telfair brought to the notice of that body the complicated state of the finances, and the necessity for taking such action as would afford immediate relief. The State owed nearly a million of dollars, under various claims, which the Governor thought might soon be extinguished from the receipts of moneys and certificates due and owing to the State, if there could at once be established a proper system in the Treasurer's department. To meet, however, "the present pressure upon the treasury, and to make provision for the sum outstanding in gratuitous claims," the Assembly, on 14th August, directed that "paper bills of credit be struck, under the direction of the Governor and Executive Council, in such form, with such devices, and of such denominations, as they shall judge fit, not exceeding £30,000;" and declared that these should be a legal tender in all cases whatsoever. On the 24th October, the Executive Council appointed Thomas Napier, Thomas P. Carnes, William Moss, William Daniell, and Joseph Jackson, to sign the bills of credit, which were issued in denominations of twenty shillings, ten shillings, five shillings, two shillings, one shilling, and sixpence.

It was at the very time that Georgia was issuing these bills of credit, to relieve her debt-burdened treasury, that Washington, writing to Jefferson, says: "Some of the States are, in my opinion, falling into very foolish and wicked plans of emitting paper money." That many extravagances were committed on this subject, by legislative enactment, in several States, is true; and that thereby much financial injury was done to the country, by showing upon what a flimsy foundation its credit stood, is also true; yet, it must be remembered, that the whole currency of the country was deranged, and in a transition state; that the war had been carried on mostly by issues of Continental bills out of the national treasury for nearly three hundred and sixty millions of dollars; that these bills, or, at least, three hundred and fifty-seven millions of them, had so depreciated that five hundred dollars of paper money only passed for one of specie; that these losses fell most heavily on the suffering soldiery and civil officers; that the several States also raised money by issuing Provincial bills; that, after a while, these partook of the general depreciation, were not received as legal tender in sister States, and, at length, caused enormous losses, in which the public faith of each State seemed almost compromised, and its credit hopelessly ruined. Influenced by considerations like these, Governor Telfair hoped that, by gathering up the different liabilities, calling in these Auditors' certificates and Continental certificates, Governor's and Speaker's warrants, &c., and funding them, upon the basis of a new issue of money, secured by new and adequate securities, to replenish the exhausted treasury, and give confidence to the languishing credit of the Commonwealth. At the time that the Assembly in Georgia ordered these bills in English money, Congress was just legislating upon the question of changing the currency of the nation; so that, instead of pounds, shillings, and pence, the money of accounts should be dollars, dimes, cents, and mills, and had not yet established its national mint, where these decimal coins were to be struck, though this institution was founded and its officers appointed in October of the same year.

At the expiration of the year for which Telfair was elected Governor, the Assembly chose to succeed him a man who had but recently come into the State, but who had rendered good service in the Continental cause during the war, as a distinguished officer of the Virginia line,—George Matthews. Whether fighting with the Indians at Pleasant Point; with the British at Germantown; or contending with the malaria on the Chesapeake; or the hardships of a prison-ship in the harbor of New York; General Matthews had displayed singular courage, sagacity, and fortitude. Having served in the southern army under General Greene, he imitated his great commander, by settling in Georgia, and had been but little over two years a resident in what is now Oglethorpe County, when, so conspicuous were his merits, that he was elevated to the highest office in the State.

The Governor was soon called upon to act with vigor, in suppressing a corps of runaway negroes, the leaders of which, having been trained to arms by the British during the siege of Savannah, still called themselves the King of England's soldiers,[5] and ravaged

[5] Jackson's letter to the Governor.

both sides of the Savannah River, plundering and murdering, to the great alarm of the people; who also feared that the presence of this body of freebooters would lead to a general and bloody insurrection of the slaves in that vicinity. Colonel Gunn was ordered to break up their camp, and disperse or capture them.

On the morning of the 6th May, 1786,[6] Lieutenant-Colonel Howell discovered their encampment on Bear Creek, and informed Gunn of the fact. A space of ground, about half a mile long and less than four hundred feet wide, had been surrounded by a kind of breastwork, four feet high, made by piling up the logs and cane, which they gathered from the cleared ground. The only entrance to this inclosure was by a place which would admit but one person at a time; and a hundred and fifty yards in advance of this was placed a sentinel, to give warning of the approach of danger. As soon as Gunn discovered the sentry, he ordered Lieutenant Lewan, with eight men, to rush on, followed by fourteen of the light infantry, with charged bayonets. These brisk movements were followed up by Captain Tatnall, with a detachment of men, on the right, and Major McPherson, with some South Carolina troops and fifteen Catawba Indians, on the left. As soon as the negroes saw the troops within their lines, they fled; and were pursued for about two miles, in all directions. Many were killed, many more wounded, their baggage and provisions were taken, and, having sent Lieutenant-Colonel Howell to search the swamp with a detachment of men, which they did as high as Zubly's Ferry, Gunn, at 5 P.M., burnt all

[6] Letter of Gunn to Jackson.

their houses, twenty-one in number, and destroyed their crops. Thus, in a tour of duty of four days, and without the loss of a man, was the State cleared of one of the most dangerous and best-disciplined bands of marauders which ever infested its borders. Great praise is due to Colonel Gunn, for the promptness and judiciousness of his operations in this important affair.

In the course of his efforts for the prevention of a war with the Creek Indians, Governor Telfair was brought into an interesting correspondence with John Sevier, the first Governor of the so-called State of Franklin. The history of the State of Franklin belongs to the annals of Tennessee; yet, being in some points interlaced with the proceedings of the Legislature and Executive of Georgia, it is important to know briefly the facts connected with its organization and temporary existence, in order to understand aright the policy and measures pursued by Georgia.

At the close of the war, the United States were burdened with an enormous debt, and harassed by unfortunate, and really needy, creditors. To relieve itself of these, Congress proposed that such of the States as owned vacant and unappropriated lands, should cede them to the United States; that these should be disposed of, for the benefit of the United States; and thus, out of what was now waste territory, the debts of the General Government could be paid. North Carolina, having large tracts of land, embraced in Sullivan, Washington, Greene, and Davidson Counties, lying west of the Alleghanies, did, in June, 1784, cede them to Congress, and authorized her delegates to execute a deed of conveyance to the United States.

Thus virtually cut off from the parent State by the law, as the western counties had long been from all sympathy, with the more favored east; and being placed in that peculiar position, of what has been well termed "political orphanage," when the mother State had offered to give up the west, and the Congress had not as yet accepted the cession, and extended over it its paternal care; the inhabitants took the matter of government into their own hands, and called a Convention, to decide upon what measures should be pursued in their anomalous position. At this Convention, it was resolved "to declare the three western counties independent of North Carolina," and a committee was appointed to draw up articles of association.

While these western settlers were rapidly progressing in their movements towards the formation of an independent State, the Legislature of North Carolina repealed the cession act, and made other provisions in favor of these ultramontane counties, which it was thought would be agreeable to them. Despite these conciliatory measures, a new Convention met, organized, adopted a Constitution, gave to the new State the name of FRANKLIN, elected its officers, placing John Sevier in the Governor's chair, and thus launched it upon the troubled waves of political existence. It was not long suffered to float there. The mother State did not tamely brook this rebellion to its authority; and after various and laborious efforts; after many and serious conflicts as to courts of judicature and the authority of laws; and after a struggle which continued until the last stronghold of Sevier's government had been by force of arms taken, the year 1788 saw the extinction of the State of Franklin, and the return of the western malcontents to the bosom of the mother country.[7]

During the existence, however, of this unique State, there were several circumstances which brought it into somewhat close relations with Georgia, and thus places it under our historical purview. On the 27th August,[8] Governor Telfair addressed a letter to Governor Sevier, in which he states that "the Creek Indians have committed murders and depredations on the persons and property of citizens of this State, which have caused the Legislature to adopt measures for the better security thereof." "It being suggested," he adds, "that you intend to march a body of men against the Creek Indians, I flatter myself it will tend greatly to the success of both armies to begin their movements at one and the same time." The time designated by the Governor, was the 1st of November, though that was to be a subject of conference between him and Messrs. Dixon and Lett, who had been appointed, by the Legislature, Commissioners on the part of Georgia. Sevier was greatly pleased at this communication, reposing, as it did, confidence in him, and a desire for co-operation; and he responded courteously to Telfair; though the correspondence had resulted in no practical benefit, when Governor Telfair's term of office expired, and George Matthews succeeded him.

In Matthews Sevier found a warm friend; and he sought to make the ties more lasting, by commissioning

[7] The Annals of Tennessee, by J. G. M. Ramsey, A.M., M.D. Philadelphia, 1853.

[8] Original letter-book of Governor Telfair.

Major Cæsar Augustus George Elholm to visit Georgia, and lay before the Governor and Assembly the affairs of the State of Franklin. This gentleman, a Pole by birth, an officer in Pulaski's legion, who had fought for Georgia in the siege of Savannah, and distinguished himself with Colonel White in one of the most daring pieces of strategy during the war, on the Ogeechee River, so ingratiated himself with Governor Matthews and the Legislature, that he was received by the Executive Council with marks of honor; was invited to a seat in their meetings, and so imparted his own enthusiasm to those around him, that "Success to the State of Franklin" was a reigning toast.

On the 3d February, 1787, the committee of the Assembly to whom had been referred Governor Sevier's letter, recommended to the House "that his honor the Governor inform the Hon. John Sevier, Esq., of the sense this State entertains of their friendly intentions to aid in the adjustment of all matters in dispute between us and the hostile tribes of Creek Indians;" that Major Elholm is "a person entitled to the thanks and attention of the Legislature;" and they recommend that "the Governor give a substantial evidence of their appreciation of him, by a gratuity of £50.

When, later in the year, Governor Sevier sought to prop up his declining government, he despatched Major Elholm a second time to Georgia, with plenary powers, to secure Governor Matthews's mediation between Franklin and the parent State of North Carolina; and when the various papers directed to Governor Matthews and the Speaker of the House were laid before the Legislature, Major Elholm was requested, by the Executive Council, to sketch out a plan of operations for the suppression of Creek hostilities. He told them that Franklin "would move in concert with the operations of your military forces, against our common enemy; and for that purpose a detachment of upwards of a thousand men, well accoutred, now waits your Excellency's chief movements and command."

The Assembly passed a law to raise three thousand men, and empowered the Executive to call for fifteen hundred more from Franklin. They also, as suggested by Major Elholm, granted the land in what is called the bend of the Tennessee, or that portion of the northern part of Alabama between the Tennessee River and the southern line of the State of Tennessee, to the officers and men from Franklin who did military duty in this movement against their common enemy. Lieutenant-Colonel George Handly was deputed by the Governor to return to Franklin with Major Elholm, and to act as Commissioner on the part of Georgia, in the preparations then going on for active exertions in the field.

The field, however, was never taken. The recruiting of troops in Georgia, to form its army of three thousand, was stopped, by the appointment of Commissioners from the United States to treat with the Indians; and the desire of making one more effort for peace, before the State was compelled to proceed to the last resort, a declaration of war.

Pending these negotiations, the State of Franklin ceased to exist as a body politic. Governor Sevier had subsided into a private citizen of North Carolina; and Governor Matthews, having finished his gubernatorial term, retired also into private life, leaving the reins of government in the hands of George Handly, the nephew-in-law of General Elbert; a soldier of prowess and a civil officer of merit, who, on the 25th January, 1788, was elected Governor of Georgia. Prior to his election, however, the Assembly had, on the 9th of January, chosen General James Jackson as Governor. General Jackson was then but thirty years of age; yet had he so distinguished himself in the field and at the Bar, that, unsolicited, this honor was conferred upon him by a large majority of the House. "To the astonishment of his friends, who believed him to be influenced by an ambition not easily satiated with public honors, General Jackson modestly refused an office, which he did not think his age or experience entitled him to. He confessed, with great candor, that such an office was too weighty for his shoulders; and that no honest patriot would assume the duties of an appointment which he had not the talents to discharge."

[9] Life of Major-General James Jackson, by T. U. P. Charlton, pt. i, Augusta, 1809.

CHAPTER III.

REVISING THE CONSTITUTION—GENERAL CLARKE'S SETTLEMENT.

IN 1785, the State of South Carolina petitioned Congress, stating that differences existed between itself and Georgia, concerning its boundaries; the said States respectively claiming the same territories; in particular, that South Carolina claimed the lands lying between the line of North Carolina and a line to be run due west from the mouth of the Tugaloo River to the Mississippi; because "the River Savannah loses its name at the mouth of the Tugaloo." South Carolina also claimed "all the lands lying between a line to be drawn from the head of the St. Mary, the head of the Alatamaha, the Mississippi, and Florida;" which last-mentioned tract was also claimed by Georgia; and praying Congress for a hearing and determination of these respective claims. That body, on the 1st June, 1785, assigned the 8th May, 1786, for the appearance of the said States, by their Agents, and to proceed in the premises.[1]

When that day arrived, the subject was again postponed until the 15th. It was not, however, until the 4th September, 1786, that the Agents of the States

[1] Journal of Congress, x, 190.

attended, and produced their credentials for adjusting this difficulty. The Agents representing South Carolina were John Kean, Charles Pinckney, and John Bull; those representing Georgia, being William Houstoun, George Walton, and William Few. Congress then resolved, that these Agents might appoint, by joint consent, commissioners or judges, to constitute a court for hearing and determining the matter in question, agreeably to the ninth article of the Confederation. As these gentlemen could not, in consequence of certain difficulties, arrange for this court, Congress, at their request, selected three persons from each of the United States, and from this number nine were finally taken by lot, viz., Alexander Contee Hanson, James Madison, Robert Goldsborough, James Duane, Philemon Dickinson, John Dickinson, Thomas McKean, Egbert Benson, William Pynchon; and these were constituted the Court. This Court were directed to meet in New York, on the third Monday in June, 1787. In the mean time, however, the two States, being desirous of an amicable adjustment of their disputes, severally appointed Commissioners—Charles Cotesworth Pinckney, Andrew Pickens, and Pierce Butler, being selected to represent South Carolina; and John Houstoun, John Habersham, and Lachlan McIntosh, to represent Georgia; to meet at Beaufort, in South Carolina, on the 24th April, 1787, and there, if possible, settle the question of claims and boundaries.

After a session of several days, and a full understanding of all the points at issue, the Commissioners agreed to six articles; by which all the lands lying north of a line drawn due west from the head of the most northern branch of the Tugaloo to the Mississippi, were by Georgia yielded to South Carolina; and all the lands claimed by South Carolina lying eastward, southward, southeastward, and westward of a line drawn from the head of the most northerly branch of the Tugaloo west to the Mississippi, were relinquished to the State of Georgia.

This treaty was unanimously ratified by Congress, on the 9th August of the same year; and these agreements were also confirmed in February, 1788, by a ratifying act passed by the Legislature of Georgia. Thus this dispute was amicably settled, and one source of irritation between these sister States was removed.

The year 1788 was rendered still further memorable in Georgia, as within it Georgia signified her approval of the Federal Constitution, and took initiatory measures for establishing a new Constitution for herself.

The Continental Congress, on the 21st February, 1787, adopted a resolution, declaring the expediency of calling a Convention, "for the sole and express purpose of revising the Articles of Confederation, and reporting to Congress, and the several Legislatures, such alterations and provisions therein as shall, when agreed to in Congress, and confirmed by the States, render the Federal Constitution adequate to the exigencies of government and the preservation of the Union."[2] Georgia saw the necessity, and approved the plan, of a general Convention; and appointed as delegates to this body, William Few, Abram Baldwin, William Pierce, George Walton, William Houstoun, and Nathaniel Pendleton.

[2] Journal of Federal Convention. Boston, 1819; p. 6.

The Hon. William Few was the only delegate from Georgia present at the opening of the Convention, on the 25th May. Major Pierce took his seat on the 31st May; William Houstoun, on the 1st June; and Abram Baldwin, on the 11th June. Messrs. Walton and Pendleton did not attend. Of these members, Mr. Baldwin took the most prominent part; and he only, with Colonel Few, signed the draft of the Constitution, as it was proposed for ratification to the several States, on the 17th September, 1787.

Agreeably to the request of the Congress of the Confederation, the Legislature of Georgia, on the 26th October, called a Convention, to meet at Augusta on the fourth Tuesday in December, to consider the proposed Constitution, "and to adopt or reject any part, or the whole thereof." This Convention was composed of the leading men of the State; and John Wereat was elected its President. After due consideration of its several articles and provisions, the Convention did unanimously, and without proposing any amendments, on the 2d January, 1788, "fully and entirely assent to, ratify, and adopt the proposed Constitution;" and, as the last name was signed to the ratification, the good news was announced by a salute of thirteen guns, fired by a detachment of Colonel Armstrong's regiment, stationed for that purpose opposite the State House.

Georgia was the fourth State to ratify this great instrument, which gave shape and permanence to a government, for which the Americans had been struggling against oppression for twenty-five years; and to reach which desirable end, they had wet the soil of every colony with blood during the war of the Revolution. In reference to this prompt action on the part of Georgia, President Wereat, as the official organ of the Convention, writing to Congress, says: "We hope that the ready compliance of this State with the recommendations of Congress, and of the late National Convention, will tend not only to consolidate the Union, but promote the happiness of our common country."

It was also found necessary, in order to bring the State Government into harmonious action with the new Constitution, and to remedy certain defects experienced in the practical workings of the State Constitution, under which the Government of Georgia had been working since 1777, to revise that instrument, or construct a new one. Accordingly, the Legislature, on the 30th of January, 1788, resolved, "that they would proceed to name three fit and discreet persons from each county, to be convened at Augusta, by the Executive, as soon as may be after official information is received that nine States have accepted the Federal Constitution; and a majority of them shall proceed to take under their consideration the alterations and amendments that are necessary to be made in the Constitution of this State, and to arrange, digest, and alter the same, in such manner as, in their judgment, will be most consistent with the interest and safety, and best secure the rights and liberties to the citizens thereof."

On the 6th of October, the official letter of the Secretary of Congress, stating that nine States had accepted the Constitution, was laid before the Executive Council; and, accordingly, Governor Handly called the members nominated and appointed by the Legislature, to meet at Augusta, on the 4th of November, "in order to carry the aforesaid resolutions of the General Assembly into execution." The Legislature was called, by proclamation of the Governor, to meet at the same time; this earlier period than usual being designated because, by a resolution of Congress, Electors for the first President and Vice-President of the United States were to be chosen in each State on the first Wednesday in January, and were to meet and cast their ballots for these officers on the first Wednesday in February, so that the new Government under the Federal Constitution might go into operation on Wednesday, the 4th March, 1789. It was necessary, therefore, that the Legislature should provide a way for the choice of these Electors, which it could not do, if the matter was delayed to its usual time of meeting.

The Convention nominated by the Legislature for the revision of the Constitution met and organized, by choosing Governor Handly, who sat as a member from Glynn County, as President, and James M. Simmons, Secretary. The counties of Chatham, Effingham, Burke, Richmond, Wilkes, Glynn, Camden, Washington, Franklin, and Greene, were represented by two or more members; and, after what they term "serious consideration" and "mature deliberation," they agreed to and signed a form, on the 24th November, which, by order of the House of Assembly, was printed; and five hundred copies thereof were to be "sent by the Executive to the different counties, and distributed among the justices and field-officers of the militia, to be communicated to the people for their consideration." The work done by this Convention was, however, to be revised by another body, created by a resolution of the General Assembly, composed of three persons from each county, chosen by the inhabitants thereof, on the first Tuesday in December, who were to meet at Augusta, on the 4th day of January, 1789, "vested with full power, and for the sole purpose, of adopting and ratifying, or rejecting," the Constitution framed by the Convention appointed by the Legislature.

The second Convention met in January, and proposed certain alterations to the form laid before them. These, by direction of the General Assembly, were also made known to the people; and Governor Walton was directed to call a third Convention, "to adopt the said original plan or form of government, with or without, all or any, of the alterations contained and expressed in the said after-plan of January last."

This Convention met in the Town Hall in Augusta, on the 4th May; considered the several articles and plans before them, and on the 6th, having accomplished the work, waited in a body upon the Governor in the Council Chamber; and the President, William Gibbons, of Savannah, delivered into his hands the Constitution which they had adopted, with a request that he would be pleased to deposit the original in the archives of the State, and cause it to be promulgated to the people. Governor Walton replied:—

"Mr. President and gentlemen of the Convention,—The Constitution for the government of this State, which you now deliver to me, shall have the great seal affixed to it, and be deposited in the office of the Secretary of the State. It shall be announced to the people at large by proclamation, and a sufficient number of copies printed for the use of the several counties. I hope and believe that it will be productive of public good and happiness, the objects of government and of society."

The act of formally accepting the new Constitution by the Governor from Mr. Gibbons, the President of the Convention, was announced to the town by a salute of eleven guns, in honor of the eleven States which had thus far acceded to the Constitution of the United States.

This Constitution, which was nearly identical with that framed by the first Convention, in November, 1788, was a great improvement on the Articles of 1777, and showed how much the people had been taught political wisdom by the experience of eleven years of self-government. Several organic changes were also introduced, as to the constitution of the General Assembly, the election of Governor, the military organizations of the several counties, and of the law courts and proceedings therein; all, however, for the good of the State, and to make the instrument more conformable to the Federal Constitution.

The new Constitution was to take effect and be in full force on the first Monday of October, 1789, when the elections for senators and representatives, prescribed by the second and third sections of Article First were to be held.

The first General Assembly under the new Constitution met on the 3d November following; and organized, by the election of Seaborn Jones as Speaker of the House of Representatives, and Nathan Brownson as President of the Senate.

The next day, agreeably to the provisions of the second section, Article II, of the Constitution, the

General Assembly proceeded to the election of a Governor. The House of Representatives balloted for three persons, and sent to the Senate the number of votes cast for each; the Senators then cast their ballots, which, when counted, were equally divided between Edward Telfair and John Houstoun. On the 9th November, the Senate again balloted, and unanimously elected Edward Telfair.

The inauguration took place in the House of Representatives, on Wednesday, the 11th November. The Governor elect; Governor Walton, and the now expiring body, the Executive Council; together with the Senate, accompanied by the Secretary of State, bearing the great seal, entered the legislative hall, where the oath prescribed by the Constitution was administered by Robert Forsyth, one of the Justices of the county of Richmond; and Edward Telfair was declared the first Governor under the new Constitution.

The House of Representatives on the same day, through a committee, presented an address to his Excellency, congratulating him on his appointment, commending the new Constitution, and assuring him, "that in all their deliberations they will steadily endeavor to keep in view the public good."

A few days after his inauguration, Governor Telfair sent a message to the Assembly, pointing out the necessity of certain additional laws, in order to carry into full effect the provisions of the new Constitution. He also urged upon the Assembly the necessity for laying a tax upon the people for the support of the Government; of reform in the Judiciary department; of a revision of the land act; and of adopting such measures as would give security to the frontier settlements.

Scarcely had they entered upon the consideration of these important topics, before they were agreeably interrupted, in order to keep, with all the people of the United States, their first national thanksgiving, since the adoption of the Federal Constitution.

On the 3d October, the General Congress, sitting in New York, had appointed Thursday, the 26th November, to be set apart as a day of public thanksgiving and prayer, in order that the people of the land might acknowledge, "with grateful hearts, the many and signal favors of Almighty God, especially by affording them an opportunity peaceably to establish a form of government for their safety and happiness." Washington, with a heart ever responsive to such pious emotions, issued his proclamation for the observance of the day; and the General Assembly of Georgia, with commendable promptness, resolved, on the 16th November, that they would, "on Thursday the 26th instant, attend divine service, agreeably to the proclamation of the President of the United States;" and the Rev. Mr. Palmer, then officiating in St. Paul's, Augusta, was "requested to prepare a discourse and form of prayer suitable to the occasion."

At the appointed time, the General Assembly met at the State House, at 10 o'clock A.M., and there, being joined by the Governor, the clergymen, and the officers of State, a procession was formed and marched to St. Paul's Church, where the services and discourse were listened to with great attention; and the thanks of the Assembly were subsequently presented to Mr. Palmer, "for the well-adapted sermon preached by him on the occasion."

It is interesting to find this most distant member of

the Union so ready, through her legislative Assembly, to respond to the resolution of Congress, and to meet her sister States around the altar upon which the religious sentiment of the people would lay its tribute of national praise and thanksgiving.

On the 8th December, 1790, the Legislature divided the State into three Congressional districts; directing that the counties of Camden, Glynn, Liberty, Chatham, and Effingham, shall compose the lower district; the counties of Burke, Richmond, and Washington, shall compose the middle district; and the counties of Wilkes, Franklin, and Greene, the upper district; and the first Monday in January was appointed as the day for the election of representatives to Congress. The elections were accordingly held, and James Jackson was chosen for the lower district, Abram Baldwin for the middle, and George Matthews for the upper district.

Thus the new Constitution was carried out in nearly all its provisions, and the Government, under the judicious management of Governor Telfair, was becoming gradually strengthened and consolidated. There were still, however, many dangers threatening the State from the French and Spanish governments on the south and west; and evils of no ordinary character marred the harmony of the legislative councils, and impeded the free action of the constituted authorities of the State. The subject of the finances of the State, so complicated by reason of the various issues of paper bills, their depreciation, and the different kinds of certificates presented at the Treasury, was full of embarrassment; for it was no easy matter to settle the eight years' accounts of troops, constituted as the American army was; operating in so many States, called out under such various proclamations, and receiving in payment so many different kinds of bills or certificates. Governor Telfair, however, brought to the subject his great experience in financial matters, and was enabled to arrange the operations of the Treasury upon a well-adjusted plan, by which the State indebtedness could be fully known, and provision for its liquidation be judiciously made.

The unsatisfactory relations which subsisted between the State and the Indians within and near its borders; the beginning of a conflict with the General Government as to the right of jurisdiction over the Indians, and the lands ceded by them; and the rise and early development of systematized schemes for stripping the State of its unoccupied territory by organized associations of land speculators; were causes of great disquiet to the Governor, and gave constant employment to his mind and energies.

In the midst of these passing cares, the Governor and the citizens of Georgia were privileged to welcome to their State the illustrious Washington.

On his accession to the Presidency, in 1789, the General Assembly presented him with a congratulatory address, to which he gave a suitable reply; but the people, who had thus approached him through their representatives, were now permitted to see and hear him, and give him such a welcome as was due to the Chief Magistrate of the Republic.

The President reached Savannah on the 13th May, 1791, and was received by the civil and military authorities of the town, with all the display and honors which it was possible for them to bestow. The occasion was one which drew to Savannah persons from the line of the seaboard and the surrounding counties, as all the citizens within reach were anxious, by their presence and congratulations, to testify their respect for the Chief Magistrate of the land. The papers of the day present a glowing account of the proceedings consequent on his visit; and evince the exhilarating effect produced upon the people by beholding one to whom had been confided the management of the war of the Revolution; and on whom had been devolved the onerous work of presiding over the Government of his country.

In reply to the address of the Mayor and Aldermen, Washington said: "While the virtuous conduct of your citizens, whose patriotism braved all hardships of the late war, engaged my esteem, the distresses peculiar to the State of Georgia, after the peace, excited my deepest regret." Such a well-deserved compliment, and such properly-expressed sympathy, was peculiarly grateful to Georgians, and made a deep impression on their minds.

Leaving Savannah, Washington, with his suite, journeyed to Augusta, the seat of government, under escort of a troop of horse sent by the Governor. He arrived there on the 18th May, and was met, five miles from town, by a large cavalcade of officers and citizens, with Governor Telfair at their head, who welcomed the President, in the name of the State, to its seat of government and to its cordial hospitalities. Two days after, the Governor presented a formal address to him in the State House. The affectionate and laudatory language of Governor Telfair expressed the general sentiment of the people; for the inhabitants of the upper counties vied with the lower, in testifying their appreciation of his august character. In the course of his reply to Governor Telfair, Washington said: "I shall always retain the most pleasing remembrance of the polite and hospitable attentions which I have received in my tour through Georgia, and during my stay at the residence of your government."

The President left Georgia, on his return, on Saturday morning, being accompanied to the bridge by the Governor and other officers; who there took leave of him, with all the civic and military ceremonies which the occasion demanded.

Under the working of the new Constitution; and sharing with the other States the advantages secured by the Federal Constitution; the political aspect of Georgia became more composed; and the judicious measures of Governor Telfair tended to augment the population, revenue, and reputation of the State. It was, however, no easy task to bring into order, and adjust to the satisfaction of all parties, inhabitants of such widely-separated districts, who had but little sympathy with each other's pursuits; but little intercourse with each other in social life; and who were but little accustomed to act together for a common end, irrespective of sectional interests; so that the legislation might be as broad as the boundaries of the State, and so nicely adapted to the wants of all, as that each should feel the benefits, and none the oppression, of the common laws of the land. Still, with all the drawbacks arising from the want of homogeneousness of material, harmony of industrial interests, and agreement as to the true policy to be pursued, in reference to the currency, the Indians, and the disposal of the unoccupied lands, the State steadily rose from the almost crushed position in which the war left it, and gave marked evidences of renewed activity and vigor.

The election of Governor for the term commencing in 1793 was a closely contested one. The three names, which the Constitution required should be presented to the Senate by the House of Representatives, were Edward Telfair, George Matthews, and Jared Irwin: Telfair receiving twenty-one votes, Irwin seventeen, and Matthews fifteen. The Senate chose George Matthews; and he was duly inaugurated, a second time, Governor of Georgia.

The record of Executive proceedings during this period is mostly occupied by orders and details as to the calling out, organizing, and posting the militia and other troops, for the protection of the State against the Indians and Spaniards; the former of whom were committing most barbarous ravages on the frontier settlers, and the latter trespassing upon the territory and rights of Georgia.

No other State had so much to impede its advancement, depress its energies, or so much frontier trouble to absorb its growing resources and harass its increasing population; yet, despite these impediments, the laying out of seven new counties in one year, was a cheering token of prosperity.

By several acts passed in 1793, a new county, called Hancock, after the President of the Continental Congress, whose name was first subscribed to the Declaration of Independence, was laid out from parts of Washington and Greene. Another county, to which, in honor of one of Georgia's bravest Revolutionary officers, was given the name of Scriven, was made out of Burke and Effingham. A third, comprising portions of Wilkes and some adjoining counties, was named Warren, in honor of the hero of Bunker Hill. The fourth county was called Oglethorpe, and was originally comprised in Elbert and Greene. The fifth, destined to bear a name which Georgia has ever delighted to honor, and which is associated with her military annals from the time of Oglethorpe, the name of McIntosh, was laid off from Liberty County. The sixth, which was called Bryan, after the venerable and suffering patriot, Jonathan Bryan, was taken out of Chatham County. The last, named from the chivalric General Richard Montgomery, who was killed while leading the American troops against Quebec, was taken off from Washington County. In these counties new towns were established; public buildings of various kinds were erected; and an impetus was given to industry and enterprise which greatly tended to draw in settlers, and diffuse over a greater area the hitherto straitened population.

In order that he might understand more truly the real situation of the frontier settlements, and see, from actual inspection, what they needed for protection and defence, Governor Matthews, in January and February, made an official tour through the northwestern frontiers, from Ward's Mill on the Tugaloo, to Carr's Bluff, on the Oconee; a distance of about two hundred miles. He found a great part of this boundary line exposed to the Cherokee Indians, and nominally protected by only two posts, occupied by the Federal troops. He communicated to the Secretary of War his views as to the necessities of this section; and suggested, as his plan of defence, that there should be stations at every twenty miles, garrisoned by an officer, sergeant, and sixteen privates; half a troop of horse to be posted at each alternate station; who should perform a scout every day to the stations on each side; and thus he thought that by two troops of horse, and two companies of infantry, he could cover the distance of one hundred and seventy or one hundred and eighty miles on the Cherokee frontier. Along the more thinly settled outskirts, on the southwestern frontier, bordering on the Creek nations, he suggested a larger number of men, as being needed to garrison the forts and protect the settlers.

The suggestions of Governor Matthews were only partially complied with. His letters to the Secretary of War were strong, earnest, and at times bore hard upon Congress and the President; and his indignation was quite aroused, when he contrasted the lavish expenditure of men and means on the northwestern frontier, in comparison with the stinted aid furnished to the equally exposed border lands of the South.

The firmness and promptness of Governor Matthews were well tested, by the illegal and dangerous conduct of General Elijah Clarke, in attempting to establish a settlement on lands reserved for the Indians, on the southwest side of the Oconee River. General Clarke had been one of the most active officers in Georgia; and had given evidence of his military qualities on several marked occasions. But when he found that the treaty which General Twiggs and himself had made with the Creek Indians, in 1785, was set aside, and new boundaries, less advantageous to the State, were declared by the treaty which was concluded with this tribe at

New York in 1790, between the President, represented by General H. Knox, Secretary for the Department of War; and Alexander McGillivray, representing the various branches of the Creek nation, on the other; he became greatly incensed, and determined to take forcible possession of the territory, which he conceived had been so improperly surrendered. Such was the military popularity of General Clark, though quite illiterate, and uncouth in his manners, that no sooner did he make known his plan than many restless adventurers joined his standard and marched with him across the Oconee, and planted themselves on the ceded lands.

It was in May, 1794, that Governor Matthews learned of the existence of this settlement, which he supposed to consist of adventurers "who had embarked in the French interest, and that in a short time they would of themselves disperse."

So soon as he was undeceived on this point, he ordered General Irwin, on the 20th May, "to direct the settlers immediately to remove;" and he was soon after informed that they had complied with his request. In the meantime, the President had taken prompt measures to terminate this illegal settlement. General Knox, the Secretary of War, wrote to the Governor of Georgia, on the 14th of May, urging that the most "effectual measures be taken to prevent entirely the expedition, and bring to punishment the authors, actors, and abettors; otherwise the United States may become responsible for the consequences." Lieutenant-Colonel Gaither, of the army, was also authorized to co-operate with the Executive of Georgia, in such way as would best secure the desired end.

On the 14th of July, Governor Matthews learned,

through Colonel Gaither, that General Clark had encamped with a party of men on the southwest side of the Oconee, opposite to Fort Fidius. Being requested by General Irwin, on the part of Georgia, to remove, he positively refused; and, on the 28th of July, the Governor issued his proclamation, as follows:—

"Whereas, I have received official information that Elijah Clark, Esq., late a Major-General of the militia of this State, has gone over the Oconee River, with intent to establish a separate and independent government on the lands allotted to the Indians for their hunting-grounds, within the boundaries and jurisdictional rights of the State of Georgia, aforesaid, and has induced numbers of the good citizens of the said State to join him in the said unlawful enterprise.

"And whereas such acts and proceedings are not only a violation of the laws of this State, but tend to subvert the good order and government thereof; I have therefore thought fit to issue this, my proclamation, warning and forbidding the citizens of the said State from engaging in such unlawful proceedings, hereby strictly enjoining all persons whatsoever, who have been deluded to engage therein, immediately to desist therefrom, as they will answer the contrary at their peril.

"And I do further strictly command and require all judges, justices, sheriffs, and other officers, and all other good citizens of this State, to be diligent in aiding and assisting in apprehending the said Elijah Clark and his adherents, in order that they may severally be brought to justice."

Clark accordingly surrendered himself to the authorities in Wilkes County, who, as they stated, "proceeded to the most mature consideration of the cause, and after an examination of the laws of the State, and the treaties made and laws passed by the United States, do give it as our decided unanimous opinion, that the said Elijah Clark be, and is hereby, discharged."

The effect of this discharge was to embolden Clark and his partisans; and the President authorized the Governor to embody the militia and call in the aid of the Federal troops if necessary, in order to disperse the settlers.

The designs of Clark became quite popular, and it was believed by many that the militia would not march against him. Accordingly, the insurgents pressed forward their operations, established a fort called Fort Advance, built houses, and began a regular and independent settlement.

A Committee of Safety was appointed, a board of officers elected, of which E. Bradley was president, while Clark was chosen the major-general and commander-in-chief of the settlement. Several garrisons, within communicating distances, were established, military stores were obtained, and the most determined resolutions taken to sustain the undertaking. "I am determinedly fixed," says General Clark, writing to Colonel Walton, "to risk everything with my life upon the issue, and for the success of the enterprise."

Before Governor Matthews, in accordance with presidential instructions, resorted to force, he once more tried the effect of negotiation, and sent Generals Twiggs and Irwin to Fort Advance; and General Gunn and Mr. Carnes had also an interview with Clark at Georgetown. "I proceeded," says General Twiggs in his official report to the Governor, "to the unauthorized settlements on the southwest side of the Oconee River, and in the presence of General E. Clark and his party, I read the letter from the War Department to your Excellency, together with Judge Walton's charge to the grand jury of Richmond County, and the law opinion of the attorney and solicitor-general. After a full explanation of the papers above recited, I entered into a friendly conference with E. Clark and his adherents, pointing out to them the danger of their enterprise without the sanction of the State. Notwithstanding all the arguments which could be advanced, they still persisted in their undertaking. Lastly, finding nothing could be done with them, I ordered them to remove within the temporary line between us and the Creek Indians. General Clark called on his officers to collect the opinion of their men, which they did, and gave me for answer that they should maintain their ground at the risk of their lives." Troops, both State and Federal, were therefore concentrated at Fort Fidius, on the Oconee; and such a disposition made of them, and such demonstrations of determination and force by them, that General Clark, upon the promise from General Irwin, "that if he would evacuate the post, himself and his men should be protected in their persons and property," marched out of the place, and the State troops took possession of the works. On the 28th of September they were set on fire, and together with Fort Defiance, another of Clark's posts, and several other garrisoned places, were completely demolished.

On the 12th of October, 1794, the Governor could write to the Secretary of War, "The posts are all burnt and destroyed, and the whole business happily terminated without the loss of blood."

The conduct of General Clark in this affair was reprehensible in the highest degree. It was a violation of the rights of Georgia, of the Indian nation, and of the United States, which had pledged its faith to the Indian tribes to secure their lands from occupation and intrusion. The plea that the grand jury of Wilkes had declared the treaty at New York inoperative, and the proclamation of Governor Matthews illegal, was a mere subterfuge; as these justices being in the interests of Clark, acted without proper power, and discharged their prisoner without due regard to the interests of the State which they were sworn to protect.

The misconduct of General Clark did not cease with the termination of this expedition. Irritated by the failure of his designs in making a settlement at Fort Advance, and condemned by all right-thinking men for his unwarrantable course, he was placed in a condition to be approached by those, who, stimulated by sympathy with the French in their revolutionary proceedings, and sharing with them a hatred of the Spanish nation, had organized a party called the "Sans Culottes," to annoy the Spaniards, and to do other things contrary to the laws of the United States.

General Clark joined this party, and received a commission as major-general, with a pay of $10,000, in the French service. With a band of adventurers, he made incursions into the territory of his Catholic Majesty in Florida, and established his camp at a place called Temple, on the St. Mary's, in the fall of 1795. The French consul in this State, Citizen Swares, disowned any connection with Clark, assured Captain Tauche, who was detailed to operate against Clark, that he had no French commission, and that "if the

French Convention had a lien on the Floridas, they well knew how to plan and execute without involving neutral powers."[3]

The only result of General Clark's movements was to seriously disturb the harmony and peace which pervaded the southern boundaries of Georgia, commit many wanton depredations, and then be compelled to abandon all his schemes and return to Georgia, humbled, defeated, and disgraced.

The 7th section of the 4th article of the Constitution directed that "at the general election for members of Assembly in the year 1794, the electors in each county shall elect three persons to represent them in a convention for the purpose of taking into consideration the alterations necessary to be made in this Constitution."

Agreeably to the provisions of this section, a convention met at Louisville, in Jefferson County, in May, 1795, and was organized by electing Noble Wimberly Jones, President, and Thomas Johnson, Secretary. This body continued in session two weeks, and most of this time was spent in debates upon the rate of apportioning senators and representatives,—the contest being between the lower district and the upper. It was finally settled that the lower counties, consisting of Camden, Glynn, McIntosh, Liberty, Bryan, Chatham, Effingham, Scriven, Burke, and Montgomery, should have twenty-five members; and the upper district, made up of the counties of Richmond, Columbia, Wilkes, Elbert, Franklin, Oglethorpe, Greene, Hancock, Washington, and Warren, should have twenty-

[3] Tauche's letter to Governor Matthews, 1st October, 1795.

six members; each county having, as before, one senator.

This body, after an excited but rather unprofitable session, adjourned on the 16th of May, having ordained and established six articles "as additions and amendments to the present Constitution, to take effect and be in full force on the first Monday in October next." The principal articles were, that the senators were to be chosen annually instead of triennially; all elections to be made by the General Assembly, were to be by joint ballot of both Houses; a new apportionment was made of representatives; the Assembly was to meet annually on the second Tuesday in January, instead of the first Monday in November; the seat of government was to be removed from Augusta to Louisville; and provision was made for further alterations of the Constitution in the year 1798.

The change which the Convention made in the time of the meeting of the General Assembly, caused, at the time, no little excitement, and but for the judicious conduct of the friends of order, might have resulted in most serious consequences.

Governor Matthews had been elected by the Assembly on the 7th of November, 1793, agreeably to the 2d section of the 2d article of the Constitution; and by the 1st section of that article, his term expired on the 6th of November, 1795. The Convention made no provision for his holding over until the meeting of the next Assembly; and therefore, by many it was conceived that Georgia was now without an Executive; and government, so far as it depended on a Governor, was at an end, until the election should be held in the January following.

Had this emergency occurred at any other time, it might scarcely have been noticed; but then the whole State was excited in reference to the speculations which were going on in western lands, and the bill which had recently passed the Legislature; and every occasion of advancing the interest of these land companies, which had been organized for the purchase of the western territory of Georgia, was eagerly seized upon and turned to their advantage.

On the 9th of November, 1795, a letter was addressed to General John Twiggs, by James McNeil, in behalf of his fellow-citizens, in which he states that they had consulted on the subject, and, "viewing with the deepest regret the political condition in which the government is placed by the late Convention, from the 6th of this instant to the 11th of January next, and doubting the civil authority, conceive that they are under a military government, or that they have a right to assume the reins of government until the meeting of the Legislature." He then requests General Twiggs, "inasmuch as the Governor did not exercise the constitutional power given him to convene the Assembly on extraordinary occasions," as the oldest Major-General, to "convene the Legislature at as early a period as possible, to quiet the minds of my fellow-citizens, and retain that order and harmony which is indispensably necessary in all well-regulated governments." Some of the most respectable inhabitants of Columbia County also signed a paper, in which they say: "Conceiving the situation of this State at present to be alarming, and that some measures ought to be taken without delay to prevent impending evils, we, whose names are underwritten, will concur in such steps as may be taken to convene the Legislature at as early a period as may be." General Twiggs consulted with General Jackson on the subject, and his letter gives striking evidence of the intense desire of the people of the upper counties that he should act according to their wishes. But he prudently declined; and while the people were discussing the exciting questions of the day, the second Tuesday in January, 1796, arrived, the Legislature met, Jared Irwin was elected Governor, and the momentarily impeded government was again set in full operation. A more inflammable, or a less law-abiding people, would, in these two months, under the influences which were then at work, have set in motion, if not carried to completion, agencies which would have overturned the government and given up the State to anarchy and misrule.

CHAPTER IV.

SETTLEMENT OF INDIAN AFFAIRS.

NEXT to the troubles incident to the war with Great Britain, were those which arose between Georgia and the Indian tribes.

To give a history of these Indian difficulties, the various turns in their treaties and negotiations, the skirmishing-like warfare so long kept up on the frontier, and the many harrowing details of massacre, cruelty, and destruction, which were perpetrated in the white man's settlements, would require more space than can be given to such detail; and therefore much must be left untold, and much more be left to the imagination, while the historian sketches a brief and confessedly incomplete outline of events connected with the Indian affairs of Georgia.

So soon as a war with the American Colonies appeared inevitable, measures were at once taken to secure the Indian tribes on the side of Great Britain, and we have already seen some of the proceedings of the Indian agents towards effecting this end.

The Indians were unable to comprehend the principles involved in the Revolutionary struggles, or the policy pursued by ministry and commanders in conducting the war. When they took sides with England, it was for gold, plunder, and personal interest; and the aim of the British agents was directed to stimulating such passions in their breasts as would make them most full of hatred towards the Americans, and most anxious to glut their passions for pelf and blood.

When the war with Great Britain was brought to a close, the assiduous attentions of the Indian agents towards the southern tribes ceased. They suddenly withdrew themselves from the nations, or remained to stir up trouble and inflame desires for further carnage. In the pacificatory measures which transpired between the Americans and English, the Indians were left unpacified, and their causes of grievance unredressed; and thus, as the ocean continues to heave and roll long after the storm which vexed it has passed away, so there remained in Georgia many disturbances originated by English machinations, and still showing their evil results, though the exciting cause had long since been removed by the treaty of 1783.

Many Tories and traders found it to their interest to keep up the hostile attitude of the frontier tribes, with a view to private revenge for losses in the war, or for personal aggrandizement, by monopolizing the trade or lands of the Indians.

A party of these men, just at the conclusion of the Revolutionary war, met together, and formed a settlement on the Etowah River, at the mouth of Longswamp Creek, in Cherokee County, and near to the Indian town of that name.

These persons were mostly desperate men, who, having imbrued their hands in Whig blood and glutted themselves with Whig spoil, had fled thither with such property as they could transport, chiefly consisting of negroes and horses, and there organized themselves into a military band, under the command of Thomas Waters. In small parties, these Tories, taking with them a few Indians, made incursions into the surrounding settlements, and even extended their forays into South Carolina, daily stealing goods, cattle, horses, and negroes, and almost daily murdering those who opposed their course.

Their depredations induced General Pickens to apply to the Governor of South Carolina for leave to conduct a small army into the Indian country, to drive them away, and to chastise the Indians. Leave was granted; and Pickens immediately wrote to Colonel E. Clark, by express, requesting him to meet him at Long Creek, with all the men he could raise, on Monday, the 16th of September, 1782, with thirty days' provisions. Clark received this letter on the 6th of September, the next day issued his orders, and, on the 17th, made the required junction, at the head of ninety-eight men, including ten volunteers under Colonel Isaac Jackson, of Richmond County. Pickens had raised and brought over three hundred and sixteen men, including officers; the whole force, therefore, numbered but little over four hundred men. Resting for a day only, to refresh the troops and concert future measures, they renewed their march on the morning of the 19th, directing their course westwardly, through the woods, to the Chattahoochee River, and crossed at Beaver Shoals on the 24th. As they approached the scene of action, General Pickens directed that the two companies of swordsmen, commanded by Captains Maxwell and Mapp, should march by turns in advance, and that silence should be observed by the whole line. All plunder was to be equally divided; and strict orders were given that the aged men and women, and the young children of the Indians, should be spared. After crossing the Chattahoochee, they struck an Indian path, and made two Indians prisoners, who told them that eight miles up the river were several Indian towns, while twenty miles before them was Waters's settlement. Colonel Robert Anderson, with one hundred men, was detached to march up to the Indian towns, piloted by one of the Indian prisoners; while the other Indian promised to conduct Pickens and the rest of the men through the woods to Long Swamp. Without a pathway, they marched till late at night; then rested a few hours on their arms; and by daybreak, having resumed their march, they reached the Etowah River, where they found a small Indian village, and made one Indian prisoner. Colonel White, with a small party, was ordered down that river, to capture some towns on the east side; while Pickens and Clark crossed over, and after a march of ten miles, came to Waters's town at Long Swamp. But the watchful Tory, having learned from his spies the approach of Pickens, had fled with his booty. The General now aimed to secure the alliance of the Indians; and having taken several prisoners, he treated them kindly and sent them to the several chiefs, with requests to meet him at that place on the 17th of October, to deliver up the white men among them, and to make treaties of peace, promising to spare their towns if they complied. In the meantime, Pickens kept his troops in motion; and Colonel Clark marched even as far as Estawnalee, sixty miles from Long Swamp, in pursuit of Waters, who had camped there for a few days, but who fled when again pursued, and continued his flight into Florida. Many negroes, horses, peltry, and a few white men, were taken from the marauders; and by the 17th, the brigade was back at Long Swamp, to receive the Indians, who had promised to meet there in order to make a treaty. Twelve head men and over two hundred others came in, and made a treaty, ceding most of their lands, and promising to meet at Augusta any commissioners that might be appointed by the Governor of Georgia to ratify the same. They also agreed to be at peace with the Americans, and to suffer no more disaffected men to dwell among them.

This treaty was no sooner signed, than the General issued orders for returning; and on the 22d of October the troops were discharged at Long Creek, near the place where they had rendezvoused on the 17th of September. Thus was accomplished the design of this expedition. In thirty-three days from the time this small army left Wilkes, well mounted, indeed, but carrying nothing but their arms and their saddle-bags, without a tent to shelter them, or bread and salt meat to eat, and subsisting entirely on parched corn and fresh beef, without salt; they had penetrated into the depths of the Indian country; had routed the marauding Tories, destroyed many Indian villages, made a treaty of peace with several large tribes, and had secured for Georgia all that country which lies between the western fork of the Chattahoochee and the upper waters of the Savannah, without the loss of a single man, and without one being sick or wounded.

Among the matters which early engrossed the attention of the Legislature in January, 1783, was the state of the Indian tribes; and, on the 11th of January, the House ordered, "that his honor the Governor be requested to prepare immediately and send a talk to the kings and beloved men of the Creek and Cherokee nations, and inform them that it is the desire of this State to meet them in Congress," "in order to demand a cession of land as a consideration or atonement for their many injuries, and to renew our treaty of peace and friendship with them." On the 21st of January the House proceeded to ballot for commissioners to hold this Congress, and chose General McIntosh, General Twiggs, Colonel E. Clark, Colonel William Few, Edward Telfair, John Martin, and General S. Elbert. Five of these, with the Governor (if the emergencies of the State would admit of his being present), were to "constitute a Board, vested with full power and authority on the part of this State, to treat, confer, and agree with the aforesaid Indian nations, on all matters relative to a cession of a claim of land, and to negotiate and agree on such other matters and things as may be conducive to the mutual interest and safety of all parties."

The Commissioners met in Augusta; and, on the 31st of May, concluded a treaty with the Cherokees, based on that of Long Swamp, and securing all the advantages and boundaries which were conceded in that.

In November, 1783, John Twiggs, Elijah Clark, Edward Telfair, Andrew Burns, and William Glascock, Commissioners appointed by authority of the State, met a deputation of the head men, warriors, and chiefs of the tribes of Creek Indians, at Augusta, and formed a brief, but effective treaty, running new boundary lines and obtaining large accessions to the territory of Georgia. The lands thus obtained were, by the act of the Legislature, in February, 1784, laid out into two new counties, called Franklin and Washington; and a Land Court was ordered to be opened at Augusta, on the first Tuesday of April, consisting of "the Governor, or President of the Executive Council, and three members of the same." A large portion of the new acquisition was reserved for bounties to the citizen soldiers, seamen, refugees, and others, who were entitled to land by any resolve of Congress, or act or resolve of the State. While these lands were being surveyed, the Indians were quite peaceable, and the old inhabitants of Wilkes County removed to their former lands and settlements; but this quiet was of short duration. The restless and bloodthirsty Creeks began hostilities again, in May, 1785, in Knox's settlement, killing the inhabitants, burning the houses, stealing the cattle, and whatever else they could carry off.

Colonel Clark heard of this incursion the next day, and, raising a small party of men, hastened after the Indians, overtook them before they had gotten thirty miles, killed one Indian, wounded several others, retook the stolen property, and returned to the settlement. The alarm, however, drew to the frontier several companies of men, who put themselves under Colonel Clark, and were by him so stationed as to protect the inhabitants and enable them to build forts for the security of themselves and families. By dividing the men into squads, and putting them on turns of duty of ten days each, Clark made the burden less heavy upon the militia; and by sending out scouting parties, and keeping up the utmost vigilance, he was enabled to give such protection that little damage was done and much confidence restored. A new treaty was concluded with these Indians, at Galphinton, on the 12th of November, 1785, by General Twiggs and Colonel E. Clark, Commissioners on the part of Georgia; and the same year a treaty was made at Hopewell, on the Keowee, between Benjamin Hawkins, Andrew Pickens, Joseph Martin, and Lachlan McIntosh, Commissioners Plenipotentiary of the United States of America, on the one part, and the head men and warriors of all the Cherokees, on the other.

Treaties with the Indians, then frequent, and councils with chiefs, then of common occurrence, have now ceased in Georgia; and therefore, as a matter of historical interest, it may be proper to give more in detail than would otherwise be needed, the proceedings of one of these councils, as illustrating the talks made, the deeds done, the usages pursued, and the influences at work, in procuring the consent of the Indians to the treaties and cessions of land which it was the object of these conventions to secure and ratify.

The following extracts from the Journal of the Congress held at Hopewell, Kiowee, in December, 1785, and January, 1786, between the Hon. Benjamin Hawkins, General Andrew Pickens, Hon. Joseph Martin, and General Lachlan McIntosh, Commissioners Plenipotentiary of the United States, to treat with the Cherokees, and all other Indians southward of them, within the limits of the United States, will illustrate this subject and give an interesting view of such proceedings. The Journal was kept probably by Benjamin Hawkins, and to it he has added explanatory notes:—

HOPEWELL ON KIOWEE, the 18th of November, 1785.

The Commissioners of the United States in Congress assembled, appointed to treat with the Cherokees, and all other Indians southward of them, within the limits of the United States assembled.

Present, Benjamin Hawkins, Andrew Pickens, Joseph Martin, and Lachlan McIntosh.

From the State of North Carolina, the Honorable William Blount, Esquire, who produced his commission as agent for that State.

The Commissioners ordered a return to be made of the Indians, and there were five hundred. The headmen and warriors having informed that the present representation of their tribes was not complete, but would be so in a few days, it was agreed to postpone treating with them until the whole representation should arrive.

November 21st, 1785.—The headmen and warriors of all the Cherokees assembled. Ordered that the interpreters inform the Indians that the Commissioners will meet them to-morrow, at ten o'clock, under the bower erected for that purpose.

November 22d, 1785.—The Commissioners assembled. Present, Benjamin Hawkins, Andrew Pickens, Joseph Martin, and Lachlan McIntosh. From the State of North Carolina, William Blount, Agent. From the State of Georgia, John King and Thomas Glascock, Commissioners. From all the tribes or towns of the Cherokees, the headmen and warriors. James Madison, and Arthur Coody, Interpreters.

The Commissioners delivered the following address to the Indians:—

Headmen and Warriors of all the Cherokees: We

are the men whom you were informed came from Congress to meet you, the headmen and warriors of all the Cherokees, to give you peace and to receive you into the favor and protection of the United States, and to remove as far as may be all causes of future contention or quarrels, that you, your people, your wives and your children, may be happy, and feel and know the blessings of the new change of sovereignty over this land, which you and we inhabit.

We sincerely wish you to live as happily as we do ourselves, and to promote that happiness as far as is in our power, regardless of any distinction of color, or of any difference in our customs, our manners, or particular situation.

This humane and generous act of the United States, will, no doubt, be received by you with gladness, and held in grateful remembrance, and the more so, as many of your young men, and the greatest number of your warriors, during the late war, were our enemies, and assisted the King of Great Britain in his endeavors to conquer our country.

You yourselves know that you refused to listen to the good talks Congress sent you; that the cause you espoused was a bad one; that all the adherents of the King of Great Britain are compelled to leave this country, never more to return.

Congress is now the sovereign of all our country, which we now point out to you on the map.[1] They

[1] We used McMurray's map, and explained with great pains the limits of the United States, as well as the occurrences of the late war, and we believe they comprehended us. Some of the Indians had visited the Six Nations; some had been up the Wabash, and down the Miami to Lake Erie; and others had been at Fort Pitt, Natchez, Pensacola, St. Augustine, Savannah, Charleston, and Williamsburg.

B. Hawkins.

want none of your lands, or anything else which belongs to you; and as an earnest of their regard for you, we propose to enter into articles of a treaty, perfectly equal, and conformable to what we now tell you.

If you have any grievances to complain of, we will hear them, and take such measures in consequence thereof as may be proper. We expect you will speak your minds freely, and look upon us as the representatives of your Father and friend, the Congress, who will see justice done you. You may now retire, and reflect on what we have told you, and let us hear from you to-morrow, or as soon as possible.

November the 23d.—Present as yesterday.

After sitting some time in silence, the Tassel of Chata arose, and addressed the Commissioners as follows:—

I am going to let the Commissioners hear what I have to say to them. I told you yesterday I would do this to-day. I was very much pleased with the talk you gave us yesterday; it is very different from what I expected when I left home. The headmen and warriors are also equally pleased with it. Now I shall give you my own talk. I am made of this earth, on which the Great Man above placed me to possess it; and what I am about to tell you, I have had in my mind for many years.

This land we are now on is the land we were fighting for during the late contest,[2] and the Great Man

[2] Hopewell is fifteen miles above the junction of Kiowee and Tugaloo. It is a seat of General Pickens, in sight of Seneca, an Indian town; at the commencement of this late war, inhabited by one hundred gunmen, but at present is a waste. Dursets Causas is forty miles east of this, and that was the eastward Indian boundary till the treaty of 1777.

B. HAWKINS.

made it for us to subsist upon. You must know the red people are the aborigines of this land, and that it is but a few years since the white people found it out.

I am of the first stock, as the Commissioners know, and a native of this land: and the white people are now living on it as our friends. From the beginning of the first friendship between the white and red people, beads were given as an emblem thereof; and these are the beads I give to the Commissioners of the thirteen United States as a confirmation of our friendship, and as a proof of my opinion of what you yesterday told us. (A string of white beads.)

The Commissioners have heard how the white people have encroached on our lands, on every side of us that they could approach.

I remember the talks that I delivered at the Long Island of Holston, and I remember giving our lands to Colonel Christie and others who treated with us, and in a manner compelled me thereto, in 1777. I remember the talks to Colonel Christie when I gave the lands at the mouth of Claud's Creek, eight springs past. At that treaty we agreed upon the line near the mouth of Limestone. The Virginia line, and part from the mouth of Claud's Creek to Cumberland Mountain, near the Gap, was paid for by Virginia.

From Claud's Creek a direct line to the Chimney-Top Mountain, thence to the mouth of Big Limestone, on Nalickackey, thence to the first mountain, about six miles from the river, on a line across the same, was never paid for by the Carolina which joins the Virginia line. I wish the Commissioners to know everything that concerns us, as I tell nothing but the truth. They, the people of North Carolina, have taken our lands for no consideration, and are now making their fortunes out of them. I have informed the Commissioners of the line I gave up, and the people of North Carolina and Virginia have gone over it, and encroached on our lands expressly against our inclination. They have gone over the line near Little River, and they have gone over Nine Mile Creek, which is but nine miles from our towns. I am glad of this opportunity of getting redress from the Commissioners. If Congress had not interposed, I and my people must have moved. They have even marked the lands on the bank of the river near the town where I live, and from thence down in the fork of the Tennessee and Holston.

I have given in to you a detail of the abuse and encroachments of these two States. We shall be satisfied if we are paid for the lands we have given up; but we will not, nor cannot, give up any more. I mean the line I gave to Colonel Christie.

I have no more to say; but one of our beloved women has, who has borne and raised up warriors. (A string of beads.)

The War Woman of Chata then addressed the Commissioners:—

I am fond of hearing that there is a peace, and I hope you have now taken us by the hand in real friendship. I have a pipe and a little tobacco to give the Commissioners to smoke in friendship. I look upon you and the red people equally as my children. Your having determined on peace is most pleasing to me, for I have seen much trouble during the late war.

I am old, but I hope yet to bear children, who will grow up and people our nation, as we are now to be under the protection of Congress, and shall have no more disturbance. (A string, little old pipe, and some tobacco.)

The talk I have given is from the young warriors I have raised in my town as well as myself. They rejoice that we have peace, and we hope the chain of friendship will never more be broke. (A string of beads.)

THE COMMISSIONERS TO THE TASSEL. We want the boundary of your country: you must recollect yourself and give it to us, particularly the line between you and the citizens, with any information you may have on that subject. If necessary, you may consult your friends, and inform us to-morrow, or as soon as possible with conveniency.

TASSEL. I will let you know the line to-morrow. I have done speaking for this day.

MUSUCHANAIL, of New Cussé, in the Middle Settlement. I speak in behalf of Kowé, New Cussé, and Watogé. I am much pleased with the talks between the Commissioners and the Tassel, who is the beloved man of Chata. I remember the talks given out by you yesterday. I shall always, I hope, remember that if we were distressed in any manner, we should make our complaints to the Commissioners, that justice may be done. There are around us young men and warriors who hear our talks, and who are interested in the success of this treaty, particularly as their lands are taken from them on which they lived entirely by hunting. And I hope, and they all anxiously hope, it is in the power of the Commissioners to do them justice. The line mentioned by the beloved man of Chata is in truth as he expressed it. I remember it; and it was formerly our hunting-grounds.

The encroachments on this side of the line have entirely deprived us of our hunting-grounds: and I hope the Commissioners will remove the white people to their own side. This is the desire of the three towns I speak for. The settlements I mean are those on Pigeon River and Swanano. It was the desire of the Commissioners that the Indians should tell all their grievances, and I hope they will do justly therein. When any of my young men are hunting on their own grounds, and meet the white people, they (the white people) order them off and claim our deer. (A string of white beads.)

CHESCOENWHEE. I am well satisfied with the talks of this day. I intended to speak; but as the day is far spent, I will decline it till to-morrow. I will go home, and consider on it.

November 24th, 1785.—Present as yesterday.

TUCKASEE. I remember the talks when I made peace. I have appointed Chescoenwhee to speak for me to-day.

CHESCOENWHEE. I rejoice that the Commissioners have delivered their talks to the headmen of the different towns. I am in hopes that these our talks will always remain unbroken. What you hear from the representatives of the towns, the young warriors will invariably adhere to. I am in hopes it is now in the power of the Commissioners, from their talks of yesterday and the day before, to see justice done to us: to see that we may yet have a little land to hunt upon. I was sent here to settle all matters respecting my country; and, being under the protection of the United States, I shall return satisfied. We have been formerly under the protection of * * * * * Great Britain; and then, when I saw a white man, I esteemed him a friend; and I hope that the Commissioners of Congress will see that times may be as formerly. I wish what I say may be deemed strictly true, for so it is; and that I may always be looked on as a friend to the thirteen United States, and that they will see justice done me.

The talks of the Commissioners are the most pleasing to us, as they do not want any lands. Formerly, when I had peace-talks, the first thing the white people expressed was a desire for our lands. I am in hopes you will adjust and settle our limits, so that we may be secured in the possession of our own. I will abide by what hitherto has been said on this subject, but cannot cede any more lands. (A string of beads.)

TASSEL. I have shown you the bounds of my country on my map, which I draw in your presence, and on the map of the United States. If the Commissioners cannot do me justice in removing the people from the fork of French Broad and Holston, I am unable to get it of myself. Are Congress, who conquered the King of Great Britain, unable to remove these people? I am satisfied with the promises of the Commissioners to remove all the people from within our lines, except those within the fork of Holston and French Broad; and I will agree to be content that the particular situation of the people settled there, and our claims to the lands, should be referred to Congress, as the Commissioners may think just, and I will abide by their decision.

UNSUCHANAIL. I and my people are to extend the line; and although our claims are well founded to a large portion of the mountains, which are of little advantage to any but hunters, and of great value to them, yet I am willing to extend the line to the southward until we come to the South Carolina Indian boundary; and we have a right, founded on the treaties at Dewitt's Corner and at Augusta, to make that line as far as the south fork of Oconee, our boundary against the white people.

November 28th, 1785.—The Commissioners assembled. Present, Benjamin Hawkins, Andrew Pickens, Joseph Martin, and Lachlan McIntosh. From the State of North Carolina, William Blount, Agent. From the State of Georgia, John King and Thomas Glascock, Commissioners. The Headmen and Warriors of all the Cherokees. James Madison and Arthur Coody, Sworn Interpreters. Major Samuel Taylor, Major William Hazzard, Captain Commandant John Cowan, John Owen, and George Ogg, merchants, with several other respectable characters.

The Commissioners produced the draught of a treaty on the plan they originally proposed to the Indians, which was read and interpreted to them with great attention; so that they agreed that they perfectly understood every article, and would with pleasure sign the same. Accordingly, two copies were signed by the Commissioners and all the headmen,—the one for the United States, and the other for the Cherokees.

Previous to the signing, the Agent from North Carolina and the Commissioners of Georgia delivered their protests against the same.

After the treaty was signed, sealed, and witnessed, the Commissioners told the headmen that Congress, from motives of humanity, had directed some presents to be made to them, for their use and comfort; and that on the next day they would direct the presents to be distributed accordingly.

November 29th.—Present as yesterday.

The Commissioners ordered a return of the Indians, and there were nine hundred and eighteen; and goods to the amount of $1311 $\frac{10}{90}$ were distributed among the headmen of every town.

The Indians having expressed a desire to say something further to the Commissioners, they attended accordingly.

TASSEL. I will now inform you of some further complaints against your people. I remember the treaty with Colonel Christie, and in all our treaties, that we referred the Long Island of Holston for ourselves, as beloved ground, to hold our treaties on. I remember the Commissioners, yesterday, in an article of the treaty, demanded all their property and prisoners. I am now going to make my demand. I desire that Colonel Martin may be empowered to find and get our prisoners: he is our friend, and he will get them for us. I am now done my talks, and I hope the Commissioners will be as good as their promise yesterday in the treaty. The white people have taken so much of our lands, we cannot kill as many deer as formerly. The traders impose on us greatly; and we wish our trade could be regulated and fixed rates on our goods. Our traders are frequently robbed when coming to and going from our nation. John Bouge was, among others, robbed of about one hundred and fifty pounds sterling worth of leather, in the State of Georgia.

TUSHEGATAHEE. I am not a chief, but will speak for my country. I shall always pay great regard to what I have heard respecting the treaty, as well as what may be sent us from Congress hereafter; and as I am within the limits of the United States, I shall always expect their protection and assistance. Our young men and warriors have heard what has passed. I expect as our boundaries are ascertained, Congress may be informed of them; and that, as peace is now firmly established, and we are all friends, we may be allowed to hunt on each other's land without molestation. On my part, being in peace and friendship with you, I shall feel myself safe wherever I go.

Many of your people on Cumberland and Kentucky have their horses on our lands: and should we find them, I wish Colonel Martin to receive them.

NEWOTA. I am fond to hear the talks of the beloved men of Congress and of ours. Your Commissioners remember the talks, and I shall always endeavor to support the peace and friendship now established. I remember the talks by Colonel Martin, and I promised to be attached to America; but, until the present, I was afraid to be in your country. I am now perfectly happy, as you are to protect us. Your prisoners I will deliver you. Formerly, Captain Cameron saw justice done to us in our land; he is gone, and I now depend upon the Commissioners. If anything depend on me to strengthen our friendship, I will faithfully execute it. You are now our protectors. When I go and tell to those of our people who could not come to hear your talks, what I have seen and heard, they will rejoice. I have heard your declarations of a desire to do us any service in your power. I believe you, and in confidence shall rest happy.

COMMISSIONERS. We will give you provisions for the

road, and wish you may be happy. We will send up to Congress all our talks.

While peace was secured with the Cherokees and the Choctaws, the Creeks continued restless and troublesome, and, in the spring of 1786, recommenced hostilities; but they were speedily chastised. In October, a Congress was held with the nation, at Shoulder-Bone Creek (a branch of the Oconee, in Hancock County), John Habersham, Abram Racot, J. Clements, James McNeil, John King, James Powell, Ferdinand O'Neil, and Jared Irwin, representing Georgia, and fifty-nine chiefs, headmen, and warriors, representing the Creek nation.

The treaty thus made, was signed on the 3d of November, 1786. The several articles of it required that the six murderers of the whites should be put to death; that full restitution of prisoners and pillage should be made; that the old boundary lines, established by treaty at Augusta, in 1783, and in Galphinton, in 1785, should be marked out; and lastly, "in proof of their good faith and sincere intentions to perform the before-mentioned articles, and for the security of the inhabitants of the said State, the Indians agree to leave in the hands of the Commissioners five of their people." "The said Indians, during their stay among the white people, shall be provided with comfortable diet, lodging, and clothing, and be well treated in every other respect."

For a few months the Indians behaved in a friendly manner; but, instigated by McGillivray, and taking advantage of the differences of opinion between the United States and Georgia, they violated their pledged faith and renewed their acts of violence. In a talk sent to them in the spring of 1787, the Executive Council state, "Not a single article of the treaty has as yet been complied with on your part;" though in full reliance upon the faith of the Indians, four of the hostages had been sent back to the nation, the fifth having committed suicide in the presence of his companions.

Without asserting that Georgia had done nothing to provoke the Creeks, and without attempting to defend all its legislation upon Indian affairs, or all the measures which were pursued in obtaining treaties and cessions of land, yet it must be confessed that the chief cause of the difficulties between the Creek nation and the Georgians was Alexander McGillivray, whose influence over that nation was almost supreme.

This man, who played so prominent a part in Indian negotiations, and ruled so regally over the Creek nation, was the son of Lachlan McGillivray, a Scotchman, resident in Georgia, who had amassed a large fortune as an Indian trader. His mother was a half-blood Creek, of high rank on the maternal side, in the tribe of the Wind; though her father, Captain Marchand, was the French commandant of Fort Toulouse. Thus the blood of three nations coursed through his veins. At the age of fourteen he was placed at school, in Charleston, South Carolina, where he was carefully instructed in English; and some years afterwards was removed by his father, who wished to make a merchant of him, to the counting-house of Samuel Elbert, afterwards General, and Governor of Georgia, in Savannah.

Young McGillivray soon discovered that he had no taste for business, though he pursued his literary studies with great eagerness and success. Before the breaking out of the Revolutionary war, he returned to his native woods, on the banks of the Coosa, and was hailed by his maternal tribe as their chief and leader. When hostilities were decided on, he was offered a colonel's commission in the British interest; and he co-operated with the emissaries of England in attaching the Indians to their interest, and engaging their services for the war against the Americans.

The defeat of the British, the confiscation of his father's large estates, and the animosities which the war had excited and cherished, left McGillivray in no very amicable mood towards the United States; and, though he was too shrewd to appear violently opposed to its interests, yet his conduct was often suspicious, always selfish, and seldom such as was productive of good, either to the Creeks, to Georgia, or to the Union at large.

Shortly after the conclusion of the war, having met with William Panton, a Scotchman by birth, a Spaniard by interest, a merchant by profession, and a member of the great commercial firm of Panton, Leslie & Co., of Florida, McGillivray was induced, under the promise of sharing in the profits of this trading house, and of large rewards and honors from the King of Spain, to enter into a treaty with the representatives of his most Catholic Majesty, pledging himself to advance the interests of Spain in her American provinces. For this treaty he was made a Spanish commissary, with the rank and pay of colonel. This was in June, 1784, before the treaty at Galphinton; and the influence of McGillivray in dissuading the tribes from sending headmen and warriors to the treaty-ground, was the reason why so few towns of the lower Creeks were represented at that Council.

It was in the power of McGillivray at any time to have made peace, and kept peace with Georgia; but it did not suit the purposes of himself and master; and hence, under pretexts specious, but false, he kept the border lands in continual trouble, embroiled Georgia in some serious disputes with the Federal Government, and kept the frontier in a state of perpetual ferment and alarm.

The attempt made by the United States Commissioner, Dr. James White, to negotiate a treaty with McGillivray, at Cusseta, in 1788, and the efforts of Governor Thomas Pinckney, of South Carolina, to effect the same end, were alike thwarted by the ingenuity and address of this man, who, under great professions of regard for the authorities of the United States, cherished the bitterest animosity and revenge.

An attempt was made by General Pickens and Chief Justice Osborne, as Commissioners of the United States for Indian Affairs in the Southern Department, to meet the Indians, in 1788; but, being frustrated, they issued the following talk to the headmen, chiefs, and warriors of the Creek nation:—

We last year appointed a time and place for holding a treaty with you to establish a lasting peace between you and us, that we might again become as one people; you all know the reasons why it was not held at that time.

We now send you this talk, inviting you to a treaty on your bank of the Oconee River, at the Rock landing. We wished to meet you at that place on the 8th of June; but, as that day is so near at hand, you might not all get notice. We therefore shall expect to meet you on the 20th day of June.

We have changed the place of meeting from that of last year, so that none of you should have reason to complain; it is your own ground, and on that land we wish to renew our former trade and friendships, and to remove everything that has blinded the path between you and us.

We are now governed by a President who is like the old King over the great water. He commands all the warriors of the thirteen great fires. He will have regard to the welfare of all the Indians; and when peace shall be established he will be your father, and you will be his children, so that none shall dare to do you harm.

We know that lands have been the cause of dispute between you and the white people; but we now tell you that we want no new grants. Our object is to make a peace and to unite us all under our Great Chief Warrior and President, who is the father and protector of all the white people.

Attend to what we say.

Our traders are very rich, and have houses full of such goods as you were used to get in former days; it is our wish that you should trade with them, and they with you, in strict friendship.

Our Brother, George Galphin, will carry you this talk. Listen to him: he will tell you nothing but truth from us. Send us your answer by him.

ANDW. PICKENS,
H. OSBORNE,
Commissioners of the United States for Indian Affairs in the Southern Department.

April 20, 1789.

This effort, however, was abortive, as McGillivray declined to make a treaty; and not only so, but he took measures to thwart General Pickens in his attempt to make a treaty with the Cherokees. "Do you not see," he says, writing to Panton in reference to his success in defeating these measures, so important to Georgia and the United States, "my cause of triumph in bringing these conquerors of the old masters of the new world, as they call themselves, to bend and supplicate for peace at the feet of a people, whom, shortly before, they despised and marked out for destruction?"

Unwilling to relinquish the efforts at Indian pacification, other and more honorable Commissioners were associated with General Pickens, and appointed to treat with McGillivray. These were General Lincoln, who had served as commander of the Southern army during the Revolutionary war; Cyrus Griffin, a former President of the Continental Congress, and David Humphreys, one of the military family of Washington, and subsequently minister to Spain. These persons sailed from New York, August 31st, for Savannah, in a vessel well laden with Indian presents; and, having reached there on the 10th of September, in safety, they prepared to enter upon their duties, by sending word to McGillivray of their arrival, and requesting him to meet them, on the 20th of September, at Rock Landing, on the Oconee. To this place they accordingly repaired, with their escort, a company of United States Artillery, under Captain Burbeck ,and pitched their tents, on the 20th of September, 1789, on the eastern bank of the river.

McGillivray, with two thousand warriors, gathered

around him to display his power and overawe the Commissioners, encamped on the western bank of the Oconee; and, after several days spent in private interviews with McGillivray, and the formalities usual on such occasions, the business of the Council was entered upon on the 24th of September, by the Commissioners presenting to the chiefs a draught of a treaty which they proposed as the basis of pacification. At the time of its delivery, the Indians seemed pleased; but when it was talked over in the council of the chiefs that night, dissatisfaction appeared, and so increased, that the next morning McGillivray wrote to the Commissioners that the boundaries proposed did not satisfy the nation, and that the chiefs had resolved to break up the Council and depart.

This announcement took the Commissioners by surprise, and they immediately addressed a note to McGillivray, imploring him to prevail on the chiefs to remain. Instead of this, however, he abruptly broke up the encampment, and, under plea of seeking forage for his horses, moved back several miles from the river; and two days after, from his camp on the Ocmulgee, he wrote to the Commissioners that he had determined to return to the nation, "deferring the matter in full peace till next spring." "We sincerely desire a peace, but we cannot sacrifice much to obtain it."

It was with great mortification, after so much toil and expense, and so large expectations of fruitful results, that the Commissioners were obliged to report to the Secretary at War, that "The parties have separated without forming a treaty."

General Lincoln and party returned to Augusta, on the 2d of October, and there spent several days in investigating the character of the treaties already made with the Creeks,—especially in reference to the treaties of Augusta, Galphinton, and Shoulder-Bone, concerning which there had been circulated such false reports, so injurious to the honor and integrity of Georgia. Their report upon this subject is important, as it fully defends the course of Georgia, and shows the flimsiness of the attempts of McGillivray and other interested parties to misrepresent the facts, deny the conclusions, and set at nought the binding authority of these treaties. "The Commissioners beg leave further to report, that, after the most accurate investigation in their power to make, after consulting the best documents, and having recourse to credible depositions, they are unable to discover but that the treaty of Augusta, in the year 1783, the treaty of Galphinton, in the year 1785, and the treaty of Shoulder-Bone, in the year 1786, were, all of them, conducted with as full and as authorized representation, with as much substantial form and apparent good faith, and understanding of the business, as Indian treaties have usually been conducted, or perhaps can be, where one of the contracting parties is destitute of the benefit of enlightened society; that the lands in question did, of right, belong to the lower Creeks as their hunting-ground, have been ceded by them to the State of Georgia for a valuable consideration, and were possessed and cultivated for some years, without any claim or molestation by any part of the Creek nation."

The Commissioners left Augusta on the 6th of October, and reached New York on the 10th of November; and, on the 17th, made a full report of their fruitless mission. In this report, they state that they "are decidedly of opinion that the failure of a treaty at this time with the Creek nation can be attributed only to their principal chief, Mr. Alexander McGillivray;" and sustain this opinion by six strong reasons, showing the deception, duplicity, selfishness, and falsehood of this chief, who, for private ends, thwarted all the efforts of the United States, and imperilled the peace and prosperity of Georgia. At the very time, however, that he was engaged in this business with the Commissioners of the United States, he was, also, as we learn from his letters to Panton (written only a few days before the meeting at Rock Landing), seeking to draw still larger honors and emoluments from Spain, by operating on the fears of the Governor of Florida, by threatening to loose the alliance with the Creeks, and on the avaricious views of Panton, by intimating the necessity of his withdrawing himself from the partnership with that trading house, which had so long supplied his nation with food.

Washington was unwilling to plunge the infant republic into the horrors and expense of an Indian war; and he determined to make one more effort to secure peace with the Creeks. He was justly incensed at the audacity and perverseness of McGillivray; yet, as no treaty could be held with the Indians without his authority and consent, he sought, by new and more private overtures, to secure the friendship of one, whose ill-will could track the whole frontier with blood—whose favor could make that same frontier peaceful and secure.

On the day after the Commissioners had reported to the President the failure of their negotiations, he sent General Knox, Secretary of War, to Colonel Marinus

Willet, an officer who had served with distinction in the Revolutionary war, with a request that he would undertake a secret mission[3] to the haughty chief. He consented, and, embarking at New York, on the 15th of March, 1790, for Charleston, he landed in that city, after a passage of fourteen days, and immediately directed his steps towards the residence of General Pickens, in the upper part of South Carolina. He reached that place on the 13th of April, and tarried there about a week, in conference with the General, to whom, and to whom alone, Washington had permitted him to confide the nature of his mission, and from whom, as from one fully conversant with Indian affairs, he gained much practical knowledge as to the best mode of carrying out his important mission.

General Pickens was a person in whom McGillivray had confidence, and with whom he corresponded; and no one, therefore, was so well qualified to advise Colonel Willet, as this sagacious and experienced General. On leaving South Carolina, Colonel Willet made a detour through the Cherokee country, guided by an Indian, called Young Corn, and attended by a single body-servant, and at length reached the Killebees, one of the Creek settlements, on Friday, 30th April. There he had the satisfaction of meeting McGillivray; and, "I went to bed," he writes in his journal, "happy in being under the same roof with the man I have travelled thus far to see."

McGillivray impressed the Colonel quite favorably. "He appears to be," he says, "a man of an open, candid, generous mind, with a good judgment and very

[3] "A Narrative of the Military Actions of Colonel Marinus Willet." New York: 1831.

tenacious memory." The Creek chief was gratified with the special mark of attention from the President, in sending to him such an ambassador; and after several days' conference with the secret agent, he appointed a council of chiefs to meet him at Ositchy, on the 17th of May.

The ceremony of the *black drink* having been conducted with due form, in the great square of the town, the chiefs assembled, at eleven o'clock on that day, to hear what Colonel Willet had to propose. "I am come to you," he said in his speech, "from our beloved town (New York), by order of our beloved Chief, George Washington, to invite you to a treaty of peace and friendship, at a council-fire in our beloved city." After stating the wishes of Washington for the prosperity of the red people, and his desire to form a lasting treaty of peace and amity with them, he informs them that the United States wanted none of their lands, but would secure them unmolested, would promote their trade, and contribute all in its power towards the welfare and happiness of the nation. He concluded by saying: "Brothers, I stand before you a messenger of peace. It is your interest, and it is our interest, that we should live in peace with each other. I promise myself that you will attend to this friendly invitation, and that your beloved chief, with such other of your chiefs and warriors as you may choose for that purpose, will repair with me to the council-fire that is kindled in our beloved town, that we may form a treaty which shall be strong as the hills, and as lasting as the rivers."

Having delivered his speech, he withdrew, and left the chiefs to confer together. An hour passed, and he was called again to the council, and informed that his talk had been acceptable, and his propositions agreed to. "Brother," said the Hallowing King, speaking in behalf of the chiefs to Colonel Willet, "you say you came from our beloved chief, George Washington, to invite our beloved chief to a council-fire, in your beloved town. The road is very long, and the weather is very hot; but our beloved chief will go with you, and such other chiefs and warriors as shall be appointed for that purpose shall go with him. Brother, all that our beloved chief shall do, we will agree to. We wish you may be preserved from every evil. We will count the time our beloved chief is away; and when he comes back we shall be glad to see him, with a treaty that shall be as strong as the hills, and last as long as the rivers."

On the 21st of May, Colonel Willet met another council of chiefs, at Nickabache; and, after the ceremony of the *black drink*, delivered to them a talk similar to the one spoken before, and received in answer nearly the same reply, from the venerable and influential chief, called the White Lieutenant. Having done all that was needful to secure the confidence of the Indians, Colonel Willet and McGillivray, with eight warriors and some few attendants, started from Little Tallasse, on the 1st of June, for New York. A long journey was before them, and the brief record of it which Willet gives in his journal, is peculiarly interesting.

On the 9th, they reached the Stone Mountain, in what is now De Kalb County; and Colonel Willet ascended to the summit. On the 14th, they reached the house of General Pickens, and were warmly welcomed.

Here they remained a few days, until some other Indians joined them; and, on the 18th, the party, increased to thirty Indians, left the hospitable mansion of the General, on their northern progress. Twenty-six of the Indians rode in three wagons, and four were on horseback; Colonel McGillivray, his nephew, two servants, and interpreter, with Colonel Willet's German man John, were also in the saddle; while Colonel Willet himself travelled in his sulky.

The party attracted great attention as they passed through the towns and villages, and were everywhere kindly received and entertained, particularly at Guilford in North Carolina, Richmond, and Philadelphia. At Elizabethtown Point they found a sloop in waiting, to transport them to New York. It was about noon, on Tuesday, the 20th of May, when they landed near the Coffee House, "and were received with great splendor by the Tammany Society, in the dress of their Order," conducted up Wall Street past the Federal Hall, where Congress was in session, and with much pomp and parade were escorted to the President. After their introduction to the President, "the Indians, with additional parade, visited the Minister of War and Governor Clinton, and then repaired to the City Tavern, where an elegant entertainment finished the day."

The party devoted some days to the scenes and excitements of their new position; and then measures were taken to bring McGillivray and the chiefs into such relationship as should make them disposed to treat with the United States. At first, the negotiations, according to the President's request, were conducted informally,—a measure rendered necessary, perhaps, by the fact, that no sooner did the Governor-General of Havana learn of the intended visit of McGillivray to New York, than he despatched the Secretary of East Florida thither; who, being furnished with a large sum of money, under the ostensible purpose of purchasing a cargo of flour, was yet directed to use his money and his influence, as an officer of his Catholic Majesty, to prevent McGillivray from forming a treaty with the United States; or, if not able to accomplish that, to embarrass his negotiations, and render them as nugatory as possible.

On the 6th of August, the President notified the Senate, that the adjustment of the terms of a treaty with the Creeks was far advanced, and that the time had arrived when the informal method, hitherto pursued, should give place to the regular form of negotiation; and hence he nominated General Knox as a Commissioner to conclude the treaty with the Indians.

General Knox found matters already shaped and prepared, so that his labors were merely the formal acts of putting the articles in due order, and, with the Indian chiefs, signing and sealing the same with the usual formalities.

The next day, therefore, Washington communicated to the Senate the treaty which had been made, and stated: "I flatter myself that this treaty will be productive of present peace and prosperity to our Southern frontier, and that it will, also, in its consequences, be the means of firmly attaching the Creeks and the neighboring tribes, to the interests of the United States." He also, in this message to the Senate, expressed the hope that the treaty would "afford solid grounds of satisfaction to the State of Georgia, as it contains a regular, full, and definitive relinquishment, on the part of the Creek nation, of the Oconee land, in the utmost extent in which it has been claimed by that State, and thus extinguishes the principal cause of those hostilities, from which it has more than once experienced such severe calamities."

The treaty which the President laid before the Senate for their ratification, was signed by Knox, sole Commissioner, on the part of the United States, and McGillivray and twenty-three chiefs, in behalf of themselves and the whole Creek nation; and, having received the confirmation of this body, it was proclaimed by the President, on the 13th of August, 1790.

This treaty did not give satisfaction to Georgia, and was the occasion of much discord between the State and the General Government, as well as the occasion of much intestine trouble.

It has been seen how continually the Creeks kept up their depredations upon the frontier, stimulated or connived at by McGillivray and others in the Spanish interest. These perpetual irritations had caused Georgia to call forth her citizen soldiers, and also to appeal to the General Government for Federal troops, to repel aggressions and protect the frontier.

The minutes of the Assembly, and the letters of the Governors, show how much thought was bestowed upon our Indian relations, and how feverishly anxious the Georgians were made by the persistency of the Creeks in their predatory, and often sanguinary, warfare.

With mercenary speculators grasping after Indian territory, on the one hand; and Spanish intrigue, stimulating savage passions, on the other; it was no cause of wonder that so many atrocities were committed, and so much done to inflame both the white man and the red man with mutual hate and revenge. "It is needless," says Governor Walton, writing to Washington, 11th March, 1789, "for commentaries on transactions so extraordinary and flagitious; but I cannot forbear to observe, that whilst proceedings of this kind are permitted, it will be wholly out of the power of this State to preserve that peace with the savages which it would seem is so much the object of the Union." Addressing the President of the Board of Wardens of Savannah, the Governor writes: "It is extremely distressing to me to be under the necessity of informing the citizens of Savannah, that our prospects of peace have changed to inevitable war." "The late arrangements for an attack upon us, demonstrate, that so far from the Indians being disposed to meet the offers of peace, they are determined for war." After stating "that the Government, as well as the Commissioners of the Union, have done everything in their power this year (1789) to bring about a treaty," and "that it is demonstrated beyond the possibility of doubting, that the war is wholly continued on the part of the Indians," he adds, "I have directed Lieutenant-Colonel Fishbourne to aid your arrangements for the defence of your valuable town, which I sincerely hope will not be exposed to any danger."

During the two previous years, as appears by a return of depredations, made by Governor Walton to the United States Commissioners, October 4, 1789, the Creeks had murdered eighty-two persons, wounded twenty-nine, taken prisoners one hundred and forty, burnt eighty-nine houses, and carried away horses and cattle and goods to the value of many thousand dollars.

However fair the promise held out by the treaty with the Creeks, at New York, seemed to be, in its provisions, yet there were two causes which led to continued disturbance between Georgia and the Indians: one, growing out of the treaty itself, and the other, out of the character of the chief, McGillivray.

It had been all along asserted by the Creeks, as a cause of their hostilities, that the treaty of Galphinton, in November, 1785, was made by only a portion of the chiefs, who had no right to act for the whole nation; that the lands ceded by that treaty were ceded under the influence of threats and the implication of force; and that they really did not comprehend, at the time, the value of the cession which the treaty demanded. The answer to these charges is found in the full refutation of them by George Walton, as Governor of Georgia (letter to Commissioners, October 4th, 1789), and by the report of General Lincoln, Colonel Humphreys, and the Hon. Cyrus Griffin, the United States Commissioners, who, after careful investigation of the subject, declared that the Galphinton treaty was made with a proper representation of the Creek chiefs; that the lands were not ceded under threats, or fear, or force; and that all the doings in reference to the treaty were according to the usual forms of such negotiations. These opinions, by men who had no interest in Georgia, supported by the views of the very intelligent Governor of the State, and by the unanimous voice of the General Assembly, were, however, virtually ignored in the treaty at New York; for the whole claim of Georgia, arising out of the Galphinton treaty, "of land to the eastward of a new temporary line, from the forks of the Oconee and the Ocmulgee, in a southwest direction to the St. Mary's River," was yielded up by General Knox, as McGillivray and the chiefs under his influence absolutely refused to surrender it. This concession was regarded as an unjust surrender, by the United States, of land, the title of which had already been extinguished by Georgia, and which consequently belonged to Georgia; and the excitement which this produced drew after it most disastrous consequences.

It brought the Indians nearer to the white settlements on the Oconee; it gave them license to break other treaty stipulations; it lowered in their minds their idea of the power and rights of Georgia; it provoked the unjustifiable settlements and military occupation of the disputed territory by General Clark; it excited hostilities and bloodshed along the frontier line; and was an occasion of continual annoyance to the citizens and government of the State.

McGillivray, upon whose promises so much reliance had been placed, and whose honor was in the keeping of the highest bidder, found himself soon opposed and weakened by the machinations of an adventurer, whose history is as romantic as the shifting scenes of the most exciting drama.

William Augustus Bowles was born in Maryland, in 1764, and when a mere lad, joined the British army, in which he was appointed Ensign to a provincial company. He was present with his corps at the battle of Monmouth, and, in the autumn of 1778, embarked at New York, with his company, first for Jamaica, and thence for Pensacola, in Florida. A wild, thoughtless boy, unfit to be intrusted with a commission, his reckless conduct brought upon him mortification and disgrace. He had not been a year in the army, before his name was stricken from the roll: and the young Ensign, friendless and almost penniless, was turned adrift from the garrison, and abandoned to the dangers and vicissitudes of a frontier life, in an inhospitable clime, and among savage tribes. Turning away with disgust from his former friends, and flinging his uniform into the sea, he attached himself to a party of Creeks, then at Pensacola, and about to return to the Indian nation; and with them he penetrated to the frontier of Georgia. In a few months, he returned to Pensacola, discontented with his uncivilized companions; and, after suffering many hardships along the coast, he again fell in with a party of Creeks, and returned with them to their wilderness homes. Here he remained for two years, during which period he acquired their language, married the daughter of one of the chiefs, and was taken into favor by the headmen of the nation.

When war was declared between Great Britain and Spain, he repaired to Pensacola with a war party from the Creek nation, and was kindly received by General Campbell, who reinstated him in the corps from which he had been expelled. Here he fought bravely, and did good service, until, on the reduction of West Florida, he went with the troops to New York, and there remained on parole until exchanged.

Having received a furlough from Lord Dorchester, he again repaired to the Creeks, visiting, on his way thither, his father, a planter, in Maryland. By the Creeks he was warmly welcomed, though his stay with them was brief, as he shortly went to the Bahamas, where the versatility of his mind displayed itself in establishing him on the stage, as a manager and actor; and among the people of New Providence, as a portrait painter. These occupations, however, were only masks, to cover up his real designs, which, all the while, through secret agents, he was actively carrying on; and, though at one time suspicion was aroused against him, and the grand jury of the island presented him "as a dangerous and suspected person, whom it behooved Government to secure," yet he adroitly extricated himself from these difficulties, and boldly vindicated, through the public press, "The Lucayan Royal Herald," his injured reputation. In 1789, in a vessel chartered by him, he set sail for St. Marks, in Florida; and, having arranged with the Creeks to meet him there, he was enabled, in the face of the Spanish authorities, to land his contraband goods and secure their transportation to the Indian country.

These trading voyages he repeated; and at last, having taught five Indians the art of seamanship, he bought a small vessel, armed it with six four-pounders, manned it with his Indian sailors, and then, as captain of the piratical craft, he cruised about the Bay of Appalachicola, capturing whatever he could take, and even fighting off the Spanish Guarda Costa, which had been sent from the Havana to take him.

The large reward of six thousand dollars, and fifteen hundred kegs of taffia (rum distilled from molasses), was offered for his capture by the Spanish authorities; but he evaded his pursuers, and, temporarily abandoning the sea, he returned to the Creek country, and was elected one of the chiefs and counsellors of the nation.

This step brought him at once into rivalry with, and

opposition to, McGillivray, and was the origin of a series of intestine wars, and contentions among the southern Indians, destructive alike to the peace and prosperity of the red people and the white.

McGillivray, so soon as he learned that Bowles was assuming a chieftain's authority, ordered him to leave the nation,—which Bowles did, though in a manner which he contrived to turn to his ultimate advantage. Proceeding to New Providence, one of the Bahamas, where Lord Dunmore was Governor, he so ingratiated himself with that officer, and so represented to him the desire of the Creeks for alliance with England, and their willingness, if aided by England, to break with their Spanish and American friends; that his lordship sent him to England, at the head of a delegation of Creeks and Cherokees, to represent their case at the British Court, and secure its favor to his plans. Accordingly, he appeared in England, as the "ambassador from the united nations of Creeks and Cherokees to the Court of London," being appointed, as was stated, "by the unanimous voice of twenty thousand warriors, ready to hazard their lives at the command of their beloved brother, son, and chief."[4]

His mission, however, was not as successful as he had anticipated. He received, together with the Indians, valuable presents, and excited much public curiosity; but his plans were not approved, and he returned to New Providence, to sink back, for a time, into a privateersman, directing his attacks principally against the vessels of Panton, the commercial partner

[4] "Authentic Memoirs of William Augustus Bowles, Esq'r, Ambassador from the United Nations of Creeks and Cherokees to the Court of London." London: Printed for R. Faulder, New Bond Street, MDCCXCI.

of McGillivray, several of which he captured,—and made himself rich and influential with his booty. Reappearing among the Creeks, as the head of a party, he made a bold stand against McGillivray, whose influence he succeeded in lessening, and stirred up against McGillivray much hatred and opposition. McGillivray found it difficult to withstand the opposing current; and, apparently yielding to it for a time, he repaired to New Orleans, and did not return until the strongest remonstrances had been sent to him, reproaching him for his pusillanimous conduct, and urging him to come back and reassert his half-vacated rights, and rule. Bowles gave it out through the Indian nation, that he was an accredited agent of the King of England; that the Americans, when they made peace with England, had no right to take the Indian lands, because the Indians were under the power of the Crown, which did not cede their lands with the territory of the thirteen colonies; hence, that the Americans had no right to their soil, or their services, and must be held as intruders, whom it was the duty of the Indians to drive away.

The Government of Great Britain, when called upon to state whether they acknowledged Bowles as their agent, distinctly repudiated him. Mr. Hammond (his Britannic Majesty's Minister to the United States), in a letter to Mr. Jefferson, Secretary of State, assured the Government "in the most explicit manner, that the assertions said to have been made by Mr. Bowles, of his pretensions having been encouraged or countenanced by the Government of Great Britain, or of his having been furnished by it with arms and ammunition, are entirely without foundation."

Between the usurpations of Bowles, and the double-dealing of McGillivray, the treaty line, as agreed upon at New York, was not run. The United States appointed surveyors and commissioners; but they were not permitted to act, in consequence of these intestine broils. The Government felt called upon to do all in its power to crush Bowles, and to throw its support in favor of McGillivray; yet the latter was unworthy of any confidence, and his hesitating and tortuous course was the occasion of much trouble both to the Indians and to the Georgians; was the cause of most of the difficulties of the State Government; and gave the Federal Government continual anxiety and alarm.

Bowles, now styling himself "General," was at last captured by the Spanish authorities, taken to New Orleans in chains, and thence sent as a state prisoner to Madrid. His capture removed from the nation one element of discord, though it did not contribute towards the accomplishment of the purposes of the Federal Government, viz., the establishing of well-defined boundaries, the protection of the frontier, and the securing of peace among the Southern tribes.

Owing to the supineness of Seagrove, the double-dealing of McGillivray, the freebooting settlement of General Clarke, the intrigues of Panton and the Spanish officials in Florida, and the irritated feeling of the Georgians at the way in which their wishes had been disregarded and opposed; the stipulations of the New York treaty were not carried out; and the horrors of a border warfare with savage tribes still hovered over the Southern frontier of Georgia.

In 1793, McGillivray, having returned the previous

autumn from New Orleans, where he had been courteously entertained by the French Governor, repaired once more to Pensacola, to enjoy the hospitality of the Spanish authorities, and the counsel of his merchant-friend Panton. It was his last visit. Already enfeebled in health, he was taken ill on his way to Florida, and died, on the 17th February, 1793, at the house of Mr. Panton, eight days after his arrival in Pensacola; and was buried, with civic and masonic honors, in his friend's beautiful garden, then redolent of the blossoms of spring, and green with the vernal glories of that land of flowers.

McGillivray was a man of strong natural abilities, which, had they been properly cultivated, would have made him eminent; and, even though imperfectly developed, he yet exhibited diplomatic powers which enabled him to baffle treaty commissioners, Indian agents, heads of departments, Governors of States, and even impose on the carefully formed judgment of Washington.

As a chief, he lacked vigor and decision; and, lowering himself from the position which he occupied, as the head of the confederacy of Creeks, he stooped to engage in trade, and bound himself down by such commercial fetters to Spanish merchants, as weakened his influence, drew off his attention from state affairs, and caused him to turn all his efforts towards enriching himself and extending his trade; while the interest of the nation of Creeks was unheeded, except when some great outside pressure roused him to action. He was, moreover, a great dissembler; and so adroitly did he manage his dealings with the Americans, English, French, and Spanish, that each feared to break with him; while each distrusted his loyalty, and watched him with ill-concealed suspicion.

His indecision, and mercantile trammels, were the cause of much of the troubles which so long afflicted Georgia; while his want of promptness and energy, enabled Bowles almost to beard him in his native forests, and well-nigh wrest from him the sceptre of the nation.

As for Bowles, after still further escapes and adventures by land and sea, he ended his life as a prisoner of state in the dungeons of Moro Castle, in Havana.

Matters had now reached such a crisis that Governor Telfair, having applied to the General Government in vain for such aid as he thought the exigencies of the frontier demanded, resolved to conduct the military operations of the State himself; and summoned a council of general officers to meet him in Augusta, on Thursday, 8th August, 1793.

The council, consisting of Governor Telfair as Commander-in-chief, Major-Generals John Twiggs, James Jackson, and Elijah Clarke, and Brigadier-Generals Glascock, Morrison, Clarke, Irwin, and Gunn, took into consideration what measures were proper to be adopted for the safety and protection of the citizens of the State. They determined that it was necessary to make an expedition against the hostile towns of the Creeks, in October; and that, for this purpose, "at least two thousand horse and three thousand foot ought to be ordered to camp for the objects that may arise in the intended expedition," to serve, after their arrival in camp, for sixty days.[5]

[5] American State Papers, iv, Indian Affairs, 370.

This line of operation was not agreeable to the views of Washington, who directed the Secretary of War, General Knox, to say to Governor Telfair, "that he utterly disapproved the measure" proposed, giving his reasons in full for such disapproval, and to express his desire that the offensive expedition should not be undertaken.

This letter put a stop to the active preparations that were going on to carry out the views of the military council, and drew from the Governor a reply, of blended remonstrance and appeal, expressive of his deep disappointment at being compelled to desist from pursuing the only measure which, in his opinion, could give ease and security to persons and property along the frontier. It required great forbearance on the part of the Georgians to refrain from carrying into execution the plans devised by the council at Augusta; and, irritated as they were by the manifold annoyances to which they were subjected, through the duplicity of McGillivray, the machinations of Bowles, the timidity of Seagrove, the recklessness of Clarke, and the imagined supineness and indifference of the Federal Government,—they displayed a commendable submission to law and authority, in ceasing to press forward the expedition which had been so enthusiastically planned.

In this feverish and unsettled condition the relations of the Government, the State, and the Indians, continued, with occasional exacerbations and remissions—now breaking out into bloody hostilities, and now apparently soothed to peace—until 1796, when Washington, having made a treaty with the Cherokees, at Holston River, and quieted all troubles with them, again sought to establish friendly relations with the turbulent and restless Creeks. Having determined, in accordance with the request of the General Assembly of Georgia, to hold another treaty with the Creeks, the President, on the 25th of June, 1795, nominated to the Senate Benjamin Hawkins, of North Carolina, George Clymer, of Pennsylvania, and Andrew Pickens, of South Carolina, "to be Commissioners for holding a treaty with the Creek nation of Indians." The place selected for holding this treaty, was Coleraine, in Camden County, and about forty-five miles above St. Mary's.

Thither the Federal Commissioners repaired, in May, 1796; there they were joined by three Commissioners, on the part of the State of Georgia, viz., James Hendricks, James Jackson, and James Simms.

The formal conferences were opened on the 16th of May, and were continued from day to day, during which speeches were made to the Indians by Benjamin Hawkins, on the part of the United States, and General James Jackson, on behalf of the Georgia Commissioners; the latter pointing out to the Indians, with great force, their faithlessness to former treaties, and presenting to them a long list of grievances unredressed, and property unrecovered, directly contrary to the provisions of the New York treaty.

After many anxious conferences with the Indians, a treaty was concluded, on the 29th of June, and signed by the Commissioners of the United States and the chiefs who represented the Creek nation.

The State Commissioners protested against this treaty, under seven distinct heads; and so decidedly were they in the right, as it respected the unconstitutionality of the Government's obtaining cessions of land from the Indians within the territorial limits of the State, that when the treaty was before the Senate for ratification, in March, 1797, that body put in a modifying proviso, which obviated that objectionable feature, and gave to Georgia pre-emption rights, and left untouched her territorial sovereignty.

In Washington's speech to Congress, December 7, 1796, he says, that the meeting of Creeks, at Coleraine, had for a principal object the purchase of a parcel of their land by Georgia. It broke up without its being accomplished, the nation having previously instructed the delegates against it. All the benefits were, that pre-existing treaties were confirmed, and permission was obtained to establish among the Creeks trading-houses and military posts.

The inefficiency of this treaty was soon seen. The troubles were varied as to place and character, but yet they continued; and it was not until several treaties had been made, and many negotiations with the Creeks entered into by Georgia and by the General Government; that, long after the beginning of this century, and within the administration of still living Governors, the Indians were removed from Georgia to the homes provided for them in the West; and with their removal came peace, security, and population.

CHAPTER V.

YAZOO SPECULATIONS.

FEW events in the history of our country, none certainly in the annals of Georgia, involved greater principles of law and equity, or were more exciting to all classes of the community, from Massachusetts to the French settlements in Louisiana, than the Yazoo sale. The questions pertaining to this matter were among the gravest which can exercise the mind of the jurist and the statesman. They involved the rights and independence, as well as the honor and integrity of the individual State; the authority and jurisdiction of the Federal Government; the privileges and immunities of the aboriginal tribes; the contracts and associated powers of several great landed companies; and the claims of Spanish, French, and English subjects, along an exposed and exasperated frontier.

For more than twenty years, these questions, in some form or other, were agitated in our courts of law, in our legislative assemblies, in the halls of Congress, and in the councils of the Cabinet,—shaping, in many respects, the political aspect of the times, and directing the measures which were finally adopted in the settlement of the vexed questions of Indian titles and Indian protection.

The southern portion of the present United States had been claimed respectively by England and Spain, on the ground of original discovery. An attempt was made, in 1604, to settle, by treaty, the pretensions of each of these powers to America, but the parties could not agree; and the claims were kept in abeyance until the year 1670, when, by the 7th article in what is called the "American treaty" between England and Spain, it is stipulated that the possessions of the English Crown, as they then existed in America, were to be confirmed to "the most serene King of Great Britain," with "plenary right of sovereignty, dominion, possession, and propriety."

Charles II, in his first charter to the Earl of Clarendon and seven others, granted to them "all that province, territory, or tract of ground, called Carolina, situate, lying, and being within our dominions of America," and between the 36° and 31° northern latitude; and "southwest in a direct line as far as the South Seas." Two years after, by a second charter, dated 30th of June, 1665, the King removed the southern boundary line, so as to cover the country claimed by right of discovery, and fixed it at 29° northern latitude. This, then, was the southern boundary of the English possessions in America five years later, when the treaty was made between Spain and England,—the 7th article of which, as we have seen, confirmed to the English King all the land which he then claimed.

In 1729, the territory covered by these two charters of Charles II was, to the extent of seven-eighths of it, surrendered to George II, by the heirs and assignees of those who held the province as proprietors under the said charters; and thus the land, to 29° south latitude, was reinvested in the Crown.

Five months later, on the 9th December, 1729, Robert Johnson was commissioned as Governor of this surrendered province; and, though no boundaries were stated, yet by title, as well as law, his commission covered the whole territory claimed under the charters of the second Charles.

In 1730, the Lords of the Committee of Council, appointed to consider the petition of Lord Percival, James Oglethorpe, &c., for a grant of lands in South Carolina, for the purpose of establishing a charitable colony, reported favorably, and recommended to his Majesty to grant to the petitioners that tract of land lying between the Rivers Savannah and Alatamaha; and accordingly, in the charter granted to these gentlemen, in 1732, the boundaries of the new colony of Georgia were fixed by those rivers on the north and south, "and westward from the heads of the said rivers respectively in direct lines to the South Seas."

This charter was surrendered to the King in 1752, when it ceased to be under the government of the trustees, and was erected by the Crown into a royal province.

In the commission appointing John Reynolds Governor of the colony, the same boundaries were recited which were recorded in the charter.

A practical aspect was soon given to this territorial question by the settlement to the southward of the Alatamaha of a party of seventy or eighty men, under the leadership of Mr. Gray, at a place called New Hanover. Lieutenant-Governor Ellis gave Gray a license to settle at the St. Mary's River, and to trade there; but this measure was reprehended by the Lords of Trade, and William Pitt particularly deplored it, "as it may disturb that peace and friendship which at present so happily subsists between his Majesty and the King of Spain,—no limits having, as we apprehend, ever been finally settled between the two crowns in this part of America." The settlement was ordered to be broken up—not because it was on Spanish soil, for it was conceded that it was on English ground—but because it might, by its proximity to Florida, give umbrage to the court of Spain.

It was well known that General Oglethorpe had made settlements south of the Alatamaha, and that lands were claimed under his rule even to the St. John's; while the establishment of Fort William, at the south end of Cumberland Island, and the keeping up a guard there by a detachment from his Majesty's Independent Company in South Carolina, under direction of the Governor of South Carolina, proved how Great Britain regarded her legal right to that territory.

The grants made by Governor Browne of large tracts of land to the southward of the Alatamaha, the *caveat* of Governor Wright against such proceedings, and the issue that was taken thereon by the Lords of Trade, complicated matters very much; but the treaty of peace of 1763, between Great Britain and Spain, and the cession of Florida to England by that treaty, set at rest all questions of boundary.

Florida was now divided into East and West Florida, and each was erected into a royal province. The northern boundary was fixed at 31° north latitude; and, on the recommendation of the Board of Trade, the jurisdiction of the Governor of Georgia was extended over the territory lying between the southern branch of the Alatamaha and the northern boundary of the Floridas. By the same treaty, also, the western boundary of Georgia, instead of being, as heretofore, the South Seas, was now made to be the middle of the River Mississippi.

By the treaty of peace concluded between the United States and Great Britain, in 1783, these were the boundaries recognized by the latter power, and accepted by the former, when the mother country acknowledged our existence as an independent nation.

Relying on these facts as full evidence of her title to this territory, the Legislature of Georgia, on the 17th February, 1783, passed "An act for opening the land office, and for other purposes therein named;" in the 13th section of which the boundaries of Georgia are thus recited: "That the limits, boundaries, jurisdiction, and authority of the State of Georgia, DO, and did, and of right ought to extend from the mouth of the River Savannah, along the north side thereof, and up the most northern stream or fork of the said river, up to its head or source; from thence, in a due west course, to the River Mississippi; and, down the said stream of the Mississippi, to the latitude 31° north; from thence, in a due east course, to the River Apalachicola, or Chatahoochee; and, from the fork of the said River Apalachicola, where the Chatahoochee and Flint Rivers meet, in a direct line to the head or source of the southernmost stream of the River St. Mary; and, along the course of the said River St. Mary, to the Atlantic Ocean," &c.

The claim which South Carolina had so long made to the tract of land lying between the Alatamaha and the St. Mary, because not originally included in that part of Carolina which was erected into the independent colony of Georgia, was relinquished by South Carolina, at the Convention of Georgia and South Carolina Commissioners, which was held at Beaufort, in 1787; and thus the last impediment in the way of the full recognition of the jurisdiction of Georgia over that portion of the territory was removed.

From these statements it appears that Georgia was the legal proprietor of these lands. In proof of this she could appeal to the cession of Florida to England by Spain; to the Royal Proclamation "for establishing the governments of East and West Florida, and extending the southern boundary of Georgia," in 1763; to the new commission of Governor Wright, in 1764; to the 2d and 9th "Articles of Confederation and Perpetual Union between the States," in 1781; to the Treaty of Peace with Great Britain, in 1783; and to the 3d Article of the Convention of Beaufort, in 1787. The Federal Government fully recognized this right of Georgia, in its official intercourse with Georgia, in its several acts of Congress, and by the instructions given to its treaty-making commissioners.

In February, 1785, the Legislature passed an act, erecting a large tract of country, bordering on the Mississippi, above and below Natchez, into a separate county, which was named BOURBON; and civil and judicial officers were appointed for that new county; but the intervention of Spanish claimants and settlers prevented the carrying the act into effect, and it was repealed in February, 1788.

Shortly after, a company of persons, stimulated by the thirst for gain, organized themselves into an association, called "The Combined Society." Its members were sworn to secrecy, and the object of it was, by means of certain influences brought to bear upon those in authority, to obtain from the State large grants of lands, either for immigration or for sale,—in either case for the end of making a large sum of money out of the transaction. Such a secret could not long be kept. It was brought to the notice of the Governor and the Legislature; and its divulgence thwarted the plans of the society, which was soon disbanded.

It existed long enough, however, to do serious mischief, by inflaming the cupidity of the citizens, by exciting visions of landed property, or golden gains to be realized in investments in western lands, and by familiarizing the minds of the people with the underhanded dealings of land speculators and political gamesters,—absolutely demoralizing to any state or people.

The evil effect of such measures soon appeared. In 1789, Thomas Washington, Alexander Moultrie, Isaac Hugee, William Clay Snipes, and certain others, associated together as "The South Carolina Yazoo Company," and applied to the Legislature of Georgia for the purchase of certain tracts of land belonging to Georgia. The principal promoters of this scheme were a certain Captain Sullivan, of the late revolutionary army, who headed the mob, in Philadelphia, which insulted the Old Congress, then sitting in the State House, and who had taken refuge in the Mississippi territory as a fugitive from the penalty which the law would have inflicted on him for his crimes; and Thomas Washington, whose real name, however, was Walsh, and who styled himself a citizen of Georgia, but who was really a swindling adventurer. These two men, bold, reckless, unscrupulous, with great address and zeal, made such representations of the desirableness of these western lands, and the facility of peopling them and bringing them into a profitable market, that many, besides the gentlemen of Georgia and South Carolina, were led away by their schemes; and "The Virginia Yazoo Company," at the head of which was the justly celebrated Patrick Henry, and "The Tennessee Company," represented by Zechariah Cox and others, made application at the same time with the Carolina company, for grants of land from the State of Georgia. Petitions from these companies were presented to the Senate, on the 20th of November, 1789, setting forth the advantages which would arise to Georgia from disposing of their western lands, and offering to purchase on certain conditions. These were referred to a committee; and a bill to that effect was shortly after introduced into the Senate, and sent to the lower House, on Monday, December 7th, for their action. The House was then engaged upon the Judiciary bill, but it was the next day set aside, in order to consider the bill for disposing of the State lands; and a joint committee was appointed, consisting of one member of the House from each county, to report specially on "the merits and propositions of the different companies proposing to become purchasers in the said territory."

Another company now appeared, and presented its claims,—"The Georgia Company," composed of citizens who were unwilling to see such large tracts of land passing into the hands of Carolinians and Virginians; while those most interested—the inhabitants of Georgia—were only to a small extent admitted into these associations. This company, however, entered the field too late. The agents of the other companies, working with indomitable zeal, and feeling that each day's delay imperilled their schemes, pressed forward legislative action with indecent haste. Nearly all other business was suspended; and though the minority were able to retard the precipitate action which the majority seemed to desire, yet they only held back the result for a few days. When, in committee of the whole, a motion was made to insert "The Georgia Company" with the other applicants, it was lost; the same fate befell a motion to increase the sum demanded for the lands; and, it appearing to the minority that there was a determination to give the lands to the three companies at a nominal value, and without allowing a fair competition, they suffered the bill to pass as it came from the Senate, without opposition.

Thus, in the course of nine days, a bill of such great importance was hurried through the House of Representatives, and every attempt to make the least amendment to it was frustrated. It received the signature of the Governor on the 21st December, and the "Act for disposing of certain vacant lands or territory within this State" became a law. By this bill it was enacted that a tract or part of the territory of Georgia, now embracing the middle counties of Mississippi, comprising over five millions of acres, should be reserved as a pre-emption for "The South Carolina Yazoo Company;" for which they were to pay the State in two years $66,964; that a tract, or part of the territory of this State, bordering on the Tennessee and Mississippi Rivers, now known as the northern counties of Mississippi, embracing over seven millions of acres, should be reserved as a pre-emption for "The Virginia Yazoo Company;" for which they were to pay $93,741 within two years; that a third tract, or part of the territory of this State, lying along the Tennessee River and Bear Creek, being a portion of what is now Northern Alabama, containing nearly three and a half millions of acres, should be reserved as a pre-emption for "The Tennessee Company;" for which they were to pay, in terms similar to the other companies, the sum of $46,875. Thus fifteen and a half millions of acres, or what proved to be in reality over twenty millions of acres, were sold to three companies for the paltry sum of about $207,000!

The passage of this act drew out strong remonstrances from the minority, and from "The Georgia Company," which had really offered a larger price and more valuable securities.

Under the provisions of this act, the South Carolina and Virginia Companies paid into the treasury some small sums in paper medium, but the full provisions of the law were not complied with by any of the companies, and the contemplated sale was not completed.

Thus the schemes of Washington, *alias* Walsh, came to nought. He himself was shortly after arrested for forging a large amount of Georgia and Carolina paper, and, being convicted and sentenced to death, was hung in Charleston in 1792.

The companies which had obtained these grants were greatly incensed at the course which the matter took, and not only charged Georgia with acting in bad faith, but even entered suits in equity against the State in the Supreme Court, for the purpose of compelling Georgia to confirm the contracts "fully and absolutely." While these suits were pending, an amendment to the Constitution of the United States passed Congress,

December 2, 1793, declaring that "the judicial power of the United States shall not be construed to extend to any suit in law or equity commenced or prosecuted against one of the United States by citizens of another State, or by citizens or subjects of any foreign State." Accordingly all proceedings thereupon came to an end. Undeterred by these failures, preparations on a more extensive scale were made for new efforts, having for their end the same general objects; and, at the session of the Legislature in November, 1794, proposals were again made by several parties for the purchase of the western territory of Georgia. These were referred to a joint committee of both Houses, who, on the 3d of December, reported, as their opinion, "that it would be right and proper to sell a part of the western territory of this State during the present session. They are also of opinion that it will be best to sell to companies; they therefore report that they are of opinion it would be right and proper, and would tend much to the advantage and population of the State, to extend the limits of the present boundary line as far as the River Ocmulgee; and that an appropriation should be made therefor, together with an application to the General Government for the holding of a treaty. Your committee further report that they have taken under consideration the several applications made for the purchase of certain tracts of country therein described; which, they are of opinion, are liberal and right to be agreed to; but this report is not to conclude the Legislature from receiving and acceding to other proposals which may be deemed more advantageous to the State, should any such be made during the passage of the bill."

A minority report was presented and offered as an amendment to the report of the committee, in which it was urged that "it is not consistent with the interests of this State to accede to the proposals made by the present companies, or any part of them, at this time." This amendment was disagreed to; and the bill, as reported by the majority, was put upon its passage.

The companies applying, and incorporating their claims and terms in the bill, entitled, "An act declaring the right of the State to the unappropriated territory thereof," &c., were "The Georgia Company;" "The Georgia Mississippi Company;" "The Tennessee Company;" and "The Virginia Yazoo Company." To these, on the 11th December, was added, "The Georgia Union Company," composed of General Twiggs, William Few, John Wereat, William Gibbons, Jr., &c., who made certain proposals to the committee for a tract of land, supposed to contain at least twenty-three millions of acres, and for which they offered the sum of $500,000.

The committee, to whom was referred this last proposal, reported, "That on examination of the boundaries of the district proposed to be purchased by the above-named gentlemen and their associates, it appears to be composed of the two districts proposed to be purchased by the 'Georgia' and 'Georgia Mississippi Companies,' and no more; that the sum offered is $90,000 greater than that offered by both the other companies; and that the new company proposes to reserve for the citizens double the amount indicated by the other companies; and they submit the advantages and disadvantages of each to the decision of the House."

The application of the Georgia Union Company, notwithstanding their larger offers and more liberal reserves, was, however, rejected by a vote of—ayes 12, nays 14.

Various amendments were offered to this bill by those opposed to this measure, but they were severally voted down by a steady and determined majority, and the bill was passed and sent to the Governor for his signature. Fearing that Governor Matthews might veto it, the leading men of the several companies interested addressed a letter to him on the 25th December, in which they sought to show the policy, expediency, and advantage of the bill,—setting forth these in brief, but strong terms,—urging his Excellency not to interpose his executive authority, and intimating how unpleasant it would be to him to have the bill passed over his veto.

Despite the urgent appeal of these parties, the Governor, on the 29th December, sent his dissent to the bill to the House; in which communication he stated his objections to it to be: "1st. I doubt whether the proper time is arrived for disposing of the territory in question. 2d. If it was the proper time, the sum offered is inadequate to the value of the lands. 3d. The quantity reserved for the citizens is too small in proportion to the extent of the purchase. 4th. That greater advantages are secured to the purchasers than to the citizens. 5th. That so large an extent of territory being disposed of to individuals will operate as monopolies, which will prevent or retard settlement, population, and agriculture. 6th. That should such disposition be made, at least one-fourth of the lands should be reserved for the future disposal of the State. 7th. That if public notice was given that the lands were for sale, the rivalship in purchasers would most probably have increased the sums offered."

After reading this dissent of the Governor, a committee of five was appointed to confer with his Excellency upon his message.

The next day, Mr. Watkins, from this committee, made the following report: "That so intimately connected is the 'act for appropriating a part of the unlocated territory of this State for the payment of the late State troops,' &c., with the bill returned to the House, the same cannot be separately carried into effect without a dangerous anticipation of funds already pledged in the most solemn manner to the soldier and suffering citizen in a common cause; or a derangement of the finances of the State, which the Legislature view with the utmost regret. That on comparing the purchase contemplated by the several companies with the map of the western territory of this State, they find that eighteen millions of acres still remain the right of the State for future appropriations, independently of the immense tract of country lying eastward of Chattahoochee, and within the temporary line of the Indian hunting-ground. That his Excellency the Governor's reasons for dissent, being founded upon opinions as to legislative operation, and not on constitutional grounds, a supplementary act, embracing the objects of this report:—

"1. That the whole sum of $600,000 deposited should become subject to the immediate use of the State, and be considered the first payment; that the Governor do thereupon issue grants to the several applicants, taking mortgage on the territory sold to secure the after-payments.

"2. That the further sum of $10,000 be added to the fund already appropriated to the extinguishment of Indian claims south of the Oconee, and eastward of the Chattahoochee.

"3. That a fair and equal representation in the several companies be therein provided and secured to the citizens, subscribers for the land reserved, on the same footing with the original purchasers.

"4. That the further quantity of five million acres, in addition to the two million five hundred and eighty thousand,—already reserved by the companies for the citizens of Georgia,—to be subscribed for and held in trust for the use of the State, subject to future disposal, and represented in like manner (if assented to by the companies) as tenants in common with the purchasers,—affords the State an additional check on the monopolies apprehended, and should be deemed an adequate reserve on the part of the State and the citizens thereof; and your committee are clearly of opinion ought finally to reconcile the several objections of his Excellency the Governor. Your committee further report that his Excellency has conceded in part, and that a further conference is appointed."

On the question of agreeing to the report, there were—yeas 20, nays 8.

The following morning, Mr. Watkins brought in a further report, in which he stated that they had adjusted the matter satisfactorily with the Governor; and that the committee had prepared and brought in a bill, "embracing the several objects therein contained."

It was objected that, by the rules of the House, no bills of a general nature could be introduced, unless a committee had been previously appointed for that purpose; and that, as the committee in this instance were not vested with power to introduce any bill, but merely to confer with the Governor on the subject of his objections to a bill already passed, therefore the bill reported by this committee could not be taken up by the House.

This objection was overruled, and the bill, entitled "An act supplementary to an act for appropriating a part of the unlocated territory of this State for the payment of the late State troops, and for other purposes therein mentioned, declaring the right to the unappropriated territory thereof, for the protection and support of the frontiers of this State, and for other purposes therein mentioned," was read the first time in the House.

This was an ingenious grafting of a rejected bill, improved, indeed, in some of its features, but still greatly objectionable, upon a bill, in which the inhabitants of Georgia felt a deep interest, and for the passage of which they were most anxious. It was a bold policy to make the vetoed bill a rider upon an unobjectionable bill, so that they should sink or swim together. The plan produced intense excitement, and threatened serious commotions.

While the new bill was pending, the "Georgia Union Company" again addressed a letter to each branch of the Legislature, inclosing proposals for purchasing the whole of the territory specified in the vetoed bill, and offering as considerations for the same, "a deposit (by way of forfeiture) of $40,000 in bills of exchange on Philadelphia, at double usance, with indisputable indorsers;" "to pay to the State the residue of the purchase-money, amounting, in the whole, to $800,000, on or before the first day of December next; promising to reserve 4,000,000 acres to the State, to be disposed of as this, or a future Legislature, shall direct; and also to reserve 4,000,000 for the citizens themselves."

Through the influence of the agents of the other companies, this proposition, by which so many and greater advantages would come to the State, met with as little favor as their former petition. The Legislature, goaded on by an outside pressure not easily withstood, within three days after bringing in the new bill, or rather the old bill slightly modified and riveted into a previously pending one, passed the same; the scruples of the too pliant Governor were overcome; and, on the 7th of December, the bill received his signature, and became the law of the land.

The preamble of the bill recites, in various paragraphs, the several grounds upon which the State based its right to the territory which it now disposes; and then enacts, 1st, That the State "is in full possession and in the full exercise of the jurisdictional and territorial right, and the fee simple thereof," of these western lands. 2d, It grants to James Gunn, Matthew McAllister, and George Walker, and their associates, called "THE GEORGIA COMPANY," &c., "all that tract or parcel of land, including islands, situate, lying, and being, within the following boundaries,—that is to say:

Beginning on the Mobile Bay, where the latitude 31° north of the equator intersects the same; running thence up the said bay to the mouth of Lake Tensaw; thence up Lake Tensaw to the Alabama River, including Curry's and all other islands therein; thence up the said River Alabama to the junction of the Coosa and Oakfuskee Rivers; thence up the Coosa River above the Big Shoal, to where it intersects the latitude of 34° north of the equator; thence a due west course to the Mississippi River; thence down the middle of said river to the latitude of 32° 40′; thence a due east course to the mouth of Tombigbee River; thence down the middle of the said river to its junction with the Alabama River; thence down the middle of the said river to the Mobile Bay; thence down the said Mobile Bay to the place of beginning," for the sum of $250,000,—$50,000 to be deposited in the treasury previous to the passage of the act, and the remaining $200,000 to be paid on or before the first day of November next. The 3d section directs, that whenever the said company shall produce to the Governor a receipt by the Treasurer, that they have deposited the $50,000, then grants were to be issued,—the last payment to be secured by a mortgage given to the Governor on the whole of the land so granted. The next section requires the company to reserve, for the use of the citizens of Georgia, a million of acres; and the next directs how the subscription money shall be received.

The 6th section of the bill grants to Nicholas Long, Thomas Glascock, Ambrose Gordon, and Thomas Cumming, and their associates, called "THE GEORGIA MISSISSIPPI COMPANY," for the sum of $155,000, "all that tract of country, including islands, situate, lying, and being, within the following boundaries,—that is to say: Beginning on the River Mississippi, at the place where the latitude of 31° 18′ north of the equator intersects the same; thence a due east course to the middle of Don or Tombigbee River; thence up the middle of the said river to where it intersects the latitude of 32° 40′ north of the equator; thence a due west course along the Georgia Company's line to the River Mississippi; thence down the middle of the same to the place of beginning.

The 7th and 8th sections relate to the mortgage to be given, and the quantity of land to be reserved by them, viz., 620,000 acres for the use of the citizens of Georgia.

The 9th section grants to John B. Scott, John C. Nightengale, and Wade Hampton, called "THE UPPER MISSISSIPPI COMPANY," for the sum of $35,000,—$5,000 previous deposit,—"all that tract of country, including islands, situate, lying, and being, within the following boundaries,—that is to say: Beginning at the Mississippi River, where the northern boundary line of this State strikes the same; thence along the said northern boundary line due east to the Tennessee River; thence along the said Tennessee River to the mouth of Bear Creek; thence up Bear Creek to where the parallel of latitude, twenty-five British statute miles south of the northern boundary line of this State, intersects the same; thence along the said last-mentioned parallel of latitude, across Tombigbee or Twenty Miles Creek, due west to the Mississippi River; thence up the middle of the said river to the beginning." This company was nearly the same as the Virginia Yazoo Company, having only changed its name.

The 10th and 11th sections regulates the mortgage to be given, and the amount of land to be reserved.

The 12th section enacts "that all that tract of land, including islands, situate, lying, and being, within the following boundary lines: Beginning at the mouth of Bear Creek, on the south side of the Tennessee River; thence up the said creek to the most southern source thereof; thence due south to the latitude of 34° 10′ north of the equator; thence a due east course one hundred and twenty miles; thence a due north course to the Great Tennessee River; thence up the middle of the said river to the northern boundary line of this State; thence a due west course along the said line to where it intersects the Great Tennessee River, below the Mussel Shoals; thence up the said river to the place of beginning, shall be sold unto Zachariah Cox, Matthias Maher, and their associates, called 'THE TENNESSEE COMPANY,' and to their heirs and assigns forever, in fee simple, as tenants in common, and not as joint tenants, for the sum of $60,000."

This company were required, by subsequent clauses of the bill, to give their mortgage, as were the other companies; to pay down as forfeit money, $12,000, and to reserve 242,000 acres for the citizens of Georgia.

The 18th section requires the grantees of land to "forbear all hostile and wanton attacks on any of the Indian tribes; and keep the State free from all charges and expenses which may attend the preserving the peace between the said Indians and the grantees, and extinguishing the Indian claims to the territory included within their respective purchases."

The 19th section directs how the money arising from these sales should be invested.

The 20th requires settlements to be made on the lands granted, within five years from the extinguishment of the Indian titles by the United States.

The 21st section sets apart $10,000 towards the extinguishment of these Indian titles. The 22d directs that none of the territory granted shall be disposed of to any foreign power; and the last declares that the remaining lands ungranted, estimated at about seven and a half millions of acres, shall be reserved and set apart for the benefit of this State, "to be granted out, or otherwise disposed of as a future Legislature may direct."

On the 26th of January, the Governor issued his proclamation, granting the designated tract to "The Georgia Mississippi Company;" and thus thirty-five millions of acres were granted to these four companies for the sum of $500,000; or less than two cents per acre.

It may well be supposed that such an act could not pass without calling out earnest remonstrance and decided opposition. Among the earliest remonstrants were William H. Crawford and other citizens of Columbia County, who, even before the bill was signed by the Governor, presented to him a petition, praying that his Excellency would "negative the said bill in due form, inasmuch as we do conceive it to be bad policy to give a grant to the company purchasing before the full amount of the purchase-money is paid; that if a grant should be given, the grantees may (if they think proper) refuse to give a mortgage; and, even if they should, the mortgage can only be foreclosed in that part of the State where the territory in question doth lie; and, lastly, whenever the territory is sold, the price or value thereof would be greatly enhanced by giving notice to all citizens."

This petition expressed the views of many citizens. Others objected to the bill because they were thereby, to a great extent, debarred participating in the grand speculation of the several companies. Others, because they held that there was no necessity so urgent as to require this enormous sacrifice of territory; and others still, because they saw in the bill only the legalizing of an immense swindling scheme to rob the State of her invaluable lands for the benefit, not of her citizens in general, but of a few bold and unscrupulous speculators, who were willing to advance their own fortunes upon the ruin and dishonor of the State.

The people, so soon as they heard of the passage of this bill, and began to discuss its merits, and understand its provisions, were aroused to a sense of the great injury which had been done to their own interests; and, as there was developed to them, step by step, the various means, and bribes, and machinations, which were set to work to bring over, or buy over, the several members of the Legislature, to vote for these measures, their indignation rose higher and higher, and vented itself in presentments of grand juries, in violent newspaper warfare, in stinging personal invective and insult, in threats of corporal violence, and in scenes of actual bloodshed and death.

The whole State was heaving with excitement. The bribery which had been so openly used by men high in office, on the Bench, at the Bar, in the Senate; and the corruption, intrigue, intimidation and violence which had been employed to gain over the Legislature to the plans of the speculators, constitute a dark page in the political history of Georgia. One of the most zealous advocates of this scheme was James Gunn. This man, who had risen from almost obscurity to power, by truckling to the vulgar tastes of the populace, and by some show of military genius; was at the period of which we write, a Senator of Georgia in Congress, and his presence there was needed to guard the interests of the State. Yet, sacrificing all public considerations to private advantage, he remained in Georgia; repaired to Augusta; and, by his influence and efforts, at once overbearing and unscrupulous, he became the main manager of this nefarious business. Having secured the passage of the bill, he then repaired to Congress, which he reached only the last day of February, four days before the constitutional close of the session; and there sought to carry out his Georgia schemes, by involving the General Government also in these questionable transactions.

The other Senator from Georgia was General James Jackson. This gentleman had been urged to take shares in some of these companies, and was told that "he might have any number of acres he pleased, to half a million, without paying a cent, provided he would put his name to the application."

But he firmly opposed these offers, and told the proposers, "that he, not they, had fought for Georgia, and the right to that territory; that he fought for the people, and it was their right, and the right of future generations; and, if they did succeed, he should hold the sale void, and would resign his seat in the Senate, come home, and head his fellow-citizens, and either lose his life or have the act annulled."

Having made an ineffectual attempt to return to Georgia in time to take part in the Convention for the revision of the Constitution, which was to take place in May; he yet exerted his pen in behalf of the opponents of a scheme which he had declared, in the Senate of the United States, to be "a conspiracy of the darkest character and of deliberate villany." He immediately began a series of articles, which he published over the signature of "Scillius," and, in eleven numbers, he examined "the policy, the legality, and the constitutionality of the enormous western grant,—a grant of land to a few individuals, containing more square miles than either of the German principalities, and of greater extent than some European kingdoms." These letters, which calmly and learnedly reviewed the whole proceedings, discussed all the constitutional questions involved, and showed the practical operation of the bill, had a great influence in directing and settling the opinions of the people, and enlightening them as to the real points at issue.

When the two Senators returned to Georgia, Gunn was regarded with indignation. He was in several places burned in effigy; and, in many parts of the country, did not dare to appear in public. But General Jackson was received with marks of public approbation; and all eyes turned to him as the leader who could best retrieve the error into which the State had been led, and redress the grievances under which it was burdened.

Yielding, therefore, to the solicitations of the friends of peace and equity, and more anxious to serve his country than to occupy its high offices, he consented, at the request of the best citizens in Chatham County, to resign his seat in the United States Senate, and accept a nomination as Representative for that county in the next State Legislature. He was elected and took his seat. The Legislature met on the second Tuesday in January, 1796; and, on the 14th, Governor Matthews sent to both branches a message, in which he thus speaks of this transaction: "The Senate and House of Representatives are now constitutionally convened for legislative deliberations; and at a time, too, when the minds of our fellow-citizens are, and have been, for some time past, more engaged in discussing the conduct of the last Legislature, on the subject of the act for disposing of part of our western territory to certain companies, than perhaps has ever been experienced since this State assumed rank with her sister States. It will, no doubt, be amongst the most important matters that may engross your attention, to inquire on what ground this act was founded, and if a constitutional and legal remedy can be applied to calm the minds of our fellow-citizens on this interesting subject. In my opinion, it requires, and, I flatter myself, will receive your most serious deliberation, whether a law can be constitutionally made to repeal another that has been so fully carried into effect as the one now in question,—the companies having paid into the treasury the whole of the purchase-money, and cancelled their mortgages; and whether, if repealed, the remedy may not be even worse than the disease. But, if a law can be devised that will constitutionally repeal the one referred to, and guard against future murmurs and well-grounded complaints against the repeal, I have no doubt but the man you may honor with the appointment of Chief Magistrate will readily deem it a duty cheerfully to co-operate.

"It is a matter much to be regretted (considering the unfavorable light the act for disposing of our western territory has been viewed in) that the spirit of party resentment and personal reflection should have run so high in many instances. The public mind has been inflamed by unfair representations, and our newspapers have teemed with personal abuse and invective. This, I remark, from having experienced the public slander. Endeavors have been made to calumniate my character by false reports, such as—'that the motives which induced me to give my assent to the second act proceeded from private interest, regardless of the sacred duty I owed to the station I filled, and the rights and interest of my fellow-citizens.' Conscious of the purity of my intentions, and supported by the justice and integrity of my actions, I have treated with silent contempt those base and malicious reports; and I now defy the blackest and most persevering malice, aided by disappointed avarice, to produce one single evidence of my ever having been interested in the sale to the amount of one single farthing. But, whilst I treated with neglect those reports so injurious to my character, I feel it a respect due to you, and a duty I owe to my reputation, to give you a candid and fair representation of the motives which actuated me on a subject which has so much disturbed the citizens of Georgia.

"On the 25th day of December, 1794, an act for disposing of a part of our western territory to *four* companies was presented to me for my concurrence.

After the most mature reflection my judgment was capable of, I thought it my duty to refuse my assent, and assigned my reasons, which, I flattered myself, would have postponed any further legislative proceedings in the law until the next meeting of the House; but, in that, I was mistaken. The first idea that occurred to some of the members, when the bill was returned with remarks was, that I should be impeached for an unconstitutional act; yet, the more cool reflection of the House terminated in appointing a committee to confer with me on my objections, and to know if it was in the power of the Legislature to frame a bill for the sale of the lands which would meet my concurrence. On the conference, I was led to believe, that the committee was convinced that my reasons for rejecting the law did not proceed from *Executive arrogance*, or from any wish to bring into action a power heretofore dormant in our proceedings, or from a propensity in me to do an act of so great a responsibility, but from a conviction that it would tend to the real interest of the State. The reflecting mind will easily perceive how much the responsibility would be enhanced by rejecting a bill that the Legislature might pass for the sale of the lands after being in possession of my remarks, even supposing it to be similar to the first. But, when it appears that three of the most important objections I had made to the first law were removed, I think there is no man of cool, dispassionate reflection, that would have refused his assent to it for any reasons short of a clear proof of corruption in its passage through the Legislature, and *no such information ever came to my knowledge.* After all the popular clamor this law has occasioned, I should depart from my usual candor to say I have ever blamed myself, either for an error of the head or a corruption in the heart; and, on a similar occasion, should feel myself perfectly justified in pursuing a similar conduct. Much has been said about unascertained millions of acres being sold, and that more than fifty millions of acres are disposed of to the companies by that act. After having thought it my duty to act on the second bill, I ordered the Surveyor-General to furnish me with as accurate a map of the country contemplated to be sold that any documents he had or could procure would afford. This was done, and is now on the file of the Executive; from which, it will appear, there were no more than twenty-nine million four hundred thousand acres in the whole aggregate tract that the first law had in view, and one-fourth of that quantity is now reserved to the State, and subject to her disposition. This is a true state of facts, so far as they have come to my knowledge; and, if it may afford you any useful hints in your deliberations, it will give me pleasure.

"The time for which I was appointed Governor having now expired, I have to request that, should an opinion prevail in the Legislature, that the duties of that important office have been improperly conducted, a committee may be appointed to examine the proceedings had therein."

The committee, which the Governor suggested, was not appointed. His term of office had expired, and he had sealed his political fate by signing the obnoxious bill.

Jared Irwin was elected to succeed Governor Matthews, and the Legislature at once proceeded to the important work intrusted to them. So thorough had been the change in the public mind as to the measures pursued by the last Assembly, that nearly every member, returned by the several counties, was pledged to vote for the repeal of the obnoxious act; and not only so, but most of the counties held public meetings on the subject, and sent instructions to their representatives to use all means to annul the act; and petitions, remonstrances, resolutions, and presentments, against it, were sent in from all parts of the State, and were piled upon the Secretary's table.

On the 15th of January, a large number of petitions which had been sent in to the Convention for altering the Constitution, which sat in May previous, and which were by that body referred to the Legislature, were, by order of the House, laid before it; and also other petitions, from the counties of Hancock, Greene, Burke, Chatham, Effingham, Scriven, Washington, Camden, Warren, Franklin, Bryan, Columbia, McIntosh, Oglethorpe, together with the presentments of the grand juries of Liberty and Burke, were presented and read. Whereupon it was "Resolved, That a committee, consisting of nine members, be appointed to examine and report to this House, respecting the validity and constitutionality of the said act, who shall have power to call for such persons, papers, and documents, as may be likely to give information relative thereto." "Resolved, That the petitions, remonstrances, and presentments, addressed to the late Convention and present Legislature, on that subject, be referred to them."

This committee were appointed by ballot, and consisted of General James Jackson, William Few, James Jones, John Moore, David B. Mitchell, James H. Rutherford, David Emanuel, —— Frazier, and George Franklin.

This committee entered upon their duties with promptness and energy. They met, indeed, with many obstacles, and were threatened with violence by the enraged advocates of the supplementary bill; but they were not the men to be intimidated by the threats of assassins, or turned aside from their duty by the impotent rage of those whose iniquities were recoiling upon their own heads.

On the 22d of January, General Jackson, from the committee, reported, "that they have had the same under their serious consideration, and lament that they are compelled to declare, that the fraud, corruption, and collusion, by which the said act was obtained, and the unconstitutionality of the same, evinces the utmost depravity in the majority of the late Legislature." "It appears to your committee, that the public good was placed entirely out of view, and private interest alone consulted; that the rights of the present generation were violated, and the rights of posterity bartered, by the said act; and that by it, the bounds of equal rights were broken down, and the principles of aristocracy established in their stead. The committee (whilst they thus with shame and confusion acknowledge that such a Legislature, intrusted with the rights of their constituents, should have existed in Georgia), cannot, however, forbear to congratulate the present Legislature and the community at large, that there are sufficient grounds, as well with respect to the unconstitutionality of the act, as from the testimony before the committee, of the fraud practised to obtain it, to pronounce, that the same is a nullity in itself, and not binding or obligatory on the people of this State: and they flatter themselves that a declaration to that effect, by a legislative act, will check that rapacious and avaricious spirit of speculation which has in this State overleaped all decent bounds, and which, if it were to continue, would totally annihilate morality and good faith from among the citizens of the State. The committee, for this purpose, beg leave to report, 'An Act for declaring the said usurped act void, and for expunging the same from the face of the public record; and they also herewith report testimony taken before them, on the subject of the fraud practised to obtain it."

The bill was then introduced and read the first time. In its progress through the House and Senate, it underwent much discussion and some modification; but it finally passed, by a vote of forty-four to three, in the House, and of fourteen to four, in the Senate, and was concurred in by the Governor, on the 13th of February, 1796.

This act, commonly called "The Rescinding Act," was drawn up by General Jackson, and displays marked ability in the discussion of the great constitutional questions to which it relates. The preamble declares, that "the free citizens of this State, or in other words, the community thereof, are essentially the source of the sovereignty of the State; and that no individual, or body of men, can be entitled to, or vested with, any authority which is not expressly derived from that source; and the exercise or assumption of powers not so derived, become, of themselves, oppression and usurpation, which it is the right and duty of the people, in their representatives, to resist, and to restore the rights of the community so usurped and infringed.

"That the will or constitution of the people is the only foundation of the legislative power or government thereof; and so far as that will or constitution expressly warrants, the Legislature may go, but no farther; and all constructive powers, not necessarily deduced from that expressed will, are violations of that essential source of sovereignty and the rights of the citizens, and are therefore of no binding force or effect on the State, but null and void."

The act then states, that "the last Legislature, not confining itself to the powers with which that body was constitutionally invested, did usurp a power to pass the obnoxious act, contrary to constitutional authority and repugnant to the democratical form of government of the State. That the act is repugnant to the 4th section, 4th article of the Constitution of the United States, and to the 16th section of the 1st article of the Constitution of this State; that it was a virtual transfer of the sovereignty and jurisdiction of the State over the territory disposed of; that there was no necessity or pressing urgency for the sale of such an immense tract; and that it exposed the State to a great loss of revenue from the relinquishment of taxation." The bill then recites, in a clear and succinct manner, the ground on which Georgia bases its right to the western territory; and states, that "the same and every part thereof is hereby declared to be vested in the State and people thereof, and inalienable but by a convention called by the people for that express purpose, or by some clause of power expressed by the people, delegating such express power to the Legislature, in the Constitution."

It then proceeds to state, that fraud had been practised to obtain this bill; and the evidences of such fraud, establishing thereby cause which "would be sufficient in equity, reason, and law, to invalidate the contract, even supposing it to be constitutional, which this Legislature declares it is not." Having in this long preamble laid down the principles on which the act was based, the bill declares—Be it therefore enacted, 1st. That the act of the 7th January, 1795, entitled "An Act supplementary," &c., "be, and the same is hereby, declared null and void," &c.

The 2d enacting clause orders this act to "be expunged from the face and indexes of the books of record of the State; and the enrolled law or usurped act shall then be publicly burnt, in order that no trace of so unconstitutional, vile, and fraudulent a transaction, other than the infamy attached to it by this law, shall remain in the offices thereof."

The 3d clause directs that none of the laws, grants, deeds, agreements, &c., respecting any contracts under that law, shall be admitted as evidence in any court of law or equity, to establish a title to the said territory.

The 4th section requires the return to the companies of the money which may have been paid by them into the treasury.

The 5th asserts, that the right of applying for, and the extinguishment of, Indian claims to any land within the boundaries of this State, as herein described, being a sovereign right, is hereby further declared to be vested in the people and government of this State, to whom the right of pre-emption of the same belongs.

The last clause requires that this law be promulgated by the Governor throughout the United States, "in order to prevent frauds on individuals, as far as the nature of the case will admit."

On the 25th of January, General Jackson, as chairman of the Investigating Committee, reported to the House sundry affidavits, "on the corruptions practised to obtain the act;" and by a resolution of the House, "all such proofs relating to the fraud and corruptions practised to obtain the act for the disposal of the western territory," were to be entered on the Journals of the House, "in order that the testimony so given may be perpetuated, as well for the satisfaction of the Legislature, and to show the grounds on which they proceeded, as to hand down to future Legislatures the base means by which the rights of the people were attempted to be bartered." Accordingly, some twenty affidavits, showing more or less fraud, were spread on the Journals. It is not necessary, however, to reproduce any of them here. It can serve no good end to parade before the public now, the names of men who in times of intense political strife were held up to ignominy and reproach, especially as many of the persons thus branded were subsequently received into public favor,—one having been since the act elected President of the Senate; four, members of the Senate; four more, members of the House; two, elevated to the bench, as judges; one, made a justice of the peace; and one appointed a trustee of the University of Georgia. There were circumstances, both inculpatory and exculpatory, which, had they been known at the time, would have added to that catalogue names which now are esteemed spotless, and which would have removed from it names which now are branded with legislative condemnation.

Two days after the act was concurred in by the Governor, both branches of the Legislature adopted a report, presented by the committee to whom was referred the mode by which the records were to be expunged of all traces of the usurped act, and the act itself burned,—suggesting "that, where it can possibly be executed without injury to other records, the same shall be expunged from the book of records, by cutting out the leaves of the book wherein the same may have been recorded; a memorandum thereof, expressing the number of pages so expunged, to be signed by the President of the Senate, and Speaker of the House of Representatives, and to be countersigned by the Secretary and Clerk,—which memorandum shall be inserted in the room or place of such expunged pages, in such manner as the President and Speaker may direct. That where records and documents are distinct and separate from other records, the same being of record, shall be expunged by being burnt. That the enrolled bill, and usurped act, passed on the 7th day of January, 1795, shall, in obedience to the act of the present session, be burnt in the square, before the State House, in the manner following: A fire shall be made in front of the State House door, and a line to be formed by the members of both branches around the same. The Secretary of State (or his deputy), with the committee, shall then produce the enrolled bill and usurped act from among the archives of the State, and deliver the same to the President of the Senate, who shall examine the same, and shall then deliver the same to the Speaker of the House of Representatives for like examination; and the Speaker shall then deliver them to the Clerk of the House of Representatives, who shall read aloud the title of the same, and shall then deliver them to the Messenger of the House, who shall then pronounce—'GOD SAVE THE STATE! AND LONG PRESERVE HER RIGHTS!! AND MAY EVERY ATTEMPT TO INJURE THEM PERISH AS THESE CORRUPT ACTS NOW DO!!!'"

In conformity with this programme, the House of Representatives, the same day, sent a message to the Senate, informing that body that they were ready to receive them in the Representatives' Hall, in order to proceed to the duty prescribed. The Senate proceeded to the Hall, and there joining the Representatives, marched in procession to the spot selected, preceded by the committee bearing the proscribed bills in their hands. When they reached the spot where the fire was kindled, the committee delivered the acts to the President of the Senate. That officer handed them to the Speaker of the House, by whom they were passed into the hands of the Clerk, who gave them to the Messenger,—who, uttering the prescribed words, laid them on the fire, and the Legislature stood in solemn circle around until the documents were burned to ashes.

Tradition states that the more enthusiastic friends of the rescinding bill resolved that the usurped act should not be burned by common fire; and, therefore, with a sun-glass, one of them drew down fire from heaven and kindled the funeral pile of the condemned documents, which were thus consumed as by the burning rays of the lidless eye of Justice. No authentic document of the day alludes to such a method of kindling the fire, though it is not impossible, in the ardor of the moment, that such may have been the fact.

The scene, aside from such a romantic circumstance,

was sufficiently striking and impressive. The sudden revolution in public opinion in one year, by which the citizens so changed their views upon the subject of the western territory, was a marvellous reaction in the popular mind. The passing of such an act, rescinding and nullifying the doings of a previous Legislature by so large a majority (almost unanimous), in the face of obstacles and dangers so numerous, was still more astounding as an index of the people's will. The expunging from the records of the State the acts and doings pertaining to the bill for disposing of the western territory, was a higher manifestation of feeling than had ever been known to exist in Georgia before, and one which had rarely been done in any legislative assembly; but, the ordering of these documents to be burned, the legislative procession, the formal delivery of them from the archives of the State, through its high officers to the humblest servant of the Representatives, the solemn appeal to God, as the papers were laid upon the fire, and the stillness which marked the few minutes which it required to consume them, was a spectacle not only never beheld in Georgia before, but unknown to any Assembly on this continent; and it indicated, as nothing else could, the intense sense of indignation at the dishonor cast upon the State, and the equally intense desire to burn out the infamy; purifying, as by fire, the archives of the State from such fraud-begotten records.

It was a scene worthy to employ the pencil of some gifted artist; and a picture that should, as far as possible, reproduce the old State House and its surroundings; the features and dresses of the men of those times; the circle just formed around the kindling fire, and the Messenger in the act of uttering the words,—God save the State! as, lifting up the acts on high, he is about to lay them upon the blazing fire,—would grace, with peculiar propriety, the hall of legislation,—telling to the eyes of future generations, what history tells to the mind, how nobly Georgia, though for a moment overborne by intrigue and deception, threw off the odium, and purged herself of the infamy of the usurping act.

The people of Georgia were prepared for the passage of the rescinding bill, and hailed its signature by the Governor with every demonstration of joy. Not so, however, the several companies, whose rights were thereby revoked, and whose claims summarily rejected. The news of the rescinding act was to them an astounding measure. Some of the companies had disposed of parts of their lands to other companies at a great advance on their purchase. The lands themselves had become suddenly enhanced in value, by reason of the Spanish treaty, which confirmed the territory, unmolested by the authority of the King of Spain, to Georgia; and the New England Mississippi Company, made up of many reliable and excellent men, had already invested large sums in the grants which had been issued.

All persons thus interested viewed the act with dismay. The friends of the former bills were loud in denouncing it as a fraud, overtopping even their own so-called fraudulent act; and it excited intense animosity and bitterness throughout the Union. Several pamphlets were written on both sides; suits at law were entered in various courts; appeals to Government were sent in from different quarters; and the controversy between the companies and Georgia was maintained for several years. It is not necessary to follow the results of this annulling act through all its tortuosities in law and equity; or to repeat the objections which were made against its validity and binding force. Suffice it to say that the question was sifted to its very foundation. The testimony and proceedings of the two Legislatures were scrutinized with an analytical skill that brought every fact to the crucible; yet, after all the war of opinions, and the clash of interests, and the thunder of volleying pamphlets, and the crimination and recrimination of individuals; the well-grounded and sober judgment of the people has settled down into the opinion that the act of '95 was an abuse of legislative authority, and a wasteful and shameful surrender of territorial rights; and that the act of '96 was necessary, as a self-protecting law, to bring back alienated territory, to efface public infamy, to settle the great question of constitutional rights, and to vindicate anew the title of Georgia to her western territory.

In March, 1798, the subject having been brought before Congress, a bill, entitled, "An act for an amicable settlement of limits with the State of Georgia, and authorizing the establishment of a government in the Mississippi territory," was passed, empowering the President "to appoint three commissioners,—any two of whom shall have power to adjust and determine, with such commissioners as may be appointed under the legislative authority of the State of Georgia, all interfering claims of the United States and that State to territory situate west of the Chattahoochee, north of the 31° of north latitude, and south of the cession made to the United States by South Carolina. And also to obtain and accept, through said commissioners, or otherwise, a relinquishment or cession of the whole, or any part of the territory, both as to jurisdiction and soil claimed by or under the State of Georgia, and out of the ordinary jurisdiction of the same."

After various modifications of this bill, commissioners were appointed by the United States and Georgia,—those for the United States being James Madison, Albert Gallatin, and Levi Lincoln,—and those for the State of Georgia being James Jackson, John Milledge, and Abram Baldwin. These commissioners, after careful and deliberate conference, entered into a convention, or agreement, which Mr. Jefferson, the President, laid before Congress, on the 26th of April, 1802. Agreeably to this convention, Georgia ceded most of her western territory to the United States for the sum of $1,250,000,—Congress agreeing to confirm the titles of all actual settlers within the ceded territory who were there prior to October, 1795; agreeing, also, to extinguish for Georgia the Indian title to the country between the Alatamaha and the St. Mary's, and all other lands in Georgia. Congress approved these measures, the cession was made, and thenceforth the contest of claimants was transferred from Georgia to the Federal Government; and there it remained for many years before a final disposition of the whole subject was made by Congress in 1814.

CHAPTER VI.

THE CONSTITUTION OF 1798, AND CONCLUSION.

In accordance with the 4th Article of the Amendment of the Constitution, established at Louisville, in May, 1795, there were elected, in the year 1797, three persons from each county to form "a Convention for the purpose of taking into consideration the further alterations and amendments necessary to be made in the Constitution."

Before the meeting of that Convention, the term of office of Governor Irwin had expired; and James Jackson was, on the 12th January, 1798, a second time elected to the Executive Chair. This honor he did not, as in 1788, feel at liberty to decline, and he was accordingly inaugurated into his high office.

Considering the prominent part which General Jackson had acted in opposition to the Yazoo sale,—being regarded by all parties as the principal person in crushing these gigantic monopolies,—this election displayed at once the opinions of the people as to the measures which he had introduced, and their confidence in him personally.

The Speaker of the House, in communicating to him the fact of his election, said, "Your appointment by a large majority of the House, evinces the great confidence which the representatives of the people repose in you. The critical posture of our affairs renders it peculiarly necessary that the Chief Magistracy of this State should be filled by a person of experience and approved patriotism. Your repeated exertions in the service of your country, leave no room to doubt that you will accept the office which has been thus honorably conferred upon you; and that you will discharge the duties of this important trust in such a manner as shall give general satisfaction."

Governor Jackson entered upon his duties with zeal, intelligence, and patriotism. He found many questions to be decided, which demanded all his wisdom; many concurring events which it required great prudence and energy to control; and difficulties to be adjusted with the General Government, the State of South Carolina, and the Indian tribes, which taxed the powers of his statesmanship; but in each he maintained the honor of Georgia, and his own official dignity.

Many of the questions which then largely occupied the public mind, were local and temporary, and are of but little historical value: such as depredations committed by the Indians; difficulties connected with running the Indian line; troubles incident to the Yazoo and Rescinding Acts; the settlement of a proper militia system; the apportionment of representatives; and the raising and investment of State funds.

The subject which rose in importance above all the others, was, the evident necessity for a new Constitution for the State. Experience had shown some serious defects in the Constitution of 1789, which the Convention at Louisville, in 1795, was not able to remove, on account of the intense excitement occasioned by the recent passage of the Act for the disposal of the Western Territory.

That Convention, therefore, in their troubled and hasty session, made but few amendments to the Constitution, and left the instrument to the calmer and wiser deliberation of the Convention which had been elected to meet in 1798.

Much of the excitement, which prevented sober action in 1795, had passed away; and the people, and their representatives, were prepared to act with true energy and discretion. The delegates elected to Convention, met in Louisville, on Tuesday, the 8th of May, and twenty-one counties were represented by fifty-six members. Jared Irwin, the late Governor, who had signed the Rescinding Act, was elected by ballot President, and James M. Simmons, Secretary.

After appointing a committee, "to prepare and report such rules as may be necessary for the good order and government of the Convention," and resolving that it would attend Divine service the next day, "at 11 o'clock, in conformity to the Proclamation of the President of the United States," the Convention adjourned till Thursday. On Thursday two more counties were represented, and a code of rules was adopted for the government of the body.

On Friday, 11th of May, the Convention resolved to take into consideration the Constitution and amendments, section by section; and on Monday following, resolved itself into a Committee of the Whole upon it; and in this way they sat, day by day, until the 30th of May. Some of the more important sections were referred to committees, to examine and report; all propositions, however, were first discussed in committee of the whole, and then reported to the Convention, which took final action upon them. As the several parts of the Constitution were not passed in the order in which they are now arranged, a committee, of which Mr. Powell was chairman, was appointed to arrange the different sections under the proper articles; which, being done, and the same being engrossed upon six pages of parchment, was read, article by article, and then signed, the members being called upon to sign by counties. It was signed by all, except General Gunn, of Camden, and Colonel Thomas Glascock, of Richmond, who asked and received leave to decline signing, because by the 23d Section of Article I, the State claimed and reasserted its right of possession and jurisdiction over territory which they claimed as grantees under the usurped act of 1795.

A committee was then appointed, consisting of James Cochran, of Liberty, Jesse Mercer, of Wilkes, and John Morrison, of Burke, to have the great seal of the State affixed to the instrument, and to have the same deposited in the office of the Secretary of State. This being done, after voting the thanks of the Convention to the presiding officer, Ex-Governor Irwin, the body adjourned *sine die.*

The signing of the Constitution was announced to the public by the discharge of sixteen rounds of artillery; and the people everywhere received it with peculiar joy.

It is not necessary to analyze this Constitution, but it is proper to state, that, while it took as its basis, the Constitution of 1789, with the amendments of 1795, it is yet an independent structure, erected by the able hands, to whom was intrusted by the State the difficult, yet honorable task.

The principal actors in the Convention were James Powell, of Liberty, the Chairman of the Committee of the Whole House; James Jones, and Dr. George Jones, of Chatham; General Jackson, then also occupying the Governor's chair; Peter J. Carnes, of Jefferson; Rev. Jesse Mercer, of Wilkes; Robert Watkins, of Richmond; Benjamin Taliaferro, of Wilkes; James Cochran, of Liberty; Jonas Fouche, of Green; William Stith, Jr., of Warren; William Barnett, of Elbert. Each of these gentlemen has the honor of having framed one or more sections of the Constitution.

That defining the territorial boundaries and declaring the contemplated purchases or sales of the Western Companies "constitutionally void;" as also the 1st Section of the 3d Article, defining and establishing the Judiciary, were written by General Jackson. The Article on the Executive power, was the production of Mr. James Jones.

That requiring self-purgation of all fraudulent attempts to secure election, to be made by Senators and Representatives, was by Mr. Robert Watkins.

That calling for a Digest of all State Laws and Ordinances, within five years, was proposed by Mr. Jonas Fouche. That respecting freedom of the press, and trial by jury, honesty in office-holders, and security for honest debtors; and that for the promotion of the arts and sciences, were suggested by Dr. George Jones. That prohibiting any further importation of slaves, was penned by Mr. Carnes; and that securing liberty of conscience, in matters of religion, was written by the Rev. Jesse Mercer.

To borrow the words of one of the most eminent jurists of Georgia, "The experience of sixty years has demonstrated the wisdom of the Constitution of '98. It has undergone but few changes, and these were rendered necessary by the changes in the condition of the country."[1] The great principles enunciated in that state paper are still preserved; and that Constitution, and the Judiciary Act of 1799, which was the fitting complement of the former, will long remain to evince the political sagacity, the judicial wisdom, and the elevated statesmanship of those Georgians who framed these memorable instruments.

Thus has been briefly traced the history of Georgia, from its discovery by Europeans to the adoption of the Constitution of 1798. This period seems to be a natural terminus for the labors of the historian.

The events since that day are too closely interwoven with the transactions of more recent legislation, or too immature in their results, or too much connected with the statesmen of the present generation, to be ripe for the historic harvest.

The pathway along which we have travelled, in tracing this history, has been a devious one, but exceedingly interesting and instructive. It has led us into the far past, among French chieftains and Spanish hidalgoes; amid virgin forests and Indian tribes; now we have passed the prisons of the unfortunate debtors in London, or the homes of the persecuted Protestants of Salzburg; and now we have journeyed with them over the stormy ocean, landing with them on the bluff of Yamacraw, and following them in their

[1] Letter from Hon. Joseph Henry Lumpkin.

new homes in the colony, which mercy erected on these shores, that the poor and the unfortunate might find rest and peace.

The history of Georgia is the record of striking providences. The colony, based upon one of the great principles of Christianity, has been signally preserved amidst all vicissitudes; and though at times on the verge of ruin, has yet, by the interposing hand of God, been relieved, restored, and lifted up to its present high position.

We have seen the nursling of Charity become the foster-child of Royalty, and though chastened in youth by the scourge of war, for its leanings to liberty, we behold it at last standing erect and free in the manhood of an independent State.

These changes in its corporate and political life, have been marked by events of deep interest, and of lasting importance; and the attempt has been made to arrange them in such a manner, and portray them in such colors as shall best develope the inner and outer life of the State, and give it a truthful and enduring biography. Once freed from Parliamentary shackles, the ravages of war, the depredations of Indian tribes, the intestine strifes consequent on imperfect legislation, and the conflicting interests of a people not yet fused into one homogeneous body politic, the young State rose gradually in all the elements of national growth and prosperity. In proportion to its age and its population, it has furnished as staunch defenders of liberty, as distinguished soldiers in the field, as learned jurists on the bench, as eminent statesmen in Congress, as valuable members of the cabinet, as judicious ministers at foreign courts, and as patriotic citizens, as any colony of the Old Thirteen.

In Commerce, Georgia takes rank among the States which employ the largest amount of tonnage. In Agriculture, but few exceed her in the variety and value of her productions. In Manufactures, she is fast rising to eminence in the number of her mills and spindles. In Mining, she has nearly all the imbedded elements of mineral wealth. In Educational efforts, she has shown remarkable zeal and diligence in multiplying her Colleges, Academies, and Schools. In religious privileges, there are but seven States which can show a larger number of church buildings and accommodations. In the industry and intelligence of her people, she has but few rivals.

In the good order of her internal government, in the law-abiding character of her citizens, in the freedom from those more shocking crimes which blot the fair fame of many other States, she presents herself for high commendation.

In the surgings of political opinion, which have unsettled for a time, other States, Georgia has held true to the Constitution. In the convulsions which have threatened sectional ruptures, Georgia has been ever on the side of Union. Her weight in the political scale has been fully recognized, and her position as a power-wielding State has been acknowledged by Executive favor and Congressional influence.

Such is her present position. God has bestowed upon her a territory, which for situation, fertility, and beauty, is unsurpassed. With an extended line of sea-coast, along the outside of which stand so many island-sentinels, from the Savannah to the St. Mary's, she is destined to possess a yet greater commerce than now fills her ports.

With noble rivers, which give her a water-power rarely equalled, she will be enabled to increase her inland tonnage and her busy factories to an almost unlimited extent. With a climate ranging from the cold of the Alleghanies to the tropical heats of Florida, her soil easily brings forth the cereal grains of the North, the products of the Middle States, and the great staples of the South.

With a population rapidly increasing, her waste places will soon be filled with a busy yeomanry, and her mines and workshops with industrious artisans.

Her lines of railroads covering, with their iron tracery nearly every section of the State, will rapidly develope her mineral resources, her agricultural wealth, and her mechanical products. Her system of common schools, projected and soon to be introduced, which shall make it possible to give to every one the benefits of a common learning, will make her children educated and enlightened. And above all this, and better than all this, with the legend of her Great Seal, "Wisdom, Justice, and Moderation," as her guiding motto; and with the smiles and protection of God, through whose favor the Colony was planted, and by whose care it has reached its maturity—Georgia shall more than realize the dreams of its founders, in all that gives to a State true greatness, and enduring glory.

INDEX.

THE END.

www.ingramcontent.com/pod-product-compliance
Lightning Source LLC
LaVergne TN
LVHW021314110826
845150LV00003B/565

9781425557980